MISSION FROM THE CROSS

Mission from the Cross

THE LUTHERAN THEOLOGY OF MISSION

Klaus Detlev Schulz

CONCORDIA PUBLISHING HOUSE · SAINT LOUIS

I dedicate this book to my father, Georg Schulz (1928–2004), who from 1955–93 patiently and faithfully served in South Africa as teacher at Enhlanhleni Theological Seminary and as bishop and missionary of the Lutheran Church in Southern Africa (LCSA). His ability to enunciate clearly and defend our Lutheran faith and mission has inspired me to come forward with a book that he should have written but never was able to write.

Published by Concordia Publishing House

3558 S. Jefferson Ave., St. Louis, MO 63118-3968

1-800-325-3040 • www. cph.org

Unless otherwise indicated, Scripture quotations are from The Holy Bible, English Standard Version®. Copyright © 2001 by Crossway Bibles, a publishing ministry of Good News Publishers, Wheaton, Illinois. Used by permission. All rights reserved.

Quotations marked KJV are from the King James or Authorized Version of the Bible.

Scripture quotations marked NIV are taken from the HOLY BIBLE, NEW INTERNATIONAL VERSION®. NIV®. Copyright © 1973, 1978, 1984 by International Bible Society. Used by permission of Zondervan Publishing House. All rights reserved.

Manufactured in the United States of America

Library of Congress Cataloging-in-Publication Data

Schulz, Klaus Detlev.
  Mission from the cross : the Lutheran theology of mission / Klaus Detlev Schulz.
      p. cm.
  Includes bibliographical references and indexes.
  ISBN 978-0-7586-1350-9
  1. Missions. 2. Lutheran Church—Doctrines. 3. Lutheran Church—Missions. I. Title.
  BV2061.3.S33   2009
  266—dc22   2009015257

1 2 3 4 5 6 7 8 9 10   18 17 16 15 14 13 12 11 10 09

CONTENTS

FIGURES

Abbreviations
and Acknowledgments

AC	Augsburg Confession (1530)
AE	American Edition, *Luther's Works.* Volumes 1–30: Edited by Jaroslav Pelikan. St. Louis: Concordia, 1955–76. Volumes 31–55: Edited by Helmut T. Lehmann. Philadelphia/Minneapolis: Muhlenberg/Fortress, 1957–86. Quotations used by permission of the publisher of the source volume.
Ap	Apology of the Augsburg Confession (1531)
BSLK	*Die Bekenntnisschriften der evangelisch-lutherischen Kirche.* Göttingen: Vandenhoeck & Ruprecht, 1976.
CWME	Commission on World Mission and Evangelism
ELCA	Evangelical Lutheran Church in America
Ep	Epitome of the Formula of Concord
FC	Formula of Concord (1577)
GW	Wilhelm Löhe. *Gesammelte Werke.* Edited by Klaus Ganzert. 7 vols. Neuendettelsau: Freimund, 1951–86.
Kolb-Wengert	Robert Kolb and Timothy J. Wengert, eds. *The Book of Concord: The Confessions of the Evangelical Lutheran Church.* Minneapolis: Fortress, 2000.
LC	Large Catechism (1529)
LCMS	The Lutheran Church—Missouri Synod
LWF	Lutheran World Federation
PE	Philadelphia Edition, *Works of Martin Luther: With Introductions and Notes.* 6 vols. Philadelphia: Muhlenberg, 1930–43.
SA	Smalcald Articles (1537)
SC	Small Catechism (1529)
SD	Solid Declaration of the Formula of Concord
Tappert	Theodore Tappert, ed. *The Book of Concord: The Confessions of the Evangelical Lutheran Church.* Philadelphia: Muhlenberg, 1959.
Tr	Treatise on the Power and Primacy of the Pope (1537)
WA	*D. Martin Luthers Werke. Kritische Gesamtausgabe.* Weimar: Herman Böhlau, 1883–.
WA Br	*D. Martin Luthers Werke. Briefwechsel.* Weimar: Herman Böhlau, 1930–.
WCC	World Council of Churches
WELS	Wisconsin Evangelical Lutheran Synod

Acknowledgments

Quotations from Stanley Hauerwas and William H. Willimon, *Resident Aliens: Life in the Christian Colony* (Nashville: Abingdon, 1989), used by permission.

Quotations from *The Cost of Discipleship* by Dietrich Bonhoeffer. Copyright © 1959 by SCM Press Ltd. Reprinted with permission of Scribner, a Division of Simon & Schuster, Inc.

Quotations from Wilhelm Andersen, *Towards a Theology of Mission: A Study of the Encounter between the Missionary Enterprise and the Church and Its Theology* (London: SCM, 1955), used by permission.

Quotations from the Lutheran Confessions in this publication marked Kolb-Wengert are from THE BOOK OF CONCORD: THE CONFESSIONS OF THE EVANGELICAL LUTHERAN CHURCH, edited by Robert Kolb and Timothy J. Wengert, copyright © 2000 Augsburg Fortress. Used by permission of Augsburg Fortress.

Quotations from the Lutheran Confessions in this publication marked Tappert are from THE BOOK OF CONCORD: THE CONFESSIONS OF THE EVANGELICAL LUTHERAN CHURCH, edited by Theodore G. Tappert, published in 1959 by Fortress Press.

PREFACE

The great missiologist and ecumenicist Walter Freytag (1899–1959) stated: "There is no Christian life, no life with Christ, without the missionary task."[1] The search for a correct definition of that missionary task is challenging. From Martin Luther we are referenced to the first chief article of justification by faith in the person and work of Christ, together with the futility of human works under the Law.[2] This sinner/saint duality of futility and hope accompanies the missionary task, and its sole resolution rests on the *theologia crucis* (theology of the cross).

This truth has by no means remained obvious to the Church in the world. In the 1950s, Freytag famously assessed his concern over the waning interest for mission by stating: "Mission always had its problems, but now it has become a problem."[3] Today, mission deals with problems such as the drift toward humanitarian and worldly concerns to the exclusion and denial of eschatology and life eternal. Yet as a visible phenomenon and expression of Christianity, mission today has received a renewed strength and emphasis among Christians and churches of all denominations worldwide. We are now in a time of mission. A number of factors contribute to this: the waning of Christian populations in the West; the influx of immigrating, largely non-Christian people into the United States and Western Europe; and the resurgence of missionary zeal among non-Christian religions. All these factors have renewed and intensified the call for mission among Christians. This means that Lutheran congregations and church bodies also should heed their apostolic and missionary calling in the twenty-first century.

Lutheranism's interest in mission *is* on the upswing. In 2004, the Lutheran World Federation (LWF) Department for Mission and Development published its most recent statement on mission entitled *Mission in Context: Transformation, Reconciliation, Empowerment*, which replaces a publication from 1988 entitled *Together in God's Mission*.[4] For

---

1 Freytag, *Reden und Aufsätze*, 1:111.
2 SA II I 1–5 (Tappert, 292; Kolb-Wengert, 301).
3 Freytag, *Reden und Aufsätze*, 1:111.
4 See Bibliography for publication information.

a number of years, the Evangelical Lutheran Church in America (ELCA) Evangelism Task Force studied current issues and challenges of mission and evangelism. The result of these investigations led to the publication in 2005 of *The Evangelizing Church: A Lutheran Contribution*.[5] The Wisconsin Evangelical Lutheran Synod (WELS) offered *We Believe—Therefore We Speak*, written by David Valleskey, a longtime professor at Wisconsin Lutheran Seminary.[6] The Lutheran Church—Missouri Synod (LCMS) has stepped forward with her own initiative in mission in the form of a movement called *Ablaze*. With it, the Missouri Synod hopes to invigorate her congregations and her partner churches for reaching the lost.[7] Moreover, as we shall demonstrate in a later chapter on Luther and the Reformation, there is a recent surge in Luther research on the topic of mission, which also indicates a renaissance.

In order to respond to the Lord's call, Christians, seminaries, and church bodies should be able to provide a compassionate yet *informed* response to the world concerning who Christ is and what they believe. However, as readers peruse literature on mission, they will come across proposals and models that seem to diverge from those connecting the Church to the triune God. What seems to be emphasized in too many approaches are mere cultural and social studies coupled with steps or programs clothed in innovative business-like vocabulary that promise numerical growth. Such literature, in addition to the wide range of mission activity through organizations, individuals, and denominations, contributes to a sense of bewilderment among the readers: "What is mission?"

This book intends to provide a particular informed outlook on mission by calling pastors, theologians, students, and all Christians back to basics, to our theological heritage understood particularly in light of the theology of the cross. It intends to further the missionary calling of the Church by engaging Scripture, the theological literature of worldwide Lutheranism, and contemporary discussions on the topic. In so doing, this book does not push for one particular structure or model of mission that declares all previous ones obsolete. Mission is volatile, always on the move and continuously in the process of restructuring. Our plea, however, is that the Church's mission preserve some stability and continuity with the past and anticipate where the Lord will lead the Church in the future. As the Church engages her context and translates her mission into praxis, the theological

---

5   Bliese and Van Gelder, *Evangelizing Church*.

6   Valleskey, *We Believe—Therefore We Speak*.

7   The Ablaze movement (see official website www.lcms.org) formulates its vision as follows: "Praying to the Lord of the Harvest, LCMS World Mission, in collaboration with its North American and worldwide partners, will share the Good News of Jesus with 100 million unreached or uncommitted people by the 500th anniversary of the Reformation in 2017."

component of her message may suffer as a result. Should there not be a theological framework or template for mission that provides stability?

The Evangelizing Church makes the following pertinent comment: "Lutherans have an incredible theological heritage upon which to draw, especially when viewed from a missional perspective."[8] Indeed, the argument of this study is that Lutheran theology and mission are not antithetical terms but that missionary potential springs from deep within Lutheran theological articulation. The central article of justification, for example, has for some time now received new attention in literature and in the ecumenical forum; its connection to and implication for mission, however, is rarely made.

Some might express their reservations in this endeavor (as we propose it) by requesting a perspective that is simply "biblical." Certainly, we would claim to be nothing but "scriptural or biblical" in our outlook for a theology and practice of mission. However, as history shows, what was purported to be "biblical" at one time has turned out not to be so later. Mission must therefore consist in an ongoing conversation with Scripture and its theological heritage, the Lutheran Confessions in particular. Mission must return to Scripture and be willing to submit itself to God's Word and to engage in historical and theological analysis of the past for the sake of mission in the future.

Within my study, I have reflected frequently on mission praxis, which I have accumulated over the years from my frequent travels as lecturer and teacher both overseas and in the United States. I also draw on a long experience in mission that includes my youth spent on a mission station in the hills of kwaZulu, South Africa, and my service as a missionary in Serowe, Botswana. As a professor at Concordia Theological Seminary, Fort Wayne, Indiana, I have had the privilege of sharing my insights for a number of years now with students and colleagues on campus. All these stations in life have deepened my conviction that mission strategy and practice must be guided by a serious engagement with Scripture and theology.

The title chosen for this study, *Mission from the Cross*, specifically addresses the scene in John 20:19–23 where the risen Lord appears before His disciples and commissions them with the task to offer forgiveness or retain sins. Mission is built on a *theologia crucis*, that is, it affirms the cross as the pivotal point of reference from which flows and to which returns the preaching of the Gospel. While appearing in His resurrected body, the Lord returns to the cross by showing the wounds in His hands and side, which were incurred at His crucifixion. From this unspoken reference to the context of His death and victory on the cross, Christ extends the merits

---

8   Bliese and Van Gelder, *Evangelizing Church*, 1.

of the cross to a broken world by commissioning His disciples. *Mission from the Cross* emphasizes this connection between the cross and the movement of the Gospel into the world.

I am particularly thankful to my colleague John G. Nordling, who offered his valuable time to read the manuscript and to make so many helpful suggestions. I also wish to express my sincere thanks to students and graduate assistants who accepted the task of reading some of what I had written and also had the courage to critique their teacher. And, finally, I am indebted to the staff of Concordia Publishing House, particularly Charles Schaum, who has been very encouraging throughout the process of publishing this book.

Klaus Detlev Schulz

Fort Wayne, Indiana

Christmas 2008

PART I

The Nature and Study of Mission Today

CHAPTER ONE

An Appraisal of Lutheran Mission

Bringing Mission Home

Formerly it was easy for Lutherans of North American and European back-grounds to live apart from those of other ethnicities and beliefs. That has changed, resulting in diminishing geographic distance between Christian communities and those of different cultures and beliefs. It has become fashionable to speak of the close proximity of the mission field. Mission takes place at "home," not only faraway in places called "abroad." The slogan "mission in six continents" coined already at the 1963 World Mission Conference in Mexico City reflects this reality for all countries, including those in the West.[1] In particular, the rising numbers of economic and political immigrants into countries such as the United States, Canada, Germany, Norway, and Sweden have made mission an important task. There was a time when the West was a stronghold of Christianity. That has changed. Today we need to take into account that paganism and Christianity coexist, often in close proximity. Recent statistics show that the greatest growth for Lutheranism in 2005 occurred on the continent of Africa, which has a current population of more than fifteen million Lutherans. By comparison, Lutheran denominations in North America saw an overall decrease of 1.16 percent to about 8,154,631 members, a decrease caused not only by a loss of membership through secularization and transfer to other denominations but also by a dwindling birthrate among those who are Lutheran.[2]

The decline and shift of Christianity is occurring in all Western countries. Today only 45 percent of Caucasian Europeans claim to be Christians, whereas one hundred years ago, it was still 80 percent. Over the next twenty-five years, the Caucasian portion of global Christianity will decline even further, as Philip Jenkins predicts in his book *The Next Christendom: The Coming of Global Christianity*.[3] This means that mission opportunities

---

1   Müller et al., *Dictionary of Mission*, 506.

2   The statistics were released February 14, 2006, on the LWF Web site: www.lutheranworld.org.

3   Jenkins, *Next Christendom*, 89–90.

abound not only in North America but also in the West overall. The mission task becomes even more pertinent as one looks at the current immigration of non-Christian people from central and eastern Asia. As a result, the ratio of non-Christians to Christians will increase even further and adult baptisms could become commonplace again.

Since Western Europe and North America have become mission fields in ways unlike those of times past, denominations in the West face the dilemma of where to concentrate their efforts. Should mission continue predominantly as an enterprise that sends people from one country to another, or should it focus on reaching the lost at home? Here is where questions of economics and priority of needs can intersect the mission task. Those who ask such questions do not intend to undermine the missionary enterprise overseas, but they would prefer to place a greater emphasis on mission in their own country. Germany is an example of this transition. The states of the former East Germany have a population that is almost 70 percent non-Christian. Since German reunification in 1991, church bodies and their mission societies have called missionaries to serve in their home country, especially in cities where there is a large concentration of non-Christians. Similar mission efforts take place all over the United States to bring the Church to areas where suburban sprawl continues and where foreign non-Christian communities settle. The harvest is waiting, as Donald Moorman points out: "Now, many new strangers have appeared on our doorstep, and we have the opportunity to take them in, minister to them and welcome them to the Family of God and the grand American mosaic."[4] Indeed, most congregations have begun to notice the challenge of mission in their own particular context.

THE UNFINISHED TASK ABROAD

The call for mission in the home country and that of placing it predominantly in local congregations has not diminished the overall need and support for overseas mission. This is apparent from the statistical overview that David Barrett and Todd Johnson provide in *World Christian Trends AD 30–AD 2200: Interpreting the Annual Christian Megacensus.*[5] Therein they explain how Christianity will fare in the next fifty years. In AD 2000, the number of the unevangelized in the world actually had not changed much from 1976. And for the next fifty years, Christianity will remain a steady 33 to 34 percent of the world's population. If Barrett's prognosis is true, Christianity obviously will not make a larger impact than it already

---

4   Moorman, *Harvest Waiting*, 55.
5   Barrett and Johnson, *World Christian Trends*, xiii and 4.

does. At the same time, however, Christians cannot accept the *status quo*; they must intensify the missionary task.[6]

To underscore the enormity of mission, literature frequently refers to the 10/40 window. This window depicts the regions between 10 and 40 degrees latitude north of the equator that contain not only the world's greatest population but also the major world religions: Islam, Hinduism, and Buddhism. Within these regions especially, missiologists have identified a multitude of unreached people groups. In fact, 57 percent of the world's population—three billion souls—are completely without Christ. Of this percentage, about 1.6 billion people continue to lead an isolated existence without the Bible and the Christian faith presented in the native language.[7] If Barrett and Johnson's statistics are true, then we ought to inquire into the reasons why the Christianity segment of the population in the twentieth century has not exceeded 34 percent and why some sectors of the world's population have no Christian presence.

First, according to Barrett, churches rarely deploy missionaries to areas where heavily non-Christian populations exist. He observes that "nine out of ten missionaries are sent out to work among peoples already contacted by the Christian message, and in some cases already heavily Christian."[8] The result is that Christian mission concentrates more than 95 percent of its efforts in countries where local Christians could take on missionary tasks themselves. What is the solution? Barrett argues that church bodies and their societies should deploy missionaries proportionally to the non-Christian and unevangelized populations in certain countries he identifies as World C. Then the number of missionaries present in World C would increase even as the number would decrease elsewhere. But even if churches were to change their strategy as Barrett suggests, two other factors—the human care issues and the worldwide resistance to Christianity—continue to significantly curb Christianity's growth beyond 34 percent worldwide and would make the deployment of missionaries into unreached regions difficult.

The second factor that curbs Christianity's growth and demands its resources is the social problems of this world among Christians and non-Christians alike. As a result, missionaries who are active in well-Christianized regions such as central and southern Africa will continue to reach not just the spiritually lost but also those in need of physical care. The twenty-first century, like the twentieth century, has incredible social problems among Christian and non-Christian populations alike. War, AIDS,

---

6   For a description of the state of worldwide Christianity fifty years ago, see Bingle, "World Mission of the Church," 144.

7   Van Rheenen, *Missions*, 209.

8   Barrett and Johnson, *World Christian Trends*, 5.

environmental disasters, water shortages, child labor, and urban problems and other calamities continue to plague the world's population.

The third and final reason why Christianity has not grown beyond the level of 34 percent of the world population is because of non-Christian opposition to Christianity. The *Evangelical Dictionary of World Missions* starkly depicts the various forms of resistance:

> Current estimates are that roughly 150,000 Christians are martyred each year, down from a peak of 330,000 prior to the demise of communist world powers. Some project that the numbers will increase to 600,000 by A.D. 2025, given current trends in human rights abuses and growth of militant religious systems. Those inflicting contemporary Christian martyrdom include political regimes with counter-Christian agendas (e.g. official atheistic powers, such as China and the former Soviet Union); sociopolitical regimes enforcing religious restrictions (e.g. Egypt, Sudan); ethnic tribal regimes bent on eliminating minorities (e.g. Sudan, Rwanda, and Burundi); and religious regimes (e.g. Muslim countries in which Sharia is the official legal system).[9]

Mission and Optimism

As we look at these three factors that seem to curb Christian mission, it becomes difficult to share the expansionary optimism of those who have and continue to envision total world evangelization. Christianity has voiced its optimism in this regard on repeated occasions. In 1910, at the time of the first World Mission Conference in Edinburgh, dignitaries and representatives made the visionary slogan of "evangelization of the world in this generation" their own, as many other conferences and revival meetings had done in preceding decades. Many Evangelical groups conceived of mission in unrealistically optimistic terms. Mission became a watchword for "scintillating missionary optimism," an enthusiasm and belief in an unhindered and rapid Christian expansion and transformation of the world.[10] Some of that optimism may have been the result of progressivism in the Romantic period before the Great War. Today, this optimism has surfaced again. In the late 1980s many denominations and movements prepared for global evangelization in the forthcoming decade (the 1990s), which they declared

---

9   Moreau, *Evangelical Dictionary of World Missions*, 602. Sri Lanka, for example, has banned baptisms of Buddhists. Christian pastors performing Holy Baptism are subject to reprisals from the government and neighboring Buddhist communities.

10   Bosch, *Transforming Mission*, 336–37. Stephen Neill claims that this hope for world evangelization was not an idle dream but relied on realistic logistics. The thought of world evangelization was based on a formidable army, a *"striking force of 45,000 missionaries and ten times that number of national workers,"* as well as on the potential of Christian churches and their national workers multiplying exponentially within a few years; see Neill, *History of Christian Missions*, 333–34. Sweeney, *American Evangelical Story*, 92–103.

to be the decade of evangelism. Denominations and movements of every kind—whether Protestant, Evangelical, Ecumenical, Roman Catholic, or Pentecostal/Charismatic—launched global plans and made solemn pledges to complete Christ's commission on earth in that decade. But as Barrett points out, the results of such campaigns were disappointing. The envisaged ten-year period of unstoppable expansion of Christianity did not material-ize. Despite an overall increase in expenditure during that period (topping more than $70 billion), Christianity made no substantial progress.[11]

Christianity should be realistic in terms of goals and obstacles in mission work. Here we would do well to limit our understanding and wisdom in light of God's purpose and intentions: "Trust in the LORD with all your heart, and do not lean on your own understanding. In all your ways acknowledge Him, and He will make straight your paths" (Prov. 3:5–6). All the obstacles to mission—stark opposition, financial constraints, theological confusion about the actual nature of mission, etc.—gnaw at the confidence placed in our efforts. Although missionaries have access to improved technology and medicine to check many of the hazards that plagued foreign mission decades ago, other factors challenge mission. The gap between Western economic wealth and poverty in other countries is widening and creating obstacles for missionaries and their perceived iden-tity and purpose. Additionally, the surge of new diseases and crime make mission today a precarious and daunting task.

One thing needs to be stated as we look at the growth/decline and distribution of Christian populations. It is impossible to follow Barrett's advice of relocating missionary personnel to specific non-Christian coun-tries. Careful consideration reveals that no country is exempt from receiv-ing missionaries. The so-called "plum targets"—that is, countries with a higher concentration of Christian populations—might not be that plum after all. In fact, the post-Christian context in the West makes the situa-tion extremely difficult for any missionary endeavor. Congregations and denominations may be more attracted to the so-called unreached areas of the world than to Western countries where the Gospel has been preached previously. Yet the configuration of Christian populations in the world is extremely volatile and not static; it may diminish or move on from one area to another, like a thundercloud shifts after it has dropped rain over a certain area. Christian mission is always on the move. Luther already knew this. He describes the Gospel's course in terms that invite us to be cautiously optimistic:

> The movement of the Gospel is now among us, but our ungratefulness
> and scorning of the divine Word, pettiness, and decadence make it so

11 Barrett and Johnson, *World Christian Trends*, xiii–xiv.

that it will not remain for long. There shall then follow after it a large rabble, and great wars will come later. In Africa, the Gospel was very powerfully present, but the liars corrupted it, and after it the Vandals and the wars came. It went likewise also in Egypt: first lying and then murder. It will also go exactly the same way in the German land. The pious preachers will first be taken away, and false prophets, enthusiasts, and demagogues will step into my place and that of other preachers and divide the church and tear it apart.[12]

The Shift in the Missionary Task

Issues pertaining to the shift in populations all over the world and how that shift impacts Christianity gives rise to the important discussion about the missionary task itself as it embraces issues of implementation. Let me briefly shed some light on this discussion. In the section above, I observed that mission remains an indispensable task in the life of the Church wherever she exists, both at home *and* abroad. Scripture speaks of a commission to loose from sin that will remain with the Church till the end of time: "And this gospel of the kingdom will be proclaimed throughout the whole world as a testimony to all nations, and then the end will come" (Matt. 24:14). None other than the Lord Himself placed on His disciples and His Church the mandate for the proclamation and Baptism of "all nations" (see Matt. 28:18–20). For us today the question is not whether mission should be done; rather, it is *how* and by *whom*. The implementation and strategic execution of mission is indeed an interesting topic of discussion, and the following chapters engage that subject. Ideally speaking, we would expect this much: All Christians are involved in mission after having received the good news of their reconciliation with God through Christ. They have the desire of sharing that wonderful news with others without selfishly protecting and withholding it from people who live estranged from God. Mission is the measure of the Church's health. According to Newbigin, mission tests our faith, inasmuch as it inquires about "our readiness to share it with all peoples."[13]

Putting mission work into practice is more organized and transitory than that ideal suggests. It is more organized because the focus and logistics of mission have become more specific than they were in the past. It is more transitory because missionaries expect to hand over their task to local people far more intentionally than in the past. True, there is still a resemblance to Protestant mission as it began two hundred years ago when William Carey (1761–1834) cried out in *Enquiry into the Obligations of Christians, to Use*

---

12 Sermon on Matthew 24:8ff. (1539) in Stolle, *Church Comes from All Nations*, 82.

13 Newbigin, "Logic of Mission," 24.

Means for the Conversion of the Heathens (1792) for a renewed commitment to apostolic mission.[14] Just as in the past, missionaries today are also called, trained, and sent to specific areas. But their job description and sphere of duty have little in common with the classic pioneer model of mission that was employed throughout most of the eighteenth century to the better part of the twentieth century. Missionaries at that time went to remote regions to preach and baptize and with the task of establishing churches where none existed. Today missionaries are only indirectly involved in those tasks since the major part of their work concentrates on teaching and training indigenous leadership. Missionaries today are more likely to be teachers or facilitators who enable local indigenous leaders to assume the task of church planting.

Representatives in mission should carefully consult Scripture for the validity of a shift in strategy. "Old-fashioned" ideals of what missionaries once did are perhaps not that outdated after all. It seems as if the Great Commission texts point out a method that should remain with the Church for all times. They encourage the sending of individuals authorized to make disciples through Baptism and instruction (Matthew 28) and of imparting the forgiveness of sins through preaching and absolution (John 20).

What, then, explains this shift of mission strategies and roles in recent years? One logical explanation lies in today's attempts to correct the failures of past mission practices. As stated, traditionally missionaries preached, baptized, and planted churches. In this capacity, they generally also held leadership positions in the young emerging churches, but unfortunately, in many cases, they did so for far too long, thus curbing the process of building indigenous churches and leadership. Missionaries of the 1990s will recall Tom Steffen's *Passing the Baton: Church Planting That Empowers.*[15] The author makes the important point that missionaries should work them- selves out of a position from the outset. The byword chosen to describe the negative phenomenon of missionary dominance is "paternalism." Ever since Protestant mission started three centuries ago, paternalistic attitudes have strained relations between young churches and foreign missionaries. In extreme cases, some churches, such as those in Japan, even declared a moratorium on mission, a stop to foreign missionary presence. Christians wanted to assess their national situation apart from foreign intervention so as to emerge with a renewed and better sense for a mission of their own.[16]

Another factor explaining the shift to a new paradigm is that mission has become an inclusive affair for all Christians. In the past, Christians

14 See Bibliography for publication information.

15 See Bibliography for publication information.

16 In many countries, governments took forceful measures to expel missionaries; see Neill, *History of Christian Missions,* 422–33.

primarily fulfilled their missionary obligation by supporting foreign mission through tithing and donations. In the years after 1847, when the LCMS was founded, congregations supported German mission societies across the Atlantic, such as those located in Leipzig, Hermannsburg, or Neuendettelsau. They did this by staging annual mission festivals at which members heard through sermons and presentations about the life and work of career missionaries in faraway countries such as India, and members affirmed their support for missionaries by funding these societies. Christians understood mission as a foreign enterprise that engaged specially trained experts for overseas duties without having to engage in that missionary activity themselves. David Bosch explains the common perception of the Great Commission:

> After all, the Great Commission (Matt. 28:19) explicitly says: "Go ye therefore . . ." The locality, not the task, decided whether someone was a missionary or not; he is a missionary if he is commissioned by the Church in one locality to go and work elsewhere. The greater the distance between these two places, the clearer it is that he is a missionary.[17]

That picture has largely changed. The statement "involvement leads to commitment" captures this overall shift. Many Christians want to become shareholders of the Church's mission, and they criticize it if they find no personal place in it. Apart from fasting and prayer in Acts 13:1–3, one wonders how much of a role the individual members of the congregation actually played in the mission of Barnabas and Paul. Today, the answer is simple. While the sending of specially trained individuals still goes on, numerous volunteers have also stepped in for service at home and abroad. The world has become a global village not only in terms of technology but also in terms of accessibility through travel. Christians have easy access to funds, and many wealthy congregations have stepped forward to offer their members the opportunity for mission and service overseas. The whole "sentness" character of mission has thus given way to a more inclusive model in which every Christian congregation and its members serves as agents in organized mission, rather than just a few individuals.

One wonders, however, whether the focus on "inner" mission and the inclusive approach will not eventually deplete the number of long-term *career* missionaries deployed overseas. Unlike a century ago, churches exist in almost all parts of the world and to a large measure could take on the task of mission in their area themselves. Dare we thus ask this provocative question: Why not radically abort foreign mission and let the indigenous churches concentrate on reaching out to their neighbors?

---

17 Bosch, *Witness to the World*, 46. One may see also Gensichen, *Living Mission*, 38.

The answer is, again, simple. We cannot abandon foreign mission because of the enormity of the task. Also, partner churches often find themselves with severely limited resources. They need the financial and personnel support of larger, wealthier church bodies. When one factors in the so-called "unreached" regions of the world, it should be apparent that foreign mission must continue as a strategic deployment of trained individuals over a longer period.

In recent years, church bodies in the West are recruiting foreign missionaries in new ways to limit costs. The LCMS, for example, may choose to deploy a missionary from a Brazilian partner church into Portuguese-speaking regions in Angola or to support a missionary from Argentina who works in Chile. This new triangular arrangement is partly a result of the sad reality that many countries harbor anti-American sentiments, which renders the sending of American missionaries a dangerous enterprise. Unless missionaries from the United States who wish to serve overseas entertain the prospect of martyrdom, the triangular strategy seems to be a better option and comes with a far smaller human price tag.

WHAT IS MISSION?

This chapter has engaged various facets of the complex situation that arises when Christians struggling in the sinner/saint dichotomy engage the missionary task. They cannot do it merely of their own will. They need to avoid attaching to this task false notions of identity, economy, motivation, culture, and requirements for salvation or the lack thereof. Yet, after sifting through these issues, the question emerges: What should we identify as the core concern of mission and who qualifies as a missionary? This question addresses a contemporary concern that best remains unanswered. Thus the Church finds herself in a position where "everything goes," missionally speaking, and perhaps that is how it should be. Missiologist Andrew Kirk attempted to identify the nature of mission in his book entitled *What Is Mission? Theological Explorations.*[18] However, within Protestantism, it would be hard to find a common consensus on the basic theological principles and definition of mission. Some associate themselves with classical soteriology, that is, the traditional call to faith and conversion, whereas others project mission as humanitarian service.[19] But as the Christian population dwindles in the

---

18 See Bibliography for publication information.

19 The identification of mission as humanitarian service often foregoes the evangelistic activity out of respect for the belief systems of other religions. The Ecumenical or Conciliar movement is known for supporting such a position. It is led by the WCC and its missionary arm, the Commission on World Mission and Evangelism (CWME). See some of the Ecumenical/Conciliar documents such as "Your Kingdom Come" (Melbourne, 1980), the "Stuttgart Consultation" (Stuttgart, 1987), "Mission in Christ's Way: Your Will Be Done" (San Antonio,

West, it seems as if church leaders are again revisiting the core activity of mission. I suggest an operating definition of mission's core concern made by the missiologist Walter Freytag many years ago: "In the biblical sense nothing can be called mission that is not geared toward conversion and baptism."[20] This statement, I believe, should not discriminate against other activities from being part of the Church's mission, but it serves as a guiding principle and constant reminder of what the Church should keep in sight as she serves as an instrument in God's mission. The Church may not lose her focus on the crucified Lord who stood before His disciples and who still offers redemption to the world through the means that dispense forgiveness. Through these means, He creates His people and leads them on to serve in His mission—mission from the cross.

1989), "Come, Holy Spirit" (Canberra, 1991), in which basic tenets such as the nature of the Gospel, peace, sharing the faith with people of other faiths in a plural context, Christ's substitution, the nature of sin and the unity of the Church are either changed or abandoned. One may see Scherer and Bevans, *New Directions in Mission and Evangelization*, 1:27–35, 65–72, 73–81, 84–88. Thus since the mid-1960s the theological legacy of Karl Hartenstein (1894–1952), Georg Vicedom (1903–74), or Walter Freytag (1899–1959) in the Ecumenical movement gradually waned. During their lifetimes, these men managed to direct and unite the Evangelical and Ecumenical interests shared also by many Lutherans of their time; see Yates, *Christian Mission in the Twentieth Century*, 199, and Van Engen, *Mission on the Way*, 150–53. In the 1960s, when the shift became evident, a few voices expressed concern. One of these was the Lutheran evangelical missiologist of Tübingen, Peter Beyerhaus. He perceptively diagnosed the events around the 1968 WCC assembly in Uppsala and the 1973 World Missionary Conference at Bangkok as those that had clearly shaken Christianity's foundation; see Beyerhaus, *Shaken Foundations* and *Missions—Which Way?*

20 Freytag, *Reden und Aufsätze*, 2:85.

CHAPTER TWO

Synonyms and Concepts of Mission

Mission or Missions?

In the previous chapter, I discussed the current status of mission and its challenges, in particular, Christianity's ongoing search to define the missionary task. To offer some guidance, I pointed out that the Gospel of Christ crucified calls all people to repentance and Baptism. For that task to take hold in this world, the Church enlists the services of all Christians in various ways. Some will witness while they remain in their particular calling; others have decided to make it their profession by becoming pastors and career missionaries. In all of these ways, the Gospel proclamation, handed down first to the apostles, continues to reach out to people, confronting them and calling them to Christ.

The question that we should ask now is, How should we designate the activity of calling people to faith in Christ? We are accustomed to the word "mission," as I will explain below. However, the reader should be aware that other terms are also used to describe the task of bringing the Gospel to others. Some authors talk of expanding God's kingdom; others suggest we should make disciples; and others imprint on us the need for the Church to be planted and to grow. I will explain some of these terms in this chapter and argue that all of these terms, if properly understood from Scripture, offer important insights into the missionary task.

To begin the discussion, I would point out that a reader may often encounter in literature the use of the term "mission" in the singular and "missions" in the plural. Missiologists employ both terms for specific reasons, though not always with consistency. "Mission" is reserved for describing the activity of God, in particular His work in reconciling sinful humankind to Himself, whereas "missions" implies the activities of the various denominations or congregations as they plan to accomplish the mission of God. The reader should note specifically that it is customary today to use the Latin *missio Dei* to mean the mission of God.

> We have to distinguish between mission (singular) and missions (plural).
> The first refers primarily to the *missio Dei* (God's mission), that is, God's
> self-revelation as the One who loves the world, God's involvement in and
> with the world, the nature and activity of God, which embraces both the
> church and the world, and in which the church is privileged to partici-
> pate. *Missio Dei* enunciates the good news that God is a God-for-people.
> Missions (the *missiones ecclesiae*: the missionary ventures of the church),
> refer to particular forms, related to specific times, places, or needs, of
> participation in the *missio Dei*.[1]

Hans-Werner Gensichen is helpful in pointing out that the use of "mission"
preserves the notion of the "divine dimension"; and "missions," the "kerygmatic intention" or human element. But he points out that both concepts
cannot stand in isolation from each other.[2] God's mission, the *missio Dei*, is
never separate from the Church's activity. God voluntarily binds Himself to
His Word and works through it as the Church administers it to the world.
God's mission leads the Church's missions and remains bound to it. For
this reason, and because it is difficult to be consistent in the distinction, we
will confine ourselves to the use of "mission" in the singular.

Scholars have suggested many other terms and concepts to replace
"mission." Remarkably, none have managed to push it aside. "Mission" has
embedded itself in the life and language of the Church for centuries. Both
Roman Catholic and Protestant Christians have used it since the sixteenth
century. In addition to this historic argument, I should point out that the
English term "mission" is anticipated by the Greek word ἀποστέλλω in
the New Testament (John 17:18; 20:21). Christ the crucified and risen Lord
sends out His disciples, and after their death the Church continues that call
of the Lord by sending Christians into all parts of the world. In this way, the
Church may call herself "apostolic" because of the mission she does, a point
to which I shall return on frequent occasions.

Let us now proceed with a presentation of a few associations made with
mission, so that we become aware of some of the nuances Scripture makes
concerning this activity.

MISSION AS PROCLAMATION OR WITNESS

A key biblical and theological concept for mission is the proclamation and
witness of faith. In fact, preaching the Gospel is the central activity of mission.[3] The Great Commission texts, in particular, clearly oblige the church

---

1   Bosch, *Transforming Mission*, 10. See also Van Rheenen, *Missions*, 20; and Newbigin, "Logic of
    Mission," 121.
2   Gensichen, *Living Mission*, 36. Muck, "Missiological Perspective," 419–20.
3   See Cheesman, *Mission Today*, 127; Jongeneel, *Philosophy, Science, and Theology of Mission*, here
    2:274.

to proclaim the Gospel to all nations (Matt. 28:18–20; Mark 13:10; 16:15–16; Luke 24:46–48). Within that proclamation or preaching activity, we should include also a broader array of communicating the Gospel—namely, private witness, the nonoral forms such as the lifestyle of believers, and the use of symbols. Our concentration on preaching activity gives credit to Paul's kerygmatic activities (Rom. 16:25; 1 Cor. 1:21; 2 Tim. 4:17), whereas the broader use of the word "mission" allows for the type of informal proclamation that goes on between Christians and their non-Christian family members, friends, and neighbors.[4]

The Roman Catholic Church has underscored a commitment to proclamation with the adoption of the term "propaganda." In 1622, Pope Gregory XV founded the *Sacred Congregation for the Propagation of the Faith* (Latin: *Sacra Congregatio de Propaganda Fide*). In 1982, Pope John Paul II decided to exchange "propaganda" for "evangelization" by renaming the agency to *Sacred Congregation for the Evangelization of the People* (Latin: *Sacra Congregatio pro Gentium Evangelisatione*). This name change indicates that the Roman Catholic Church is aware of society's negative associations with the term "propaganda," particularly since the Nazi regime in World War II.[5] Protestant mission avoids the use of "propaganda," too, solely using the term to indicate negatively how the preaching of the Gospel has been mingled with colonial and imperialistic interests.

Martin Kähler uses the term "propaganda" with his allegation that mission efforts had been connecting the preaching of the Gospel with ulterior or impure motives. Missionaries are propagandists when they try to create carbon copies of themselves and impose their own moral and cultural systems on others. Modern missiologists, therefore, prefer the use of the word "mission" to that of "propaganda." By "propaganda," I mean the interest of promoting racial and cultural superiority over others in place of the Gospel.[6]

Kähler and others also speak of propaganda when they see missionary activity promoting a confessional interest, that is, a specific interpretation of the scriptural truths. This, they claim, stands in the way of the Gospel's ecumenical claim and stifles the Holy Spirit's work of faith. I maintain, however, that it is impossible to understand the confession of doctrine solely in the negative light of "confessionalism" in the sense of a primarily human template. Scripture points out that the Gospel was confessed on a number of occasions without stifling the Spirit. Peter's simple statement, "You are the Christ, the Son of the living God," is faith answering a question that the

---

4   See Senior and Stuhlmueller, *Biblical Foundations for Mission*, 333.

5   Oehler, *Geschichte der Deutschen Evangelischen Mission*, 1:80.

6   Kähler, *Schriften zur Christologie und Mission*; Bosch, *Witness to the World*, 138–39.

Lord put before Peter and explained as one revealed not by man but by God (Matt. 16:16). Paul demands a faith that knows how to confess (ὁμολογέω, Rom. 10:9); and in the letter to the Thessalonians, he praises the Christians for their boldness of faith (1 Thess. 1:8–10). From a scriptural point of view, making a confession is part of the Christian life. The believer speaks his faith and, as he does so, he furthers the truths about the identity of Jesus Christ and rejects those who teach against it (Gal. 1:8). In this regard, confessing the faith cannot be simply a selfish interest of promoting one's own identity, but rather the content of Scripture. To drag "confessionalism" purely into the negative with a term such as "propaganda" does not give full justice to its purpose.

As said earlier, "proclamation" frequently occurs in Scripture. Consider, for example, the phrase κηρύξατε τὸ εὐαγγέλιον ("preach the Gospel") (Matt. 10:27; cf. Mark 16:15). The verb εὐαγγελίζομαι can mean "evangelize a city" (Acts 14:21; cf. Luke 20:1; Acts 5:42; Rom. 1:15; 1 Cor. 15:1). Jesus Christ Himself, the apostles, and Philip (called an εὐαγγελιστής, "the evangelist," in Acts 21:8) were engaged in that activity of proclamation or evangelizing. In the Book of Acts, the apostles spent day after day in the temple and in the homes where "they never stopped teaching and *proclaiming* the good news that Jesus is the Christ" (Acts 5:42 NIV, *emphasis added*). The evangelist Philip met the eunuch and *proclaimed* to him "the good news about Jesus" (Acts 8:35). Furthermore, it is said of some men—who are only identified as those from Cyprus and Cyrene—that they "went to Antioch and began to speak to Greeks also, *proclaiming* about the Lord Jesus" (Acts 11:20, *author's translation*). Very rarely are all believers associated with this activity, only on one explicit occasion, in 1 Pet. 2:9. In this passage, the verb ἐξαγγείλητε includes the Christians' declaration of God's glory in the setting of worship and their confession of faith to the world.[7]

Thus both verbs, κηρύσσειν and εὐαγγελίζεσθαι, portray an outward activity of preaching the Gospel to the world. Even the noun τὸ εὐαγγέλιον ("the good news") is often used in a missionary context (Luke 2:10). In Jerusalem, Peter addressed the apostles and elders and reminded them "that in the early days God made a choice among you, that by my mouth the Gentiles should hear the word of the gospel and believe" (Acts 15:7). In Rom. 1:16, Paul announces his programmatic statement: "I am not ashamed of the gospel, for it is the power of God for salvation to everyone who believes, to the Jew first and also to the Greek."

Moreover, the verbs κηρύσσειν and εὐαγγελίζεσθαι express an activity that is very specific and purposeful. Proclamation seems to mean

---

7   Lewis W. Spitz demonstrates convincingly that declaring the praises is an activity that goes beyond the worship setting to the world; see "Universal Priesthood of Believers," 321–41.

something more than the act of witnessing or testifying (μαρτυρεῖν), even when such bold testimony was conducted publicly (for example, Acts 22:20; Rev. 2:13). Overall, the evidence points to an explicit, authorized, and commissioned preaching activity such as Paul did, and as missionaries do today. To underscore his task, Paul appropriates for himself the title of κῆρυξ (a "herald" or "preacher"), indicating thereby that his sole purpose and devotion is to the specific activity of proclaiming the Gospel. He is both "herald and apostle" (1 Tim. 2:7; 2 Tim. 1:11 NIV). Heralds are proclaimers. They call out the news in the name of the king and share in his honor, authority, and immunity as the Hebrew world knew of the *shaliach* (שליח), a duly called and sent representative of his master.[8]

Paul repeatedly referred to himself as an "apostle" (Rom 1:1; 1 Cor. 1:1; 9:1f.; 15:9; 2 Cor. 1:1; Gal. 1:1; Eph. 1:1; Col. 1:1; 1 Tim. 1:1; 2:7; 2 Tim. 1:1, 11; Titus 1:1). Although he considered himself unworthy of that task (1 Cor. 15:9; Gal. 1:13, 23), God gave it to him by grace (1 Cor. 15:10). Paul did it because of a revelation he received (Gal. 1:16), which came directly from Christ (Rom. 1:1; Gal. 1:1), who assigned to him the explicit task of preaching the Gospel to the heathen. Paul would not make his authority dependent on a delegation received by another apostle. His conversion near Damascus, which includes his subsequent meeting and Baptism, was thus the definitive moment and turning point in his life at which his service to Christ began (Gal. 1:15–16; Acts 9:1–19; 22:6–16).

Christ charged all apostles to continue His mission in His name. After they had been with Christ and witnessed His death and resurrection, they testified these events to others. But that testimony must continue even after the death of the apostles. Thus, if today's missionaries call themselves "preachers or proclaimers of the Gospel," they have good reason to do so. For it is precisely to their ministry of preaching the Gospel that the Lord connects His own presence in this world (Matt. 24:14; 28:20). To this day and until the end of the world, the message that preachers proclaim remains the new, unknown, and "official" news about the person Christ. Preaching falls under the Lord's authority and, in terms of purpose, surpasses all other messages in this world.

Mission as the Expansion of the Kingdom of God

Frequently, Scripture points to the kingdom of God (βασιλεία τῶν οὐρανῶν or τοῦ θεοῦ) that the ministry of Jesus Christ and the continued preaching of the Gospel bring into this world. The kingdom began with the

---

8   Rengstorf, *Apostleship.*

activity of preaching by John the Baptist and continued with Jesus Himself before it moved to His disciples. Everyone who hears the news of the coming kingdom is received into it through conversion by coming to faith in Christ (Matt. 4:17). For this reason, the kingdom of God is established through the Gospel and faith. It is by definition a spiritual entity that stands apart from all worldly attempts to promote it through power and force (John 18:36).

It thus comes as no surprise that, on many occasions, the mission of God identifies itself with the expansion of the kingdom of God. The famous Lutheran hymnologist Philip Nicolai (1556–1608), for example, wrote *Commentarii de regno Christi*[9] (*Commentaries on the Kingdom of Christ*, 1597), laying out in great detail the expansion of the Gospel and the strategic plans of Lutheran Orthodoxy. In this treatment, Nicolai also promoted a common claim of Orthodoxy that the Gospel had actually reached all parts of the world. Yet he discovered from his research that in many places it was no longer present, for example, in parts of Brazil. Nicolai attributed the reason for the absence or loss of the Gospel in many parts of the world to mankind's guilt. They had heard it once upon a time but had turned away from it. Positively, Nicolai, and all Orthodox theologians, underscored God's universal salvific will as one that seeks to embrace all nations. They saw that claim inherent in the Gospel itself. Thus the Gospel must be preached and heard by all, as the Jesuit missionaries were already proclaiming the Gospel in parts of India and China. Although they were not engaged in mission directly themselves, Nicolai and the Lutheran Orthodox theologians recognized that the kingdom of God was expanded also through the preaching and teaching of the Roman Catholic missionaries.

Martin Luther frequently embraces the "kingdom of God" in his theology. The Large Catechism contains a mission prayer under the Second Petition: "Thy kingdom come." Luther observes that though God's kingdom comes without our prayer, we should pray that it may also come to us through the preaching of the Word and the Holy Spirit. This is an important point, because Luther thereby underscores the divine and spiritual dimension of the kingdom. God furthers it through His means, the Word.[10]

Past missionary efforts often confused the means of promoting the kingdom of God. Many times, the Gospel was confused with worldly kingdoms, and missionaries sought to hasten its final coming by their own efforts. Today, the "kingdom of God" theology is receiving renewed attention. In 1980, the World Mission Conference in Melbourne convened

---

9 Heß, *Das Missionsdenken bei Philip Nicolai*. One may see also Größel, *Die Mission und die evangelische Kirche*; Schulz, "Lutheran Missiology," 4–53.

10 LC III 50, 54 (Kolb-Wengert, 446–47).

under the theme of the Second Petition of the Lord's Prayer, "Thy kingdom come." The kingdom of God inaugurates itself in this world with transforming powers that change society and rectify problems in this world. Unfortunately, this concept of the kingdom of God is promoted not so much through the Word of God in the contrite hearts of those plagued by personal guilt and sin, but instead by the mission of the Church when she corrects the social plights and abject conditions of suffering humanity. As much as we would like to affirm the Gospel's transforming power of changing social structures and concerns, it serves in essence as the vehicle of restoring the relationship between God and the sinner through the atoning sacrifice of Jesus Christ.

Mission as Conversion

Another important concept connected with the "kingdom of God" is that of conversion (Matt. 3:2; 4:17; Acts 2:38). The call to "convert" (μετανοεῖν) implies literally a change of mind and heart as one encounters the Gospel. The Gospel does not make any exceptions here, such as accepting a greater tolerance for religious pluralism; it calls every person to repentance and faith in Christ. Scripture summons everyone to turn away from every other religious affiliation to an exclusive faith in Christ alone (Mark 1:4; Luke 24:47). Thus the call to repent and believe in Christ embodies the quintessence of mission. More positively, conversion signifies a turn to the joyous news of salvation and the beginning of a new life in Christ enacted through the Holy Spirit.

The discussion on conversion has raised the issue of "proselytism," which not only stands for bringing adherents of other religions into Christianity but also Christians from one denomination to another. It is commonly called "sheep stealing." Many perceive proselytism, or sheep stealing, as violating the common courtesy and respect churches should have for one another. However, as long as various denominations exist and as long as some church body offers itself as a better alternative over others, people will be inclined either to "hop churches" or to be drawn to a fellowship elsewhere. Members of one church might move to another church because they find that the pastor preaches and teaches the Gospel with greater clarity. Thus, even if Christians think that every church presents a part of larger Christianity, they would still prefer to attend a church of their own liking and preference. And that choice might be based on an intentional outreach program of a particular community that has no problem "wooing" members from other churches. Issues related to "proselytism" mostly seem to emerge in areas where numerous churches coexist and where the community of unbelievers has dwindled substantially. In that situation, prior agreements of "minding one's own business" and mutually respecting one another give way to competing for the remaining unbelievers in the surrounding areas as well as competing for other believers.[11] The bottom line is perhaps this: our preaching and teaching of the Gospel deserves to be heard by all people, and that conviction validates our presence in areas where other denominations and churches have already established a presence.

Conversion impacts the lives of people and bears many sociological ramifications and consequences. In communities where the social network of family and kinships are greatly respected, single conversions typically have the potential of alienating and separating families from one another. For this reason, Christian Keysser (1877–1961), the Lutheran missionary to Papua New Guinea, debated the benefits and liabilities of baptizing single individuals against the consent and agreement of the family.[12] Conversion signifies a transition from old allegiances to new ones; it places one into the body of Christ and a new circle of people. It creates a community of those who share a common faith in their Lord and anxiously await His return. That switch, however, is never clear-cut. A tension between the "old" and the "new" world continues to exist. New converts must readjust their former family relationships and continue the struggle against syncretism. Thus every converted Christian will struggle with his past, even if it implies that a new life has begun that sets itself apart from this world (John 15:18–25).

Mission as Church Planting

Next to the goal of conversion, every missionary enterprise must confront the task of planting churches. What type of a church should be planted? One should, for example, inquire about the theological nature of the church and then what human goals would be part of that project. Henry Venn (1796–1873) and Rufus Anderson's (1796–1880) "three-selfs" formula (self-propagating, self-supporting, and self-governing) has dominated Protestant mission for more than a century. Although these goals express a certain human logic, their scriptural support is less clear. The Church at large and local congregations remain dependent on God and His Word and, in this regard, always independent of human goals that seem to be self-serving (such as the "three-selfs" formula). Nevertheless, it must be acknowledged that human ingenuity and hard work are crucial in church planting. Human standards are applied to bring a church planting "project" to a close. There

---

11 In Sri Lanka, for example, I met a Lutheran pastor of the Sri Lanka Evangelical Lutheran Church who shared with me an unpleasant experience. After he had completed a building project for a church in the central highlands, the local Roman Catholic and Buddhist priest united and had the newly built Lutheran Church burned to the ground out of fear of competition.

12 Keysser, *People Reborn*.

must be an exit strategy for the withdrawal of foreign mission presence. The purpose behind such measures is an attempt to ensure a national church's survival apart from foreign mission support.

Many other housekeeping issues form part of church planting efforts, even if these go beyond the theological definition of a church. Matters such as setting up a constitution, electing elders, nominating treasurers, or opening bank accounts fulfill the goal of church planting. Theologically speaking, however, a church must be considered planted once faith comes about and the believers meet together to be nurtured and strengthened through the Gospel. That would agree closest with the Lutheran definition of the church as "the assembly of saints in which the gospel is taught purely and the sacraments are administered rightly."[13] The Third Article of the Apostles' Creed, too, confesses the church as "the holy, catholic Church, the communion of saints." When we thus apply these definitions to the overall goals of church planting, we must draw the distinction between those goals that speak of the true essence of a church and those goals that we humans set in terms of ecclesiastical structure and organization.

Our theological definition of the church as the "communion of saints" includes the important aspect of "community." While each individual goes through repentance and believes on his own, the goal of church planting inserts the notion of community and a sense of belonging to a larger fellowship (Romans 12; 1 Corinthians 12). Church planting is thus important for individual believers to see themselves as part of a worshiping community where faith is strengthened and nurtured. One should thus argue for an understanding of mission that sees conversion embedded in a broader context where individual believers are led on their path to salvation through the spiritual nourishment of the Word and communal fellowship with the triune God and one another.[14]

MISSION AS MAKING DISCIPLES

One could speak of mission also as the task of making disciples. That would find agreement with explicit biblical texts such as Matt. 28:19: "Go therefore and make disciples of all nations." In this regard, the goal of making disciples is the same as making Christians and also includes Baptism and proper instruction (v. 20). In the Gospel of John, μαθηταί ("disciples") is often used as an alternate term for "Christians" (e.g., John 8:31; 13:35; 15:8). Donald McGavran (1897–1990), the pioneer and founder of the Church Growth Movement, and Peter Wagner, his successor at Fuller Seminary's

---

13 AC VII 1 (Kolb-Wengert, 43).
14 Margull, *Hope in Action*.

School of World Mission since 1984, prefer to speak of a two-tiered concept of discipleship that distinguishes between "discipling" and "perfecting" Christians. The former signifies their initial incorporation into the Church, and the latter, their spiritual and ethical growth.[15] Some take a similar approach with the use of the phrase "equipping disciples," and it has become common mission jargon. It includes the ethical goal of turning disciples into actual disciplers of others.[16] The ethical leanings toward discipleship indicate the widespread concern that mission produces disciples who often fail to live out the missionary obligation. It reflects the concern for a laxity of faith as expressed in the Epistle of James, a faith that fails to display its fruits adequately. Scripture, however, in addition to secular Hellenistic writings, employs the term "disciple" in the single sense of learner, apprentice, follower, and associate of a master. Thus the push for a two-tiered discipleship with the term for "disciplers" added to "disciples" is unwarranted. Being a disciple embraces a missionary witness from the very beginning. A disciple will not see witness to others as an arbitrary expression or something that one must acquire at a later stage. In fact, the argument is often made that first-generation Christians have a far greater zeal to share their faith with non-Christians than those of second and third generations. Moreover, Lutherans claim that faith is always a living faith; with justification, someone's sanctification is already fully in place, as I shall explain in full in a later chapter. Thus, as soon as one has been justified, the fruit of faith, such as sharing the Gospel with others, is part of being a Christian. The Spirit makes dead sinners alive in faith (John 3:3–8; Titus 3:5). Being a disciple implies that one possesses this living faith that confesses Christ to others. This makes the use of the term "discipler," or a two-tiered concept of discipleship, superfluous.[17]

To a degree, these considerations also answer the crucial question of just how much "equipping" is necessary during a Christian's life before one can be considered fully fit for mission involvement. Christians remain disciples of Christ all their life. Thus continual, lifelong instruction will deepen their faith and lead them to confess it and live a proper lifestyle. Admittedly, however, faith is engaged in a continual struggle to survive, so the quest to create the "perfect" disciple is more an ideal vision for missiologists and much less based on facts and reality. Daily growth in faith stands in constant battle against sin's corrosive nature. Thus discipleship seems less a progression from one stage to the next as it is a constant fall and rise,

---

15 Engle and McIntosh. *Evaluating the Church Growth Movement*, 84; Wagner, "Church Growth Movement," 199–200; McGavran, *Understanding Church Growth*, 123–32.

16 Barna, *Growing True Disciples*, 8–9.

17 Vicedom, *Mission of God*, 77–80.

a vacillation between failure and success (Romans 7).[18] True, the desire for sharing the Gospel should never be made a mere incidental component of discipleship on par with any other good work. However, the expectations for perfect discipleship must be realistically seen in view of the dialectic of "sinner and saint," of falling and rising.

Mission as Crossing Boundaries

Often, the missionary task of the church is viewed as an activity that crosses borders and boundaries. A cursory review of literature shows that these borders are overwhelmingly culturally or geographically defined. This has impacted also the understanding of who the missionary is and what he is to do. For example, the Commission on World Evangelization and Mission (CWME) of the WCC places a cultural aspect into its definition of a missionary: "The missionary is a servant of the church, who leaves *his own culture* to proclaim the Gospel in partnership with the church if already present or with the intention to plant a church where it has not been planted before."[19] The Evangelical Movement especially associates itself with the cultural aspect in mission. Its scholars have advanced into the science of cultural anthropology (ethnography) to such a degree that the concept now has taken a dominant seat in the missiology of Evangelicalism. Peter Wagner, a student of Donald McGavran, defines missiology as the "study of cross-cultural communication of the Christian faith."[20] And Ralph Winter's proposal of a multilevel approach to cross-cultural or cross-geographic communication that targets hidden people groups has become an integral component of the Evangelical or Lausanne Movement.[21]

It is certainly true that missionaries should not overlook the distinctive cultural traits and subtleties of people groups as they communicate the Gospel to others. As one discusses communication in the context of culture, it becomes evident that there is the challenge of preserving the integrity of the Word of God in all its truth. As the Gospel meets a specific context, a tension arises that seems hardly solvable. For example, missionaries may at first struggle to learn the language and have difficulty in expressing themselves well enough for the people to understand the message. Yet it is

---

18 One may see, for example, the Engel Scale of Conversion Stages or the Spiritual Decision Process as proposed by James F. Engel and Wilbert H. Norton, *What's Gone Wrong with the Harvest?* 45.

19 Peter Beyerhaus, "Missionar I," 278 (*emphasis added*).

20 See Jongeneel, *Philosophy, Science, and Theology of Mission*, 1:64.

21 Next to the E-0 level of communication (to nominal Christians), Ralph Winter has added three further categories: E-1 Evangelism (same language and same culture), E-2 Evangelism (similar culture and new language), and E-3 Evangelism (different culture and language). One may see Stott, *Making Christ Known*, 29; Van Rheenen, *Missions*, 83.

helpful that Christians already are mindful of this challenge and engage in a learning process of discovering the language and customs of the people to whom they go.[22]

We should add one more important biblical insight on the cultural aspect of missionary witness that often seems to escape current discussions. It pertains to the meaning of the term *ta Ethne* (τὰ ἔθνη, "nations") in texts that pertain to the Great Commission. On the one hand, it could be interpreted in geographic and cultural terms, as those people who are regionally and culturally removed from us. Generally, this is how it is understood. Once one then combines *ta Ethne* with the aorist participle πορευθέντες ("going") (Matt. 28:19), the interpretation takes on a cultural and geographic dimension. The words "go therefore" point the missionary to nations who live in faraway places, across the oceanic divides. This has been the traditional understanding of the eighteenth and nineteenth centuries, where locality and geographic distance seem to determine the nature of mission.

As we look at the missionary task, we realize that it crosses another border—namely, a spiritual one. The term *ta Ethne* could—besides its cultural or geographic connotations—imply all those who stand outside of the Christian faith in need of the Gospel and Baptism. "Nations" then indicates all those who are distanced from the Gospel and Jesus Christ. According to this sense, the boundary in need of crossing is that of unbelief, and biblical "nations" means in fact the heathen who reject the Gospel or are ignorant of it. This spiritual border runs in close proximity to the Christian church. In fact, we should acknowledge it as a reality within the Christian church wherein "paganism" in all its subtle forms exists. Hermann Dörries, a Luther scholar, traced the meaning of the word "heathen" in Luther's writings. In one sense, Luther would point to the prevalence of heathenism within Christianity. Christians are strongly forewarned by Luther not to appropriate for themselves the name "Christian" when they embrace idolatry, superstition, or false security. Luther thus assigns a missionary dimension to every preaching of the Gospel as it addresses paganism within the Christian community.[23] This spiritual barrier's existence is anticipated in the Augsburg Confession, for it describes the Church here on earth in a wider sense as a body in which believers and hypocrites coexist.[24]

Thus, if we apply a missionary dimension to every proclamation of the Church and pastorate, yes, to the very existence of the Church on earth itself, then we are certainly not defining mission only by locality—

---

22 Van Rheenen, *Missions*, 93.

23 Dörries, "Luther und die Heidenpredigt," 330.

24 AC VIII (Kolb-Wengert, 43).

that is, in geographic terms. Rather, we wish to ensure that all Christians see themselves also as recipients of exactly that same divine grace that is brought to outsiders. The Church needs to acknowledge the barrier of sin and heathenism in its midst and seek to overcome it by preaching the forgiveness and riches of the Gospel. Mission, then, becomes an integral part of the Church's life. In his definition of mission, James Scherer takes that boundary into consideration: "Mission as applied to the work of the church means the specific intention of bearing witness to the gospel of salvation in Jesus Christ at the borderline between faith and unbelief."[25] The Lutheran World Federation's *Together in God's Mission* (1988), discusses the complex nature of mission frontiers and includes observations in addition to the ones presented here:

> The cutting edge of mission is at the points where faith in Jesus Christ meets unbelief, i.e. non-recognition or rejection of Christ. It is to these points that the church in mission is called again and again. They are to be found in every continent, country and community. They are present even among members of the church. It is characteristic of a mission frontier that it is a focal area of the conflict between the Reign of God as revealed by Jesus Christ and the forces which are opposed to the claims of Christ and which prevent people from recognizing the love of God.[26]

MISSION AS "SENDING" AND THE OLD TESTAMENT

An indispensable component of mission has always been and continues to be the very act of sending. In the Old Testament, that sending was associated with isolated cases, such as the going of Jonah to Nineveh. Obviously, the concept of sending in the Old Testament also includes the work of the prophets. Nevertheless, the concept of sending comes to full expression in the New Testament. Andreas Köstenberger and Peter O'Brien debate the character of the Old Testament mission in the following terms: "To contend that Israel had a missionary task and should have engaged in mission as we understand it today goes beyond the evidence. There is no suggestion in the Old Testament that Israel should have engaged in 'cross-cultural' or foreign mission."[27] Instead, we are told that Israel approached their missionary task in two ways. First, as a *historical incorporation* with examples such as the "mixed crowd" that accompanied Israel out of Egypt (Exod. 12:38), the adoption of Rahab and her family (Josh. 6:25), and the acceptance of

25 Scherer, *Gospel, Church and Kingdom*, 37.
26 LWF, *Together in God's Mission*, 13.
27 Köstenberger and O'Brien, *Salvation to the Ends of the Earth*, 35.

foreigners within the kingdom of David (2 Sam. 11:3; 15:19–23). Ruth, the Moabitess, is also a good example of this historic incorporation into the tribe of Israel. Second, the Old Testament projects mission also as an *eschatological ingathering* of the Gentiles that is expected as a future action of God. This feature begins with the hope of the unification of the northern and southern tribes so that they would no longer be two nations (Jer. 31:31; Ezek. 34:12–13, 15; 37:15–23), and it broadens with the eschatological expectation of the ingathering of the Gentiles (Isa. 2:2–4; chs. 60–61).[28]

In the New Testament, the Latin term *missio* is a rendering of the Greek verb ἀποστέλλειν ("to send," e.g., Matt. 10:16; John 17:18; 20:21) or its noun, ἀποστολή ("the sending"). An important question in this regard is: What kind of sending is necessary before one qualifies as a missionary or before that task may actually be called mission? We observed from the Old Testament paradigm of mission that the explicit sending moment was rare; it was more common in its *centripetal* form, as a coming together or incorporation of people to the tribe. But the *centrifugal* aspect of mission as an explicit *sending* or *going* out needs to be considered. Part of the reason why Gustav Warneck and other scholars have so harshly judged the Reformation is because, to them, it lacked an intentional or deliberate act of sending out. Warneck, for example, opens his *Evangelische Missionslehre* with a very explicit concept of mission that would disqualify ordinary Christians from being called missionaries unless they are authoritatively sent.

> We understand Christian mission as the total activity of Christianity of planting and organizing a Christian church among non-Christians. This activity bears the name mission because it is founded on the commission of the head of the Christian church, is executed through missionaries (apostles), and reaches its goal as soon as such sending is no longer necessary.[29]

The underlying understanding of this definition is that many scholars like Warneck perceive mission along the lines of an authoritative and explicit sending. They would thus find completely unacceptable a broader definition of mission that either identifies mission as the "total activity of the church" or that includes every Christian. Mission would have to be more than Christians being in contact with non-Christians.

David Hesselgrave thus suggests that mission cannot dispense itself of a specific task that is associated with the missionary. He is intent on protecting the missionary, who, sent by the church, performs a specific task and not simply everything. We should note his observation:

---

28 Köstenberger and O'Brien, *Salvation to the Ends of the Earth*, 35–36.

29 Warneck, *Evangelische Missionslehre*, 1:1. Likewise, see Scherer's understanding as quoted above: *Gospel, Church and Kingdom*, 37.

> It would be well if, instead of using the word *mission* to describe all that the church is sent to do, we would use a word like *task* instead. Or, if instead of using the word *missionary* we would use the New Testament word *apostle* just as we use the New Testament words *prophet* and *evangelist*. But that is wishful thinking. In any case, let us not allow terminological confusion to undermine the primary task of sending missionaries into all the world to do precisely what the first missionaries did—evangelize and gather believers into local congregations where they can be taught the ways and words of Christ. *That is their specialized task. Whatever else they do by any way of doing good to all people (Gal. 6:10), they do, not because they are missionaries, but because they are Christians and belong to the larger church of Christ!*[30]

Indeed, given the biblical mandate and the worldwide need for the Gospel, we should underscore that the Church has an obligation to set apart individuals and commission them on behalf of those Christians who remain behind (Acts 13:3). Although mission can include spontaneous outreach and works of love and mercy arising from all Christians, it also represents the intentional targeting of people in the state of unbelief to whom the Church sends individuals. Obviously, mission and the idea of "going" to another area should not be determined on the basis of the distance covered. As much as distance is part of mission, the immediate neighborhood of every congregation may demand an organized campaign to address unbelievers that goes beyond a general mission paradigm including all Christians. The Church's task is also to set apart and commission individuals to ensure that the mission of the Church continues intentionally next to the sporadic witness of all Christians. The Lord Himself gave the example when He spoke to His disciples and included therein the commission to go. For some, such going meant the close proximity of Jerusalem, the place of the Lord's crucifixion. For others, it implied taking the Good News of the cross and resurrection in the task of mission to Samaria, Judea, and the very ends of the world.

---

30 Hesselgrave, *Today's Choices for Tomorrow's Mission*, 90.

CHAPTER THREE

Missiology as a Discipline
and Setting Priorities

Synonyms?

I mentioned in the opening chapter that global changes challenge the term "mission" on a number of levels. In the last chapter, I examined synonyms for *mission* based on the biblical witness to various dimensions of mission. In this chapter, I shall engage the pros and cons of possible alternate terms for mission in light of the changing human situation. All over the world, countries have closed their doors to Christian missionaries, showing thereby that they have taken a stand against Christian mission and its intentions. In the West, pluralism and secularism dismiss mission as an enterprise to convert non-Christians, representing an antiquated task from a bygone era of colonialism and Western domination. Those who have attained a Doctor of Missiology degree in mission or missiology at Western institutions discover upon returning home that such a degree has become more a liability than an asset for finding work.[1] This, in turn, has motivated universities to drop their degree in mission or missiology or to offer a less contested term for the degree, such as, for example, the doctorate in cultural anthropology.[2]

Even if we are reluctant to drop the term *mission* entirely from the Christian vocabulary, we may ask hypothetically, at least, what term could potentially replace it. Ever since missiology became a discipline at institutions, scholars explored the biblical data for alternative terms for mission. In his five-volume *Evangelische Missionslehre* (1897), the missiologist

---

1 When, for example, Concordia Theological Seminary, Fort Wayne, Indiana, dropped the name "Doctor of Missiology" and instead adopted the title "Doctor of Philosophy" for its program, there was relief among many students. Korean and Indian students, especially, welcomed the decision to have such a nomenclature change.

2 The Institute of Ecumenics and Religious Studies at the University of Tübingen closed its missiology program after its director, Professor Peter Beyerhaus, retired.

Gustav Warneck was the first to investigate the issue.[3] The Dutch missiologists Johannes Verkuyl (in his *Contemporary Missiology*) and Jan Jongeneel (in his two-volume *Philosophy, Science and Theology of Mission in the 19th and 20th Centuries*[4]) repristinated Warneck's proposals. Both these scholars, however, concluded that all alternative suggestions to mission offered little help in replacing "mission." They were simply too cumbersome to pronounce. However, they still highlight a number of important facets of mission. For this reason, I shall offer a brief overview of the investigation of alternative terms.

HALIEUTICS

The term *halieutics* ("fishing") is derived from the Greek verb ἁλιεύειν ("to catch fish") or the noun ἁλιεύς ("fisherman"). Obviously, the purpose here is not to refer to the mundane task of catching fish (which Peter and others were doing as a profession before they met Christ, John 21:3; Matt. 4:18; Luke 5:2; Mark 1:16). Rather, it symbolizes the task of becoming fishers of men to which Christ called them: "Follow Me, and I will make you fishers of men" (Matt. 4:19; Mark 1:17; Luke 5:10; Matt. 13:47). It is true that mission is the task of fishing in the sea of a non-Christian world. For that reason, the theory of mission could be called "halieutics," the study of fishing. But proposals to use this term have been short-lived and are no longer in circulation. Gustav Warneck clearly expresses his dislike for the term. Even if it captures the task of mission, he claims the term is neither tasteful nor appropriate for representing what mission does or the historical study of mission. It is also too narrow and too symbolic.[5]

KERYTICS

What about the term "kerytics" or its alternatives "kerygtics" and "kerygmatics"? These terms point to the task of preaching. Proclaiming the Gospel is certainly the most prominent task associated with mission. The term comes from the verb κηρύσσειν ("to preach," Mark 16:15; Rom. 10:14–15) or from the noun κῆρυξ ("herald," 1 Tim. 2:7; 2 Tim. 1:11; 2 Pet. 2:5). Undoubtedly, mission has at its core the task of proclaiming the Gospel. That also includes, of course, the broader conversation Christians have with non-Christians. But like the previous term, this fails to represent the comprehensive nature of mission. Along with calling out the unbelieving

---

3   Warneck, *Evangelische Missionslehre*, 1:18–26.

4   Verkuyl, *Contemporary Missiology*, 1–9; Jongeneel, *Philosophy, Science, and Theology of Mission*, 1:6–27.

5   Warneck, *Evangelische Missionslehre*, 1:19.

world to come to Christ, missionaries also instruct and baptize. "Kerytics" thus identifies only part of the missionary enterprise, not the whole task.[6]

EVANGELISTICS

Alexander Duff (1806–78) had already proposed "evangelistics" as perhaps the most likely term to replace *mission*. There are good reasons for such a substitution since the word on which "evangelistics" is based occurs frequently in the New Testament in both noun (76 times) and verb (54 times) forms. As stated above with "kerytics," mission associates itself with the task of proclaiming and sharing the Gospel. Very often, someone engaged in proclamation will be called an εὐαγγελιστής ("evangelist"). "Evangelist" is listed among the offices of apostle, prophet, shepherd, and teacher (Eph. 4:11). The early church theologian Jerome draws the distinction that while all apostles are evangelists, not all evangelists are apostles.[7] A similar distinction should apply today as well when we compare missionaries to evangelists: all missionaries are evangelists, but not all evangelists are missionaries. Although individuals who are sent out as missionaries to proclaim the Gospel may rightfully be called "evangelistic missionaries," a missionary is something more than an evangelist; he is also a teacher, translator, administrator of the Sacraments, organizer, and shepherd of a congregation.

What I said about "kerytics" also applies to the term "evangelistics" as a replacement for *mission*. We are dealing with a term that examines one task within mission, a task that forms only a fraction of the entire discipline of missiology.[8]

APOSTOLOGY

Perhaps the most compelling term to replace "mission" would be the one derived from the Greek verb ἀποστέλλειν ("to send"). Usually, the verb is translated into Latin as "missio," thus the term "mission." One could suggest that we retain the Greek element by using the phrase "apostology" instead of "missiology." The Greek verb ἀποστέλλειν occurs 131 times in the New Testament. It points particularly to the sending of the apostles by Christ (Matt. 10:5). Jesus sent them out like sheep into the midst of wolves (Matt. 10:16). And, though they were sent with no possessions such as a purse, bag, or sandals, they lacked nothing (Matt. 10:9–10; Luke 22:5).

---

6   Warneck, *Evangelische Missionslehre*, 1:20.

7   "Omnis apostolus evangelista sed non omnis evangelista apostolus," Warneck, *Evangelische Missionslehre*, 1:20.

8   Warneck, *Evangelische Missionslehre*, 1:20; Jongeneel, *Philosophy, Science, and Theology of Mission*, 1:27–28.

Paul refers to this sending with an important rhetorical question: "And how are they to preach unless they are sent?" (Rom. 10:15). The one sent by Christ is called in Greek ἀπόστολος ("the sent one") to give testimony to the resurrection of the Lord Jesus (Acts 4:33). This title occurs 79 times in the New Testament in reference to those sent, including the apostle Paul (Rom. 1:1; 11:13).

The argument, however, that the term "apostolics" or "apostology" should replace *mission* or the study of mission (missiology) is ultimately not strong enough. Jongeneel points out that "apostology" might be a good replacement since there is a great deal of agitation against Christian "mission." The use of the terms "apostology" or the "theology of the apostolate" might avoid the negative connotations of mission.[9] Yet the term sounds peculiar, foreign to the ear. The Church would have difficulty growing accustomed to it. But the Church, in order to confess fully its apostolic character, must confess and practice the concept of identifying and sending individuals. Missiology should therefore investigate thoroughly what the apostolate means beyond the traditional understanding, which is that the Church builds on the word and witness of the apostles. The apostolate of the Church must also have something to do with the missionary dimension of the Church.[10]

AUXANICS AND PROSTHETICS

We shall refer briefly to two other terms. "Auxanics" derives from the Greek verb αὐξάνειν or αὔξειν: "to grow, to increase, to multiply, or to advance." It emerges as an obvious choice for those within Church Growth circles who concentrate on numerical growth. The term occurs in the New Testament 22 times, especially in the Book of Acts (Acts 6:7; 12:24; 19:20), which shows that numerical growth, next to that of spiritual or internal growth, plays a part in Scripture. The term highlights the important work of the Holy Spirit who, through the preaching of His messengers, works faith in people and incorporates them into the Church. This process leads to the other term— namely, "prosthetics." The latter term also plays an important role in the Book of Acts. Frequently, we read of new believers being added to the body of believers (Acts 2:41, 47; 5:14; 11:24), and the Greek word used to indicate that "adding" is προστίθημι. We could thus suggest that we call the study of mission something like "auxanics" or "prosthetics." However, the fact that both terms deal with the work of the Holy Spirit speaks against their use. The Spirit causes the Church to grow by adding members to the Body

---

9   Jongeneel, *Philosophy, Science, and Theology of Mission*, 1:58.

10   Recent discussions point out the importance of understanding the apostolic role of the Church. See, for example, Guder, *Missional Church*, 83; Scudieri, *Apostolic Church*.

of Christ. It should be clearly said that both the activities of "growing" and "adding" are not man's doing but belong exclusively to God's free operation through the Holy Spirit. Both terms are thus difficult to study from a scholarly point of view.[11]

In summary, though the above terms reflect mission in varying degrees, they have a limited value to replace "mission" or "missiology." Even if the term "missiology" reflects, from a linguistic perspective, an unnatural marriage of Latin *missio* ("sending") and Greek *logos* ("study"), which might also sound offensive to a purist's ears, it has gained wide acceptance in describing the scholarly study of the Church's mission.[12]

Defining Missiology as a Discipline

In an essay entitled "Missiology as a Discipline and What It Includes," James Scherer reflects on the confusion that exists worldwide concerning the word "mission."[13] I noted earlier the British missiologist Andrew Kirk, who chose the simple title *What Is Mission?*[14] Scherer argues that the problem of definition derives from the theological imprecision. Once the theological elements for mission are in place, then the definition of missiology and the answer to the question about its branches would come far easier. A perusal through literature reveals an engaging debate among scholars over this question.[15] After giving a tentative definition of missiology, I shall list a few theological elements that will help to describe the mission of the Church and the study of that task:

> Missiology is an academic study that reflects critically on the mission of the Church as the instrument of the salvation activity of the triune God. It integrates various disciplines (it is multidisciplinary) such as biblical and ecclesiastical theology, mission history, and empirical studies, and it aims to contribute positively and constructively toward the Church's faithful stewardship of the mission of God.

The first conclusion that one can draw from this definition is that missiology is a multidisciplinary endeavor embracing insights from all classical

---

11 Jongeneel, *Philosophy, Science, and Theology of Mission*, 1:22–24.

12 Warneck himself proposes that the Church stay with mission and hence calls the study of it the science of mission (*Missionslehre* or *Missionswissenschaft*): *Evangelische Missionslehre*, 1:21.

13 Scherer and Bevans, *New Directions in Mission and Evangelization*, 173–87.

14 See Bibliography for publication information.

15 Bosch, "Theological Education in Missionary Perspective," 26. One may also consult other essays or studies on this topic: Farley, "Reform of Theological Education," 93–117; Findeis, "Missiology," 299–301; Hesselgrave, "Science Orientation," in *Today's Choices for Tomorrow's Mission*, 131–46; Hogg, "Teaching of Missiology," 487–506; Jongeneel, *Philosophy, Science and Theology of Mission*; Jongeneel, "Missiology of Gisbertus Voetius," 47–79; Medeiros, *Missiology as an Academic Discipline*; Myklebust, *Study of Missions*.

theological disciplines—biblical, historical, systematic, and practical theology, as well as from empirical studies such as linguistics and translation, history, statistics (on the growth of Christianity, the number of missionaries deployed, and the areas of deployment), cultural anthropology, psychology, education, and studies of other religions. Undeniably, the material is far too exhaustive for one discipline; therefore, missiology has no choice but to become an eclectic discipline. But the selection process of subject matter should be done carefully, lest missiology lose its focus and, with that, its integrity.

Second, missiology needs to be given its own right to exist within the framework of theological education or theological curricula. Scherer and Verkuyl argue that missiology is a complementary discipline that should stand on its own.[16] By making it an integrative discipline, that is, by merging it into one or all of the classical theological disciplines, missiology is in danger of being left to those among those disciplines who might not be comfortable with the task of reminding theology of its missionary dimension. That notwithstanding, it would still be necessary to argue for an integrative character of missiology in the curriculum. There is a missionary dimension to *all* theology that should become part of every theological discipline. In order to bring out this aspect of mission in theology, missiology should, as Bosch affirms, "provoke theology as a whole to discover anew that mission is not simply a more or less neglected department of the church's life that only enters the picture when a specialist from outside appears on the scene when a collection is taken."[17]

Third, missiology must choose an appropriate methodology. Some missiologists may be deductive, engaged in the task of drawing lines from Scripture and theology to today's context, while others may proceed more inductively by making the situation or context a starting point. The latter group must first gather data, after which they approach theology and draw conclusions on their observations. At any rate, it seems impossible to confine oneself to a single methodology. Ultimately, missiology is accountable to Scripture, the Church, and theology. Our definition thus points to the fact that missiology is a study that stands in solidarity with the Church and constructively contributes to the mission of the Church. Missiology does more than engage in descriptive or inductive methodology, it is *normative* and *prescriptive* as well. It analyzes the missionary task, and then proceeds to posit from theology *what* needs to be done to accomplish that task. Theological study purposefully and intentionally promotes the

---

16 Verkuyl, *Contemporary Missiology*, 7.
17 Bosch, "Theological Education in Missionary Perspective," 26.

proclamation of the Word of God for the conversion of nonbelievers and for building up the Body of Christ.

The diagram below shows the approaches taken by the method of deduction and induction. Each takes a different starting point. They either chart a collision course, or at least they pass by each other. One starting point is a set of principles that may be known either directly from Scripture or from valid logical conclusions based soundly on Scripture. I call this *principle*-oriented to show where the stress lies in the fundamentals. Another starting point consists of findings gleaned from the human context in the world. I call this principle *pragmatic*-oriented because it puts the stress on *praxis* in order to know certain fundamentals. Both have the opportunity to engage each other as Scripture is proclaimed in the human context throughout the world.

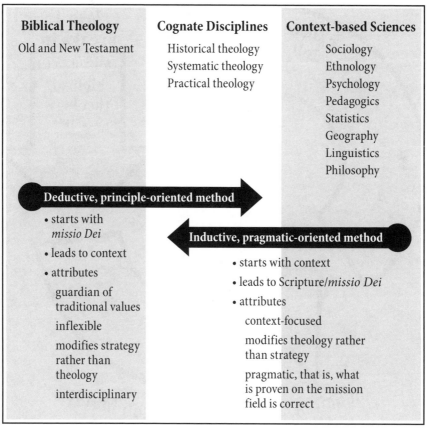

Fig. 1: Missiology as a Discipline

Both methods must serve each other to give justice to missiology's integrative and holistic character. Figure 1 suggests that sometimes this may fail to happen. In its hermeneutic and study, missiology draws together information from all sides and goes after all the available data. It moves from gathering data to a critical analysis, from description to prescription. It would thus be more appropriate to compare missiology to the hermeneutical circle. Its methods move in concentric circles; one leads to the other. The diagram below illustrates the point.

Missiology as a Discipline: A Prescriptive Approach

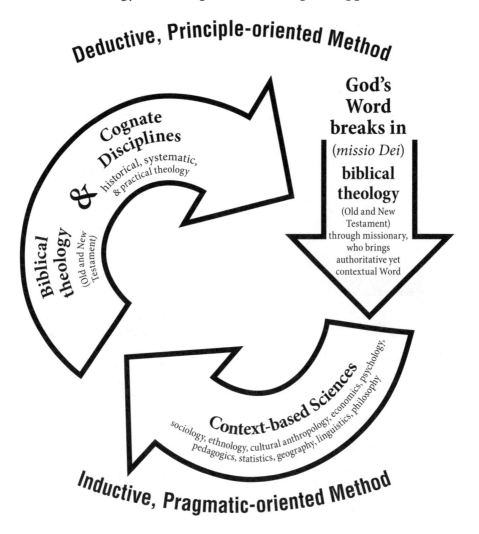

Fig. 2: Missiology's Holistic Character

Setting Priorities
for a Theology of Mission

It can be disconcerting to see the mission of the Church in a state of constant change. One would expect that mission is based on an unshaken foundation that, within reason, keeps changes in check and prevents methods and strategies from being constantly replaced by others. Indeed, a "theology" of mission should attempt to establish guiding principles that withstand the torrent of time and offer an element of stability.

However, as one actually pursues a theology for mission, the question is: Where should one begin? Where is an appropriate starting point, and which principles should one choose? For Lutherans, the answer to these questions is perhaps not as difficult as one might imagine. Lutherans have had an organizing principle all along. Call it the criterion around which all other theological principles gather. In the following chapter, we shall examine the doctrine of justification. Justification forms the centerpiece of Lutheran missiology, and around it clusters a series of principles that are influenced and normed by it. Meanwhile, let me more briefly point to some important aspects that would be indispensable for the emerging missionary task and missiology.[18]

Mission is rooted in the mystery of the triune God, whose entire being is a communication and a giving of Himself to the world. The triune God is the subject of mission and, as the Church pursues her mission, everything she does emanates from God and reflects His very being.[19] Mission is embedded in the eternal relationship of love that God has with this world. As the Church speaks of her mission, she should, above all, point to the mission of God, the *missio Dei*. Mission affirms the primary work of God, and that should serve as the vantage point. God plans and wills salvation

---

18 One may also see a list of theses I offered in "In Search of the Proprium of Lutheran Mission." The mission of the Church should commit herself to (1) the triune God; (2) the one Church of Jesus Christ, the *una sancta ecclesia* (and not the *proprium* of this or that particular church); (3) the purity of the means of grace as the only reliable marks of the Church; (4) the salvation of all sinners through justification; (5) the entire person as a human being in a particular context; (6) the goal of gathering and nurturing emerging congregations for worship through Word and Sacrament and their catechization for service and witness in this world; (7) an appropriate structure in the ministry between the ordained clergy and the priesthood of all believers; and (8) the ecclesial fellowship of Christian churches and congregations on the basis of an existing unity in doctrine.

19 In a theological statement on mission, the Commission on Theology and Church Relations (CTCR) of The Lutheran Church—Missouri Synod (LCMS) traces mission back to the very heart of God, stating that: "Mission begins in the heart of God and expresses his great love for the world. It is the Lord's gracious initiative and ongoing activity to save a world incapable of saving itself" (Commission on Theology and Church Relations, *Theological Statement of Mission*, 7).

for all (1 Tim. 2:3–4), and He ensures that this salvation is brought to those in need.

Mission is concerned with salvation and a particular understanding of it. God wishes to free people from their guilt and have them receive a new life. This means that mission represents the task of calling every individual to turn away from sin and toward God. Mission also calls these individuals into the family of God, that is, the Church. Such salvation is spiritual in nature. At the same time, mission does not reject physical concerns, those associated with the First Article of the Creed, with creation. While mission is concerned with bringing salvation in the narrow, spiritual sense, an integral part of it also implies a care for people in need.

Mission always deals with a community of believers. In the Apostles' Creed, we confess that community as the "communion of saints," which agrees with Article VII of the Augsburg Confession. This implies that God planned and created the human being in such a way that he does not exist separately from the Christian community (1 Cor. 12:13). Christians do not go their own way independently from one another. Rather, they nurture and support one another as a body. Only together, through the divine means of Word and Sacrament, will they find the important support and nurture for life eternal.[20] The Church represents the haven of salvation. The communion of believers shares God's Word as the gift of salvation, and the Church becomes an instrument of the Holy Spirit to further the salvation of the world.

A further essential element of mission is the world or context, particularly those people who have not yet heard the Gospel and those who are not members of the Church. Mission is never active in a vacuum or in the abstract; it happens where God meets the world, where the divine and the human dimensions come together. A case in point is the life and ministry of Jesus Christ. As the incarnate Son of God, He walked the earth in human form while still the divine Logos. For us, the human element includes the entire existence and reality of people as they order and structure their lives, both as individuals and as groups. However, as the Church confronts the world with the Gospel, not all Christians will agree how the Gospel informs the culture. The late theologian Richard Niebuhr claimed that Christians see the Gospel at work in culture in five different ways: (1) Christ against culture (antithesis); (2) Christ of culture (accommodation); (3) Christ above culture (synthesis); (4) Christ and culture in paradox (polarity); and (5) Christ the transformer of culture (conversion).[21] It would be difficult to choose any one of the five as definitive. In a way, each possibility repre-

---

20 Luther beautifully outlines this aspect: LC II 52–53 (Kolb-Wengert, 438).

21 Niebuhr, *Christ and Culture*.

sents a part of this complex subject matter. In fact, the late Lesslie Newbigin observed that "there can never be a culture-free gospel."[22] Christians ought to contemplate Newbigin's observation carefully as his insight may free up all those who serve in cross-cultural witness. Christians come to grips with their own cultural setting and thus avoid potential mistakes and misunderstandings as they witness to the Gospel in varying contexts.

METHOD AND APPROACH

As one peruses theological literature, one notices various principles of orientation and methodological differences. For example, Thomas Thangaraj suggests in *The Common Task* that Christian mission should make the concept of *missio humanitatis* and the common bond of humanity between Christians and non-Christians the important starting point for reaching out. He pleads for the widest circle possible as Christians and non-Christians engage in dialogue, so that a common conversation with nonbelievers is made before Christians share specific tenets of the faith with non-Christians. Scripture, he argues, cannot be made the starting point since the conversation would be substantially narrower and dismissive of others from the outset.[23]

Other missiologists prefer to follow the more traditional and deductive role of explaining mission from Scripture and then advancing to contemporary questions. In *Transforming Mission*,[24] the South African missiologist Bosch chooses God's self-communication in Christ as his point of departure. In *Contemporary Missiology*, the Dutch missiologist Verkuyl has little to offer in terms of providing the integrating principle or central pillar. The British missiologist Andrew Kirk ultimately follows classic methodology of proceeding from Scripture to contemporary questions, but he fails to establish any single principle or criterion as a hermeneutical device or organizing principle to his missiology.[25]

Today, a significant number of missiologists have delved into scientific or empirical studies. They see mission predominantly in cultural terms. For example, in *Translating the Message*, Lamin Sanneh simply places mission into the context of culture and communication, seeming to have left theology by the wayside. He takes both culture and communication as a heuristic device to determine the success or failure of Christian mission.[26]

---

22 Newbigin, *Foolishness to the Greeks*, 4.

23 Thangaraj, *Common Task*, 31–60.

24 Bosch, *Transforming Mission*, 22.

25 Items such as "Overcoming Violence and Building Peace" and "Care for the Environment" are also given central place in his subject matter. See Kirk, *What Is Mission?* 143–83.

26 Sanneh, *Translating the Message*, 6–8.

Overall, social sciences such as cultural anthropology have taken up the substantial part of the theology of mission in Evangelical circles. The seminal statements of the Evangelical Movement, the *Lausanne Covenant* (1974) and the *Willowbank Report on Gospel and Culture* (1978),[27] set the stage for many later works that investigate these themes further. Gailyn Van Rheenen's *Missions: Biblical Foundations and Contemporary Strategies* and Alan Tippet's *Introduction to Missiology* choose an inductive approach, where particular contemporary cultural issues dominate. As a consequence, the theological principles of missiology are treated only lightly.[28] One important contribution that is still worthy of study is Georg Vicedom's *The Mission of God.*[29] This book served earlier generations of students well and remains an important theological treatment of Christian mission, even if it is lacking in contextual issues. Vicedom was really the first theologian to systematically unfold the important theological concept of *missio Dei.*[30] Today, *missio Dei* is a regularly used term, but it needs to be understood once again in light of the more important priorities of mission. We will commit ourselves to that task in a later chapter.

The Ecumenical Movement has established its own mission priorities. The interest for mission began as early as the late nineteenth century and emerged in strong force with the World Missionary Conference at Edinburgh (1910). There has always been the quest to build mission on as broad a "consensus" as possible. For the Ecumenical Movement, theological discussions that could cause divisions should be abandoned in favor of those that unite. And yet, a disregard for the truth would make our Christian message ultimately meaningless for the world and thereby erode the integrity of mission itself (John 17:11-17). To paraphrase Paul, the quality of the tone of the trumpet is set by the quality of the trumpet player (1 Cor. 14:8).

The Value of Historical Study

Missiology and those involved in mission practice can learn a great deal from the past. There is great value in studying the history of mission, for it provides great lessons from which contemporary mission efforts can learn. As the saying goes, those who cannot remember the past are condemned to repeat it. The missiologist Gustav Warneck (1834–1910) from Halle, Germany, acknowledged the important role of studying the history of mission. Indeed, Warneck was almost inclined to place the academic

---

27   Both statements are found in Stott, *Making Christ Known*, 1–55, 75–113.

28   This, I believe, is evident, for example, from the works of Van Rheenen, *Missions*, and Tippet, *Introduction to Missiology*.

29   See Bibliography for publication information.

30   Kirk, *What Is Mission?* 25.

study of missiology into the discipline of historical theology. Next to the primacy of Scripture, he ranked history second as a nearly inexhaustible reservoir of information. Eventually, however, he chose to place missiology in practical theology, for it gave the final important advice on how to organize and plan for mission.[31]

When so much can be learned from history, it becomes important to provide regular updates of past records. Two seminal works on this topic, those by Kenneth Scott Latourette and Stephen Neill, should be acknowledged for their invaluable contribution.[32] But each resource is considerably dated. Since then, a worthy study by Timothy Yates, *Christian Mission in the Twentieth Century*, has provided an important update on the history of mission since Neill's treatment.[33] There is a wealth of information. Indeed, the continual expansion of mission makes the task of keeping abreast of current affairs extremely difficult. Whereas Latourette still described mission as a largely Western enterprise—and at his time it arguably still was—Neill perceptibly broadened his history of mission to churches in other areas of the world, such as Africa, India, and China. These regions look back over more than two hundred years of Protestant missionary presence and, in India's case, a very early presence of missionaries reaching as far back as the apostle Thomas. Recently, indigenous scholars from these regions have stepped forward and traced their local mission histories to their very beginnings.[34]

A further ethical challenge to the study of the history of mission is that every scholar must avoid generalizations and conspicuous omissions. A case in point is the formidable research project of the late David Bosch, who in *Transforming Mission*, his *magnum opus*, harmonized the epochs into greater theological paradigms. While helpful, the shortcomings of such an attempt are evident. One seeks in vain for any mention of the numerous missionary movements that persist within each of the paradigms.[35] The

---

31 Warneck, *Evangelische Missionslehre*, 1:35. Unfortunately, this *magnum opus* still awaits a translation into English.

32 Latourette, *History of the Expansion of Christianity*; Neill, *History of Christian Missions*. When Hans Peter Moritzen translated Stephen Neill's edition, he added some additional updated commentary.

33 Next to Yates's excellent study *Christian Mission in the Twentieth Century*, we have Tucker, *From Jerusalem to Irian Jaya*. It can hardly be regarded as an adequate coverage of past events. That must be said also of Anderson, *Biographical Dictionary of Christian Missions*.

34 For example, Kuriakose, *History of Christianity in India*, and Isichei, *History of Christianity in Africa*.

35 The periods mentioned: (1) the apocalyptic paradigm of primitive Christianity; (2) the Hellenistic paradigm of the patristic period; (3) the medieval Roman Catholic paradigm; (4) the Protestant (Reformation) paradigm; (5) the modern Enlightenment paradigm; and (6) the emerging Ecumenical paradigm. Cf. Bosch, *Transforming Mission*, 182–83. For a critical reflection on Bosch's second paradigm, the Greek patristic period, see Kreider, "Beyond Bosch," 59–68.

nineteenth century, for example, though closest to the paradigm of the modern Enlightenment, embraced also within its time period a number of other mission movements that emerged or had continued unabated from earlier centuries. It is true that the Ecumenical Movement that arose under its energetic organizer, John R. Mott (1865–1955), has become the dominant Protestant paradigm of the late nineteenth century; it was, however, not the sole movement during that time. One only needs to mention the continued mission efforts of the Moravian Brethren or the emerging Lutheran Confessional mission, as insignificant as these latter movements may seem. For inexplicable reasons, Bosch also omitted influential and formative pioneers of Lutheran foreign mission, such as Wilhelm Löhe (1808–72) at Neuendettelsau and Ludwig Harms (1808–65) in Hermannsburg.[36]

Within the Ecumenical paradigm—as ours is supposedly called today—there are also those theologians who do not share its direction. Concerned theologians separated from the Ecumenical Movement of the WCC in 1974 to protest its theology. They formed the Lausanne, or Evangelical, Movement, named after their *magna Carta*, the Lausanne Covenant.[37] Other major denominations, though ecumenically oriented, maintain their own denominationally oriented mission. In his comparative study on the various missionary movements of Lutheranism, Roman Catholicism, Evangelicalism, and Eastern Orthodoxy, James Scherer demonstrates that each of them affirms distinctive principles and agendas.[38] Thus even if Christianity of the twentieth and twenty-first century appears at first glance to be ecumenically oriented, denominations still feel obliged to argue the validity of their own existence and mission.

An important benefit from a careful study of the history of mission is a deepened appreciation for Christianity's struggles through time and varying contexts. Through her mission, the Church confronted the world and as a result was compelled to formulate her faith and practices. For this reason, Martin Kähler once called the mission of the Church "the mother of theology." As the Church preached the Gospel to others, "it was forced to theologize."[39] Within the history of mission, there is a seedbed of information that assists us in mapping out a theological road for today and tomorrow. We can, for example, see that the Lord's mandate for mission has survived the centuries and speaks in undiminished intensity to us, even as it did centuries ago. But in terms of its execution throughout these centuries, the mission of the Church has displayed various faces.

---

36 The German period is examined in Aagaard, *Mission, Konfession, Kirche.*
37 Yates, *Christian Mission in the Twentieth Century*, 199.
38 Scherer, *Gospel, Church and Kingdom.*
39 Bosch, *Transforming Mission*, 16.

Admittedly, our era of mission will be subjected to scrutiny, just as we appraise and critique the past. We may be reluctant to concede to the stark reality of being conditioned by times and circumstances. Our natural reaction is to command for ourselves a purity and objectivity that looks askance at defective practices of the past. As we look back into history, for example, it seems inconceivable that missionaries could ever have forsaken obvious Christian and biblical principles such as love and compassion, falling prey to oppressive expansionist ideals. The bloody conquest of the Saxons by Charlemagne in the ninth century, the crusades in the eleventh century, and the invasions into foreign lands by the conquistadors from Portugal and Spain in the sixteenth century are all evidence of an illegitimate fusion of political and religious motivations. As we dismiss so readily this disastrous entanglement of the objective missionary enterprise with personal and political interests, we should know that we will hardly be spared from future criticism against the way we do mission in the world today.

One disturbing point in the collective portrayals of the history of mission is the harsh treatment that Lutheranism has received, particularly during the time of the Reformation and the age of Orthodoxy. Sixteenth- and seventeenth-century Lutheranism is charged, quite undeservedly, with having been quiescent, even reticent, toward overseas mission. Fortunately, great defenses of the Reformation have demonstrated quite persuasively that such accusations are biased and unfair. Most modern renderings of the history of mission apply a hermeneutic that understands mission as an activity of mission societies. Because of William Carey and the era of Pietism, mission became largely an enterprise of societies, and the nineteenth century has been hailed as *the* century in mission.[40] But whether that century should actually hold the key to a properly understood mission is a different matter. Protestant mission rests on the theological heritage of the Reformation, which places mission in the hands of the Church and every believer, not a syndicated group of people. With that proviso, the Reformation suddenly comes alive as an important missionary movement of the Church, mission from the cross, as we shall demonstrate in the following chapter.

---

40 Winter, "Long Look," 168–69.

CHAPTER FOUR

THE REFORMATION[1]

REASONS FOR NOT RESPONDING
TO A WORLDWIDE OBLIGATION

The Reformation is known for bringing the Gospel to light, but it lacked an intentional and operational missionary enterprise to bring it to the world. The reasons for not being more missional are manifold. First, congregations had no immediate connection to overseas countries and thus could not pursue foreign mission. Second, the reformers spent their energies largely on reforming the church's internal problems. Third, even if overseas mission had been an option, the territorial ruler who had authority over ecclesiastical affairs in that region, including the dispatching of personnel, would have had to grant permission to go ahead with a mission project. Then it would have been necessary to raise funds, primarily solicited from the nobility and rising merchant class. Thus the lack of missionary intent and enterprise is mostly a case of historical circumstance, which many scholars—who often level scathing criticisms against the reformers—are loath to admit. Instead, they gloss over the underlying mission component in Luther's theology and focus instead on what they see to be a failure on the reformer's part to be more intentional with respect to mission.

THE CHALLENGE OF DEFINING MISSION

The famous missiologist Gustav Warneck (1834–1910), the father of mission science, who taught in Halle, Germany, at the end of the nineteenth century, is one of those scholars who judged Luther negatively for what he perceived

---

1 Some portions of this chapter are based on "From Wittenberg with Love: Martin Luther's Theology of Mission," a conference paper delivered March 31, 2005, at the Congress for Lutheran Confessions, Association of Confessional Lutherans, Indian Lakes Resort, Bloomingdale, Illinois. Permission to use this paper as the foundation for this chapter has been granted by Luther Academy and the Association of Confessional Lutherans.

to be a lack of mission emphasis in Luther's theology. Warneck based his negative evaluation on his particular understanding of mission. He writes:

> For by "mission" we understand and we must not understand anything else than this sending [i.e. a regular sending of messengers of the Gospel to non-Christian nations, with the view of Christianizing them], continuing through every age of the church, which carries out the commandment, "Go and make disciples of all nations."[2]

Warneck promotes a sociological and organizational concept of mission that encourages a "sending" pursued deliberately by an institution, such as a mission society or a core group of individuals, and that works in geographic terms of leaving one territory for another, preferably across an ocean.

If one were to approach Luther with such a concept of mission, perhaps Warneck's criticisms would seem justified. For the intentional sending of individuals through mission societies to faraway countries came into being only centuries after Luther. The concept of sending out missionaries became possible through newly discovered lands in which one found no Christian communities. Protestant rulers gained power over some of these countries, to which the rulers could then send missionaries. In the late sixteenth and early seventeenth century, European Christians sent missionaries to the Scandinavian countries, to the Eskimos in Greenland, to the northern Lapps, and to indigenous populations in both India and the Americas.

There were and are, however, many more scholars who point out aspects of Luther's theology that are clearly missiological.[3] They operate with a

---

2   Warneck, *Outline of a History of Protestant Mission*, 10. Warneck must be seen as the major instigator of this negative discussion as it emerged in his groundbreaking essay, "Mission unter den Heiden," 128. In his *Outline*, Warneck makes the following conclusion to his observations: "If, however, the Reformers and their immediate disciples have no word either of sorrow or excuse that circumstances hindered their discharge of missionary duty, while they could not but see that the Church of Rome was implementing this duty on a broad scale, this strange silence can be accounted for satisfactorily only by the fact that the recognition of the missionary obligation was itself absent. We miss in the Reformers not only missionary action, but even the idea of mission, in the sense in which we understand them today. And this not only because the newly discovered heathen world across the sea lay almost wholly beyond the range of their vision, though that reason had some weight, but because fundamental theological views hindered them from giving their activity, and even their thoughts, a missionary direction" (10). This citation is also found in Bürkle, *Missionstheologie*, 43. Since then, many scholars have discounted Luther for similar reasons. See Latourette, *History of the Expansion of Christianity*, 3:25; Rosenkranz, *Weltmission und Weltende*, 43–44; Littell, "Protestantism and the Great Commission," 26–42; Ohm, *Machet zu Jüngern alle Völker*, 113; Hogg, "Rise of Protestant Missionary Concern," 95–111; Tucker, *From Jerusalem to Irian Jaya*, 67; Müller, "Missionarischer Gemeindeaufbau bei Martin Luther," 31–37.

3   The list provided is not complete. The scholars Gustav Leopold Plitt, Karl Holl, and Werner Elert should be given credit as the first scholars who provided support for missionary accents in Luther's theology. See Plitt, *Geschichte der lutherischen Mission*, 1:3–15; Holl, "Luther und die Mission," 234–43; Elert, *Structure of Lutheranism*, 1:385–402. These additional scholars

broader definition of mission than the one that Gustav Warneck follows. David Bosch offers a broader concept of mission, which is more sympathetic to Luther: "[M]ission does not only begin when somebody goes overseas; it is not an 'operational theory' nor is it dependent upon the existence of separate agencies."[4] If we can agree on the idea that mission is by definition far broader and far deeper in meaning than forming organizations and operations for overseas mission, then Luther and his theology suddenly become very pertinent for mission. In this book, I shall maintain that the Reformation must be seen as a missionary movement. The Church—not societies—expands through the preaching of pastors, through the witness of Christians, and through translation and publication of texts.

ARE WE PREPARED TO LEARN FROM LUTHER?

In recent years, several studies on Luther's role in mission have been published. Some are worthy of mention: First, Volker Stolle's *The Church Comes from All Nations* provides helpful source material. Second, Ingemar Öberg's *Luther and World Mission: A Historical and Systematic Study*. Third, and perhaps the best study, is that by Paul Wetter: *Der Missiongedanke bei Martin Luther.*[5] Other essays add little to what has been contributed by Werner Elert and Paul Wetter.[6]

Elert and Wetter admit that the Reformation did not originate primarily as a call to missionary or evangelistic obedience but as a movement for the reform and renewal of existing Christian life. Yet they and others have searched Luther's theology and thus conclude that it is truly a

---

follow Plitt, Holl, and Elert: Drews, "Die Anschauungen reformatorischer Theologen über die Heidenmission," 1–26; Holsten, "Reformation und Mission," 1–32; Gensichen, "Mission und Luthertum," 546–48; Maurer, "Reformation und Mission," 20–41; Gensichen, "Were the Reformers Indifferent to Missions?" 119–27; Koschade, "Luther on Missionary Motivation," 224–39; Peters, "Luthers weltweiter Missionssinn," 162–75; Dörries, "Luther und die Heidenpredigt," 327–46; Schmidt, "Die missionarische Dimension der Theologie," 193–201; Aagaard, "Missionstheologie," 250–74; Blöchle, "Die missionarische Dimension in der Theologie Luthers," 357–68; Bürkle, *Missionstheologie*, 42–46; Scherer, *That the Gospel May Be Sincerely Preached*, 4–15; Bunkowske, "Luther, the Missionary," 54–91; Laman, "Origin of Protestant Missions," 728–74; Bosch, *Transforming Mission*, 239–48; Wetter, *Der Missionsgedanke bei Martin Luther*; Stolle, *Church Comes from All Nations*; Schulz, "Lutheran Missiology," 4–53; Öberg, *Luther and World Mission*.

4 Bosch, *Transforming Mission*, 244.

5 For detailed references on these works, see Bibliography for publication information. Although Luther receives the most attention, numerous scholars include the reformers Calvin and Melanchthon in their observations and discuss commonalities. See, for example, Gensichen, "Were the Reformers Indifferent to Missions?" 119–27. Holsten, "Reformation und Mission," 14, recognizes a common thread in the theology of Luther, Melanchthon, Bugenhagen, Veit Dietrich, and even Calvin but sets apart from them Martin Bucer, Zwingli, and Bibliander.

6 See texts listed in pp. 46–47 n. 3 above.

Brunnenstube[7]—that is, a valuable source for missionary theology and practice. In his essay *Die missionarische Dimension in der Theologie Luthers,* Herbert Blöchle states it pointedly: "Luther did not speak just on occasions and periodically to the questions about mission to the heathens. His entire theology is rather permeated by a 'missionary dimension.'"[8] Wilhelm Maurer, too, argues similarly: "While Luther did not run an organized mission operation, he clearly brought out principles of evangelical mission work; and we must begin with him to recognize these principles."[9] In this chapter, we will turn first to various mission accents in Luther's theology. Then, we will cite several places where Luther actively promoted actual missionary intents and activities. In none of this material does Luther suggest passivity or quietism. Let us start with the realization that Luther understood faith to be a busy and living thing, which impels Christians to share their faith with others.[10]

CONFIDENCE IN THE DYNAMIC WORD

The Word of God sets down the tenets of what we must believe. *Sola scriptura*, the verification of doctrine through the agency of Scripture alone, serves as a principle against which other teachings must be measured. Luther demonstrated this understanding best at Worms on April 17–18, 1521, when he pleaded his case before the emperor and stated that he would retract all his writings if he was proven wrong from Scripture. But Luther also added a strong dynamic character to the Word of God that has missiological implications. Bosch points out that Luther rested his entire mission paradigm on Rom. 1:16: "I am not ashamed of the Gospel."[11] In Luther's theology, the Word of God has the dynamic missionary character of being constantly in motion and not limited to time and space.[12] In his sermon for Ascension Sunday in 1523, Luther provides the following well-known illustration:

> With this message or preaching, it is just as if one throws a stone into the water. It makes waves and circles or wheels around itself, and the waves roll always farther outward. One drives the other until they reach the shore. Although it is still in the middle, the waves do not rest; instead,

---

7   Schmidt, "Die missionarische Dimension der Theologie," 193.

8   Blöchle, "Die missionarische Dimension in der Theologie Luthers," 367.

9   Maurer, "Reformation und Mission," 28.

10   "O it is a living, busy, active, mighty thing, this faith. It is impossible for it not to be doing good works incessantly. It does not ask whether good works are to be done, but before the question is asked, it has already done them, and is constantly doing them" (*Preface to Romans,* AE 35:370; Bosch, 244).

11   Bosch, *Transforming Mission,* 240.

12   Maurer, "Reformation und Mission," 30.

the waves continue forward. So it is with the preaching. It is started through the apostles and always proceeds and is driven farther through the preacher to and fro in the world, driven out and persecuted; nevertheless, it is always being made more widely known to those that have never heard it before. As it travels, however, in the center, it may be extinguished and perverted by heresy. Or as it is said, if someone sends a message out, the message has been sent even though it has not arrived at the intended place or at a particular point, but is traveling en route, as when one says: "The emperor's message has gone out," though it has not yet arrived at Nuremberg or in Turkey where it now should go. This is how the preaching of the apostles should also be understood.[13]

This oft-quoted illustration not only offers insight into Luther's confidence in God's Word and its continual expansion, but it reveals also Luther's critique of a position regarding mission that by his time had become traditional. This belief held erroneously, on the basis of texts such as Rom. 10:18, that the Gospel had reached all parts of the world and thus the preaching of the Gospel was no longer necessary. Luther, however, was of another mind. He explicitly mentions his own knowledge of new lands being discovered and that the preaching of the apostles had not yet reached them but would do so as the Gospel continues its expansive course. In other words, Luther considered that the Word had not yet reached all parts of the world; it is in the process of doing so. And so we may conclude with Elert's words:

The idea of many later theologians—that the church of the present time is no longer obligated to preach among the heathen, because the apostles have already reached all—is totally foreign to him, just as it is to Melanchthon. Furthermore, it would be opposed to the dynamic view of the Gospel and the church. It is self-evident that Luther knows that no apostle came to the Germans.[14]

This ongoing dynamic view of God's Word or, as Elert puts it, this impact of the Gospel (*evangelischer Ansatz*) establishes two important principles for mission. First, we should have faith in the omnipotence and the universal teleology of the Gospel. Second, we should commit ourselves to the mission of proclaiming the Gospel.[15]

Both aspects come to bear in the second petition of the Lord's Prayer, "Thy kingdom come." There, Luther asks that the kingdom may come through the Word and the Holy Spirit "to those who are not yet in it." He thus prays: "Dear Father, we ask you first to give your Word, so that the gospel may be properly preached throughout the world and then that it

13 Stolle, *Church Comes from All Nations*, 24–25.
14 Elert, *Structure of Lutheranism*, 1:387.
15 Elert, *Structure of Lutheranism*, 1:385; Blöchle, "Die missionarische Dimension in der Theologie Luthers," 362.

may also be received in faith and may work and dwell in us so that your kingdom may pervade among us."[16] For what is Luther praying? Clearly, it is for the mission of God to continue to all those outside of the Church and for God's mission to remain with us—in other words, to keep the kingdom among us until its final vindication. We see here once again the missionary dimension to Luther's theology: God's mission takes place within the life of the Church, and yet it also extends beyond the Church to those still held in unbelief. From the above, we learn the following: though Luther did not use the contemporary phrase *missio Dei*, he nonetheless was conceptually the forerunner of much of what the term denotes. God is the subject. Our activity must subordinate itself to God's doing, and any success is due to Him.

Let us now ask the question, With whom does mission contend? Who opposes it? Luther's understanding is that the mission of the Church primarily plays itself out as a spiritual battle between the Word of God and diabolical forces. A little further on in his petition, Luther concludes: ". . . so that your kingdom may pervade among us through the Word and the power of the Holy Spirit and the devil's kingdom may be destroyed so that he may have no right or power over us until his kingdom is utterly eradicated and sin, death, and hell wiped out."[17] In other words, mission is not done in a neutral zone. Rather, it contends with ultimate powers. During Luther's time and according to his understanding, these powers were embodied in the papal church and in Islam, the religion of the Turks. Throughout his life, he thus made these two missionary fronts part of his ministry of refuting and correcting them.[18]

Eschatology, Judgment Day, and Predestination

The diabolical front opposing the efforts of the Gospel also brings us to the topic of Luther's expectation: the coming of Judgment Day. Indeed, Luther lived a life that was immersed in the thought of the end times. Calamities and events were interpreted as signs that Judgment Day was imminent. But his confidence was such that God's Word would prevail over Satan within history, and that such victory would become fully manifest at the end on the final day of consummation.

Some scholars argue that the nearness of Judgment Day actually inhibited Luther's activity and his support for preaching the Gospel. Warneck observes:

---

16 LC III 53–54 (Kolb-Wengert, 447). See also Peters, *Kommentar zu Luthers Katechismen*, 3:83.

17 LC III 53–54 (Kolb-Wengert, 447).

18 Stolle, *Church Comes from All Nations*, 75–76, 89–90.

Account has also to be taken of his [Luther's] doctrine of Election and of his Eschatology. To lay the whole stress upon the former . . . is certainly one sided. But when Luther considers the Turks as the obdurate enemies in the last time by whom God visits the sins of Christendom, and looks upon the heathen and the Jews as having fallen under the dominion of the Devil—and that, too, not without their own fault—this view must from the outset paralyze every thought of missionary work among them. God, to be sure, has everywhere His elect, whom by divers means He leads to faith; but how He brings this to pass, that is a matter of His sovereign grace—a human missionary agency does not lie in the plan of His decree. Add to this that Luther and his contemporaries were persuaded that the end of the world was at hand . . . It was the general view, shared both by Luther and Melanchthon . . . that in the middle of the 16th Century, some time in the year 1558, the last day would come. This eschatological conception of the Reformers . . . clearly explains how we find in them no proper missionary ideas.[19]

In terms of Luther's expectation of Christ's return, one may perhaps offer a few words of correction. Luther was extremely critical of the calculations of a close associate of his, Pastor Michael Stifel, who in a publication projected the exact date of Christ's return on October 19, 1533, at 8 a.m. Luther turned down the request to write a foreword to this publication by correcting the pastor with a statement similar to Augustine's invective against his own contemporary end-time calculators that all those who make calculations should relax their fingers and give them a rest.[20]

Thomas Ohm also considers Luther's doctrine of election and his eschatology as a reason for what he calls a "fatalistic-quietistic" attitude for mission. Ohm asserts that Luther would place everything in God's hands to call His elect to salvation in His own way without summoning Christians to mission. Ohm's opinion, however, ought to raise the hackles of any Luther scholar. Ohm's views impose on Luther an alien doctrine of predestination that has more similarities with Calvin than with Luther. For, as we shall show in a later chapter, the hallmark of the Lutheran doctrine of predestination is a conscious decision for the universal salvific will of God, over against a restricted duality of the elect and the condemned. God's will that all be saved was extended through the preaching of the Gospel to all nations worldwide.[21]

We should note, however, Luther's sober realism in interpreting the Church's affairs and her mission in these end times. There is a significant

---

19 Warneck, *Outline of a History of Protestant Missions*, 15–16.

20 Luther assigned Pastor Michael Stifel to a neighboring parsonage after Stifel had fled his home area in northern Austria as a result of the Counter-Reformation. Stifel entered his calculations in the book *Rechenbüchlein vom Endchrist: Apocalypsis in Apocalypsim*. One may see Brecht, *Martin Luther*, 3:20.

21 Wetter, *Der Missionsgedanke bei Martin Luther*, 45.

difference between Luther's views and today's unguarded confidence in our activities of making pledges and taking oaths of achieving results within specific time frames. Luther was realistic and sober enough to realize that until the final consummation arrives, resistance and hostility to God's Word will dominate and Christianity will never attain the status of becoming a dominant religion in this world. The coming end heightens the urgency of mission for Luther, but at the same time, the world's deep estrangement from God and its opposition to God will always bring the cross upon the Church.

So, will the whole world become Christian? Luther would deny this possibility: "You must therefore not understand it in such a way that the whole world and all people will believe in Christ. Because we must always have the holy cross, the greater portion will be those who persecute Christians."[22]

With respect to Germany, the land where the Gospel had been rediscovered, Luther observed:

> The movement of the Gospel is now among us, but our ungratefulness and scorning of the divine Word, pettiness, and decadence make it so that it will not remain for long. There shall then follow after it a large rabble, and great wars will come later. In Africa, the Gospel was very powerfully present, but the liars corrupted it, and after it the Vandals and the wars came. It went likewise also in Egypt: first lying then murder. It will also go exactly the same way in the German land. The pious preachers will first be taken away, and false prophets, enthusiasts, and demagogues will step into my place and that of other preachers and divide the church and tear it apart.[23]

The Central Role of the Church

Luther complements the missionary dimension of his theology with a call to missionary activity. Often when he spoke of furthering the Gospel, he would do so in ecclesiological terms. Human activity represents the activity of preaching the Word and administering the Sacraments, and this activity extends the kingdom of God. As unbelievers hear preaching and as they are baptized, they are incorporated into a Christian community. Mission has much to do with the core activities of the Church: preaching, teaching and administering the means of grace. Luther explains the role of the Church in God's mission as follows:

> The Holy Spirit will remain with the holy community or Christian people until the Last Day. Through it he gathers us, using it to teach and preach the Word. . . . [I]n this Christian community we have the forgiveness of

---

22 Stolle, *Church Comes from All Nations*, 26.
23 Stolle, *Church Comes from All Nations*, 83.

sins, which takes place through the holy sacraments and absolution as well as through all the comforting words of the entire gospel. . . . For he has not yet gathered all of this Christian community, nor has he completed the granting of forgiveness.[24]

This Church-centered approach to mission suggests that the Church, and not a mission society, serves as the catalyst and base for missionary outreach.[25] Expansion ultimately takes place at the level of the congregation. The mission of every congregation stands in the service of expanding the universal Church; it moves toward the heathen as the Gospel is preached and as believers witness to Christ.[26] Undoubtedly, the activities associated with the Word and Sacraments in the local church is the most original and appropriate form of mission. Already the Early Church undertook mission in a way that the life of the congregation filled the surrounding world (e.g., 1 Thess. 1:8). When Luther encouraged mission work, his thought embraced the winsome force of the local churches and that of individual Christians moving into the unbelieving world. Luther speaks with renewed relevancy to our own situation.

All this implies that congregational work, directly or indirectly, stands in service to the goal of mission. Even the liturgical worship of a congregation plays a role, as Luther observed: "The second is the German Mass and Order of Service, which should be arranged for the sake of the unlearned lay folk and with which we are now concerned. These two orders of service must be used publicly, in the churches, for all people, among whom are many who do not believe and are not yet Christians."[27] The hymns of the congregation advance the mission of the Church:

> God has made our heart and spirit happy through his dear Son, whom he gave for our salvation from sin, death and the devil. Whoever honestly believes this, cannot leave it alone, but he must cheerfully and with joy speak about it in order that others might listen and draw near. If, however, one does not want to sing and speak about it, it is a sign that he does not believe and is not in the new cheerful testament but belongs under the old, rotten, unhappy testament. Therefore, the printers do very well when they diligently print songs and make them pleasant for the people, with

---

24 LC II 53, 54, 62 (Kolb-Wengert, 438–39). See also Gensichen, "Mission und Luthertum," 546.

25 Maurer, "Reformation und Mission," 33–44; Stolle, *Church Comes from All Nations*; Aagaard, *Mission, Konfession, Kirche*, 208; Koschade, "Luther on Missionary Motivation," 236–37.

26 Three hundred years later, the theologian and man of mission Wilhelm Löhe reaffirmed this concept: "Mission is nothing but the one church of God in its motion, the actualization of the one universal, catholic church" (Löhe, *Three Books about the Church*, 59); Elert, *Structure of Lutheranism*, 1:390.

27 Stolle, *Church Comes from All Nations*, 43–44.

all kinds of ornamentation so that they are stimulated to this joy of the faith and gladly sing.[28]

Catechesis Serves Mission

Luther's ecclesiology also includes the witness activity of every Christian. But the proper foundation needs to be built. A Christian must be properly instructed through catechesis: "I strongly urge that the children be taught the catechism. Should they be taken captive in the invasion, they will at least take something of the Christian faith with them."[29]

Every Christian's faith must be informed on the biblical truths about Christ, the Savior. This is evident from Luther's explanation of the Second Article of the Apostles' Creed:

> Study now, while you still have room and place, the Ten Commandments, the Lord's Prayer, the Creed, and learn them well, especially the article in which we say, "And in Jesus Christ, his only-begotten Son, our Lord, who was conceived by the Holy Spirit, born of the Virgin Mary, suffered under Pontius Pilate, crucified, died and buried, descended to Hell, on the third day again raised from the dead, ascended to Heaven, sitting on the Right of God, the almighty Father, from whence he shall come, to judge the living and the dead, etc." Because everything lies in this article. From this article, we are called Christians and are also called through the Gospel to the same, baptized and counted in Christendom and accepted, and receive through the same Holy Spirit the forgiveness of sins.[30]

On the basis of this instruction, the distinctive contours of our Christian belief become evident over and against those of other religions. Already in the identity of God, distinctions are apparent. According to Luther, Jews, Muslims, and false Christians together all equally reject the triune God. Luther states that "our faith is distinguished from all other beliefs on earth. The Jews don't have it, the Turks and Saracens also do not, furthermore a Papist or false Christian or any other unbeliever does not have it but only the orthodox Christian."[31]

As Luther speaks on the service of all Christians, he devotes particular attention to those situations where he sees that regular circumstances no longer exist. Under such extraordinary circumstances, the witness of the laity must be unyielding and firm in their Christian testimony. "If, he [a Christian] is in a place where there are no Christians he needs no other call than to be a Christian . . . . Here it is his duty to preach and to teach the

---

28 Stolle, *Church Comes from All Nations*, 47.
29 Stolle, *Church Comes from All Nations*, 46.
30 Stolle, *Church Comes from All Nations*, 71.
31 Stolle, *Church Comes from All Nations*, 71.

gospel to erring heathen or non-Christians, because of the duty of brotherly love, even though no man calls him to do so."[32] Luther contrived no fictitious cases; real threats were imminent. The Turks were close, and he advised Christian prisoners of war to remain constant in faith.

> I must here be of encouragement and give a word of comfort to those Germans who already have been captured or may still be captured in Turkey . . . they should be patient in captivity and remain firm in the faith until the time of their redemption, in order that they may not be scandalized by the Babylonian faith and worship. . . . Pay attention, therefore, my dear brother. Be warned and admonished, that you remain in the right Christian faith and neither deny nor forget your dear Lord and Savior Jesus Christ, who died for your sin.[33]

If, however, a believer finds himself among many other Christians, he should step back and let regular rules dictate the situation. Luther explains: "If he is at a place where there are Christians who have the same power and right as he . . . he should let himself be called and chosen to preach and to teach in the place and by the command of others."[34]

We shall repeat the above observations in a later chapter as we discuss the meaning and implications of emergency situations. We shall also devote ourselves then to Luther's concept of the priesthood of all believers as it impacts this issue.

THE CULTURAL MOTIVE

Finally, Luther's remarkably sensitive views on customs and cultures ought to inform the modern Church's attempts to bring the Gospel to diverse groups of people the world over. Not only should the Gospel be taught and preached in the indigenous people's language, but the newly converted should also find their own expression of faith within their particular cultural context. The preaching of the Gospel must be heard and understood in the language of those being evangelized. Luther furthered the cause and value of translation. A good preacher and missionary must take great pains in his choice of words by mingling with his audience and watching them closely. Here Luther opined:

> We do not have to inquire of the literal Latin, how we are to speak German . . . Rather we must inquire about this of the mother in the home, the children on the street, the common man in the marketplace. We must be guided by their language, the way they speak, and do our translating

---

32 Stolle, *Church Comes from All Nations*, 21.

33 Stolle, *Church Comes from All Nations*, 71.

34 Stolle, *Church Comes from All Nations*, 22.

accordingly. That way they will understand it and recognize that we are speaking German to them.[35]

Luther's efforts at learning about others included also other nations with whom Christians in the sixteenth century could potentially come into contact. In 1529, he addressed the German people's ignorance of the Qur'an and Muslims by translating and prefacing a monograph on the "Custom and Religion of the Turks" (*Libellus de ritu et moribus turcorum*), written by a Dominican monk, Georgius of Hungary, between 1475 and 1481. And in 1542, Luther followed up with translating *Confutation against the Koran* (*Confutatio Alcorani*), written by Italian Dominican monk and missionary Ricoldo da Monte Crucis (d. 1320) in the fourteenth century.[36] We have already seen how Luther debated the question of how one should behave appropriately as a Christian in a war against the Turks.

Luther admired the disciplined life of the Turks and promoted it as a helpful example for Germans to follow suit. Nevertheless, Luther had a negative opinion of the religion of the Turks and of the Muslim faith. In general, Luther supposed that Islam was a religion of the Law that rejects free grace in Christ and thus leads to eternal condemnation, set on equal par with that of the Roman Catholic faith and Judaism.

In his later years, Luther was so critical of Judaism that he came to be seen as the precursor of the Jewish Holocaust in the twentieth century.[37] Paul Wetter rightly points out, however, that Luther looked at the Jewish people not as a nation to be exterminated, but rather as a religion that was in error and had to be corrected.[38] Rumors had already reached Luther's ears of synagogues serving as centers to convert Christians. His irritation and vexation over the continual resistance of the Jews to Christ burst forth by 1543 in his tract *On the Jews and Their Lies*. Therein he published his most vocal indictment on Judaism by invoking the government to apply "harsh mercy" (*scharfe Barmherzigkeit*) in order to bring the Jews to their senses about the falseness of their religion. Just as God uses an alien work of punishing man to bring about his conversion, so, too, Luther thought, the government could use harsh measures to cause the Jews to recognize their spiritual bondage.[39] Indeed, over time, Luther slowly abandoned the hope

---

35 *On Translating: An Open Letter* (1530), AE 35:189.

36 German title of Luther's tract: *Vorlegung des Alcoran Bruder Richardi, Prediger Ordens: Verdeutscht und herausgegeben von M. Luther* (1542), WA 53:274. For a discussion on Luther's position to Muslims, see Miller, *Muslims and the Gospel*.

37 See also Siemon-Netto, *Fabricated Luther*.

38 Wetter, *Missionsgedanke bei Martin Luther*, 286–89.

39 Wetter, *Missionsgedanke bei Martin Luther*, 284.

of mass conversions of Jews, though he always entertained until the end the hope that individual Jewish people would convert to Christianity.[40]

FINAL OBSERVATIONS ON LUTHER

Luther's missiological accents have implications for modern mission work in a number of ways. First, we cannot be satisfied with attempts that select just a few *loci* of Luther's theology as valuable for mission, whereas other parts are left by the wayside. A mission consciousness ought to integrate Luther's theology in such a way that the very nature of God, the Gospel, the Church, the means of grace, ministry, and eschatology all become meaningful.[41] Stated in another way, all parts of Luther's theology must be explained in such a way that their missiological implications become apparent. The unfortunate situation of taking diverging paths that can describe theology and mission in the Church today results in the isolation of Luther's theology in the mission field. It is a tragic circumstance that those involved in mission are still seen as an odd group engaging in an activity with which the majority in the Church has little to do. That phenomenon has unfortunately taken root in Pietism where the motto *ecclesiola in ecclesia* ("little church in the Church") actually became a positive trait of this movement. Even today, this way of thinking is still widely prevalent in Lutheran circles. In all fairness to Luther, however, mission is not just a core enterprise of a few committed members, but it is a part of the entire Church and of every Christian.

At several points, I have touched upon the missiological implications of one important aspect of Luther's theology, and that is the justification of the sinner. In the next chapter, the discussion will embrace this in greater detail. Despite the awesome distance between God and the world, God, in His sovereignty and by *grace (sola gratia)*, took the initiative to forgive, justify, and save human beings. Thus justification expresses and brings about God's truest salvific intentions. The soteriology underlying this article on which the Church stands and falls functions as both a support for Luther's theology and indeed as a mission motive. Luther did in fact bring the Gospel to full expression not just for his own sake or for that of the German nation but also for all people.

Luther's theology and his efforts to reform and renew Christianity in Germany were not an end in themselves. They were all part of the preparation of the Church for its primary task of proclaiming the Gospel to the world. Major parts of this preparation were also Luther's labors to expose

---

40 See Siemon-Netto, *Fabricated Luther*.

41 Bosch, *Transforming Mission*, 492–96. For an extended list of doctrines, see Braaten, *Apostolic Imperative*, 71–72.

the fronts that opposed the course of the Gospel: the Jewish and Turkish religions. Luther alerted Christians to protect themselves against these intrusions, lest they destroy faith and the willingness to give better witness.[42] In fact, Luther's efforts at making the Christian Church doctrinally sound were designed to strengthen Christians for their witness and confession to the world. His emphasis on the Word of God, the Sacraments, faith and obedience, catechesis, worship and liturgy, and translation makes most sense in view of the Church's primary mission of preaching the Gospel and bringing in the lost.

In the Lutheran Church, an unfortunate divide between the preservation of pure doctrine and the proclamation of doctrine to the world has developed. Indeed, these two orientations need not oppose each other in Luther's theology. Preserving the doctrine of the Gospel without intending to preach it to the world fundamentally undermines the *raison d' être* of pure doctrine.[43]

Luther identified the Jews and Turks as people in need of the Gospel. But the missionary task was broader already in the sixteenth century. The entire country of Germany and its citizens constituted a mission field. Over time, that notion changed. Germany evolved instead into a nation sending missionaries overseas. Today, we have come full circle as Germany and Europe represent prime mission fields. Europe's situation, and North America's, has much in common with the geopolitical state of affairs that Luther knew in the days of the Reformation. Christianity finds itself again in an alien context among people who will have little or nothing to do with it. In his preface to his selection of Luther's texts, Volker Stolle thus makes the following observation:

> Mission is no longer understood as a thing which plays itself out chiefly on the outer edges of Christendom, but instead as a way of life or, rather, as a lifestyle for every Christian congregation within its particular surrounding. Here, Luther now begins to speak with surprising wisdom. He has expressed insights on the topic of mission which are to a certain degree of exciting relevance. One notices the close relationship between the concern of the Reformation and of mission. One is made conscious of the connection of life and doctrine in missionary witness. Luther becomes meaningful for various questions concerning the missionary task of the Christian and the church.[44]

In the West, the world around us has abandoned the Christian faith, and mission-minded pastors and church members are needed who—through preaching, Baptism, liturgy, and personal witness—use the congregation to

---

42 As argued by Wetter, *Der Missionsgedanke bei Martin Luther*, 283.

43 See Kolb, "Primary Mission of the Church," 117–29.

44 Stolle, *Church Comes from All Nations*, 11.

assimilate newcomers into their midst. In contrast to Luther's time, there are no restrictions placed on the Church by the territorial rulers. Today, Christians profit from religious freedom and may thus engage in mission without governmental censure.

THE LUTHERAN CONFESSIONS

THE QUESTION OF AUTHORITY

Many have thought that the Lutheran Confessions also fail to refer directly to mission. In their defense, we should say that they were not written primarily as missionary tracts or manuals in instructing the church how to reach out to an unbelieving world. Instead, they affirmed and corrected theological positions within the church. Despite their theological emphasis, however, the Lutheran Confessions have clarified the content of the church's message and thereby served indirectly the church's mission. As the church preaches and teaches Christian doctrine to its members, Christians approach their neighbors with a clearer understanding of the content of the Gospel and thus make a more effective witness. It is true that the Confessions speak a theologically distinct language that pertains to their immediate circumstances. But since the Confessions represent an interpretation of Scripture, Christians will—through proper catechization and instruction in the Confessions—relate biblical truths to neighbors with greater clarity and effectiveness. Thereby, the Confessions serve as a template (so to speak) on which the Lutheran Church builds all her activities of preaching and teaching, including her witness to the unbelieving world. Just as the theology of Luther has much to say for a theology of mission, so also the Lutheran Confessions direct our attention to important principles laid down in Scripture. The Confessions add a stamp of integrity to the church's mission, and thus provide the answer to James Scherer's plea:

> The Lutheran church needs to do mission and evangelism with theological integrity. This requires the trust and support of the entire church. In order to merit this support it should avoid doing mission or evangelism on the basis of an alien foundation or motivation that might bring its work into contempt or cause it to fall under suspicion. Therefore, the search for a theological and ecclesiological rationale for mission is necessary and justified. It cannot be postponed.[45]

---

45 Scherer, *That the Gospel May Be Sincerely Preached*, 1. Kurt E. Marquart raises a similar concern: "Lutheran congregations and synods must learn again to treasure the Book of Concord as their best and most authentic 'mission statement,' and to implement its doctrinal and sacramental substance full-strength in the actual shaping of their church-life" (*Church and Her Fellowship*, 185 n. 30).

In order for the Lutheran Confessions to make a positive and critical contribution to mission, the church must concede to them authority. In such a case, the Lutheran Church must be prepared to adjust her mission to theological standards set forth by Scripture and the Confessions. The church may be reluctant to do so, especially because mission literature has—as the German missiologist Walter Holsten once claimed—shown little respect for Luther and the Reformation.[46]

What type of authority do the Lutheran Confessions provide? Traditionally, the normative and binding authority of the Lutheran Confessions for the Lutheran Church and her mission has always been one of a *quia* ("because") subscription. This implies an unconditional subscription *because* the Confessions are understood as the correct exposition of Scripture. This is more affirmative of the Confessions' authority than the *quatenus* ("insofar as") subscription. In the latter case, the reader may determine the Confessions' authority as he sees fit and entertain the thought that their exposition of Scripture might contain potential error.[47]

Both *quia* and *quatenus* subscriptions exist in the worldwide Lutheran community today. I make my case on the basis of a *quia* subscription. In fact, during the middle and latter periods of the nineteenth century, most supporters of mission turned to the Lutheran Confessions as the true means of promoting the Christian and catholic faith on the mission field. Theologians such as Wilhelm Löhe from Neuendettelsau, Ludwig Harms from Hermannsburg, and the Leipzig mission society stood as great promoters of a Confessional Lutheran approach to mission. This tradition bore fruit both in North America and worldwide. It led to the so-called *Sammelmission,* the gathering of German settlers into American Lutheran communities through circuit riders, such as Friedrich Wyneken, and to mission in faraway countries such as India and South Africa. All these efforts occurred during a period in church history when ecumenism became the dominant movement.

A glance into missiological research reveals that few touch upon the role of the Lutheran Confessions in mission. In contrast, the scholarly debate over mission in Luther's theology is widely known. Apart from occasional references to Luther's catechisms, few scholars have attempted to engage the Lutheran Confessions from a missiological point of view.[48]

---

46 Holsten, "Reformation und Mission," 2; see also Gensichen, "Were the Reformers Indifferent to Missions?" 120.

47 Two documents discuss the issue of subscription: Walther, "Why Should Our Pastors, Teachers and Professors Subscribe Unconditionally," 241–53, and Preus, "Confessional Subscription," 43–52.

48 Wiebe, "Missionsgedanken in den lutherischen Bekenntnisschriften," has made the first and, to date, the most significant attempt to engage the Lutheran Confessions in missiological research. He bypasses, however, such major themes of the Reformation as the doctrine of the Trinity

These few contributions cannot mitigate the general impression that a chasm between confessional and mission theology continues to exist. In fact, Franz Wiebe, in his treatment on the missiological dimension in the Lutheran Confessions, speaks candidly about an unfamiliarity between confessional and mission theology, which has yet to be overcome.[49]

Today's hermeneutic of greater tolerance for other people's points of view makes it difficult to argue in favor of the Confessions. The statements of absolute truth and condemnations of falsehood in the confessional documents do not speak in today's popular spirit of reconciliation, agreement, and pluralism. We live in a postmodern discussion in which many advocate freedom from all claims for religiosity based on dogma and determinate religious confession. That skepticism, however, is not a correct reflection of the spirit of our times. Rather, it is still a remnant from the times of modernity. Instead, it is quite permissible to accept the reality that a faith community embraces a particular conviction based on revelation and confession, supported by a confessionally governed church.[50]

Therefore, I propose that the postmodern argument for faith-communities actually makes the Lutheran Confessions a perfect document to use as the voice of a faith community in the twenty-first century. Clearly, the Lutheran Confessions extol the trinitarian love for mankind and the primary impulse to communicate divine love that has existed in truth and in God from all eternity. Yet as this truth breaks forth as the Gospel message in a world that has cast off absolute truth, the community that receives this Gospel could elevate the Confessions to the special status of serving as a means of promoting and preserving unity within the community's own ranks.[51] In this sense, the Lutheran Confessions function as

and justification. For a treatment of both, one may see Schulz, *Missiological Significance of the Doctrine of Justification*. The author is also in possession of an unpublished presentation by the late Georg Schulz, "Die Bedeutung des Bekenntnisses der lutherischen Kirche," which was offered at an International Theological Convention on September 4, 1980, in Heiligenstein, Elsaß (Alsace).

49 Franz Wiebe calls it a "noch nicht behobenen *Fremdheit* zwischen Bekenntnis- und Missionstheologie" ("Der Missionsgedanken in den lutherischen Bekenntnisschriften," 18). Even the Lutheran missiology of Georg Vicedom (*Mission of God*) is disappointing in this respect. Only one reference to the Confessions (namely, to AC VII) appears on p. 86.

50 Smith, *Who's Afraid of Postmodernism?* 122.

51 This ecclesiological interest of unity is expressed, for example, in the preface to the Augsburg Confession (1530). Therein the authors formulate that the goal of the Lutheran party was to remove dissension and misunderstandings so that all Christians might "exist and fight under one Christ . . . to live in one Christian church in unity and concord" (AC Preface 4, Kolb-Wengert, 31). It is also important to be aware of the Confessions' comprehensive and ecumenical claim so that Lutheran missionaries not look upon them as confessions of a particular denomination. See Schlink, *Theology of the Lutheran Confessions*, xvi–xvii, especially in terms of the doctrine of justification as the *doctrina catholica et apostolica*. See also Vajta, "Confessions of the Church as an Ecumenical Concern," 176, 179. The concern for the ecumenical nature of the Lutheran Confessions is also argued by Meyer-Roscher, "Die Bedeutung der lutherischen

a form of *paradosis* (1 Cor. 10:2; 15:3) in the community, preserving and handing on from one generation to the next a condensed form of the faith. Indeed, any church claiming its roots in the sixteenth century should see the Confessions as a timeless source for guidance and not just as a historic document limited in its applicability.[52]

Skeptics of this proposed endeavor might see here a violation of the principle of *sola scriptura* and would prefer to have Scripture alone provide the missiological agenda of a church body. Such a concern is unwarranted. The integrity of Scripture as the ultimate norm that itself norms (*norma normans*) all missionary thought and action remains an inviolate premise of this study. And since the Lutheran Confessions are nothing but a correct explanation of Scripture, this work will not violate the *sola scriptura* principle, but rather give it an enhanced role.

THE MISSION OF THE TRIUNE GOD AND THE ARRANGEMENT OF ARTICLES

What missionary impulse, then, do the Lutheran Confessions provide? We have already considered the ecclesiology of Luther's Large Catechism, and we shall touch on others in forthcoming chapters. Let us first consider the arrangement of articles in the Augsburg Confession.

The articles are not chosen at random but reflect a sequence of events that comprise the triune God's mission in this world. It is a structure that reflects salvation history (*Heilsgeschichte*).[53] The first article on God frames the sequence. To a degree, the theological debate on the Trinity had been settled many centuries before, precisely in the fourth century during the events of the ecumenical councils of Nicaea (AD 325) and Constantinople (AD 381). Since then, Christians generally have accepted what was said about the Trinity. Hence, the Trinity represents a finished and settled doctrine that is affirmed with the confession of the creeds of the Church of every time and place.[54]

On the other side of the sequence, there is the second coming of Christ in Article XVII of the Augsburg Confession. Theologian Peter Brunner lends distinctive terms to describe both the beginning and the end of our faith. Since the former aspect throws the reader back to the beginning,

---

Bekenntnisschriften," 19–34, and Brunner, "Die bleibende Bedeutung des lutherischen Bekenntnisses für die Mission," 8–22.

52 An example how the *Sitz im Leben* of the Augsburg Confession can be explored is Maurer, *Historical Commentary on the Augsburg Confession.*

53 Öberg, "Mission und Heilsgeschichte," 25–42.

54 This observation is shared by Edmund Schlink: "In the Confessions the doctrine of the Trinity is evidently quoted as a presupposition rather than developed and proved dogmatically. After all, it is taken over as a finished and settled doctrine" (*Theology of the Lutheran Confessions*, 65). Compare also Brunstäd, *Theologie der lutherischen Bekenntnisschriften* 28.

Brunner calls it the primordial-protological event, whereas the latter is forward-oriented and called the final-eschatological horizon.[55] Between these two poles, God performs His special and extensive saving plan. Melanchthon traces the trinitarian mission in the very ordering of the Augsburg Confession. The triune God (AC I) sends to fallen humanity (AC II) Christ the Redeemer (AC III). This deliverance and renewal is accomplished in the justification of the sinner (AC IV). Through the beneficial influence of office, Word and Sacraments (AC V), new spiritual powers and forgiveness are given to humanity (AC VI). These powers carry out their historical work within the one, holy, Christian Church (AC VII), and though hypocrites continually threaten that work (AC VIII), it continues to exist through the use of the Sacraments (AC IX–XIII). The Church's existence is humanly guaranteed through the active participation of incumbents in the spiritual office and through establishing church orders (AC XIV, XV), for which civil order provides the presuppositions (AC XVI).[56]

In his Large Catechism, Luther expounds in detail who God is and what He does by basing it on the Apostles' Creed:

> Here in the Creed you have the entire essence of God, his will, and his work exquisitely depicted . . . In these three articles God himself has revealed and opened to us the most profound depths of his fatherly heart, his sheer, unutterable love. He created us for this very purpose, to redeem and sanctify us. Moreover, having bestowed upon us everything in heaven and on earth, he has given us his Son and his Holy Spirit, through whom he brings us to himself. As we explained before, we could never come to recognize the Father's favor and grace were it not for the Lord Christ, who is a mirror of the Father's heart. Apart from him we see nothing but an angry and terrible judge. But neither could we know anything of Christ, had it not been revealed by the Holy Spirit.[57]

Luther's observations on the nature of the triune God taken from the Apostles' Creed effectively depict God's activity to the world in missionary terms.

Note, then, that Luther and Melanchthon show us how the Christian Church may affirm the trinitarian statements of old, but they also expound on them in descriptive and narrative forms. Much of what the trinitarian statements affirm embraces God's saving intentions for this world. All

---

55 Brunner calls creation and fall the "urgeschichtlich-protologischer Horizont" of man's existence in contrast to his "endgeschichtlich-eschatologischen Horizont" ("'Rechtfertigung' heute," 136).

56 Wilhelm Maurer demonstrates that Melanchthon's editorial intention was to rework Luther's *Great Confession* (AE 37) into a trinitarian history of salvation by drawing the reader's attention to the sequence of the articles within part 1 of the Augsburg Confession. See Maurer, *Historical Commentary on the Augsburg Confession*, 112–24.

57 LC II 63–65 (Kolb-Wengert, 439–40).

theology that concerns the triune God should always explain the entire divine essence of God—as three persons and one substance—in view of His salvific will to bring all to salvation and that He does so through His work of creation, redemption, and sanctification.

THE GREAT COMMISSION TEXTS

Although the Lutheran Confessions do not use the term "mission" to underscore a specific activity, there are a few places where the biblical verses from Great Commission texts—those associated with the preaching of the Gospel and Baptism—convey a missionary motive.

The Great Commission texts in the Augsburg Confession and elsewhere in the Lutheran Confessions are used in very specific ways. Several texts in the Confessions use Matt. 28:19–20 or parts thereof as a reference to the Office of the Holy Ministry, as does Walther's second thesis on the ministry in the citation of Johann Gerhard's *Loci Theologici*.[58]

These texts are quoted to establish the ministry of the Church, the *ministerium verbi divini*, and to explain the functions of that ministry. On occasion, the link to the priesthood of all believers is established by inference, as is done in the tradition of the LCMS. This is the case in Melanchthon's Treatise, where he observes that the keys have been given to the Church "principally and immediately" (Tr 24). This is taken as a reference to the priesthood of all believers, and we may assume that they are possessors of that ministry specifically through Holy Baptism, however not through an assumed set of rights.[59]

---

58 There is a diverse use of the Commission texts. In FC VII and VIII, it refers to the Lord's Supper and the person of Christ, where it uses Matt. 28:18 specifically for the doctrine of Christ and the Words of Institution. AC I and SA I both imply Matt. 28:19 and the three creeds of Western Christianity for the Trinity. AC IX, SC IV, Luther's short preface to the LC, and LC IV speak of the Trinity in the context of Baptism and of Baptism as God's action. LC III, covering the First Petition of the Lord's Prayer, applies the triune name through Baptism to all Christians. AC XXVIII draws on Matt. 28:19–20 regarding the power of bishops (Latin) and the power of the Church (German). The Treatise speaks likewise of the Church's authority to teach the Gospel and administer the Sacraments over against the worldly powers of arms and civil law that some Roman Catholic bishops also wielded. Both sources understand this authority to be exercised by the Church through the ministry. FC VIII uses Matt. 28:20 with the person of Christ. See Kolb-Wengert, 36–37, 92–93, 184, 300, 335, 359, 385, 445, 457, 511, and 600. See also Walther, *Church and Ministry*, 186.

59 See Walther, *Church and Ministry*, 51, 273. Also the *Brief Statement* of the Missouri Synod notes Treatise 23–24, as well as 1 Cor. 3:21–22: "All things are yours." The *Brief Statement* also confesses that Christ Himself commits the Keys to all believers (Matt. 16:13–19; 18:17–20) and commissions all believers to preach the Gospel and administer the Sacraments (Matt. 28:19–20; 1 Cor. 11:23–25). Yet the Missouri Synod affirms that preaching the Gospel and administering the Sacraments occur publicly, that is, in a church setting beyond the scope of private Christian witness, through a specific office established by God through the Church; see Walther, *Church and Ministry*, 161–97.

Indeed, Melanchthon uses some Great Commission texts to highlight the divine mandate for the important functions of the Office of the Holy Ministry. The basis for the ministry of preaching and forgiving sins is taken from John 20:21–23: "to preach the gospel, to forgive and retain sins, and to administer the sacraments." Melanchthon also cites Mark 16:15: "Go . . . and proclaim the good news to the whole creation."[60] In the Smalcald Articles, Luther quotes Luke 24:47: "You must preach repentance and forgiveness of sins in my name to the whole world."[61] Luther describes the proper function of the Gospel as "the spoken word, in which the forgiveness of sins is preached to the whole world."[62] In his Large Catechism, Luther refers to the preaching of the Gospel as the work of the Holy Spirit through which a church is founded: "For where Christ is not preached, there is no Holy Spirit to create, call, and gather the Christian church, apart from which no one can come to the Lord Christ."[63] To this, compare the statement made in the Formula of Concord, the Solid Declaration:

> In his immeasurable goodness and mercy God provides for the public proclamation of his divine, eternal Law and of the wondrous counsel of our redemption, the holy gospel of his eternal Son, our only Savior Jesus Christ, which alone can save. By means of this proclamation he gathers an everlasting church from humankind, and he effects in human hearts true repentance and knowledge of sin and true faith in the Son of God, Jesus Christ. God wants to call human beings to eternal salvation, to draw them to himself, to convert them, to give them new birth, and to sanctify them through these means, and in no other way than through his holy Word (which people hear proclaimed or read) and through the sacraments.[64]

All these references lead one to conclude that the preaching of the Gospel is also pointing to a missionary context, that is, an activity to the unbelieving world through which the Gospel wishes to draw all nations to Christ.[65]

Luther also quotes Matthew 28 and Mark 16 to support the doctrine of Baptism in terms of its institution and benefits. This is significant insofar as the use of the Great Commission texts highlights the value of Baptism as an integral act of Lutheran mission once the Church preaches the Gospel to the world.[66] Luther speaks of the world in need of preaching and Baptism

---

60 AC XXVIII 5–7 (Kolb-Wengert, 93).
61 SA III III 6 (Kolb-Wengert, 313).
62 SA III IV (Kolb-Wengert, 319).
63 LC II 44–45 (Kolb-Wengert, 436).
64 SD II 50 (Kolb-Wengert, 553).
65 Schulz, "Das geistliche Amt nach lutherischem Verständnis in der missionarischen Situation," 167.
66 SC IV 4 (Kolb-Wengert, 359).

when he connects Mark 16:16 to Cornelius's baptism (Acts 10:47–48). Cornelius represents all those who once did not believe but have come into contact with preaching and the Sacrament and have now been saved.[67] In his Large Catechism, Luther looks at Baptism under the missionary aspect of delivering "from sin, death, and the devil, to enter into the kingdom of Christ and to live with him forever."[68] In fact, Baptism in the Confessions is not lowered in importance as later happened during the period of Lutheran Orthodoxy. Baptism simply is affirmed as a necessary sacrament, without which salvation cannot be attained.[69]

ANTHROPOLOGY

One helpful aspect to the Confessions is the anthropological statements. They strongly affirm the total depravity of man, and they strongly dismiss any notion to the contrary. One article that speaks of this in great clarity is the first article of the Formula of Concord, where original sin is said to have totally corrupted man so much that he becomes entirely dependent on outside divine assistance. This outward assistance is the work of Christ and justification by Him through faith. That depravity has also affected man's will so that the only causes of one's conversion become God's Word and the Holy Spirit. Indeed, the first two articles of the Formula of Concord posit an important principle for missionary address to a world that, spiritually speaking, is overconfident in its natural abilities.[70]

ADIAPHORA, PROVISIONALLY NEUTRAL THINGS

Finally, there is the question of *adiaphora*, namely, those practices in the Church that Scripture neither commands as being necessary for salvation, that is, essential to saving faith, nor forbids as sin. What comes to mind in this connection are the rites and ceremonies in the liturgical context. A radical application of the principle of *adiaphora* has the potential to erode the uniformity of liturgical practices in the Church. Article X of the Formula of Concord addresses the issue of ecclesiastical practices with the question of what to do with them under severe persecution, when these provisionally neutral or "middle things" lose their neutrality because they are either imposed or removed by force. In either case, the authors rule that "nothing is an adiaphoron in a time when confession of the faith

---

67 SA III VIII 7–8 (Kolb-Wengert, 322).

68 LC IV 25 (Kolb-Wengert, 459).

69 On two occasions, the Lutheran Confessions argue this point: the Augsburg Confession high-lights the need for Baptism and the Holy Spirit for salvation (AC II, Kolb-Wengert, 39) and the Formula of Concord rejects those who hold that children are saved without Baptism (FC XII 11, Kolb-Wengert, 657).

70 FC I–II (Kolb-Wengert, 531–62).

is necessary."[71] This means that the Church should not accept imposed practices unless agreed upon, nor should the Church cede any of them if forcefully removed. Naturally, here, the Confessions speak to a context of severe tribulation, a situation that is not ours today. But even in peaceful conditions, the context of the Reformation would reject pleas for unlimited freedom in middle things, particularly in allowing each congregation to choose its self-determined "middle things" as it sees fit. The discussion on *adiaphora* should be seen in view of the numerous agendas published during the time of Johannes Bugenhagen (1485–1558), parish pastor of Wittenberg and personal friend of Luther. Bugenhagen's efforts at compiling agendas for states such as Pomerania show the Reformation's interest in expressing unity as a church body through a common and ordered structure.

I maintain that liturgical order and the ecumenical nature of the liturgy should always accompany the mission of the Church. An overt congregationalism that pleads for its own right in unlimited freedom of practice does not square with the Lutheran Church's understanding of *adiaphora* in the sixteenth century.[72]

SUMMARY

The age of the Reformation provides an important stepping-stone into a missiology from the cross. Thus it would be a fatal mistake to ignore the fundamental contributions that this period has brought to the Church and her mission. Every congregation and visible communion in the Church, all believers, have received a faith built on the words of Scripture. But our heritage and tradition still speak to us today, or at least offer words of advice for our faith and practice. For this reason, we engaged in a careful examination of the Reformation's history and its theology. Significant aspects and principles came to light, of which the theology of the cross and the work of Christ for our salvation as depicted in the central doctrine of justification invigorate our mission the most. The next chapter will examine how that material principle in particular applies to our mission from the cross.

---

71 FC X 10–11 (Kolb-Wengert, 637).

72 When the founders of the LCMS organized its constitution in 1847, they, too, pleaded for uniformity, as Carl Mundinger points out: "Another control device was a codified attitude on the part of the Synod concerning the question of uniform liturgy. While the framers of the constitution remained faithful to Article VII of the Unaltered Augsburg Confession in that their demand for uniformity was not absolute, they did insist rather vigorously that then member congregations leave no stone unturned in their efforts to introduce uniform ceremonies. The constitution even goes so far as to claim the uniformity in liturgy, especially if this liturgy is increased and developed according to Lutheran standards, will be helpful in purifying the American Lutheran Church of its Reformed excrescences" (*Government in the Missouri Synod*, 191).

CHAPTER FIVE

JUSTIFICATION

THE ORGANIZING PRINCIPLE OF MISSION

INTRODUCING THE ORGANIZING PRINCIPLE

Anyone who studies theology knows how much content it covers. Theology gathers information from Scripture about God and His dealings with the world and neatly lays out this information into numerous statements called doctrines. Every Christian who reads Scripture engages in theology and constructs doctrines in some way or another. The reader may not always take a learned approach by following a clearly defined methodology of interpreting Scripture, but as one gathers information on God from Scripture, the reader processes it into a coherent whole so that the Word of God speaks one message without contradiction.

What a reader of Scripture might not know is that there is a key that helps him to process the content of the Word of God. The key, as Lutherans believe to be revealed in Scripture, is the doctrine of justification (Acts 15:11; Rom. 1:16–17; 3:28; Eph. 2:9). Some refer to justification as the central or concretizing principle in Scripture because it truly represents the central content of the Bible, which becomes concrete in the person and work of Christ. Justification talks of a God who, through the death of His Son, Jesus, on the cross, has lowered Himself to mankind and has chosen to save us from eternal damnation through the forgiveness of sins that we receive as a gift through faith. This doctrine brings out the good news, the Gospel, that pervades Scripture from beginning to end. Justification moves through all texts like a red thread, and, even where it is not apparent, the reader should still keep it in mind. All statements in the Bible about God, man, the Church, eternal life, and so forth are tied together by the central doctrine of justification; it gives meaning to the entire Word of God and lends itself toward unraveling difficult texts in Scripture.

Theologians have long pointed out that justification serves as the integrating principle that keeps Scripture and theology together. Gottfried

Thomasius, an important nineteenth-century Lutheran theologian at Erlangen, speaks of justification as the "principle of life" (*Lebensprinzip*) of the Church and the constituting center (*konstitutiver Mittelpunkt*) of theology.[1] More recently, Carl E. Braaten explains that justification is "not merely a single article among many others, but . . . the foundational truth with generative power affecting the entire organism of Christian faith, life, and thought. The relative importance of any Christian doctrine [is] determined by its proximity to the central article of faith. All doctrines, in fact, must somehow be corollaries of the vital principle of justification."[2]

Thus all other articles of theology connect to one another, and all in turn point to justification. This explains Luther's statement that "all that we teach and practice against the pope, the devil and the world stands on the article of justification."[3] In unison with Luther, the confessors of the sixteenth century also hailed the doctrine of justification as the "principle article of the Christian doctrines."[4]

The fact that justification assumes the status of being not only the central article of theology but also the integrating principle explains why it has been called "the doctrine on which the Church stands and falls." We do not know the exact origin of this oft-quoted statement, but it does underscore the undiminished prominence of justification.[5] In the sixteenth century, Martin Luther and his close associate Philip Melanchthon must be given credit for pointing to the doctrine of justification as the hermeneutical key for interpreting Scripture and the life and tradition of the Church. Justification serves as the arbiter of all doctrinal statements made by the Church throughout the centuries, which includes a critical analysis of her traditions, structures, and practices. In a recent study by Heinrich Holze, the argument is made that Luther was not blinded by romanticism when it came to judging the past centuries; instead, Luther measured every confession against the hermeneutical key of justification and the Gospel before he was willing to grant any statements a normative character.[6] Thomas C. Oden has boldly defended the Early Church by pointing out that a broad consensus on the doctrine of justification already existed prior to the

---

1   Thomasius, *Das Bekenntniß der evangelisch-lutherischen Kirche*, 4–5.

2   Braaten, *Justification*, 28. See also Bayer, *Living by Faith*.

3   SA II 1–5 (Kolb-Wengert, 301).

4   E.g., SD III 6 (Kolb-Wengert, 563).

5   Mahlmann, "Zur Geschichte der Formel 'Articulus stantis et cadentis ecclesiae,'" 187–94.

6   Rittner, *Was heißt hier lutherisch!* 56–86.

Reformation.[7] Oden may be overstating the case in view of other studies.[8] The reformers' more cautious estimate of the Church's tradition comes from the fact they gave justification central status in theology and practices in the Church.

In their struggle to provide clarity to justification as the article for defining salvation, Luther and Melanchthon chose very distinctive terms that were borrowed from the courtroom setting; justification is a forensic declaration.[9] A sinner is justified by Christ imputatively and reckoned righteous through a verdict that is pronounced by God and that acquits the sinner of all his sins just as a judge would exonerate the accused of his crime. We are dealing here not merely with a play on words but with a truthful and indispensable choice of descriptions based on Scripture (e.g., Rom. 4:1–12). Luther encountered a soteriology within the Church that demanded clarification because the glory and honor of Christ were at stake in the face of ceremonies, relics, indulgences, and traditions that took authority and trust away from Christ and put it in human works and ideas. Both rulers and theologians joined Luther's struggle and stood firmly at his side as he defended the position that, in terms of salvation, man cannot accomplish anything (Rom. 3:28). God presents the gift of salvation to man, while human sin causes every human being to rely totally on this gift from God and not works; faith passively receives this gift. The doctrine of justification as so understood is no less contradicted today. Life on a day-to-day basis looks at ways to achieve things and to overcome adversities. Such accomplishments are hailed as victories of the will. Even in courtroom situations, the defendant is expected to plead his innocence before the judge and the plaintiff's accusations. Such thinking likewise infiltrates a Christian's understanding of his relationship with God. The Church and its preachers are thus challenged to preach continuously against the thinking of the world since Christians and non-Christians typically forget this biblical concern. It becomes necessary to explain justification and its terms clearly, and ways must be found to apply the principles of justification by Christ through faith in a world that has difficulty comprehending it.

Often, preachers consider other issues more pressing and may eventually lose sight of justification. Some abandon justification intentionally and find alternative ways of entering theology because they think justification

---

7   Thomas Oden's underlying motive is to establish an ecumenical consensus among the traditions of the East and West, Catholic, Protestant, and Orthodox, including Charismatic and Pentecostal teaching; see Oden, *Justification Reader*.

8   Needam, "Justification in the Early Church Fathers," 25–53, and Pelikan, *Riddle of Roman Catholicism*, 50.

9   For an example of the "forensic usage," see Ap IV 252 (Kolb-Wengert, 159).

has lost its appeal. The late theologian Hans Joachim Iwand cautions the Church not to go that route:

> An evangelical church that views the teaching of the righteousness of faith as self-evident—but about which no one should trouble himself further because other issues are more important—has in principle robbed itself of the central solution by which all other questions are illuminated. Such a church will become increasingly more splintered and worn down. If we take the article of justification out of the center very soon we will not know why we are evangelical Christians or should remain so. As a result, we will strive for the unity of the church and will sacrifice the purity of the gospel; we will have more confidence in church organization and church government and will promise more on the basis of reform of Christian authority and church training than either can deliver. If we lose our center, we will court pietism and listen to other teachings and we will be in danger of being tolerant where we should be radical and radical where we should be tolerant. In short, the standards will be lowered and along with them everything that is necessary and correct in the reforms that we sing about now will be incomprehensible.[10]

THE CENTRAL ARTICLE UNDER ATTACK: EXAMPLES

Lutherans should be mindful of the article of justification's central status in theology and missiology and be sensitized to the imminent dangers that could lead to its being pushed to the margins. These are not just hypothetical concerns but valid in view of past attempts at marginalization. Let five examples suffice.

1. In ecumenical discussions, the temptation has always been to find agreement on individual points of theology apart from asking about their relationship to the central article of justification. This problem became evident in the discussion on the doctrine of justification between representatives of the LWF and the Roman Catholic Church that led to the signing of a *Joint Declaration of the Doctrine of Justification* (*JDDJ*) in the city of Augsburg, where the Confession was originally presented on June 25, 1530. The date chosen for signing the *JDDJ* was October 31, 1999, the anniversary of Luther's posting the Ninety-five Theses. Although a common consensus was established, it soon became apparent after careful reading that this agreement failed to honor a number of points that would have been crucial to Luther and other reformers. Thus, for example, it was unclear

---

10 Iwand, *Righteousness of Faith*, 16.

whether the doctrine of justification actually served as *the* criterion of all doctrine or only *a* criterion among all other doctrines.[11] As Oswald Bayer observed with respect to ecumenical attempts at reaching consensus on the doctrine: "Ecumenical discourse is to be welcomed, but not at the price of mistaking justification as just one *façon de parler.*"[12] This procedure of isolating and compartmentalizing individual doctrines facilitated the task of finding broader consensus. Certain beliefs still practiced in the Roman Catholic Church, such as pilgrimages, purgatory, and satisfaction actually still oppose Luther's position on justification serving as *the* criterion of all doctrine. In other words, though the *JDDJ* expressed unanimity between Lutherans and Roman Catholics in view of terms and expressions chosen to describe the doctrine, it failed to have a full bearing on the theology and practice of the Roman Catholic Church and, arguably, also on those churches that compromise the LWF. For concerned Lutheran and Reformed theologians, the *JDDJ* operates with deliberate ambiguity to cover deeper theological distinctions that continue to divide the two churches.[13]

2. The failure to see the impact of justification on theology is also a fault within Protestantism. Generally, justification receives central place, but at times not as the integrating principle. All Protestants may agree on the *solas*, namely, that salvation is based on *sola fide, solus Christus, sola gratia,* and *sola scriptura* ("faith alone," "Christ alone," "grace alone," and "Scripture alone"). When, however, it comes to explaining how justification works in theology, each denomination has its own interpretation. Lutherans believe that justification is mediated through the preached and sacramental Word of God. The majority of Protestants, however, connect justification to the work of the Holy Spirit, though a Spirit not necessarily connected to divine grace and faith through the Sacraments. Take, for example, the

---

11 Other points of concern with the *JDDJ* are the failure to address the sinner *and* saint relationship (*simul iustus et peccator*), concupiscence after Baptism, and the *monergism of God* in justification, namely, a believer's total dependency on God for justification as a gift throughout his life, that is, how it applies also to a believer's good works in his sanctified state.

12 Bayer, *Living by Faith,* xiv. One may see Nürnberger, "Thesen zum Stellenwert der Rechtfertigungslehre," 67–86.

13 Consider the following response and assessment by the faculty of Concordia Theological Seminary: "Joint Lutheran/Roman Catholic Declaration on Justification" and "Formula of Agreement" in *Concordia Theological Quarterly.* A helpful discussion on the *JDDJ* that also includes a Reformed perspective is Blocher, "Lutheran—Catholic Declaration on Justification," 197–217.

Sacrament of Holy Baptism. Baptism is a visible form of the Gospel; it comprehends God's objective imputation of His righteousness and thus is more than just a mere human work. It is essentially the work of the Holy Spirit who, in this Sacrament, applies the gift of forgiveness achieved for the baptized through Christ's work on the cross. Confusion in this matter obscures the nature of the gift inherent in Baptism. When justification is divorced from the proper mediation by the Word, it falls into the realm of abstraction. Lost is a concrete, personal coming of Christ as a gift.

3.   The discussion over the *JDDJ* reveals also a controversy over how best to interpret to the theology of the sixteenth century, particularly the Lutheran Confessions. The basic question is whether the condemnations, such as those expressed in the Augsburg Confession, should stand in the way of today's efforts toward rapprochement. It was important for the original confessors to articulate—next to every positive statement on the faith—also an explicit condemnation of error. The authors of the *JDDJ*, however, defined the condemnations as historically conditioned. They argued that, since the historical situation is different today, the condemnations were of no further relevance.[14] Thus the Lutheran Confessions become documents from which nuggets can be extracted at the whim of a reader. This hermeneutical approach was already evident at the fourth meeting of the LWF in Helsinki in 1963, and it surfaced again at the Leuenberg Concord agreements on the Lord's Supper in 1971.[15] It is evident that this haphazard approach widens the doors for ecumenical agreement.

4.   A new interpretation of the traditional explanation of justification itself began in the mid-1970s by scholars of the School of Finnish Luther Research at the University of Helsinki. They approached the Eastern Orthodox churches in the interest of furthering ecumenical relations. As justification became the topic of discussion, common strings were threaded around this doctrine, and the term *theosis* was chosen as its synonym. In the

---

14   See the text of the *JDDJ* in Commission of Theology and Church Relations, *Joint Declaration on the Doctrine of Justification*, 14.

15   Braaten, *Justification*, 13. It seems puzzling why Carl Braaten, despite his clear articulation of the important central and integrative status in theology, is such an avid supporter of the *JDDJ*. A critical assessment of Helsinki is offered in Schlichting, *Rechtfertigung und Weltverantwortung*, and Martens, *Die Rechtfertigung des Sünders*.

discussions, however, the Finnish theologians soon realized that rapprochement with the Eastern Orthodox could apparently be reached only with Luther's theology of justification, but not with Melanchthon and the Lutheran Confessions. As a result, a wedge was driven between the reformers themselves, most notably between Melanchthon and Luther.[16] Melanchthon was unappealing for his forensic-declaratory character of justification that the Finns claimed did not represent Luther's concept of justification. The Finnish theologians based their argument on a few selected statements in Luther's writings, such as his *Lectures on Galatians* (1535) in which Luther states that the believer is "in Christ" and "Christ in us." These theologians posited justification essentially as an ontological union between the believer and Christ, so that the indwelling (the presence of Christ in the believer through faith) marks the true nature of justification, not the declaration of pardon to the sinner. Such an interpretation of Luther's theology would strike a chord with Eastern Orthodoxy's motif of *theosis* (divinization). However, more recent research has persuasively shown that the portrayal of justification as *theosis* cannot cover all nuances of Luther's interpretation, and it disrespects the sequence of justification as Luther and Melanchthon both represented it.[17]

Consider, for example, that the Christian must daily die and rise with Christ. Properly speaking, justification does not constitute an upward spiral of the believer's righteousness that leads to an eventual blend with the divine chorus, which is how the Eastern Orthodox conceive of *theosis*. In a careful study on all these issues, Reinhard Flogaus convincingly concludes that the apparent distinction on the nature of justification lies within Luther himself rather than in the differences between him and Melanchthon or with the Formula of Concord.[18] In other words, Luther and Melanchthon did not have that apparent disparity in understanding as the Finnish theologians claim. After a careful analysis of all of Luther's statements, it is evident that Luther indeed was of the opinion that the prerequisite and basis for a concept of Christ's indwelling is the forensic-imputative declaration. The

---

16 Mannermaa, "Why Is Luther So Fascinating?" 1–20, and "In ipsa fide Christus adest," 11–93.

17 One may read the following helpful contributions: Mattes, *Role of Justification in Contemporary Theology*, and "Future for Lutheran Theology?" 439–57; Kolb, "Contemporary Lutheran Understandings of the Doctrine of Justification," 153–76.

18 Flogaus, *Theosis bei Palamas und Luther*, 321.

problem, then, is not so much with the thought of an inhabitation of Christ—something the confessors had encountered in Andrew Osiander's proposal[19]—but *more so the sequence.* The divinization or inhabitation of God *follows* the act of declaration based on Christ's righteousness that remains alien. Christ's righteousness can never dwell within the Christian ontologically apart from faith, to which it is bound.[20] Finally, as we look at the sequence, it is puzzling how scholars have completely ignored the concept *unio mystica* in the discussion. Although appropriated as a term and concept by dogmaticians after Luther, the mystical union became the descriptive term of highlighting the believer's renewal and life in Christ.

5.   Finally, justification reminds us of the core content of the Gospel that must withstand cultural relativism. It is true that the Gospel is always culturally embodied. Thus it is delivered in a particular language and a particular lifestyle. In his book *The Gospel in a Pluralist Society,* Lesslie Newbigin debates the related questions: "How can it be possible for the Gospel to have a critical relation to culture?" and "Will it (the Gospel) accept all elements of human culture?"[21] In contrast to those who want to dismiss the critical role of the Gospel in culture, Newbigin affirms that the Gospel must serve in a countercultural capacity. The Gospel opposed barbaric practices that missionaries encountered in their travels, such as cannibalism in Papua Guinea, the Indian custom of *sati* (the burning of a man's widow with his body on the funeral pyre), and slavery. It is thus clear that "the Bible speaks of things which are not simply products of human culture but are Words and deeds of God, creator and sustainer of all that is."[22] Not everything in culture can be condoned.

Newbigin points to the double event of Jesus' death and resurrection, according to which "we are called neither to a simple affirmation of human culture nor to a simple rejection of it."[23] It

---

19 Andrew Osiander's position is summarized as follows: ". . . Christ is our righteousness before God only according to his divine nature . . . That when the prophets and apostles speak of the righteousness of faith, the words 'justify' and 'be justified' do not mean being pronounced free from sin and receiving the forgiveness of sins but rather being made righteous in fact and in truth on account of love and other virtues infused into us through the Holy Spirit and on account of the works that result" (FC III 60, 62, Kolb-Wengert, 573).

20 FC III 54 (Kolb-Wengert, 571–72).

21 Newbigin, *Gospel in a Pluralist Society,* 185, 191.

22 Newbigin, *Gospel in a Pluralist Society,* 192.

23 Newbigin, *Gospel in a Pluralist Society,* 195.

seems that Newbigin detects the critical element in the content of the Gospel, which includes justification as the act that accuses sinners of their sin and then acquits them. Justification uncovers the constant murderous rebellion of man against God and then extols the forgiveness earned by Christ on the cross. This content of the Gospel is universal and countercultural in that it is brought to all peoples around the world, no matter their indigenous cultural context and behavioral patterns.

JUSTIFICATION AND THE CROSS

Does the making of justification the central article of Christianity result in a shift of focus from the objective reality of Christ's death and resurrection to the actual subjective appropriation of that reality through faith? We would argue that both the objective (justification) and the subjective (faith) dimensions are essential to Christianity. Braaten is of the opinion, for example, that the cross "provides the criterion of all Christian thought and life; it offers a perspective on all Christian knowledge and shows the way to do theology that is truly Christian."[24] There is certainly no disagreement between the cruciform character of our theology and affirming the doctrine of justification as the integrating principle. For justification is more than just the subjective description of the believer appropriating salvation through faith. It embraces the "lofty articles of the divine Majesty" and those "that pertain to the office and the work of Jesus Christ, or our redemption" (2 Cor. 5:19–21; Eph. 2:1–10).[25]

An example of how the cross itself forms the backbone of our theology and is part of justification can be seen in Luther's *Theses on the Heidelberg Disputations*. There, Luther describes the task of theology and of every theologian as follows: "He deserves to be called a theologian, however, who comprehends the visible and manifest things of God seen through the suffering and the cross."[26] By the expression "theology of the cross" (*theologia crucis*) Lutherans mean a lens through which Christians evaluate all theology and practice. Christ's death on the cross offers a crucial correction to a person's overbearing confidence in himself and his abilities (1 Cor. 1:18–25). It also represents our own suffering that is inflicted upon us for being believers in Christ: "For where God's Word is preached, accepted, or believed, and bears fruit, there the holy and precious cross will also not be

---

24 Braaten, *Apostolic Imperative*, 17.

25 SA I–II (Kolb-Wengert, 300).

26 Thesis 20, AE 31:52.

far behind."[27] The cross of Christ thus serves as the basis for all theology and of mission as well, and the doctrine of justification points to Christ alone as our salvation. Jesus Christ, our God and Lord, died for our trespasses and was raised for our justification (Rom. 4:25). His suffering and death was satisfactory for all humanity and opened access to God (Rom. 5:2); the cross represents the payment for all the sins of the world (Phil. 3:9). And righteousness as the forgiveness of sins before God can be found only in the person of Christ (1 Cor. 1:30).

Thus the doctrine of justification includes the doctrine of Christ's death and resurrection. The total accomplishment of Christ in achieving righteousness for the world compels one to confess Luther's dictum that "the cross alone is our theology" *(crux sola est nostra theologia)*.[28]

Yet, having affirmed the event of the cross as a *fait accompli* for our salvation to which nothing must be added or subtracted, we should not fall into the trap of a false universalism that relieves the Church of its missionary obligation of proclaiming the Good News to the world so that it may hear and believe (Rom. 10:14–17). The message of reconciliation must go out to all.

Mission is the act of extending the gift of righteousness and forgiveness to the world through its preaching of the Word and administering of the Sacraments. Just as justification by Christ through faith embraces the objective moment of the cross, it also includes a strong evangelical and personal dimension. The righteousness wrought by Christ on the cross for the world is offered to the individual, and he or she appropriates it as salvation through faith. As was pointed out earlier, it is also very important that the actual delivery of Christ's righteousness to the believer includes the concept of imputation, namely, the act of appropriating righteousness through a declaration of the spoken Word. God declares through His spoken Word that sinners who believe the promise are righteous. We commonly identify that personal appropriation of the Word as subjective justification. But as was said before, the act of believing the Gospel is also based on the objective reality of the cross of Christ. In other words, both the objective and subjective side of justification remain indissoluble as the two sides of the article of justification (Rom. 5:17–19; Eph 2:8–9).[29]

27 LC III 65 (Kolb-Wengert, 448–49).

28 Theses 20–21, AE 31:52–53.

29 Braaten, *Justification*, 23–25.

The Missiological Dimension
of the Organizing Principle

The main focus of our discussion must rest upon the missiological character of justification. Although that connection might not seem that difficult to make, in fact most discussions on justification do not go this far. Justification is missiological in its very essence, since it describes what mission is at its core: imparting salvation through the forgiveness of sins. Thus justification represents, in a nutshell, the truth of the biblical message about our salvation in narrative form (e.g., the prodigal son, Luke 15:11–32) or what Paul set forth so brilliantly as the quintessence of his mission to the Gentiles (Romans 1, 3–5, 10; Galatians 2–3). Paul posits our salvation as an activity of the triune God, in other words, as divine monergism (e.g., Rom. 3:21–26). The world receives the divine gift of salvation apart from its own doing. For the apostle Paul, this principle of *sola gratia* signified his theology and motivation for mission to the Gentiles; it had to be defended at all costs, even when contested by the apostle Peter himself (Gal. 2:11–21).

As we have just stated, the implications attached to the doctrine of justification are familiar to most students of theology; its far-reaching missiological implications, however, are rarely mentioned. Clearly, since justification by grace through faith is synonymous with what we call salvation, it imbues and promotes a strong mission motif and motive. For this reason, any theology of mission and activity of mission deprived of justification will remain in a kind of Babylonian captivity.

Justification as the Critical
Yardstick in Mission

In making justification central to theology, it also becomes the critical yardstick of all theology and the mission of the Church. Making justification the critical key to mission will expose many false perceptions of missiology. Three examples may illustrate this point.

1. There is the tendency to confine mission to the Church. In other words, as the Church concentrates on her mission, she is susceptible to making herself the starting point as well as the bearer of mission. Justification by Christ through faith, however, broadens a Church's scope by pointing to God as the sole initiator and source of mission. Even in terms of all accomplishments in mission, Christians glorify and honor God's work through the Holy Spirit. Fishing for compliments and praise by claiming

credit for oneself truly diminishes the work of the triune God in mission.

Justification by Christ through faith also dismisses the erroneous notion of equating mission solely with the numerical expansion of the Church at the expense of internal growth.[30] A proper missiology underscores the existence of sin among Christians and their continuous need of forgiveness, imparted through the divine sending of the Holy Spirit. The spiritual growth within the Church is equally as important as the outward expansion of numbers. To use Luther's description, Christians "have not lost their old skin. There are so many hindrances and attacks of the devil and the world that they often grow weary and faint and at times even stumble."[31] As Christians plan to reach out to the non-Christian world, justification by Christ through faith also points to our own continual need for forgiveness and the Holy Spirit's work of sanctification.

The doctrine of justification promotes an important task for mission, namely, of giving glory and honor to Christ alone and honestly disclosing natural man's condition before God. If there ever is a central theme that permeates Lutheran theology, it is this combination of the doxological and hamartological motives (e.g., Rom. 3:23). A proper hamartology steadfastly affirms Christological doxology. Failing to speak of our own fallen state represents a deviation from the doxological motive and would "rob Christ of his honor as mediator and propitiator" and "our consciences of their comfort."[32] Justification by Christ through faith invites a theocentric perspective in mission that pays full tribute to the Lord "as the founder and perfecter of our faith" (Heb. 12:2). "To Him be given all the glory" *is* the final purpose of all mission. Justification disciplines Christians to hold their actions accountable to God Himself and to His Word.

2. Mission is commonly associated with the art of communication and proclamation. At its core, mission is all about proclaiming the Gospel and learning the mechanics of communication itself. The most influential contribution in this area began with Eugene A. Nida's *Message and Mission*.[33] Nida's insights,

---

30 Ap IV, with its definition of growth in faith, confirms this (Kolb-Wengert, 167).
31 LC V 23 (Kolb-Wengert, 469).
32 Ap IV 157, 285; Ap XXVII 17 (Tappert, 130, 150, 272). Cf. also SD V 1 (Kolb-Wengert, 581).
33 See Bibliography for publication information.

particularly in Scripture translation and revision, have set the course for many linguists after him. There is an inherent danger, though, when such studies begin to concentrate exclusively upon cultural sciences and secular anthropology. A proper missiology allows biblical theology and the divine operation through the Word to reign supreme. The study of the Word of God is more than an investigation into linguistic rules or communication theories. Linguistic studies that are based on empirical investigations and human insight must be willing to admit potential shortcomings.

3. Justification by Christ through faith stands for traditional soteriology. It is identified as personal freedom from the bondage of sin and divine wrath gained through forgiveness of one's sins. David Bosch describes how many theologians and church leaders have squeezed this traditional concept of salvation into ideas of peace and liberation that apply to life in this world and related concerns and thereby ignore the vertical dimension between God and the individual sinner. This shift has brought about a "crisis in the modern understanding of salvation."[34] With respect to salvation, Bosch states that the classical interpretation "dangerously narrows the meaning of salvation, as if it comprises only escape from the wrath of God and the redemption of the individual soul in the hereafter and . . . that it tends to make an absolute distinction between creation and new creation, between well-being and salvation."[35]

The consequences of this shift result in justification being compromised. Thus mission is no longer devoted to the task of restoring the impaired relationship between God and the believer and bringing about spiritual peace, nor would the Church be primarily devoted to the proclamation of the forgiveness of sins. Against this theological shift and confusion in soteriology, justification provides an important correction. Indeed, it projects an eschatological motif that bars idealistic and romantic notions of establishing an inner worldly peace. Justification demands a sober outlook on worldly affairs where human ability is limited

---

34 Bosch, *Transforming Mission*, 397. Bosch identifies this crisis occurring within the Conciliar-Ecumenical Movement in which the term "liberation" is now used to describe salvation. Obviously, supporters of liberation theology within Roman Catholicism engage in the same error. See Núñez, *Liberation Theology*, 175–206. But liberation theology is also controversial within Roman Catholicism for its ideological character, as the late Pope John Paul II courageously opposed various aspects of it.

35 Bosch, *Transforming Mission*, 398.

in changing events. The doctrine of justification thus fills and guides our perceptions of how we seek to promote the kingdom of God in this world. Its coming into this world has to do with an individual's bondage to sin and his restoration with God. Thus, in place of promoting mission as "liberation," Lutheran missiology continues to operate with the term "justification" to underscore salvation as "forgiveness of personal guilt" and "spiritual freedom."

Contributions in Literature

These previous examples over the last three sections involve situations, ways of thinking, paths to resolution, and implementation of ideas that engage serious issues requiring critical self-reflection. In the spirit of such reflection, I now consider existing scholarly literature to see if it presents the doctrine of justification as the integrating principle for mission and whether it adequately describes soteriology. In answer, consider that scholars have drawn attention to the missiological significance of the doctrine of justification. In his essay "Luther und die Mission," Adolf Schlatter hailed the doctrine of justification through faith as the formative motif in all evangelical missionary activity, and freedom from legalism as its missionary corollary.[36] Georg Vicedom's brief monograph *Justification as the Shaping Power of Mission*[37] accentuates the doctrine of justification as the foundation of any missionary endeavor for bringing out the facts of salvation— that is, God's judgment and merciful intention of saving the world. In his book *Das Kerygma und der Mensch*,[38] Walter Holsten follows the Bultmann tradition by concentrating on the "nowness" of the Gospel message. For him, Christian mission can be based only on God's own kerygmatic action. In fact, the kerygma itself, the message of justification, evangelizes. Holsten presents missionary activity as the verbal witness of the Pauline kerygma of justification. This insight validates the proclamation of the Word of God (the *kerygmatic motive*), but it lacks mooring in the historic events of the death and resurrection of Jesus Christ. Another point of contention against Holsten is that his one-sided emphasis on the verbal witness weakens the missionary tasks of human care and service that have been part of Christian mission since its inception.[39]

---

36 Schlatter, "Luther und die Mission," 281–88.

37 Vicedom, *Die Rechtfertigung als gestaltende Kraft der Mission.*

38 See Bibliography for publication information.

39 Müller, *Mission Theology: An Introduction*, 20–21.

In his presentation "Missiologische Aspekt der Rechtfertigungslehre" ["The Missiological Aspect of the Doctrine of Justification"],[40] Hans Schwarz stresses the hamartological motif, the world's sinfulness. He thus defines the goal of mission as overcoming man's estrangement from God, a goal founded in the reconciling event of Christ's death on the cross. Seen from the doctrine of justification, mission should therefore be nothing other than bringing faith, thereby strengthening the Christian.

All these scholars have shown that the missiological dimension of the doctrine of justification lies in its soteriological significance. Justification embodies and epitomizes God's saving acts upon man. Justification is concerned with the worldwide and universal distribution of Christ's presence to the whole world and stresses faith received through proclamation. Thus justification motivates the missionary enterprise and points away from applying it selfishly to oneself or from making it an inner-ecclesial issue. Rather, justification exposes the deeper underlying missionary cause and motivation for the proclamation of the Christian message to *all* those in need of salvation.[41] It frames the setting for mission from the cross.

Proposing the Synthetic and Doctrinal Method

In taking justification as the integrative principle, this study now turns to other theological themes. I pursue a *synthetic* rather than an *analytical* approach to theology. I do not plan to discuss each article separately in full detail, but I will argue the integrative nature of each doctrine of faith. One begins with the work and mission of the triune God (*missio Dei*) as the Creator, Redeemer, and Sanctifier. God reaches out to the entire world and embraces the Church as His instrument of reaching the lost. I thus include the proclamation of the Church and how God ensures that His Word is preached to the world so that each individual is received through forgiveness into His kingdom. Then we shall consider the nature of the Church, the service of all Christians, the means of grace, the ethical character of mission as an outflow of new obedience, and how justification holds the key to the proper discernment of Christendom from other religions. Thus one will not simply behold a panoramic view of theology and practice, but one will be engaged in a paradigm that has a particular missiological thrust. As a result, I will argue that a proper theology of mission is

---

40 Schwarz, "Missiologische Aspekt der Rechtfertigungslehre," 209–17.
41 Bürkle, *Missionstheologie*, 45.

deductive, not inductive, and one that is not merely descriptive but also prescriptive and normative in its approach. In other words, as we discuss missiological issues, we shall remain predominantly in the parameters of a doctrinal and dogmatic missiology.[42]

---

42 One may see here Jongeneel, *Philosophy, Science, and Theology of Mission*, 1:177–80; 2:49–50. Paul Heerboth defines the relation of systematic theology to mission as follows: "Systematic Theology seeks the meaning and application of Christology and Soteriology in mission, and the interaction of Christian faith with the secular world" ("Missouri Synod Approach to Mission in the Early Period," 26). The same study concludes that "every aspect of theology has an inescapable missiological dimension." Gensichen, *Glaube für die Welt*, 250, states that missiology should be "the theme of all theology" ("Gegenstand aller Theologie"), or, as Bosch, *Transforming Mission*, 494, suggests: "Missiology may be termed 'the synoptic discipline' within the wider encyclopedia of theology."

PART II

THE MISSION OF THE TRIUNE GOD

CHAPTER SIX

THE TRINITARIAN STRUCTURE OF MISSION

MISSIO DEI AS MISSIO TRINITATIS

Today, most theologians present their theology on mission in the context of the theology of the triune God; that is, they expound mission in trinitarian dimensions.[1] Lesslie Newbigin, for example, argues: "The mission of the church is to be understood, can only be rightly understood, in terms of the trinitarian model."[2]

On July 5–17, 1952, the International Missionary Council conference held at Willingen, Germany, laid the foundation for discussion by positing the first seminal definition of the mission of God: "Mission has its source in the Triune God. Out of the depth of his love to us, the Father has sent forth his own beloved son to reconcile all things to himself that we and all men might through the Holy Spirit be made one in him with the Father in that perfect love which is the very nature of God."[3] That itself arose from preliminary work by German missiologist Karl Hartenstein. In 1934, Hartenstein coined the phrase *missio Dei* in response to Karl Barth's use of *actio Dei* ("the action of God").[4] The phrase recalls traditional Western thought such as Augustine's doctrine of the Trinity and finds allusions in his *Confessions*, but its major application to missiology appears first in Willingen.[5]

---

1 Consider especially Vicedom, *Mission of God*. Many contemporary missiologists of his time— inspired by the conference of Willingen, July 5–17, 1952—share this soteriological paradigm: Neill, *Unfinished Task*; Andersen, *Towards a Theology of Mission*; Hartenstein, "Theologische Besinnung," 51–72; Freytag, "Sendung und Verheißung," 217–23; Newbigin, *Trinitarian Faith and Today's Mission*; LWF, *Together in God's Mission*; LWF, *Mission in Context*; Wagner, "Das lutherische Bekenntnis als Dimension des Missionspapiers," 149–61.

2 Newbigin, *Gospel in a Pluralist Society*, 118.

3 In the sectional "Missionary Calling of the Church," in *International Review of Mission* 41 (1952): 562. See also Thomas, *Classic Texts in Mission and World Christianity*, 103–4.

4 Van Sanders, "Mission of God and the Local Church," 24.

5 See Augustine, *Conf.* 1:18, 38; 3:6, 61–62; 6:5, 117; 8:12, 178.

Under the tutelage of leading missiologists and theologians such as Walter Freytag, Karl Hartenstein, and Karl Barth, the byword *missio Dei* was soon widely adopted to express mission as God's mission.[6] What is so groundbreaking in this? Speaking of mission as *missio Dei* signifies a theological shift from the common perception of mission as substantially a human endeavor to a theocentric approach that makes God, and not humans, the source and initiator of mission. Lest there be any confusion over which God this is, the *missio Dei* term reflects the mission of the triune God, the *missio Trinitatis*.

Perhaps this insight does not seem particularly overwhelming. A few years after World War II, however, there was every reason to refocus missiological thinking. By that time, mission had reached an all-time low. Both wars had depleted the resources for foreign mission, the fateful mingling of mission and politics had destroyed the credibility of the missionary motives on the mission field, and the hopes of achieving world evangelization as stated at the Edinburgh Conference of 1910 seemed entirely dashed. This state of affairs occasioned the laudable return to the basics of mission and made theologians and church bodies realign their motives and strategies to that of God's will and intentions.

HEILSGESCHICHTE, GRACE OF CREATION, AND REDEMPTION

Theologians at the Willingen conference added important theological components to the *missio Dei*, such as salvation history, eschatology, and the activity of the Church as the instrument through which God works in this world. Let us examine briefly each concept in turn. The eschatological direction made the Church's mission focus on the coming kingdom. Much of what the Church does is still preliminary in the sense that with the Lord's return all things will come to completion.[7]

The term *Heilsgeschichte* ("salvation history") explains God's saving activity in time. *Heilsgeschichte* describes God's intention to bring salvation through the proclamation of the Word in and through the Church.[8] Salvation history dismisses the thought that God uses other activities and events in the world as His means in the same way as He does His Word. Through His providential care, God continues to guide and protect the world until eternity so that His mission through the Church may continue.

6   For the history of the concept *missio Dei*, see Bosch, *Transforming Mission*, 389–93. For a more detailed survey of the term, see Rosin, *Missio Dei*.

7   See in particular Walter Freytag's treatment, "Mission im Blick aufs Ende," 186–98.

8   Oscar Cullmann is noted in particular for his discussion of salvation history in Scripture. One may see his *Salvation in History*, as well as Bosch, *Transforming Mission*, 498–510.

God's goodness is shown as He guides and protects the world by holding "the world in readiness for the gospel and keep[ing] it from collapsing into the chaos which threatens His salvific plans."[9] The divine providential care is thus not equal with the gift of salvation, but neither is it wholly separate. God's care for mankind and world through His established orders and channels of human activities is preemptive in nature as it awaits salvation in Christ.[10]

Thus God uses His grace of creation *(gratia creatoris)* in support of His saving grace *(gratia redemptoris)*. Put differently, in Protestant theology, this divine act of salvation comes as justification. Justification stands for the grace of redemption that is embedded in a broader framework that describes a greater *extensive* activity of God. Georg Vicedom makes this observation: "Justification . . . is . . . included in the totality of God's dealing with mankind. This dealing involves more than declaring man righteous and accepting him into divine fellowship."[11] It is true that God deals with man on a broader level. However, justification points to the Lord's preservation of the world with His salvific mission in mind. Thus events within the broader framework of God's dealings—even those devastating ones such as earthquakes and wars—have often moved people to seek out God and have driven them back to Church. Such ideas about how an unbeliever might come to faith are not new. Even Augustine of Hippo described being moved through external and internal trials in order that he truly learn Scripture and regain faith.

Once a person has been brought to that point, the certainty of the forgiveness of sins becomes the event that truly saves. For this reason, salvation history focuses on the activity of the triune God within history that has been happening since the beginning of the world. Adam and Eve, the prophets, the house of Israel, the disciples of Christ, the first believers, and Christians all over the world today are beneficiaries of the divine salvific plan.

The center of God's reconciliation with the world is the cross. The event of Christ's death on the cross is the world's salvation, redemption, and justification. Salvation history thus brings out God's salvific acts as these acts have occurred and will continue to occur in time. Yet there remains a "vertical" dimension to these divine acts. They continue to transcend the framework of merely "horizontal" evolutionary plans to transform the world or any other influence of human intention. Missiological agendas sometimes fail to draw these distinctions.

---

9 Forde, "Forensic Justification and the Law," 301.

10 Beißer, *Hoffnung und Vollendung*, 75.

11 Vicedom, *Mission of God*, 14; Pannenberg, *Faith and Reality*, 72–73; Martens, *Die Rechtfertigung des Sünders*, 32.

THE DISPUTE OVER THE *MISSIO DEI*

Sadly, many of the above tenets, which once were part of the *missio Dei*, may no longer be assumed as a given. While many missiologists agree on the term *missio Dei*, it has largely been divested of theological meaning. Indeed, as one focuses upon particular points of definition, agreements and misunderstandings ensue immediately. Most disputed is the description of God's salvific mission, which we have identified with justification. Not all Christian circles choose justification as the most important concept of salvation, but prefer "liberation" instead. This viewpoint would be most prevalent among theologians of the Conciliar or Ecumenical Movement, as can be seen from the following statement of the Conciliar Movement: "The Christian understanding of liberation is informed by the biblical understanding of justice . . . Its goal is nothing less than the peace (shalom) of God in a qualitatively new community in which the role of the oppressor and oppressed is completely done away with. The values of God's kingdom become the touchstone for a comprehensive and authentic liberation."[12]

The contemporary emphasis upon so-called "liberation" provides reason for us to assert a specific Lutheran approach within current missiological discussions. Past attempts to promote the Lutheran understanding of justification are Georg Vicedom's *Mission of God* and the LWF studies *Together in God's Mission* (1988) and *Mission in Context: Transformation, Reconciliation, Empowerment* (2005). A recent attempt by the ELCA is *The Evangelizing Church: A Lutheran Contribution*.[13]

However perplexing apparent differences on the content of the *missio Dei* may be, ascribing mission to God as its source still remains the crucial point for a proper theology of mission. Despite the confusion over the content of the term, I would not suggest that we abandon it altogether. Instead, we should make the extra effort of discussing all its aspects from Scripture and historical theology. A proper *missio Dei* was fixed already in language and concepts in the first four centuries of the Christian Church, particularly in the first two ecumenical councils of AD 325 (Nicaea) and

---

12   WCC-CWME, *Statement on Urban Rural Mission*, and Scherer and Bevans, *New Directions in Mission and Evangelization*, 1:62, 65–72. See also its documents "Mission and Evangelization" (1982) or its latest World Missionary Conference of the CWME in Salvador in 1996. Seeing the social plight of many citizens in South America as they suffer because of exploitation by large landowners and corporations, Roman Catholic theologians, too, have pleaded for a *missio Dei* that promises the oppressed "liberation." For an overall discussion of the meaning of "salvation," see Bosch, *Transforming Mission*, 397–99. See also Krusche, "Die Kirche für andere," 151. The Conciliar Movement's emphasis on "liberation" has been strongly contested by Peter Beyerhaus, one of the important authors of the "Frankfurt Declaration." See the two tracts: Beyerhaus, *Missions—Which Way?* and *Shaken Foundations*. The following scholars follow similar lines as Beyerhaus: Ji, "Evangelization and Humanization," 176; Gensichen, *Glaube für die Welt*, 203.

13   See the preface for references to these works.

AD 381 (Constantinople). Some may be concerned about drawing attention to the Early Church in explaining the mission of the triune God instead of proceeding directly from Scripture. Scripture, too, points to the Trinity in texts such as Matt. 28:18–20 and 2 Cor. 13:14. It is tempting to suppose that trinitarian statements are a later product of theological and confessional reflections in the early history of the Christian Church. Indeed, during the first few centuries, the Church took upon herself the task of clarifying and rejecting errors associated with the doctrine of the Trinity. However, the Church articulated the doctrine of the Trinity by referring back to Scripture. Already in the New Testament, confessions of Jesus Christ as the Son of God, Son of Man, Son of David, and Messiah became a necessary complement to the belief in the one God of the Judaic tradition.[14] The same applies to the person of the Holy Spirit who is sent by God to all believers to be the Counselor and Comforter (John 15:26; Gal. 4:6). The triadic formulas of the New Testament, including Matt. 28:19 and 2 Cor. 13:14, speak for the New Testament faith in a God who is the Father of Jesus Christ and who is present in the Spirit of love and reconciliation in the life of the Church. On these passages, informed by the Spirit teaching them to the Church and the latter's response in the great creeds, rests the true sense of the *missio Dei*.

GOD'S OUTWARD ACTIVITIES TO THE WORLD

Philip Melanchthon opened his *Loci Communes,* the first Lutheran dogmatics, with the observation that Christians should not merely admire or probe the mysteries of the Trinity but also believe in God's self-revelation to the world through His Son and Spirit.[15] Since then, Western theology has undertaken many efforts to describe the salvific implications of God's work to the world. Scholars such as Robert Jenson, Wolfhart Pannenberg, and Karl Rahner have contributed to the doctrine of the Trinity, particularly with respect to the inward and outward relations of the three persons. However, Melanchthon is certainly correct in his observation that the doctrine of the Trinity is meaningful only in terms of highlighting its salvific intentions in Christ. Thus without the ministry of Christ, His suffering and resurrection, God would remain an alien and an apathetic entity. There is thus no discussion of God and His mission except through Jesus Christ, who became incarnate and died on the cross (John 3:16; 1 John 4:10; Rom.

---

14 The pertinent passages are: Mark 1:11 (Jesus' Baptism); Mark 8:29 (Peter's confession); Matt. 17:5 (Jesus' transfiguration); Matt. 21:9 (Jesus' triumphal entry into Jerusalem); Matt. 27:54 (the centurion's confession); Luke 24:26 (meeting with the disciples of Emmaus); Rom. 1:3 (Son of David); also 1 Cor. 15:3–11; Phil. 2:5–11; Col. 1:15–20.

15 Melanchthon, *Loci Communes*, 20–21.

3:25). The *missio Dei* is only fully understood when one discovers the intention of God's loving will as it became known in Jesus Christ.[16]

The *missio Dei* thus presupposes the ontological definitions of the unity of the triune God—in other words, that God *is and exists as one* (Deut. 6:4: "Hear, O Israel: The LORD our God, the LORD is one").[17] The missiological significance of the Godhead lies in the economic activity of the three persons to the world. God's mission must be seen in terms of what He *does* according to the personal acts of creation, redemption, and sanctification. Martin Luther made a significant contribution toward this understanding in his Large Catechism. It is true that Luther did not write the Large Catechism in a specific missiological framework, but he nonetheless provides a theological blueprint for mission as it lays out God's mission. Therein, Luther parts with the traditional division of the Apostles' Creed into twelve sentences and chooses instead a tripartite rendering of the Creed, with each article addressing a specific outward activity of one of the persons in the Trinity. In doing so, Luther did not abandon the important rule that the external activities of God are indivisible: *Opera trinitatis ad extra sunt indivisa*.[18] Nor did Luther fall prey to a form of modalism or naive tritheism that destroyed the actual unity or divinity of the three persons. Luther explicitly mentions that his tripartite division was done for pedagogical reasons.[19] The reformer knew full well that he had abridged the scriptural witness and the confession of the Church for the simple folk. And so a student in search of a greater fullness of Luther's understanding of the doctrine than what is presented in his catechism may turn to his exegetical-dogmatic writings and to his Trinity sermons.[20]

The external acts of creation, redemption, and fulfillment project an intricate and inseparable unity of the triune God: "God sends His Son; Father and Son send the Holy Ghost. Here God makes Himself not only the One sent, but at the same time the Content of the sending, without dissolving through this Trinity of revelation the equality of essence of the divine

---

16 Gensichen, *Living Mission*, 252.

17 Schlink, *Theology of the Lutheran Confessions*, 63. E.g., AC I 3 (Kolb-Wengert, 37).

18 Schlink, *Theology of the Lutheran Confessions*, 66; Gensichen, *Glaube für die Welt*, 81; Wagner, "Das lutherische Bekenntnis als Dimension des Missionspapiers," 153; Mueller, *Christian Dogmatics*.

19 LC II 5–6 (Kolb-Wengert, 431–32).

20 Peters, *Kommentar zu Luthers Katechismen*, 2:38. See also Maurer, *Historical Commentary on the Augsburg Confession*, 246–49. In the Smalcald Articles, Luther affirms that the "three distinct persons in one divine essence and nature, are one God, who created heaven and earth" (SA I 1, Kolb-Wengert, 300). The seriousness that the Confessions place on the trinitarian dogma is most apparent when one looks at the condemnation of a wide variety of ancient antitrinitarians (AC I 5–6, Kolb-Wengert, 37) and the antitrinitarians during the time of the Reformation (SD XII 1.37–38, Kolb-Wengert, 656, 659–60). See Schlink, *Theology of the Lutheran Confessions*, 64.

Persons. For in the every Person of the deity God works in His entirety."[21] These outward trinitarian operations reflect in every way the one God at work. The mission of Jesus Christ may at times defy human logic and stand in contention with natural man's perception of God, especially with respect to the mission of the Son of God, the incarnate Christ, who displays His divinity and divine mission even in His death on the cross (1 Cor. 1:18–31). Such titles of the Second Person of the Trinity as are given in the Gospels (Christ, Messiah, Rabbi, Master) may not reflect the divine character of Christ's person and mission. But there are also statements that present His unity with the Father (John 10:30; 17:21) and indicate the full divinity of His person (Phil. 2:6–11; Col. 1:15–18; 2:9).

The Church has always worshiped Christ as the preexistent, incarnate, and co-creating divinity. It thus rejected at the council of Nicaea in AD 325 attempts at subordinating Christ to the Father as claimed by Arius. It was precisely Arius's reluctance to have God dragged into the mission of the incarnate Christ—His human birth, suffering, and death—that became the controversial issue. For this reason, the decision of Nicaea safeguarded the deity of the incarnate Christ by affirming Christ to be of the same substance (*homoousios*) with the Father.

The theologians quickly realized that the equation of Father with the Son must also include the Holy Spirit. Otherwise, the Spirit would be treated as inferior to the other two persons. According to John 16:15 and 17:26, the Third Person's activity is to make known to the world the glory of Christ which, in turn, is the Father's glory. Although the Church confesses God as one, God in Christ also establishes His presence in the life of the Church through the presence and work of the Holy Spirit. In the year 589, the regional council of Toledo affirmed the divine status of the Holy Spirit by adding the famous *filioque* ("and from the Son"), which states that the Holy Spirit, as the Lord and Giver of life, proceeds from the Father *and* the Son. The *filioque* ensured that the Holy Spirit, who, in turn, is worthy of worship with the Father and Son, shares the majesty of the Father and Son.

Thus God's mission includes His outward operations toward the world, that is, in time and in relation to God's creation. We could formulate the divine mission in this way: God the Father, driven by His loving will, sends His Word through which He creates the world. Fallen man is not simply ejected from creation, having spurned the Word of God for the devil's lies in Genesis 3. God's Word became flesh in Jesus Christ, the first missionary, through whom God the Father is reconciled to man. Jesus Christ makes way for His Spirit, through whom creation is brought back to Christ and to

---

21 Vicedom, *Mission of God*, 8.

the Creator. Mission therefore has its origin in God Himself. The one God acts out of love to this world; in three persons, God creates, redeems, and sanctifies the world.

These external trinitarian operations are not the same as the intratrinitarian relationships. The latter establish that, within God, each person subsists of Himself through the actual internal motions of generation of the Son from the Father and the spiration of the Holy Spirit from the Father and the Son. These activities are considered divisible *(opera ad intra sunt divisa)* and express in some ways an internal hierarchy within the Godhead. The external activities, on the other hand, discuss God's work to the world and affirm the unity of God.[22] The Church uses the concept of *perichoresis* ("mutual coinherence" or "interexistence") to underscore that the three persons of the Godhead do not only interpenetrate the same essence and share their lives but also that all three are involved in the divine works of the one God. Certainly, as one sees in Luther's catechisms, each external work is attributed to one person of the Godhead in the sense that one of the persons primarily does the work. However, all participate in what is done by appropriation to one person of the Trinity. Creation is associated with the work of the Father, redemption with the Son, and sanctification with the Holy Spirit. However, each of the other persons also participates in the divine actions that are specific to each person.[23]

THE VALUE OF THE *FILIOQUE*

We do not affirm the internal personal acts and the economic Trinity just to pay homage to its scriptural and historical authority. The acts and economy of the Trinity are extremely relevant for the mission of God. One aspect of the Trinity includes the *filioque* clause that the Western Church inserted into the Nicene Creed.[24] The *filioque* clause affirms the explicit connection between the Holy Spirit and Jesus Christ. The Spirit is the Spirit of Christ and brings the gift of salvation to the world that Christ has won. Putting it this way may be considered a limitation of the Spirit's freedom to work independently of Christ and His presence. For many scholars, the *filioque* is thus seen as a hindrance to a genuine dialogue with other religions. Since the *filioque* ties the Spirit to Christ, the result is that salvific elements in other religions should be disqualified as false. Other scholars may dismiss

---

22 Nicene Creed (Kolb-Wengert, 22–23); SA I 2 (Kolb-Wengert, 300). See here for further explanation: Brunstäd, *Theologie der lutherischen Bekenntnisschriften*, 30; Schlink, *Theology of the Lutheran Confessions*, 66; Mueller, *Christian Dogmatics*, 156.

23 See Erickson, *Making Sense of the Trinity*, 64.

24 Here, the Confessions follow the Western tradition; see Athanasian Creed 22 (Kolb-Wengert, 24); Nicene Creed 7 (Kolb-Wengert, 23); and SA I 2 (Kolb-Wengert, 300). Fagerberg, *Die Theologie der lutherischen Bekenntnisschriften*, 128.

the value of the *filioque* for ecumenical reasons, seeing it as an impediment to improving relations between the Eastern and the Western Churches. One notices here two different interests. The East preserves the person of God the Father as the source in the Godhead in contrast to the West's emphasis of the unity of all three persons.

We can see how missiological disaster would result from waiving the *filioque*. The classical concept of mission consists in the profession of the uniqueness of Christ, to whom the Spirit must lead adherents of all religions. If the Holy Spirit were to be divorced from the person of Christ, the Spirit's role and His outward salvific economy would change from making Christ present to some different role. Moreover, there is the very real danger that if the Holy Spirit is given pivotal attention apart from His connection to Christ, the role and relevancy of Christ Himself is changed. An example in which our concern would apply is in the current interreligious dialogue. Here, it is important to note that the Holy Spirit is connected to Christ and brings Christ to all people through the proclamation of the Word. We should not delve into investigations that espouse sentiments of religious pluralism by seeking out evidence or testimonies of the presence of the Holy Spirit in other religions apart from the presence of Christ and the Word as His vehicle.[25] Once the pendulum swings in favor of selling off the *filioque*, Christ is pushed back into the historic past and most probably also into irrelevance. It should thus be obvious that the *filioque* continues to serve as a helpful reminder of the Spirit's work in God's mission and thus also a correction to religious pluralism.[26]

THE CHURCH

These external or economic activities of the triune God as captured by the three articles of the catholic Creeds have become most helpful in expounding upon the status and the nature of the mission of the Church today. The Church affirms that mission begins with God, and not man. "The missionary obligation of the church is grounded in the outgoing activity of God, whereby, as creator, redeemer, governor and guide, God establishes and includes the world and men within his fulfilling purposes and fellowship."[27] A continual task of the Church's mission is thus to align and realign itself to all three activities of the Trinity: creation (Father), incarnation (Son), and

---

25 See Schulz, "Tensions in the Pneumatology of the Missio Dei," 99–121. See also a most helpful contribution by Smail, "Holy Spirit in the Holy Trinity," 149–65.

26 Braaten, *Justification*, 137–38. One may also consult an earlier treatment by Weber, "Mysterium Trinitatis," 355.

27 Günther, *Von Edinburgh nach Mexico City*, 74–76. See also Günther, "Gott selbst treibt Mission," 57.

sanctification (Spirit). Indeed, the Church relates her mission to all three articles of the Creed, but it would be most true that the Church's mission is most clearly defined by the Third Article, the economic activity of the Holy Spirit. This definition does not diminish the Christocentric perspective, but underscores the point that the reconciliation of God with fallen mankind through Christ is made present through the activity of the Spirit in Word and Sacrament. Luther's perspective on the Spirit's work remains relevant:

> Neither you nor I could ever know anything of Christ, or believe in him and take him as our Lord, unless these were first offered to us and bestowed on our hearts through the preaching of the Gospel by the Holy Spirit. The work is finished and completed, Christ has acquired and won the treasure for us by his sufferings, death, and resurrection, etc. But if the work remained hidden and no one knew of it, it would have been all in vain, all lost. In order that this treasure might not be buried but put to use and enjoyed, God has caused the Word to be published and proclaimed, in which he has given the Holy Spirit to offer and apply to us this treasure of salvation.[28]

The nature and characteristic of today's mission undoubtedly finds its place in the mission of the Holy Spirit. While mission becomes in part a holistic endeavor of human care services as the First Article would suggest, and while it is wholly based on the objective and reconciling work of Christ on the cross, mission's lasting relevancy lies in its being a kerygmatic and sacramental act (Rom. 10:9–17).

Although there may be some that consider this approach an illegitimate aggrandizement, I nevertheless maintain that the mission of the Church flows from the theocentric and trinitarian impulse and revelation itself. In emphasizing the theocentric dimension of mission, one might think that the concept of *missio Dei* would have difficulties in incorporating and defining the human enterprise. But the mission of God in time continues through the activity of human preachers and workers throughout the world, while the success of mission remains God's alone. Newbigin discerns both aspects of mission in this way: "But the Church is not the source of the witness; rather, it is the locus of witness."[29] Van Rheenen states similarly: "Mission does not originate with human sources, for ultimately it is not a human enterprise. Mission is rooted in the nature of God, who sends and saves."[30] This mutual and bilateral nature of mission may not be completely grasped with the term *missio Dei*. For this reason, Hans-Werner Gensichen suggests that one should drop the term *missio Dei* altogether and

---

28 LC II 38 (Kolb-Wengert, 436).

29 Newbign, *Gospel in a Pluralist Society*, 120.

30 Van Rheenen, *Missions*, 14.

speak instead of the theological dimension and the kerygmatic intention of the mission of God.[31] Other missiologists, led by the late Dutch ecumenical theologian Johannes Christiaan Hoekendijk (1912–75), oppose the central place of the Church in the *missio Dei* and propose instead that the world is a direct forum of the divine mission apart from, and not through, the mediation of the Church.[32] David Bosch rightly defines such a proposal as "a view that leads to absurdity" because it then becomes impossible "to talk about the church's involvement in the world if its very right to exist is disputed a priori."[33] The mission of God is only accomplished through the service of the Church as she proclaims the Gospel and administers the Sacraments. The instrumentality of the Church in God's mission is thus without any doubt essential for God's mission to continue.[34]

The concept of salvation history serves as a safeguard against a complete boycott of the Church's central role in the *missio Dei*. Obviously, we do not wish to abandon the First Article of the Creed, that protective and guiding activity of God the Father over creation, but salvation history conveys the important point that God's special salvific activity is not dissolved in, say, world events. Instead, salvation is located within and through the proclaiming activity of the Church. Salvation history necessitates the mission activity of the Church, for it suggests an interim period of time and space between the Christ event and the Day of Judgment in which the *missio ecclesiae* actively participates in God's mission. Vicedom's insight seems highly apropos: "The church has the obligation in the interim between the completion of salvation and the final judgment (when salvation will be revealed as redemption) to call men to repentance and to transmit the saving faith."[35] In light of the above, it would perhaps be appropriate to provide my own definition of the *missio Dei*. This definition affirms a specific perception of the nature of the *missio Trinitatis* and the role of the Church within the activity of the doctrine of the Trinity in the world:

> The *missio Dei* is the trinitarian redemptive and reconciling activity in history, motivated by God the Father's loving will for the entire world, grounded in the atoning work of Jesus Christ, and carried out by the Holy Spirit of Christ through the means of grace. God justifies man through the means of grace; delivers him from rebellion, sin, and death; subjects him under His kindly reign; and leads him and the redeemed community toward the final goal in history.

31 Gensichen, *Living Mission*, 34–38; see also Gensichen, *Glaube für die Welt*, 80–95.
32 Guder, *Missional Church*, 99.
33 Bosch, *Transforming Mission*, 385, 392.
34 See Scherer, *That the Gospel May Be Sincerely Preached*, 13–14.
35 Vicedom, *Mission of God*, 65.

CHAPTER SEVEN

CREATION AND PRESERVATION
IN GOD'S MISSION

UNPACKING TRINITARIAN MISSION

In chapter 6, we looked at the *missio Dei* and defined it as the *missio Trinitatis*. All three persons are involved. Now it is time to unpack in some detail their role in the mission of God. Chapters 7–9 look to the persons of the Trinity and the external works of the Trinity as they relate to mission. This chapter engages God's role as Creator, looking at a proper sense of God as the ultimate, universal truth. Various aspects include the image of God, *diakonia*, Christian vocation, and natural law. Chapter 8 focuses on Christology, including the cross, sin, and the person and work of Christ as central to mission. Chapter 9 addresses the Holy Spirit's role in the life of the Church and the Christian, the means of grace, and the importance of that to mission.

UNIVERSAL PERSPECTIVE

The fact that the world is God's creation has huge implications for the mission of the Church. Creation gives Christianity a central place among all other religions and spiritual expressions, since it identifies the God of creation with no other God but the triune God. The triune God is the one who created the world. This makes Him also the God over all nations and the world's Redeemer. Christian mission thus does not illegitimately usurp rights over other nations as missionaries proclaim the Gospel. Rather, the cry is that all need to be reconciled with the sole, true, triune God from whom they have fallen away. Such important individuals of the Old Testament as Jonah and Ruth demonstrated that the God who created all nations also wants the latter to become recipients of His salvific mission.[1]

---

1   For expositions of how God's mission in these Old Testament books is fulfilled in the ministry of Jesus Christ and continues in the mission of the Christian Church, see Lessing, *Jonah*, 151–69, and Wilch, *Ruth*, 25–28, 58–60, 83–86, 101–7.

The doctrine of creation thus lays the groundwork for the universal motif and motive connected to the cross of Christ. When the Lord pointed the apostles toward all nations in Matt. 28:19–20 as the beneficiaries of His death on the cross, the apostles—and all readers of Scripture—have in mind the vast number of "nations" who live in this world under the one true God who made heaven and earth (e.g., Gen. 1:1; Ps. 24:1) and who are His possession (Genesis 10; Ps. 86:9; Deut. 32:8). The Old Testament demonstrates that God's message and action is not aimed solely at a particular nation, but that God cares about all nations.[2] Thus the doctrine of creation promotes not particularism but a proper universalism. Biblically, universalism presents God's salvation plan in an all-embracing sense. This means that God's mission not only includes the nation of Israel or a chosen remnant but also the entire human race. God calls all people through His Word, which presents Christ as the Savior for all that they may come to Him (1 Tim. 2:4). If we define universalism as just discussed, then we should dismiss false definitions of universalism that declare salvation to all apart from the Word and Christ and exclude the reality of God's judgment.

Restoring the Image of God

The doctrine of creation reminds one that salvation entails the restoration in sinners of the image of God in which all humanity was once created (Gen. 1:26–27). Through the fall, all humanity lost the image of God (Genesis 3). No distinction exists among humans in this world with respect to the loss of God's image; everyone who is descended from Adam and Eve shares Adam's image and likeness (Gen. 5:3) and partakes in wickedness (Gen. 6:5; Rom. 5:12–21). In regard to an exact, mechanical, or empirical description of the loss of the *imago Dei*, Scripture remains silent.[3] There is, however, an important impairment in man's relation to God as far as the image of God applies to the First Commandment. All humans share the loss of the original state of integrity before God. Christians are in solidarity with non-Christians since "there is no real difference between a justified Christian insofar as he still is the old human and an unbelieving and unrepentant non-Christian."[4] But God does not abandon His creation after the fall. God still protects human life by virtue of the image of God (Gen. 9:6). Humans are thus in a constant search to resume a relationship with God,

---

2   Rzepkowski, "Creation Theology and Missiology," 90.

3   Gerhard von Rad states: "Certainly, the story of the Fall tells of grave disturbances in the creaturely nature of man. But as to the way in which these affected the image of God in man, the Old Testament has nothing explicit to say" (*Old Testament Theology*, 1:147). Peters, *Kommentar zu Luthers Katechismen*, 2:86.

4   Bayer, *Living by Faith*, 68.

but they create a religion of their own. Therefore, the initiative must come from God. God's redemption alone leads to the restoration of a proper relationship and attitude toward God. That restored relationship to God is a spiritual one and comes about through the proclamation of the Gospel and faith in Jesus Christ. God will not rest until "every tribe and language and people and nation" and "a great multitude that no one could number" has been gathered around His throne (Rev. 5:9–10; 7:9–17).[5] For this reason, the Church's mission is committed to the proclamation of the Word of God to bring about that restoration: "The goal and content of the *missio Dei* and the lordship of God is to conquer this hostile area, to bring man once more into the proper place of the vis-à-vis, to restore him to fellowship with God, and to liberate him from sin."[6]

Broadening the Scope
of Mission for *Diakonia*

The priority of the Church's mission is to restore the broken relationship of sinful humanity with God. But the doctrine of creation informs the Church that her mission reaches out to a human being according to the manner in which God created male and female in His image, in the human entirety of body and soul, and not just as a spiritual object targeted for conversion.[7] The Western world, building on Greek philosophy from Thales and Anaximander to Plato and Aristotle, has the tendency to draw philosophical distinctions between body and soul. This interprets human existence in dichotomies between a life here on earth and eternal life, giving the physical and temporal things less worth than the spiritual, eternal things. If the missionary enterprise concentrates exclusively upon bringing someone to eternal life, then the missionary could very easily neglect humanity's bodily needs for which God Himself daily and richly provides. Conversely, if all stress is placed on bodily needs, then the spiritual condition of man could be ignored. Mission thus must take on a holistic practice that carefully attends to a service that conserves human dignity in every way. A proper mission seriously considers the physical side of human existence and cares for man's body, earthly life, and environment. In addition, the holistic

---

5 Verkuyl, *Contemporary Missiology*, 91.

6 Vicedom, *Mission of God*, 15.

7 In 1973, the LCMS officially adopted *Statement of Scriptural and Confessional Principles*, which contains a section on the mission of the Church. This states: "We believe, teach, and confess that the primary mission of the Church is to make disciples of every nation by bearing witness to Jesus Christ through the preaching of the Gospel and the administration of the Sacraments. Other necessary activities of the Church, such as ministering to men's physical needs, are to serve the church's primary mission and its goal that men will believe and confess Jesus Christ as their Lord and Savior" (2).

nature of mission includes elements such as language, culture, religious sensitivity, and social realities, and it responds in particular to needs of God's created people in the form of diaconal services. Diaconal service was part of the life of the Early Church. For example, in Acts 6:1–7, individuals were chosen to address the needs of the Hellenistic widows in Jerusalem while the apostles continued to preach the Word. Since then, the Church makes the effort to have love through deeds complement the preaching of the Word. While some are preachers of the Word, Christians step forward to express their faith through loving and caring service to all people in need. Like the preaching of the Word, human care is a joint concern of all Christians. It takes on an organizational form for the Church as she looks at the needs of the people.

Diaconal service carried out by organizations within the Church complements mission work very well, and, wherever possible, it should accompany the proclamation of the Word of God. Ideally speaking, all Christians are motivated to human care by their love for the neighbor just as Christ exemplified works of outreach and love in person and through His ministry. Christ's great mercy and holy love to those in physical need motivate Christians to act likewise. The Word of God also inspires mission to acts of love and service. An explicit command to emulate the Lord in His acts of mercy to the neighbor in need is provided in the parable of the Good Samaritan (Luke 10:25–37): "Go, and do likewise." These words inspire the Christian to acts of love and service. Likewise, the great Judge invokes a blessing upon those on His right who have in fact demonstrated their love to "the least of these" (Matt. 25:31–46). According to the Lord, "signs" of mercy to the neighbor will accompany His missionaries (Mark 16:17), and in fact He confirmed them as the apostles went about their respective ministries (Mark 16:20).

Often, the term "integral mission" is used to define the holistic nature of mission. All this indicates is that a wide array of services addressing life in this world accompany mission.[8] However, "integral mission" flows from "integral salvation." In other words, all diaconal services are auxiliary to the preaching of the Word so that the proclamation of the Good News may also spill over into temporal blessing, recalling Jesus' own ministry. Peter Brunner provides the following distinction: "The church must take seriously the entire spectrum of this [human] need and attempt to address it ... The danger exists when this diaconical service of the church to the world is made the proper, meaningful and norming function of her existence ... thereby the message of justification through faith is truly inverted to the

---

8   Verkuyl, *Contemporary Missiology*, 197.

opposite."[9] The humanitarian service of the Church assumes its rightful place next to the proclamation of the Word. Proponents of the document *Together in God's Mission* likewise affirm the supremacy of the Word of God in Christian mission: "Among all the ministries of the church, the ministry of Word and Sacrament occupies, however, a special place because of its responsibility for the means of grace."[10]

Thus as visible communions or entities within the Church integrate diaconical services into mission, they would do well to follow the precedent set in Acts 6 where the twelve apostles prioritized their ministry to the Word by establishing a supporting ministry of seven "deacons" to care for those in need.[11] For this reason, Christian mission should enlist auxiliary services that specifically support and enhance the primary task of missionary proclamation. Failure on the part of evangelistic missionaries to demonstrate love to indigenous populations can seem heartless and disingenuous. Unfortunately, on many occasions the absence of such auxiliary services has forced evangelistic missionaries to be tied to human care activities such as initiating and overseeing building projects and assisting in food and clothing ministries. As important as the latter activities are, they ought never displace a missionary's primary job, which is preaching and teaching the Word of God. Auxiliary services, therefore, free the missionary to be faithful to the Word but also see to it that the human needs of the indigenous populations are accounted for.

The relationship between mission and social care has been posed before. For example, the proponents of the Lausanne Movement expressed their fears that such social services may become a distraction or even a betrayal of the primary task.[12] However, after deliberations, a reasonable solution was offered with the following statement:

> Evangelism and social responsibility, while distinct from one another, are integrally related in our proclamation of and obedience to the Gospel. The partnership is, in reality, a marriage. In practice, as in the public ministry of Jesus, the two are inseparable, at least in open societies. Rather than

---

9 Brunner, "'Rechtfertigung' heute," 128.

10 LWF, *Together in God's Mission*, 14.

11 While the later, formal office of deacon and deaconess today cannot be traced to Acts 6 as a kind of "institution," nevertheless this passage does show that God permits the Church in its Gospel freedom to appoint people to carry out auxiliary offices that perform works of mercy and other tasks.

12 Finding the proper relationship of social services to mission was discussed at great length in the Evangelical Missionary Movement (Lausanne Movement) at their International Consultation in Grand Rapids (June 19–25, 1982). For a list of the options, see Scherer, *Gospel, Church and Kingdom*, 182–83.

competing with each other, they mutually support and strengthen each other in an upward spiral of increased concern for both.[13]

The preceding statement presents a well-reasoned proposition for Lutherans. Some sense of this has led to the recruitment of medical doctors, nurses, deaconesses, and agricultural advisors in missional contexts.[14] Mission typically penetrates areas where the negative effects resulting from man's inability to be good stewards of God's creation are starkly apparent. Werner Elert once compared our failure to be good stewards to riders in a closed paddock where the horses are allowed to trample everything under the hoof.[15] Therefore, not everything brought into this world through the progress of civilization should be seen in a positive light. The alarming increase of the world's population, the ongoing drain on the world's resources, the destruction of pristine rain forests, the pollution of land and water, and atomic radiation are all a result of human failure. The myriad of such failures prove that in order to be better stewards of God's world and creation, we must use our reason in a faithful and conscientious way. For God placed the obligation of taking care of His creation into the hands of humans (Gen. 1:28–30; 2:15).

As one looks at the First Article of the Creed, one might be inclined to think that the mission of the Church must remain open for new challenges. Andrew Kirk proposes that the mission of the Church should include such issues as "justice for the poor," "overcoming violence and building peace," and "care of the environment."[16] There is perhaps less disagreement over the legitimacy of these issues as there is over the attitude that guides the tackling of such concerns. It is important to note that a paradise-like situation in this world cannot be brought about through human efforts. Mission cannot forsake the Gospel for a dream-vision of a comprehensive "shalom" that aims at overcoming all oppression and poverty in this world. Such goals can only lead to disappointment and frustration. To be sure, Christians should work to preserve the world and improve abject conditions as best as possible. But the sober truth remains that the world will not become perfect under the stewardship of sinners. Likewise, salvation cannot be brought about through human efforts but only through the preaching of the Gospel.

---

13 International Consultation of the Relationship between Evangelism and Social Responsibility (CRESR) at Grand Rapids, June 19–25, 1982. Scherer and Bevans, *New Directions in Mission and Evangelization*, 1:279–80.

14 Hopf, "Zur Begründung unserer Hospitalarbeit," 143–44.

15 Voigt, *Was die Kirche lehrt*, 72.

16 Kirk, *What Is Mission?* One may see also Gensichen, *Glaube für die Welt*, 204. Elsewhere, in his article "Ambassadors of Reconciliation," 242, Gensichen speaks of "mission in two gears." For a similar argument, see Bürkle, *Missionstheologie*, 142.

VOCATION AND THE CULTURAL MANDATE

By raising the issue of stewardship over God's creation, we have arrived at the important concept of vocation. Martin Luther and the Lutheran Church instruct Christians on how to live out their vocation in this world. The Small Catechism, the Ten Commandments, the Second Table of the Decalogue (Commandments 4–10), the Fourth Petition of the Lord's Prayer (daily bread), and the Table of Duties are all sources of encouragement for Christians to receive God as Creator into their lives and participate in everyday activities alongside their unbelieving neighbors.[17] A theology of creation teaches Christians to uphold this specific Lutheran concept of *vocatio*, which is the Latin form of "vocation" or "calling." It is not of human invention, but Christians are called to it in Scripture (Eph. 4:1; 1 Thess. 2:12). Vocation contains great mission potential, for it demonstrates how Christians may contribute in the civil sphere toward the promulgation of the Gospel: "The priesthood of all believers lives out its Christian vocation within their daily occupations and in their sharing responsibility for the corporate witness of the church."[18] Just as a church body and congregations support the organized diaconical service, vocation also broadens the scope of mission by taking into consideration that, through their everyday service, Christians contribute to the spread of the Gospel. Indeed, every Christian with his or her special talents, abilities, and gifts contributes to the mission of God in his or her particular way. They may do so by helping to prepare the way for witnessing the Gospel through their own personal acts of mercy, and then through their witness of God's Word to the neighbor. Both activities may occur in the context of their vocation. As Christians devote themselves unselfishly to the well-being and protection of the neighbor, they reflect the love of Christ to the world. Gene Veith summarizes vocation as follows:

> The purpose of one's vocation, whatever it might be, is serving others. It has to do with fulfilling Christ's injunction to love one's neighbor. Though justification has nothing to do with good works, vocation does involve good works. The Christian's relationship to God is based on sheer grace and forgiveness on God's part; the Christian's relationship to other people, however, is to be based on love put into action.[19]

It should be obvious, however, that a Christian, through his vocation, does not focus on special Christian activities. He rather shares with his neighbor

17 These may be found in SC I 1–22 (Kolb-Wengert, 351–54); LC I 1–333/SC III 12–13 (Kolb-Wengert, 386–431, 357); LC III 71–84/SC IX 1–15 (Kolb-Wengert, 449–52, 365–67).

18 LWF, *Together in God's Mission*, 14.

19 Veith, *Spirituality of the Cross*, 77. A detailed treatment of vocation is given by Wingren, *Luther on Vocation*.

a common sense for what must be done through their professions.[20] Christians reflect in an exemplary way on what is considered good and right in the eyes of God as they participate with others in their everyday roles. Christians uphold with their fellow citizens the common good by demonstrating what precisely the common good is.

Christians share common convictions with non-Christians because, in a certain sense, the Ten Commandments have to do with natural law; thus non-Christians can in a limited degree understand the Ten Commandments in an external sense. Moreover, to Christians, both the Ten Commandments and natural law are summarized in the command to love one's neighbor (Matt. 22:39). Thus all Christians together with their fellow citizens are directed to the natural sphere of life in which God has placed them and where their neighbor is in need of help and love. Melanchthon already noted: "Love goes forth upon earth among the people, and does much good, by consoling, teaching, instructing, helping, counseling privately and publicly."[21] Clearly, the commandment of loving one's neighbor compels Christians especially to participate in social life rather than to abandon civil responsibilities. And though the duties vary from person to person according to his or her station or calling, everyone is held equally account-able to the Ten Commandments in word and deed; as Luther once stated: "Here reflect on your walk of life in light of the Ten Commandments."[22]

God the Creator orders and preserves creation through the vocations of Christians and non-Christians alike. Humans participate in God's love for creation and in His care over it so that it may not fall into chaos. God uses people in their respective vocations as "the hands and channels of his goodness."[23]

For the purpose of living their vocation responsibly, God has provided humans the ability to manage everyday matters with their own reason. Otherwise, we might be inclined to think that God determines human fate in everyday life by shuffling people around like figures on a chessboard. There

---

20 Holsten Fagerberg points out that natural law agrees in content with the Decalogue. He thus concludes that there is no need for a unique Christian ethic: "It is therefore to a certain extent unnecessary to speak of a unique Christian ethic. In an external sense, the Christian behaves the same way as the non-Christian" (*New Look at the Lutheran Confessions*, 68). The same can be said from Luther in *How Christians Should Regard Moses*: "Thus I keep the commandments which Moses has given, not because Moses gave the commandment, but because they are implanted in me by nature, and Moses agrees exactly with nature" (AE 35:168). "We will regard Moses as a teacher, but we will not regard him as a lawgiver—unless he agrees with both the New Testament and the natural law" (AE 35:165).

21 Author's translation of Ap IV 104 from the German in the *Triglotta*. Also AC XVI 4 (Kolb-Wengert, 49).

22 The German conveys the idea of one's standing in the vocation far better: "Da siehe deinen *Stand* an nach den 10 Geboten" (see SC V 20, Kolb-Wengert, 360).

23 LC I 26 (Kolb-Wengert, 389).

is, however, autonomy for humans to arrange everyday matters themselves through the use of reason. That does not apply to spiritual matters in which reason and will are completely inadequate. But the Augsburg Confession points to a liberty of reason in worldly affairs: "a human being has some measure of free will, so as to live an externally honorable life and to choose among the things reason comprehends."[24]

One important lesson learned from the theology of vocation is that the scope of the Church's mission cannot be reduced to spiritual or eschatological concerns alone—that is, matters pertaining to the life hereafter. Christians are not quietistic or passive as they prepare for eternal life. On the contrary, the best preparation for proper Christian living comes through active participation within this world. Within their vocations, all Christians recognize the world as the realm in which they perform their new obedience to Christ in answer to the "indicative" of grace they received as forgiveness. Such ethical action flows from a worship life in which the gifts of God are given through the Word. And so in their reply to the divine gifts, Christians present and offer their loyal service to God within their particular vocation. Yet, as Christians, they also draw from that Word in order to share it. The Holy Spirit will provide the opportunity to do so and the words to use (Matt. 10:19–20).[25] The idea of sacrifice applies here. Christians offer their life and service to God and their neighbor in nonmeritorious ways in order that God may draw their neighbor into His kingdom. Faith alone, and not merit, saves. Through the Holy Spirit, vocation and Christian service are rooted in a Christian's justification.[26] We shall discuss the ethical dimensions of Christian mission in a later chapter (see ch. 14), yet justification always points through and beyond ethics to Baptism and to Christ as the source of new life with God.

---

24 AC XVIII 1 (Kolb-Wengert, 50). In regard to spiritual matters, the AC continues: "However, without the grace, help, and operation of the Holy Spirit a human being cannot becomes pleasing to God, fear or believe in God with the whole heart."

25 All Christians, as members of the priesthood of all believers, have as part of their calling a responsibility to speak the Gospel to their neighbors. 1 Pet. 2:5, 9 states, "You yourselves like living stones are being built up as a spiritual house, to be a holy priesthood, to offer spiritual sacrifices acceptable to God through Jesus Christ. . . . You are a chosen race, a royal priesthood, a people for His own possession, that you may proclaim the excellence of Him who called you out of darkness into his marvelous light." First Peter 3:15 affirms this continual readiness to give witness on account of the hope of the Gospel.

26 Fagerberg, *New Look at the Lutheran Confessions*, 279.

Natural Law, General Revelation, and the Role of Government

Non-Christians' general knowledge of God and of His will (Rom. 1:19; 2:15) may be extremely limited. And yet, positively speaking, man can, through his vocation, benefit society with the use of such limited knowledge of natural law—of what is right and wrong—and contribute through communal laws toward civil justice and righteousness. As the Confessions put it: "God wants this civil discipline to restrain the unspiritual, and to preserve it he has given laws, learning, teaching, governments, and penalties."[27] In this way, the natural law performs a positive, socio-ethical role of regulating and safeguarding life, and thus of safeguarding righteousness in this world.[28]

All humans thus become co-workers of God: "the hands, channels, and means through which God bestows all blessings."[29] They order and protect life on earth and restrain the evil and destructive powers, even if, strictly speaking, human beings are unaware of their divinely sanctioned role. Unfortunately, humans distance themselves from God and, as a result, abuse and tarnish their vocation and leave society in disarray. This fact becomes a sober warning to those who look upon cultures through romantic eyes, especially social systems that exist outside of any Christian missionary influence.[30] For example, in *National Geographic*, the author of an article on isolated Amazonian Indians lamented the onslaught of our so-called civilization and its negative influences, claiming that "uncontacted Indians live in a lost paradise." A reader, presumably an anthropologist, took exception to that quote, stating that even prior to any missionary and Western contact these people groups still experienced death by disease, interpersonal violence, and war.[31]

Governments and rulers serve—even unknowingly—as instruments of divine providential care and are guided by divine laws. God makes an ordered and regulated life among humans possible and sustains His

---

27   Ap IV 22–24 (Tappert, 110).

28   Lutheran theology contains the thought of a twofold righteousness in this world: The spiritual righteousness through faith and the civil righteousness (*iustitia civilis*) that equals at times the righteousness of reason (*iustitia rationis*), Ap IV 22, 224 (Tappert, 110, 138). Here, caution must apply because the Lutheran Confessions (e.g., Ap IV 9, Tappert, 108) oftentimes dismiss the righteousness of reason when applied to spiritual matters, especially when it addresses the Roman Catholic Church's idea of earning the merit of God's forgiveness. For comments on the twofold righteousness, see Maurer, *Historical Commentary on the Augsburg Confession*, 89–97.

29   LC I 26 (Kolb-Wengert, 389); Peters, *Kommentar zu Luthers Katechismen*, 2:64.

30   Consider, for example, Richardson, *Peace Child* and *Eternity in Their Hearts*.

31   *National Geographic* (December 2003), in the Forum section in response to the article by Sydney Possuelo in the August 2003 edition.

creation through established institutions. God provides civil rule so that, among humans, a form of righteousness may prevail that will prevent self-destruction. The Law is known in its political or civil use. Indeed, the Law is applied, to use the Lutheran doctrine of the two kingdoms, to the kingdom on the left-hand, apart from the Church. This way of thinking about the Law safeguards the Church's mission and helps her all the more promote the Gospel and redemption.[32] For if the first creation were to be understood as salvific, then man through his participation in society could bring it about himself without the mediation of Christ.

As history repeatedly shows, governments and rulers abuse their role as guardians of God's inscribed Law. The Lutheran Confessions are thus cautious about human ability to establish civil righteousness: "But so great is the power of concupiscence that men obey their evil impulses more than their sound judgment . . . For these reasons even civil righteousness is rare among men, as we see from the fact that even philosophers who seem to have wanted this righteousness did not achieve it."[33] In fact, societal systems and structures are under the influences of evil forces. Mission thus witnesses such failures and deals with victims of such flawed systems. The appropriate approach for the Church to take is to address such failures with the Word of God and the Ten Commandments in order to offer guidance to her members as they live out their vocations in a fallen world. But in doing so, the Church may be blamed for either violating the two-kingdom distinction or for being too political. On other hand, if she fails to speak up, she will be accused of having failed to use her prophetic voice. Either way, the Church is challenged in finding the correct form of advice to Christians living in a fallen world.[34] The situation of the Lutheran Church in the Third Reich reflects this dilemma. Dietrich Bonhoeffer opposed those of the Reich Church who complied with Nazism, but as he did so he reaped the criticisms of other observers. A similar situation arose in South Africa under the apartheid regime that greatly challenged Christians and church leaders to find a suitable answer.

---

32 Beißer, "Mission und Reich Gottes," 51; Öberg, "Mission und Heilsgeschichte," 27.

33 Ap IV 23 (Tappert, 110) continues: "To some extent, reason can produce this righteousness by its own strength, though it is often overwhelmed by its natural weakness and by the devil, who drives it to open crimes." See also Ap II 9–12 (Tappert, 102); Ap XVIII 5–6 (Tappert, 225).

34 Schlink, *Theology of the Lutheran Confessions*, 226, 240; Öberg, "Mission und Heilsgeschichte," 27.

DIVINE CARE
THROUGH THE ORDERS OF CREATION

God established such "orders of creation" as vocation, government (i.e., political and societal orders), marriage, and family. As a result, many look at culture as if the orders within it must be treasured and kept inviolate at all costs. However, the orders of creation are subject to evil influences and abuses. Scripture testifies that the world-governing bodies are institutions by God (Romans 13), but at the same time, they have also become perverted by sin (Revelation 13). In light of Scripture's testimony, we cannot view world governments only positively. Also the form of established orders may be subject to change. Before popular forms of democracy, the monarchial system was thought to be the only divinely instituted form of government. However, the many forms of democracy today might cause one to think that God only favors democratic forms of government.

Just as man is God's creation and at the same time sinner, so, too, are the established orders in this world. They are not merely neutrally created entities, but they are, as Helmut Thielicke affirms, "also the structural form of fallen existence."[35] Since the orders take their place between creation and sin, they have the signature both of fallen creation and human rebellion on them. Thielicke observes: "The Noachic world conceals the true order of creation [Schöpfungsordnung]. If we overlook this concealment, if we count upon an unequivocal world which does not exist, or no longer exists, we inevitably become fanatics."[36]

So, just as government, marriage, family, and societal culture are good orders in the sense that they make life among humans possible, they are also subject to man's abuse because of sin. They are not a priori guarantees for harmony in this world but need to be called to repentance through periodic restructuring and correction that looks to the goodness of the natural order and natural law of God with an eye to mitigate sinful human abuse. For example, marriage must look to the basic established order in Gen. 1:28 and 2:24, as well as the Christological and eschatological motifs from the Song of Solomon to the Gospels to Revelation. It cannot be redefined to embrace human depravity without causing incalculable harm in both physical and spiritual dimensions. Governments and other institutions also stand under the Lord, whether or not they desire to recognize that. The extent that they are a blessing is determined by their faithfulness to God's created order. Deviation from that will bring persecution and misery. In other words, "orders of creation" are realistically seen in the context of an "infralapsarian

---

35 Thielicke, *Foundations*, 440.
36 Thielicke, *Foundations*, 611.

theology," that is, of being caught in the reciprocal relationship of having been established by God yet being abused through sinful people.

Nonetheless, in many positive ways, society manages to arrange its life. In fact, the Gospel may encounter certain societies or cultures in which positive traits exist that agree with the intentions of the divine Creator. It would thus be false to assume *a priori* that the Gospel will encounter natural knowledge and its application in society only in its totally corrupted form. We concur with the following statement of Paul Althaus: "We do not mean that the Gospel takes the place of all religions' traditions among nations; it rather steps into an association with them, and that not only in the negative, in the form of judgment."[37]

CREATION AND PRESERVATION: AN EXPRESSION OF DIVINE GOODNESS AND LOVE

Creation reveals also one important fact about God Himself and His intentions toward the world as He seeks to preserve it. Christian theology often presents God as the angry and wrathful judge over a world that has abandoned Him. This way of looking at God obscures God's reasons for preserving creation. If God's relationship to the world is only as a vindictive judge, then creation would be subject to a god who deals with it in inexplicable and unpredictable ways. Greek tragedies present gods in this way. The term *deus ex machina* portrays a god who was let down on a machine onto the stage to solve the problems that the actors, that is, the humans, could not themselves discover. After resolving a complicated matter quickly, the god would withdraw from the world and leave circumstances to man. The Christian God, however, is a God who does not deal with His creation only at sporadic times and in wrathful ways. Nor is He withdrawn from the affairs in this world. God's intentions for the world are entirely good because He loves it and is willing to preserve it. In fact, a straight line can be drawn between God's love for creation and the cross. As Johannes Blauw points out: "The will to save, on the part of the God of Israel, is one with His will to create."[38]

God thus actively preserves His creation. He does not withdraw Himself from it to let it take its own course as the doctrines of theism or open theism seem to imply. In other words, the common fallacy of theism is that God

---

37 "Wir meinen auch nicht, daß das Evangelium sich einfach an die Stelle aller religiösen Traditionen der Völker setze; es tritt in Beziehung zu ihr, und zwar nicht immer nur in die negative des Gerichts" (Althaus, "Um die Reinheit der Mission," 52). For a discussion on Althaus's position on what he calls *Uroffenbarung*, see Pöhlmann, "Das Problem der Ur-Offenbarung bei Paul Althaus," 242–58.

38 Blauw, "Biblical View of Man in His Religion," 34.

removed Himself from His creation. Creation becomes an arbitrary or for-gotten act of God. Theism emerged with Galileo and Descartes and still marks much of the thinking of modern society. Modernity states that God initially was responsible for creating the world, but afterward withdrew to let creation take its own course.[39] We affirm, on the contrary, that creation is both a single event in the past, signifying a beginning from nothing, and a continual act of God that ceases only with the end of this world. Preservation of creation should be thought of in the perfect tense to indi-cate that all existing life that God created at a specific point in time is still preserved and protected by Him. As created beings, we humans are com-pletely dependent upon our Creator, as are all other creatures.[40]

In her creedal confessions, the Christian Church points to God not only as the omnipotent Creator of heaven and earth, *ex nihilo* ("from nothing"),[41] but also a Being who continues to keep and preserve His creation, the *creatio continuata* ("continual creation"). God is both initiator and conser-vator. Both dimensions of creation are part of the Lutheran Confessions: "Everything we possess, and everything in heaven and on earth besides, is daily given, sustained and protected by God."[42] Luther portrays God as the continual provider for His creation not only in broad cosmic terms but also in a very personal and existential way. In other words, no human being looks at God's activity in this world from a distance and is unaffected by it. Luther's comments on God's personal role in creation are worth noting:

> I hold and believe that I am God's creature, that is, that he has given me and constantly sustains my body, soul, and life, my members great and small, all my senses, my reason and understanding, and the like; my food and drink, clothing, nourishment, spouse and children, servants, house and farm, etc. Besides, he makes all creation help provide the benefits and necessities of life: sun, moon and stars in the heavens, day and night; air, fire, water, the earth and all that it yields and brings forth; birds, fish, animals, grain, and all sorts of produce. Moreover, he gives all physical and temporal blessings—good government, peace, security.[43]

---

39 Pannenberg, *Systematic Theology*, 2:65–66.

40 Blauw, "Biblical View of Man in His Religion," 32.

41 Apostles' Creed 1 (Kolb-Wengert, 21); Nicene Creed 1 (Kolb-Wengert, 22).

42 LC II 19 (Kolb-Wengert, 433); SC II 1–2 (Kolb-Wengert, 354). Peters, *Kommentar zu Luthers Katechismen*, 2:63.

43 LC II 13–14 (Kolb-Wengert, 432); Peters, *Kommentar zu Luthers Katechismen*, 2:65.

THE GRACE OF CREATION
AND GOAL OF REDEMPTION

The significant point in the doctrine of creation is that God chose to become Creator and Preserver. He stooped to His creation and establishes communion with it quite voluntarily and purposefully. There was no need for God to do so, as if He needed any created thing. Yet His love compels Him to act, as Luther would say, "out of pure, fatherly, and divine goodness and mercy."[44] The world that God called into being was perfect and revered God, who called it very good and hallowed it. Oswald Bayer comments: "The world was called into being without any worldly condition, in pure freedom and pure goodness. Creation out of nothing means that everything that is exists out of sheer gratuity, out of pure goodness."[45] Sadly, the world does not recognize God's fatherly heart and His boundless love toward it in all that He does. The biblical accounts of the fall, the flood, and the tower of Babel (Genesis 1–11) vividly portray the world's negative response to God's loving care. And yet, God repeatedly and faithfully renewed His unbroken relationship with man. The Noah covenant (Gen. 8:15–9:17) becomes an indelible reminder of God's loyalty to creation for posterity. Even as sin and destruction persisted and increased, God, out of love, did not falter in His bond to the world, which ultimately led to the suffering of His Son. As stated earlier, God's original design of creation was perfectly good (Gen. 1:31), but the realities of abuse and destruction that soon followed finally led to the intervention of God the Father sending His Son into the fallen world. Through Christ's suffering and through the proclamation of the message of justification, an arch is strung back to the original state of creation through and with the person of Christ who has become the restorer and firstborn of creation (Col. 1:15).[46]

Divine care over life thus continues to this day as a blessing despite man's fall and corruption. The theologian Wolfhart Pannenberg coins here the term *agapism* to express God's benevolent attitude. *Agapism* implies that love becomes the creative and universal principle of God toward the world. *Agapism* represents love in its unique and unselfish way, related also to the love God the Father has for His Son. And since creation was the object of His love, God had Christ act as the mediator of creation (Heb. 1:2; John 1:3).

Agapism asserts that God's creative actions are oriented wholly to His creation. God's love cannot be confused with the self-seeking form of love

---

44 SC II 2 (Kolb-Wengert, 354); LC II 23 (Kolb-Wengert, 433).

45 Bayer, *Living by Faith*, 80.

46 Vicedom, *Mission of God*, 13.

that Pannenberg calls *amor*. As he states: "We cannot say . . . that in the first instance God sought his own glory by giving existence to creatures."[47] It is true, that the glory of God is manifest in created heaven and earth (Ps. 9:2), and on the basis of perceiving God behind creation, man must honor Him as God (Rom. 1:21; cf. Luke 17:18). Overall, the destiny of man is to praise and glorify God as Creator (Ps. 19:2; Rev. 19:1–7). In glorifying and praising God, man also joins with the Son and with the Holy Spirit (John 17:4). Humans, too, are asked to demonstrate an *agapism*, an unself-ish love for God, their Creator, and for one another (Deut. 6:5; Lev. 19:18; Matt. 22:37–39).[48] Sadly, through sin (Gen. 1:26), the relationship to God and fellow neighbor has changed for the worse, morally wounding the once perfect relationship between God and creation. Man constantly fails to love selflessly in a way that withholds from God that honor He deserves (Rom. 1:21).

Thus it would be incorrect to suggest that God was *explicitly* self-seeking His glory and honor by creating the world. For if He were seeking mere glory and honor, then one could compare God's intention with man's corrupt, selfish attitudes. God does not have to prove His deity; He was God already before creation.[49] Furthermore, in Christ's condescendence in the incarnation, particularly in His suffering and death, God contradicts or inverts man's self-seeking standards of glory and praise. For in His lower-ing Himself in such a way, God made Himself subject to scorn.

One may call God's benevolence toward this world the grace of creation (*gratia creatoris*). The words of Christ in Matt. 6:26–34; 10:29–30 aptly illu-minate divine benevolence and love toward creation.[50] Redemptive grace (*gratia redemptoris*) is best described as a deliberate intention of God to guide and steer His creation toward its final end through and against inces-sant harmful influences of the evil one and his forces. The Latin term *guber-natio* is often used to portray God as *gubernator*, a helmsman and a guide, who steers the world in a direction as a pilot would steer a boat. However, this preservation and guiding function should not be seen as an end in itself. For implicit within the article of creation is the divine plan of its sal-vation. In other words, God as *gubernator* is motivated soteriologically "in order to redeem and fulfill his creation."[51] Whether or not the term *teleol-ogy* is fully appropriate in this connection, it does express the important

---

47 Pannenberg, *Systematic Theology*, 57. Schlink, *Theology of the Lutheran Confessions*, 39; Peters, *Kommentar zu Luthers Katechismen*, 2:58, 86.

48 Deuser, *Kleine Einfuehrung in die Systematische Theologie*, 75.

49 Pannenberg, *Systematic Theology*, 74.

50 Nowhere in the Confessions is the term *gratia creatoris* used to correspond to the *gratia redemp-toris*; Schlink, *Theology of the Lutheran Confessions*, 40; Pöhlmann, *Abriß der Dogmatik*, 140.

51 Pannenberg, *Systematic Theology*, 57.

thought that the events indeed follow an intentional course, "a goal or *telos*," designed by God, who has salvation in view.[52] Certainly, "teleology" would be falsely understood if it were to imply that God's will and intention with His creation were not already clearly defined prior to all events—as if God has to make up His mind during the course of events! History is marked by God's intervening acts (Prov. 16:4), but behind them is God's eternal and changeless self-identity. Pannenberg concludes that "the object of the divine will has to be thought of as already realized, even though God ties the realization to the conditions of creaturely life and conduct."[53]

Thus in view of the subject, goal, and object of God's dealing with creation, we may hold that there is a linear course taken with the history of creation; it progresses from the first protological event of creation (*proton*) to the final completion (*eschaton*). "The protological and the eschatological relate to each other as do promise and fulfillment, origin and goal."[54] It is by divine design that the once uncorrupted creation must be regenerated through faith in Jesus Christ and be fully restored at resurrection through the work of the Holy Spirit. The sequence of creation, redemption, and complete restoration engages logical conclusions stemming from creation. This sequence does not merely describe incidental events. The Creator is revealed as the triune God, with the implied roles of Son and Holy Spirit. In terms of the Holy Spirit, all His activity aims at the resurrection and the new creation. The First Article, the doctrine of creation, finds its continuation and completion in the Second and Third Articles. Redemption and sanctification culminate in the restoration of the work of creation on the Last Day, with the appearance of the new heaven and earth, the eternal Jerusalem.

CREATION: AN ARTICLE OF FAITH

Lutheran theologians deny the ability of unbelievers to recognize God's goodness and blessings behind creation and preservation. Natural knowledge has been corrupted through the fall (Genesis 3), so that natural man's response will also be inadequate. For example, it is doubtful whether Luther's closure of his explanation to the First Article of the Apostles' Creed, "for all of this I owe it to God to thank and praise, serve, and obey him," also includes natural man apart from faith.[55] Neither on the basis of the inherent understanding of God (Rom. 2:14–15) nor from the empirical observation

---

52 Brunner, "'Rechtfertigung' heute," 35.

53 Pannenberg, *Systematic Theology*, 57; Peters, *Kommentar zu Luthers Katechismen*, 2:90.

54 Brunner, "'Rechtfertigung' heute," 49; Pöhlmann, *Abriß der Dogmatik*, 154; Prenter, *Spiritus Creator*, 240.

55 SC II 2 (Kolb-Wengert, 355); LC II 19 (Kolb-Wengert, 433).

of the created world (Rom. 1:19) would the unbeliever bring forth true thankfulness and recognition of God's benevolence. Natural knowledge of God is so defective that it holds to a false picture of God and leads man to promote his own works-righteousness. Luther observes that "the heathen, the Turks, and the Jews know that God is, but they do not know what He is really like in the essence of His being."[56] To be exact, natural man fails to grasp and fulfill the First Table of the Law—namely, those laws that dismiss idolatry and demand true worship.[57] Fallen man has no power to fulfill such demands. The heart and will of fallen man cause him not only to commit actual sins, but also, from the very start, he is unable to fear and love God. In fact, he hates and despises God and puts all his trust and fear on other powers and goods, thereby creating his own gods.[58]

Positively speaking, the reverse side of this argument is that through faith in Christ the believer appreciates God's divine care and is thankful for a life before God the Creator. In faith, God becomes an object of love to the believer, and He receives thanks, praise, and servitude: "All who know that they are reconciled to the Father through Christ truly know God, know that God cares for them, and call upon him."[59] As the believer invokes God the Creator, with the title "Father," it implies that he does so with a faith in the triune God. Albrecht Peters thus makes a helpful observation: "Thereby the born Son of the Second Article, through whose cross and resurrection we have been received in Baptism as sons of God, is secretly present in the word 'Father' of the First Article."[60]

---

56 Fagerberg, *New Look at the Lutheran Confessions*, 67, paraphrases Luther's statement in LC II 66 (Kolb-Wengert, 440).

57 "All human beings . . . are conceived in sin . . . and cannot by nature possess true fear of God and true faith in God" (AC II 1, Kolb-Wengert, 37–38). "This passage testifies that in those who are born according to the flesh we deny the existence not only of actual fear and trust in God but also of the possibility and gift to produce it" (Ap II 3, Tappert, 101).

58 See here Luther's explanation to the First Commandment, LC I 1–3 (Kolb-Wengert, 386); Peters, *Kommentar zu Luthers Katechismen*, 2:110–12.

59 AC XX 24 (Kolb-Wengert, 57); Mildenberger, *Theologie der lutherischen Bekenntnisschriften*, 74.

60 Peters, *Kommentar zu Luthers Katechismen*, 2:83, 67. See also Meyer, *Historischer Kommentar*, 274.

CHAPTER EIGHT

The Foundation and Goal
of God's Mission

The Sending Motive

When God created the cosmos, He chose of His will and purpose to enter into communion with it by hallowing it and dwelling in it, particularly by having a special rapport with mankind, made in His own image. Despite Adam and Eve's rebellion, having fallen from grace and losing the image of God, that same God did not forsake them. He gave His Son, Jesus Christ, for the world as Savior. We have already pointed to the centrality of the Christ event in the *missio Dei*. The Christ event describes the mission of Christ, which includes His coming to earth, His entire ministry on earth, His lordship, and His second coming. The Church awaits our Lord's return with great expectation. She is thus eschatologically motivated; that is, in anticipation of our Lord's return, she senses an urgency to preach the Gospel to all people.

The person and work of Christ opens up a plethora of issues for the topic of mission. For example, in the Early Church, the Nicene-Constantinopolitan Creed of AD 381 laid down the doctrinal position that Christ is of the same substance (*homoousios*) as the Father, and at the councils of Ephesus (432) and Chalcedon (451), the relationship of the divine and human nature in the one person of Christ was settled doctrinally. Today, new religious movements and cultures raise new issues. Christology must grapple with such issues as the pluralistic claims made by the religions of the world and the context of poverty and socio-economic needs. As Christianity responds to all contexts and issues, it must do so meaningfully, yet not at the price of giving up Christ's death on the cross as the basis for salvation.

Missiological literature often affirms Christology merely in passing. It takes for granted all aspects of Christology. I shall, however, discuss some of the issues of Christology as they pertain to mission.[1] The underlying hermeneutical principle is clearly devoted to the theological task of describing the mission of Christ in order to illumine and magnify the honor of Christ.[2]

Christ's mission begins with His being sent to the world (John 3:16), not for its judgment but for its salvation. "It is again through the Son that we know God loves us. In that way the mission of the Son discloses itself to us: he comes not to judge and to slay but so that we might have life in him."[3] The mission of Christ differs from creation and God's providential activities. On the cross, God revealed Himself in a unique way as the Incarnate Word, and He became the world's Redeemer. In sending His Son into the world, God's mission becomes a mission of mercy. Christ not only proclaims and brings God's grace, but He actually becomes its foundation and the cause of its extension to us.[4] We affirm both the objective reality of the cross and the atonement on which the subjective appropriation of salvation rests, that is, justification through faith. God's mission points to the cross of Christ as a past event, unique and final in its meaning for all people. At the same time, the cross becomes a present reality in the life of every person as the Gospel is proclaimed. Yes, as much as the objective historic facts of the Christ event are true, the proclamation must go on today to bring Christ into the lives of all people. Christology is thus also *kerygmatic* theology. Through the preaching and teaching of the Gospel, all the blessings of the atonement from two thousand years ago must reach the ears of all unbelievers today, if they are to be saved (Rom. 10:14–17).

In order that this treasure that Christ has achieved on the cross "might not be buried but put to use and enjoyed, God has caused the Word to be published and proclaimed, in which he has given the Holy Spirit to offer and apply to us this treasure of salvation . . . If the work remained hidden and no one knew of it, it would have been all in vain, all lost."[5] The sending motive thus compels the Church to continue with the sending of messengers. The sending began before Christ with the divine appointment of Old Testament prophets, then Christ Himself came to earth, continuing the prophetic

---

1   For a relationship between Christology and world religions, see, for example, Van Engen, *Mission on the Way*, 169–87. Contextual implications of Christology are presented in Greene, *Christology in Cultural Perspective*. For proclaiming Christ in the postmodern world, see Lose, *Confessing Christ*, and García and Raj, *Theology of the Cross*.

2   To honor and glorify Christ with sound theology is one of the main pastoral concerns of the Lutheran Confessions. E.g., Ap IV 2, 156 (Tappert, 107, 128).

3   Maurer, *Historical Commentary on the Augsburg Confession*, 252.

4   "We could never come to recognize the Father's favor and grace were it not for the Lord Christ, who is a mirror of the Father's heart" (LC II 29, 65, Kolb-Wengert, 434, 440). Vicedom, *Die Rechtfertigung als gestaltende Kraft der Mission*, 12.

5   LC II 38 (Kolb-Wengert, 436). E.g., Kretzmann, "Crosscurrents in Mission," 354.

proclamation of God's will. Jesus' disciples continued the task, and today the Church is called to continue the proclamation of the Gospel.

The Cross of Christ
as the Assertion of God's Love

The doctrine of atonement has invited much debate over God's motivation for having His Son die on the cross. Did God allow His Son to die to reconcile the world to Himself in order to appease His wrath, or did He do it out of love to reconcile Himself with the world? Well-known theologians such as Friedrich Schleiermacher or Albrecht Ritschl intentionally shunned the idea that the cross symbolizes the wrath of God and that Christ's death conciliates or placates God's wrath. To be sure, God sent Christ for our redemption's sake and not to satisfy His own desire or wish. Yet God was not only the subject but also the object of Christ's mission in the crucifixion. God not only sent Christ for the sake of the world but also to placate the Father's wrath. Both Father and Son play prominent roles in the crucifixion. While both wield divine kingship, it was Christ, the Son, who took the accursed path to the cross of utter dereliction on behalf of all people. To some bystanders, that path appeared as sheer wrath and attrition; to others it was revealed as the true love of God for His world (Matt. 27:46; Mark 15:34; Luke 23:46; John 18:33–38). The theology of the cross expresses this by using the distinction between the alien and proper work of God.

No other theologian has promoted this distinction as efficiently as Luther with his theology of the cross. Luther gained the deepest insights into the hidden and revealed God at the cross, into the "proper" and "alien work" of God.[6] Luther's insight was that the "the wrath of God, which is propitiated through Christ's death, is not the 'proper' but 'improper' work. God is only indirectly the object of reconciliation; properly speaking, he is the subject of reconciliation. For love is his proper work."[7] This means that the event of the cross does in fact communicate both God's alien work, that is, the exclamation and satisfaction of His wrath, as well as His proper work, that is, the expression of His grace and love for the world.

With the sending of His Son, God participated in what occurred on the cross. He was more than a distant observer. Rather, in the divine nature of Jesus Christ, God Himself dies on the cross. That God Himself dies on the cross is an offense to reason, or it is at least difficult to comprehend. For Luther, however, there was no negotiation on this point, as the following

---

6 With these distinctions, Luther laid the foundation for a Christian theology of history. Loewenich, "Zur Gnadenlehre bei Augustin und bei Luther," 75–86.

7 Pöhlmann, *Abriß der Dogmatik*, 226; Peters, *Kommentar zu Luthers Katechismen*, 2:138.

insight makes clear: "The Son of God suffers . . . if it cannot be said that God died for us, but only a man, we are lost . . . For God in his own nature cannot die; but now that God and man are united in one person, it is called God's death when the man dies who is one substance or one person with God."[8]

THE UNIQUENESS OF THE CHRIST EVENT

The priestly office thus points to Christ as the sacrifice offered in our stead for our redemption. The important formula "vicarious satisfaction" (*satisfactio vicaria*) is used to underscore the sacrifice of Christ in the stead of sinners. The Lutheran Confessions teach that Christ "through his death made satisfaction (*hostia*) for our sins."[9] The use of the Latin term *hostia* remains interesting. Jesus Christ died as a *hostia,* that is, as a sacrifice under the wrath of God. He was forsaken by God in order to propitiate the punitive will of God. The Lutheran Confessions actually include God's wrath *expressis verbis* by saying that Christ was both "to be a sacrifice not only for original sin but also for all other sins and to conciliate God's wrath."[10]

Biblical imagery brings out the above with the reference to Christ as high priest who then also became the sacrificial lamb "who takes away the sin of the world" (John 1:29; Heb. 9:11–12). In His own words, Jesus came "to give His life as a ransom for many" (Mark 10:45). Further on, Christ states that this outpouring of His blood would establish a new covenant (Mark 14:24; Luke 22:20). In Rom. 4:25, Paul writes that Jesus Christ "was delivered up for our trespasses and raised for our justification." Isaiah writes that "the LORD has laid on Him the iniquity of us all" (Isa. 53:6).[11] All these statements (and many more) indicate that through His death and resurrection, Christ restored the irreparably broken relationship with God. As a result, God poured out justice, mercy, and compassion on all mankind. As the high priest, Christ thus takes on the unique role as mediator and intercessor for man before God (1 Tim. 2:5) to bring about reconciliation between God and man. Christ's role here is given numerous titles: mediator, propitiator, high priest, or intercessor. However, all titles act as synonyms to indicate the important role Christ fulfilled between the world and God. Edmund Schlink observes: "No matter which terms are

---

8 Quoted in SD VIII 42–44 (Kolb-Wengert, 623–24).

9 AC III 3 (Kolb-Wengert, 39).

10 AC III 2 (Kolb-Wengert, 38). With regard to the formula "sacrifice" (*hostia*) and its ramifications in the New Testament and the Lutheran Confessions, see Franzmann, "Reconciliation and Justification," 81–93.

11 See quotes made in SA II 1–5 (Kolb-Wengert, 301) which show Luther's interest in upholding the uniqueness and exclusive character of Christ's work. See Martens, *Die Rechtfertigung des Sünders,* 33; Schlink, *Theology of the Lutheran Confessions,* 84.

used to designate the atonement, all have this common denominator that they acknowledge the obedient death of Jesus Christ to be a substitutionary death."[12] "Propitiator" means that through His sacrifice, Christ appeased the wrath of God. It may seem odd, but it is nonetheless true that for our justification Christ as God is set against God. Christ's work has as its goal to placate God so that the Father is graciously disposed toward the Son and toward all humanity.[13]

Christ contributes to our salvation solely and uniquely, as Luther reminds us: "Nothing in this article can be conceded or given up, even if heaven and earth or whatever is transitory passed away."[14] Anything detracting from Christ's unique contribution diminishes the glory and honor for Christ. So often, Christ's merits are called the treasure, the price, and the ransom to indicate that it was His work and merit alone that saves man over and against the merits of man.[15] Theologians also make use of the exclusive particles to underscore Christ's accomplishment: "by grace" (*sola gratia*), "for Christ's sake" (*propter Christum*), "Christ alone" (*solus Christus*).[16] All these phrases, in some way or another, present the atonement as one that rests on Christ's work alone.

Contextual theologies typically question the sole work of Christ vis-à-vis the competing truth claims of other religions. One sees this especially where Christianity must contend with prevalent beliefs in the broader culture. For example, African Christianity is especially in danger of compromising Christ's central role as mediator and priest as it contends with African traditional religions and Islam. The same situation of contextual theological pressure can be applied to contact with other religions as well. Islam places Christ as prophet under Allah, and Christ becomes absorbed into the numerous deities of Hinduism or identified as a great moral teacher. In Buddhism, too, Christ is often associated with the way or *Dao*.[17]

---

12 Schlink, *Theology of the Lutheran Confessions*, 85.

13 The Lutheran Confessions refer to the propitiation of the Son to the Father on numerous occasions: Ap IV 45–46, 80–81, 163, 376, 386 (Tappert, 113, 118, 129, 165–66); Ap XII 64 (Tappert, 191); Ap XXI 20 (Tappert, 232); Ap XXIV 19 (Tappert, 252); AC XXI 2 (Kolb-Wengert, 59). Christ as mediator and propitiator are often used interchangeably so that they virtually mean the same: Schlink, *Theology of the Lutheran Confessions*, 86; Elert, *Structure of Lutheranism*, 1:129.

14 SA II I 5 (Kolb-Wengert, 301).

15 Ap IV 53, 57 (Tappert, 114); LC II 31 (Kolb-Wengert, 31).

16 E.g., AC IV 1 (Kolb-Wengert, 39). The formulation *propter Christum* occurs many times in the Confessions. In the Apology, for example, it occurs 106 times, as Pöhlmann, *Abriß der Dogmatik*, 206, points out. For a presentation on *propter Christum*, see Maurer, *Historical Commentary on the Augsburg Confession*, 309–20.

17 The Christian missionary Karl Ludwig Reichelt (1877–1952) is known for his attempt at accommodating Buddhism's *Dao* principle into Christianity, which earned him criticism from Hendrik Kraemer (1888–1965). See Thelle, "Legacy of Karl Ludwig Reichelt," 35–40; Berger, *Skeptical Affirmation of Christianity*.

Although identifiable in areas of Africa and Asia, one can see analogous pressures when groups migrate from such contexts to Europe and North America in today's climate of pluralism.

THE UNIVERSAL MOTIF

The *missio Christi* teaches that all nations, with no restrictions placed on geography or race, are called to repentance and invited to believe the Gospel. For this reason, Christ has commanded "that repentance and forgiveness of sins should be proclaimed in His name to all nations" (Luke 24:47). Christ would not have commissioned His disciples to go preach unless He had completed His own mission on earth.

Some might argue that the Lutheran Confessions minimize the objective nature of salvation in order to concentrate upon the subjective appropriation of the same through faith. Plenty of evidence suggests, however, that the Confessions concentrate as much upon Christ's atoning work as our own grasp of the same through faith. For example, consider the following passage: ". . . that he might reconcile the Father to us and be a sacrifice not only for original guilt but also for all actual sins of human beings." Moreover, "it is not God's will that any are damned but that all turn to him and be saved" (1 Tim. 2:4). The latter quote has been taken from Ezek. 33:11 and is connected to John 3:16.[18]

Often, the Aristotelian term *cause* is used to hail Christ's work as the only efficient cause of salvation (*causa efficiens*).[19] Nevertheless, the Lutheran Confessions also teach that Christ's work does not stand apart from the existence of the believer. What Christ did is inseparably linked to the distribution of His benefits to believing individuals. Christ's objective work of atonement has its purpose in the subjective justification of the sinner through faith. The *extra nos* of our salvation is complemented by the *pro nobis*.[20] The *pro nobis* does not diminish the completeness and all-sufficiency of the atoning work of Christ or the theology of the cross. But the paradox of Christology is that all men are redeemed in Christ while only those who believe are justified. This shows how closely connected the cross—objective reconciliation—is to personal justification. One cannot be separated from the other without falling into error.

---

18 AC III 3 (Kolb-Wengert, 39); SD II 49 (Kolb-Wengert, 553); Ap IV 103, 262 (Tappert, 121, 145). See Schurb, *Does the Lutheran Confessions' Emphasis on Subjective Justification Mitigate Their Teaching of Objective Justification?* 76: "The Lutheran Confessions teach objective justification, and this doctrine is neither restricted nor hindered by their teaching of subjective justification. To be sure, the Symbols say that 'all are justified'—in those precise syllables—only in SA II, I, 3."

19 Ap IV 98 (Tappert, 121).

20 Pöhlmann, *Abriß der Dogmatik*, 223.

Some prominent theologians have denied the objective aspects of this juncture while others have denied the subjective. Rudolf Bultmann's existentialism has resurfaced in Gerd Lüdemann, who is renowned for denying the historicity and objectivity of the Christ event.[21] Paul Tillich pleaded for an anonymous Christianity, and Karl Barth argued his inclusive Christology, known as *apocatastasis*. Yet both, while affirming objective reconciliation, nevertheless effectively denied the need for a subjective appropriation through faith.[22] This trend cannot sufficiently account for the significant combination of the cross and the justification of the sinner by Christ through faith.[23] The *solus Christus* must be an objective and physical necessity for everyone in this world through a physical and direct connection with the historical Christ event by means of proclamation. As Peter Beyerhaus claims: "The saving event of Golgotha must be made present through the act of proclamation."[24]

THE HAMARTOLOGICAL MOTIVE

In light of the *missio Christi*, the deep depravity and sinful state of mankind becomes particularly apparent. The state of mankind therefore becomes most pertinent to discuss at this point. The account of Simon's calling as disciple illustrates well the connection between Christology and sinfulness (Luke 5:4–11). Here, Christ asked the disciple to put the boat into the deep water and fish. The time was noon—the most unlikely occasion to fish. Simon's doubt seems sensible, and yet that doubt questions Christ Himself. Peter's doubt became apparent when he stood before the person of Christ and confessed: "Depart from me, for I am a sinful man, O Lord" (v. 8).

In the presence of Christ, our sins are overshadowed by Christ's holiness. It is not by mere coincidence that Melanchthon positioned Article II ("On Original Sin") in the Augsburg Confession between Article I ("On God") and Article III ("On Christ"). For in doing so, the author demonstrates that every sinner can only be born again through Jesus Christ. The

---

21 See, for example, the most recent publication tackling Bultmannian theology as presented by Lüdemann: *Jesus' Resurrection*. Bultmann's denial of the cross and resurrection as facts is represented in this quote: "Thus, to believe in the cross of Christ does not mean to look to the mythical process that has taken place outside of us and our world or at an objectively visible event that God has somehow reckoned to our credit; rather, to believe in the cross of Christ means to accept the cross as one's own and to allow oneself to be crucified with Christ" ("New Testament and Mythology," 34).

22 See Eitel, "The Way," 279–93, who holds this point against Karl Rahner's, and similarly Karl Barth's, universalism. See Scott, *Barth's Theology of Mission*, 30. The arguments against Barth's inclusive Christology are made by Seils, "Heil und Erlösung IV," 632–33.

23 See Scherer, *That the Gospel May Be Sincerely Preached*, 84.

24 Beyerhaus, "Christi Heilsangebot durch seine Gesandten," 62.

Christology in Article III is thus not merely an abstract doctrinal statement; it is given a strong "soteriological slant," that is, a missional orientation.

Such positive expressions of reinstatement into a righteous relationship with God through Christ counter the negative reality that original sin is confessed as an "abominable and dreadful inherited disease" that has corrupted the entire nature of man (Ps. 51:5; Rom. 3:23).[25] Many today deny original sin because it seems unfair to accept responsibility for a guilt that is not a result of their own doing (actual sin). The doctrine of total depravity, however, teaches that every actual sin is the consequence of a deeply engrained estrangement from God. Humans live in total enmity toward God, and within them is a strong desire toward sin that the confessors called *concupiscence*. No one is free from concupiscence; it can only be broken and curbed by spiritual life in Christ.

Thus Paul was unwilling to make concessions to anyone who would seek to find his way to God through his own strengths aside from Christ. Although he knew that there were heathen who actually "by nature do what the law requires" (Rom. 2:14), he still placed the negative verdict against all unbelievers (1 Thess. 4:5; Gal. 4:8). Paul accuses them all of having abandoned the First Commandment for an idolatrous worship of other gods. Their worship and conduct is not directed at God (1 Cor. 10:20). Thus they are all "without excuse" (Rom. 1:20), and the wrath of God is revealed from heaven over all ungodliness and wickedness (Rom. 1:18). The Jews, too, though being in possession of the Law, are judged for not doing what the Torah teaches (Rom. 2:17–29).

The doctrine of sin thus provides a powerful reason for doing mission. The Church looks at a world that is without the one true God and engaged in idolatrous behavior. The Church desires to highlight God's love for all as the first motivation for mission. But the hamartological motive explains why the *missio Christi* is necessary. For God, out of His own volition, chose not to condemn a world that has turned against Him. Instead, He sent Christ to save and to bestow eternal life by opening the way to God for every believer (Rom. 5:2). The Church continues the Father's work by sending messengers who proclaim to an unbelieving world the Good News of salvation in Christ.[26]

INCARNATION

With Scripture and the creedal statements, the Church confesses that Christ, the Son of God, began His mission on earth by assuming human

---

25 For example: SD I 5, 11, 60 (Kolb-Wengert, 533–34, 542). AC II 1–2 (Kolb-Wengert, 37–38); Maurer, *Historical Commentary on the Augsburg Confession*, 245.

26 Romans 5:1–2 is a popular text in the Apology, e.g, Ap IV 45, 80 (Tappert, 113, 118).

flesh and thereby becoming man.[27] The Athanasian Creed, in theses 27–40, affirms the fact of the incarnation in greater length than do the two other creeds, the Nicene and the Apostles' Creed. In becoming human, the Son of God identified Himself fully with the human condition in all its limitations without succumbing to sin. As a result, Christ is found "at once God and a human being."[28] The Lutheran doctrine *finitum capax infiniti* ("the finite is capable of the infinite") teaches in accordance with Col. 2:9 that in Christ, the finite human body takes on infinite divinity: "For in [Christ] the whole fullness of Deity dwells bodily." Since Christ assumed human nature, both natures are so united in the one person of Christ that they become inseparable. To quote Luther: "He [Christ] has become one person and does not separate the humanity from himself as Master Jack takes off his coat and lays it aside when he goes to bed."[29] Thus the incarnation explains why Christ's human nature is always present in the Word and Sacraments that enliven the worshiping community.[30]

Philippians 2:5–11 is a Christological hymn devoted to describing Christ's incarnation. In fact, Christ's mission on earth embraces both the states of humiliation (vv. 6–8) and exultation (vv. 9–11). Humiliation occurs when Christ voluntarily declines the full use of divine powers. Instead, Christ humbled or self-emptied Himself, a term that has become known in Greek as the *kenosis* (from *kenoein* in Phil. 2:7). A "kenotic" Christology affirms the mind of Christ, or voluntary sacrifice and obedience to God.[31]

Traditional dogmatics has divided Christ's obedience into a passive and active obedience. These two kinds of obedience make sense in view of the will or Law of God that demands a perfect obedience from someone on behalf of humanity. From His virgin birth to the cross, Christ thus actively obeyed the divine will without guilt and is presented as a perfect sacrifice on our behalf. On the other hand, He also chose to endure passively all temptations, pain, and tribulations, as well as the punishment over humanity for not having kept the Law. Thus through His total obedience—both active and passive—Christ did what the world could not achieve on its own.

Moreover, Christ achieved this obedience with His entire person in both the human and divine natures. In Christ, both natures played an important role in becoming that righteousness which God freely bestows on us all. Christ's mission took place in the *hypostatic union* that, in turn, implies an inseparable union in one person even if "true God" and "true

---

27   The point with the preexistent Christ assuming human nature, AC III 1 (Kolb-Wengert, 39), is that His divinity does not undergo any change nor does it ever abandon the human nature.

28   Athanasian Creed 27 (Kolb-Wengert, 24).

29   *Confession Concerning Christ's Supper*, AE 37:217.

30   See here, e.g., SD VIII 29 (Kolb-Wengert, 621).

31   Bosch, *Transforming Mission*, 512–13.

man" present a paradox hardly comprehensible by reason.[32] Ever since Wolfhart Pannenberg's *Jesus: God and Man* (1968), it has become popular to use the terms "from above" and "from below" as one relates Christology to contextual issues.[33] The Asian missiologist Stanley Samartha likened Christology "from above" to a helicopter and Christology "from below" to a bull-cart Christology. He expressed his own preference for the latter as being context sensitive. The Christology "from above" has the tendency of kicking up so much "theological dust that people around it are prevented from hearing the voice and seeing the vision of the descending Christianity. A bull-cart Christology, on the other hand, always has its wheels touching the unpaved roads of Asia. For without continual friction with the ground, the cart cannot move forward at all."[34]

Hence, it would be incorrect to reduce the Christology for mission either as entirely "from below," according to which Christ effected salvation through His humanity, or entirely "from above," which would ignore the condescension of God in coming into flesh and suffering as a human.[35] Scripture represents both aspects of Christology even when the Gospels start from different perspectives. For example, the Gospel of John may begin "from above" (with Christ's coming as *logos*), and Matthew and Luke may present a Christology "from below" (with Jesus' birth). The Dutch missiologist Jan Jongeneel argues correctly that a "helicopter Christology" is of little use if it has difficulties in landing, thus being unable to explain the full implications of Christ's incarnation. On the other hand, a "bull-cart Christology" may have difficulties in taking off or bringing in notions of Christ's preexistence and second coming.[36]

CHRIST AS EXAMPLE

The uniqueness of Christ's mission seems to leave little room for any ethical interpretations, though in the past, ideals of asceticism or imitation of Christ repeatedly have surfaced within Christianity. Thomas à Kempis, a late medieval mystic, wrote *The Imitation of Christ* (*De imitatione Christi*),

32 The hypostatic union is a nonnegotiable principle for Christology in the Solid Declaration of the Formula of Concord, e.g., SD III 15, 56 (Kolb-Wengert, 564, 572). Paul Tillich is one of those theologians who have replaced the traditional Christology of *vere Deus—vere homo* with the paradox, *Christus homo essentialis—homo existentialis* ("true man and yet real man"). See Tillich, "Die Lehre von der Inkarnation," 205–19.

33 Pannenberg, *Jesus: God and Man*.

34 Samartha, *One Christ—Many Religions*, 115–20.

35 Karl Barth is a supporter of the so-called "Extra Calvinisticum" (*Logos extra carnem*, "the Word outside the flesh"), which emphasizes the transcendence of the Christology at the expense of the Lutheran condescendence of the divine logos and His total identification with His human form. See Barth, *Church Dogmatics*, 4/1:94, 140.

36 Jongeneel, *Philosophy, Science, and Theology of Mission*, 2:180–81.

which became one of the most widely distributed books in the body of literature during his time.[37] The challenge with such approaches, however, is that the message of the cross as a gift of salvation switches to one of ethics. This is particularly a result of theological rationalism that rejects the divinity of Christ and reduces Him to a historic figure. In all cases where theologians and Christians refuse to accept the divinity of Christ, Christianity becomes a moral project and Christ serves as an example or as an excellent preacher and teacher.

Other religions, to be sure, would be willing to accept Christ as such a teacher. Yet missionary proclamation is interested in passing on Christ and the cross as a gift of life to an unbelieving world, and this is much more than a moral message. Undeniably, there are limited references to Christ as an example (1 Cor. 11:1; 1 Pet. 2:21). Such passages depict Christ as the supreme example of suffering evil for doing good. Not even here, however, is Christ solely a moral example. In the Lutheran Confessions, there is no evidence that Christ's life and suffering should serve merely as an example. Even though Christians often are called to true suffering in a manner that follows the example of Christ, that suffering has no value unless it is subsumed entirely under faith and the reception of Christ's suffering for us.[38] The Lutheran Confessions repeatedly affirm this against the false understanding of the distinction of foods, against false doctrines of repentance, and against the false doctrines of sacrifice in the Roman Mass.[39] The ideal of imitation could bear the inherent danger of works-righteousness. The Lutheran Confessions guard against that by making human deeds the passive reception of divine gifts alone through faith in Christ to follow in His example. In his normative study *Luther on Vocation*, Gustav Wingren summarizes Luther's theology on this point as follows: "Christ is not to be imitated by us, but rather to be accepted in faith, because Christ also had his special office for the salvation of man, an office which no one has."[40] Ultimately, therefore, Christ serves for us less as an *exemplum* or paradigm for activity but especially as *sacramentum*—that is, a being given through faith as the price of our salvation.[41]

In literature, the cross has often been given a sociopolitical interpretation. The same has also been true among theologians, as one sees in *The Crucified God: The Cross of Christ as the Foundation and Criticism of*

---

37 Hägglund, *History of Theology*, 207.

38 AC XXIV 31 (Kolb-Wengert, 78); Ap IV 358 (Kolb-Wengert, 173).

39 AC XXIV 31 (Kolb-Wengert, 78); Ap XII 31 (Kolb-Wengert, 208); Ap XXIV 57 (Kolb-Wengert, 268); SA III III 2 (Kolb-Wengert, 312); LC I 4 (Kolb-Wengert, 387).

40 Wingren, *Luther on Vocation*, 172.

41 See Öberg, "Mission und Heilsgeschichte," 39.

Christian Theology by Jürgen Moltmann.[42] In agreement with the World
Conference on Mission and Evangelism in Melbourne (1980), theologians
of the Ecumenical Movement heralded the *kenosis* of Christ as that which
calls Jesus' followers to join Him with the poor at the peripheries and thus
challenges human power structures: "God identified with the poor and
oppressed by sending his Son Jesus to live and serve as a Galilean speaking
directly to the common people; promising to bless those who met the needs
of the hungry, the thirsty, the stranger, the naked, the sick and the prisoner;
and finally meeting death on a cross as a political offender."[43] A kenotic
Christology portrays Christ as the first missionary par excellence who in
exceptional ways displayed self-denial and one who withstood conventions in society. That interpretation would certainly inspire those in abject
conditions to follow suit with the interest of bringing about change. Such
a kenotic Christology that sees in Christ's mission a prototype or model
should note, however, that Christ emptied or humbled Himself vicariously
for us in a unique way.

To be sure, the abject condition of many people around the world poses
a huge challenge to the mission of the Church. Christianity must ask herself
how her proclamation of the cross can address in meaningful and relevant
ways the deep existential concerns of suffering people. However, holding up
Christ as the supreme example of suffering in the hope of alleviating temporal suffering cannot fully cover the eschatological meaning of the cross
as salvation for the life to come. Missionary proclamation must include the
reign of Christ by presenting the cross as a gift of forgiveness for every person's guilt, including those who suffer under abject conditions. Indeed, that
gift is not obtained through action, but through faith in Christ alone.

The Kyriological Motive or Goal of Mission

In a later chapter, we shall return to the goal of mission. For the goal of
mission is multileveled, and it relates not only to Christology but also to
anthropology and ecclesiology. Yet the ultimate goal of God's mission is
the establishment of Christ's lordship in this world. The mission of God has
as its goal the extension of Christ's rule over all people. This goal will only
conclude with the eschatological event of Christ's second coming to judge
the living and the dead.[44] The missiological implications of Christ's present

---

42 Moltmann, *Crucified God*, 25. For a critique of Moltmann's theology of the cross, see Braaten,
    "Trinitarian Theology of the Cross," 113–21. Other countries, such as South Africa, have used
    Christologically motivated strategies such as seeking political reconciliation through the "Truth
    and Reconciliation Commission."

43 Scherer and Bevans, *New Directions in Mission and Evangelization*, 1:28.

44 Andersen, *Towards a Theology of Mission*, 53. Freytag, "Mission im Blick aufs Ende," 187. For a
    description of Christ's return in the Lutheran Confessions, see AC III 4 (Kolb-Wengert, 39); AC

rule are that His death and resurrection not only serve as the foundation of mission but also that as Lord He is the dynamo that drives mission today. Christ sends His Spirit, through whom He builds and expands His rule. One may speak here of the *kyriological* motivation for the Church—namely, to pursue mission so that Christ's kingdom may come.[45]

The important point is that Christ's dominion as King and Lord is not realized only in the future; He exercises His lordship already in the present. The Lord is not an Arthurian "once and future king"; rather, He is King of both the present and the future in which He shall return. That also has implications for the gifts received through mission. Since Christ's return and His present kingdom fall together, the present gifts of forgiveness and life received through faith are already eternal and eschatological gifts.[46]

One further point concerning Christ's dominion is that it would not be correct to divide between God's kingdom and that of Christ.[47] Christ, from His seat at the right hand of His Father, is the cosmic ruler. He is everywhere present to rule as God from sea to sea and to the ends of the earth. Dogmaticians term this rule as His *regnum potentiae* to indicate His dominion over all creatures, history, and the cosmos (Matt. 28:18). However, Christ's lordship over the congregation of the saints is presented in Scripture not as an earthly rule (John 18:36), but as a soteriological and eschatological reality, that is, as a dominion over redeemed man and the redeemed community. This dominion is called the kingdom of grace (*regnum Christi gratiae*). It is into this kingdom of grace that every individual is called through proclamation and Baptism. Thus as much as one must underscore that there is only one Christ and one dominion that includes both the cosmos and redeemed man, it is necessary to relate Christ's dominion in terms of soteriology. As Werner Elert observes:

> We speak of His dominion only as He, according to His own words, became our Lord. Insofar as His cosmic dominion exceeds that, we must number it among the mysteries of God which are hidden from our sight. It suffices to know that we together with the entire cosmos to which we belong are redeemed unto His dominion and that there is nothing in heaven or on earth which may thwart His dominion over us.[48]

XVII 1–5 (Kolb-Wengert, 51); Apostles' Creed 5 (Kolb-Wengert, 22).

45 Vicedom's missiological scheme is described from the perspective of Christ's reign; see Vicedom, *Mission of God*, 13–14. Beißer, "Mission und Reich Gottes," 43. See Gensichen, *Glaube für die Welt*, 105.

46 Beißer, *Hoffnung und Vollendung*, 78.

47 "God's kingdom" and "Christ's kingdom" can be used synonymously, as Beißer, *Hoffnung und Vollendung*, 58, 80, shows.

48 Elert, *Christian Faith*, 241.

The distinction between Christ's full cosmological dominion and that of grace invites thought of the two-kingdom doctrine. The dominion of grace points to Jesus Christ extending His rule through the Holy Spirit and the preaching of the Gospel. By contrast, the kingdom on the left is ruled differently—namely, through His Law to maintain order in this world over all its inhabitants in this world.

The ecclesiological implication of Christ's dominion of grace is that the Church is the seat of Christ's reign insofar as He rules there through Word and Sacrament, bestowing forgiveness of sins to those who believe. But the Church as a human organization on an everyday level is not identical with the kingdom of grace. The distinction between the lordship of Christ and the Church as an earthly organization should be evident. The daily functions conducted in the Church to regulate its daily lives are not identical to Christ's rule over the redeemed community. Christ's lordship is identified with the divinely ordained activities of preaching the Word, of baptizing, and of celebrating the Lord's Supper. Where these functions occur, there Christ exercises His lordship. The mission of the Church thus pursues these functions intentionally, for through them alone Christ's lordship extends over the unbelieving world.[49]

THE STRUGGLE BETWEEN TWO DOMINIONS

The extension of Christ's kingdom is one that does not occur without a struggle against the evil one. Consider Luther's famous explanation to the Second Article of the Apostles' Creed:

> He has redeemed me, a lost and condemned human being. He has purchased and freed me from all sins, from death, and from the power of the devil, not with gold or silver but with his holy, precious blood and with his innocent suffering and death . . . in order that I may belong to him, and live under his kingdom.[50]

The full dimensions of the soteriological implications of Christ's reign are presented here. To paraphrase Luther from his Large Catechism, everyone who has entered the kingdom of grace previously lay under God's wrath and displeasure. But in the preaching of the Gospel, the eternal Son of God has had mercy on us and has come from heaven to snatch us sinners from the jaws of hell. Now God rules over us until the Last Day when He will completely divide and separate us, together with all believers, from the wicked world, the devil, death, and sin.[51] What Luther describes here is

---

49 Tr 31–33 (Kolb-Wengert, 335); Ap XVI 2 (Tappert, 222).
50 SC II 4 (Kolb-Wengert, 355).
51 LC II 28–31 (Kolb-Wengert, 434).

an eschatological struggle between the mission of God and the reign of the devil. No one should think that God's mission is simply opposed by the earthly powers such as atheistic governments and kings. God's mission, which is always Christ's mission, contends with the diabolical forces in this world; it is a power struggle with the devil. Christians in other cultures who are acutely aware of spiritual forces in their lives concur with this observation.[52]

Scripture describes the true enemy who opposes Christ's mission as the Antichrist, who not only stands and works outside the kingdom of grace, but actually prevails in it (2 Thess. 2:4).[53] Christ's mission thus protects all believers from further evil onslaughts. But that would not make them immune to constant attacks. In fact, as Luther would say, all believers are daily under the dominion of the devil, who neither day nor night relaxes his efforts to steal upon them unawares and kindle unbelief in their heart.[54] Thus the struggle between Christ and the devil takes hold of a Christian's life and denotes a constant battle. *Simul iustus et peccator* ("both redeemed and sinner") means that the Christian lives in Christ's and the devil's kingdom at one and the same time.[55]

The images and words used by Luther to express this struggle resemble the descriptions of the classic *Christus Victor* soteriology. Christ stands victorious as Lord, but that victory precedes a struggle with the powers of the devil. It has been rightly argued that this motif must be complemented by the traditional Anselmian doctrine of atonement to include the satisfaction or forgiveness on account of Christ's death on the cross.[56] Scholars, however, have proven that while Luther does employ imageries from the classic and heroic idea of atonement, he deepens it with the Latin tradition as to how Jesus Christ Himself endures God's wrath upon all mankind and the curse of the Law.[57] Horst Georg Pöhlmann thus appropriately coins the phrase *Victor quia victima* ("victor because the victim"), implying that, in order to become victorious, Christ had to become the victim.[58] It needs to be said

52 For a discussion of the reign of Christ, see Lochmann, "Lordship of Christ in a Secularized World," 71 n. 26. Trillhaas, *"Regnum Christi,"* 42. Cullmann, *Salvation in History*, 25. Gensichen, *Living Mission*, 23.

53 See, for example, Luther's statements in SA II IV 10 (Kolb-Wengert, 307–10). For an explanation of Luther's statements on the Antichrist, see Hendrix, *Luther and the Papacy*, and Bizer, *Luther und der Papst*.

54 LC I 100 (Kolb-Wengert, 400); LC III 104–5 (Kolb-Wengert, 454).

55 LC III 106 (Kolb-Wengert, 454). Through the strength and power provided by God, a Christian will contribute to resisting the onslaughts on himself and God's kingdom. Peters, *Kommentar zu Luthers Katechismen*, 2:138.

56 See Aulén, *Christus Victor*, 101–22.

57 Peters, *Kommentar zu Luthers Katechismen*, 2:138.

58 Pöhlmann, *Abriß der Dogmatik*, 224–25.

also that this struggle is not completed. Christ's saving mission remains a continuous struggle against Satan to the very last day when "the devil and all powers must be subject to him and lie beneath his feet."[59] This implies that every Christian's faith is filled with hope in this final completion while caught in a struggle with sorrow and pain. This is what the theology of the cross implies in contrast to a theology of glory. The former provides a realistic understanding of Christian existence in which Christians patiently expect the final triumph.

---

59 LC II 31 (Kolb-Wengert, 434).

CHAPTER NINE

The Dynamism of God's Mission

Affirming the Spirit's Person and Work

Mainline Protestantism is often faulted for its conspicuous silence on the person and work of the Holy Spirit. However, people must consider rethinking that criticism (which comes from Pentecostal and Charismatic circles) by taking a closer look at the theology of the Holy Spirit in Lutheran theology. The Danish theologian Regin Prenter points out that in the theology of Martin Luther, the Holy Spirit receives central place even in such doctrines as justification, Scripture, the Sacraments, the Church, and ethics.[1] If Luther and the Confessions do not always explicitly mention the Holy Spirit, they nevertheless always imply the Spirit's person and work.

The Church fully acknowledges the Holy Spirit as God. This person is not merely an emanation or energy of God, such as one encounters in the teachings of other religions. As Luther states, "many other kinds of spirits are mentioned in Scripture, such as the human spirit, heavenly spirits, and the evil spirit. But God's Spirit alone is called Holy Spirit."[2]

This Spirit is the Third Person of the Trinity, of the same essence and power with the Father and the Son. As the Third Person of the one true God, He is, like the Father and Son, of "immeasurable power," "wisdom," "goodness," and is the "creator and preserver of all things, visible and invisible."[3] The Nicene Creed adds that He is "Lord" and "Life-giver" and thus is worshiped and glorified together with Father and Son.[4]

In addition to His person, the Church also points to the pivotal role of the Spirit's mission or, as one generally calls it, His *economy*. The Holy Spirit continues the divine salvation plan, but in such a way that His work

---

1   Prenter, *Spiritus Creator*. The soteriological dimension is particularly strong in Luther's theology, see Mostert, "Hinweise zu Luthers Lehre vom Heiligen Geist," 26. The same applies to the Lutheran Confessions; see Kvist, "Der Heilige Geist," 206, 209.

2   LC II 36 (Kolb-Wengert, 435). See also AC XVIII 1–3 (Kolb-Wengert, 39).

3   AC I 2 (Kolb-Wengert, 37); Ap I 1 (Tappert, 100); LC II 36 (Kolb-Wengert, 435).

4   Nicene Creed 7 (Kolb-Wengert, 23).

remains inseparably tied to the person and work of Christ. For the Holy Spirit was not sent into the world to draw attention to Himself. Rather, He comes to glorify Jesus Christ and what He has done for our salvation (John 16:14). For this reason, there exists an inseparable communion between the Third and the Second Person of the Trinity (John 14:26; 15:26) that is anchored already in the procession of the Holy Spirit from the Father *and the Son* (*filioque*). Thus the Counselor or Comforter does not represent an absent Christ or God, but He conveys the presence of Christ and the Father.[5] Without the Holy Spirit, the benefits or (as Luther would say) the treasure of salvation brought by Christ's suffering, death, and resurrection would not reach man.[6] Through the Holy Spirit, the distance between God and man—obviously not merely the historical separation of almost two thousand years, but more the gap between the holy God and sinful man—is overcome.

Thus, without the Holy Spirit, the mission of God and of the Church would not continue. As Andersen observes, with the sending of the Holy Spirit "God has made it evident that He retains the missionary enterprise in His own hands and does not surrender it to any human authority."[7] The fact that God carries on His missionary enterprise through the Holy Spirit, as He did throughout the history of the Church, cautions us to "be restrained in our judgment on all the missionary organizations that have been active in the generation prior to our own."[8] All discussion of the Church's mission, such as conversion, planting a congregation, growth, and motivating members for mission are attributed, strictly speaking, to the power and operation of the Holy Spirit.

THE HOLY SPIRIT IN THE LIFE
OF THE BELIEVER AND THE CHURCH

The Holy Spirit's work impacts soteriology, the life and everyday existence of the Church. The Holy Spirit performs within creation and history the special task of conveying to people the life and blessings God intended for them. In the New Testament, the Spirit assumes responsibility for the entire order of salvation (*ordo salutis*) by giving to Christians the *new life* that Christ has wrought for us through His death on the cross and resurrection (2 Cor. 3:6). The Spirit *calls* us through the Gospel, enlightens us with the knowledge of sin and grace (Ps. 51:12; John 16:8; Acts 2:37; 1 Cor. 2:12),

---

5   Joest, *Dogmatik*, 1:310; LC II 39 (Kolb-Wengert, 439); Prenter, *Spiritus Creator*, 27.

6   LC II 38 (Kolb-Wengert, 415): Peters, *Kommentar zu Luthers Katechismen*, 2:196–97.

7   Andersen, *Towards a Theology of Mission*, 46.

8   Andersen, *Towards a Theology of Mission*, 48. See also LWF, *Together in God's Mission*, 9; SD II 55 (Kolb-Wengert, 554).

works in us repentance and faith for our *justification* through Jesus Christ, makes us the children of God, and enables us to pray to God our Father (Rom. 8:14–17, 26–27). The Holy Spirit sanctifies and renews our life (Rom. 8:13; 1 Cor. 6:11), and He brings forth in us good, spiritual fruits (Gal. 5:22). He also strengthens and keeps us in the hope for an eternal reunion with Christ upon His return (Rom. 8:23–25; 2 Cor. 1:22; Eph. 1:13–14; 4:30).[9]

This long list establishes the scriptural truth that no one can accomplish anything toward his own salvation or preserve it except through the work of the Holy Spirit. Nor can anyone call God Lord without the Holy Spirit (1 Cor. 12:3; Acts 5:32). Luther affirms these observations with his famous words:

> I believe that I cannot by my own understanding or strength believe in Christ my Lord or come to him, but instead the Holy Spirit has called me through the gospel, enlightened me with his gifts, made me holy and kept me in the true faith, just as he calls, gathers, enlightens, and makes holy the whole Christian church on earth and keeps it with Jesus Christ in the one common true faith. Daily in this Christian church the Holy Spirit abundantly forgives all sins—mine and those of all believers. On the Last Day the Holy Spirit will raise me and all dead and will give to me and all believers in Christ eternal life.[10]

On occasion, Luther would call the Holy Spirit the "Sanctifier" or define His work on us as "sanctification," that is, He made us holy and still does so.[11] Speaking about sanctification in this way may create confusion at times, since it is used in the broad and not the narrow sense. In the broad sense, the term sanctification presupposes all the means that the Holy Spirit uses to sanctify someone or make him holy: the Church, the forgiveness of sins, resurrection of the flesh and eternal life—*and* the working of the righteous faith. The broad sense of sanctification thus also includes the first initial act of the Holy Spirit bringing about faith, that is, our justification.[12] On other occasions—and generally this is what has become the rule—sanctification is used in distinction from justification, where sanctification refers to love and good works.[13] Here, the term sanctification points to all that the

---

9 For references in the Confessions to the *ordo salutis*, see SD II 54, 71 (Kolb-Wengert, 554, 557); SD III 40–41 (Kolb-Wengert, 569); SD VI 17 (Kolb-Wengert, 590). The Confessions also add an anthropological-psychological dimension to the coming to faith that the believer is moved by new spiritual motions; see Ap IV 64–65, 125, 136, 351 (Tappert, 116, 124–25, 161). The events of the *ordo salutis* present the application of redemption from various angles and should not be conceived of in terms of a "domino effect, such that, the process having begun, one follows from the other automatically" (McGowan, "Justification and the *ordo salutis*," 147). See also Kvist, "Der Heilige Geist," 210, and Peters, *Kommentar zu Luthers Katechismen*, 2:209.

10 SC II 2 (Kolb-Wengert, 355–56).

11 LC II 36 (Kolb-Wengert, 435). See Peters, *Kommentar zu Luthers Katechismen*, 2:209.

12 E.g., SC II 6 (Kolb-Wengert, 356); LC II 38 (Kolb-Wengert, 436).

13 E.g., SD III, 40–41 (Kolb-Wengert, 569). Kvist, "Der Heilige Geist," 209–10.

believer, in possession of the Holy Spirit, does in the sense that he fears and loves God, requests His help, and loves his neighbor. "Sanctification" in this sense connects to all that pertains to good works that have sprung from the faith of the justified believer.

The significance of the Holy Spirit's mission is that He not only brings a person to faith, but in doing so, He also gathers the believer into a Christian community, forgives him daily of his sins within that community, and keeps him and all Christians in the one true faith to eternal life. For some, this gathering represents a second step to becoming a believer. Both should, however, be seen as synonymous acts. As someone comes to faith, he is also placed in the Body of Christ (1 Cor. 12:14, 27; Acts 2:41–42). One might be inclined to perceive the Spirit's work in egotistical terms, as it pertains only to me privately or is reduced only to me. However, the same work that occurs to me is the same for all Christians daily who belong to the one, Christian Church. Coming to faith, being preserved in it, and being led to eternal life is a communal issue. For where the believers meet and celebrate God's Word, there the presence of the Holy Spirit is assured.[14]

As stated before, the work of the Holy Spirit represents a testimony, not to Himself but to Jesus Christ. The community of believers is permeated with the Spirit's testimony to Christ. He adds those born of water and Spirit (John 3:5; Titus 3:5) as members to the Body of Christ and temple of God (1 Cor. 12:13; Eph. 2:21–22), appoints and authorizes apostles and pastors (1 Cor. 12:28; Eph. 4:11–12; 1 Tim. 4:14), and assigns all members with His gifts according to each believer's measure of faith (Rom. 12:3) for service as the royal priesthood (1 Cor. 12:4–31; 1 Pet. 2:5–9). He is the *Paraclete* who comforts those in faith as the representative of the risen Christ. He assists all believers in their apologetic (Luke 12:11–12; 1 Pet. 3:15) and missionary witness (Acts 1:8) to the world. He leads Christians from their sins to the righteousness found only in Christ, and He will do so before the final judgment (Rev. 20:10) over the devil and all principalities of the world (John 16:7–11).

THE MEANS OF GRACE AND THE HOLY SPIRIT

According to the biblical witness, God gives His Holy Spirit after the important event of Pentecost only through the preached and written word (1 Thess. 1:5; Gal. 3:2), as well as through the Sacraments instituted by Christ (Matt. 28:19; John 6:53; 1 Cor. 10:3–4). God never chooses to work apart from these means, and the Church is thus charged (as the above references indicate) to take on a structure that adequately provides for these means.

---

14 For a beautiful treatment of the Spirit's work of gathering the Church, see Martin Luther's discussion in LC II 52 (Kolb-Wengert, 438). Also Elert, *Structure of Lutheranism*, 1:86.

In all instances, the Church must recognize that God provides His gifts through means. Such gifts cannot be enforced or coerced through human actions or called upon on certain dates (see Acts 8:18–24).[15] The Spirit's means can only be requested in prayer with a childlike faith (Luke 11:13). For this reason, God is sovereign in that the Holy Spirit is free to bring faith through the external Word where and when it pleases God.[16] This does not mean that God abandons His means to deliver faith through other avenues. It simply means that the decision whether faith will or will not be given rests with God. This prevents the Church from seeing the Sacraments as magical means that can be applied anywhere or at any place without the context of a believing community and without the faith that receives the benefits of the means. Such misconceptions occurred, for example, at the mass baptisms by the conquistadors when multitudes of Indians were given the sacrament without prior instruction in the Christian faith.

To guarantee the Spirit's means, God also has instituted the ministry in the Church. This ensures that the Church carries out her mission through the activities of preaching and the Sacraments. Indeed, it would be contrary to God's institution if the Church were to decide to abandon the preached and sacramental Word.[17]

It is true that the Holy Spirit works faith internally in man. Yet He does so through external means. These means of Word and Sacrament are absolutely necessary for the Holy Spirit to perform and impart justifying faith. As Maurer states: "It is impossible to separate the external oral Word and the physical signs, on the one hand, from the internal process of Spirit and faith, on the other."[18] The certainty of one's salvation is at stake. The objective or external means used by the Holy Spirit prevent self-deception

---

15 Maurer, *Historical Commentary on the Augsburg Confession*, 365.

16 AC V 3 (Kolb-Wengert, 41). To the "predestinarian" understanding of this quotation, see Schlink, *Theology of the Lutheran Confessions*, 289; Maurer, *Historical Commentary on the Augsburg Confession*, 363; Kvist, "Der Heilige Geist," 208. The strong emphasis on the means of grace in the Lutheran Confessions is argued explicitly and implicitly against those who deny it and teach that the Holy Spirit works directly on the heart apart from the means of grace and whose presence could be attested on the basis of spiritual experiences, such as the Anabaptists (Enthusiasts) or Schwenkfelders. See AC V 2–3 (Kolb-Wengert, 41); Ap IV 67 (Tappert, 116); Ap XXIV 70 (Tappert, 262); SA III VIII 6, 10 (Kolb-Wengert, 322–23); LC V 31 (Kolb-Wengert, 469); SD II 48–52, 80 (Kolb-Wengert, 553, 559); SD XII 30 (Kolb-Wengert, 659). Next to Baptism and Holy Communion, Absolution and the ministry of the Word are included under the term "sacrament" (see Ap XIII 3–5, 7–13, Tappert, 211–13), since all have as their content the event of justification; see Martens, *Die Rechtfertigung des Sünders*, 23–24, and Maurer, *Historical Commentary on the Augsburg Confession*, 366. Also to be rejected is the position of the Roman Church on the sacraments (*ex opere operato*), which borders on a magical understanding and does not include faith as the means of appropriating the gifts; see Grane, *Augsburg Confession*, 76.

17 AC V 1–2 (Kolb-Wengert, 40–41). See Nagel, "Office of the Holy Ministry," 289. Maurer, *Historical Commentary on the Augsburg Confession*, 360; Gensichen, *Glaube für die Welt*, 125.

18 Maurer, *Historical Commentary on the Augsburg Confession*, 361; Kvist, "Der Heilige Geist," 207.

in the believer that he may have brought about or produced his own salvation.[19] The believer must acknowledge that there are only two causes for his coming to faith: the Word and the Holy Spirit. The person himself passively receives (*pure passive*) the work of these causes through means.[20] The Book of Acts (often called the book of the Holy Spirit) features a number of places where sinners were brought to faith by the action of the Word. In short episodes, we see that it is not the person who takes initiative to approach God, but God Himself acts through the testimony of the Holy Spirit, Baptism, and the Word. Consider, for example, the listeners in Jerusalem who congregated for the first time (Acts 2:41–42), those who heard the preaching of Peter and John (Acts 4:4) and Philip (Acts 8:12), the Ethiopian eunuch (Acts 8:38), Paul (Acts 9:18), Cornelius (Acts 10:44, 48), and Lydia (Acts 16:14–15). All were reached by God through the Holy Spirit and Baptism. The Holy Spirit's coming to them through the external means of Word and Baptism marked important change in their lives. And though on occasion the number of those saved are mentioned (Acts 2:41, 47; 6:7; 9:31; 11:21; 12:24; 14:1; 16:5; 19:20), it was never mere numbers that were emphasized. These vignettes represent glimpses of the personal encounter between God and the individual through the Word and what results from that meeting.

Sometimes, however, God's messenger was persecuted and the message rejected (Acts 8:1; 13:50) or not understood (Acts 8:31). These negative examples reveal natural man's inability to perceive or be open for God's Word: "the natural person does not accept the things of the Spirit of God, for they are folly to him, and he is not able to understand them because they are spiritually discerned" (1 Cor. 2:14).[21]

HUMAN EXPERIENCES
AND "POWER ENCOUNTERS"

The above discussion raises also the issue of spiritual and religious experiences in a person. It is true that in the conversion process the saving work of the Holy Spirit takes hold of the man's entire existence, thus his thinking, feelings, and desires. When God comes to man, the Holy Spirit can also seize the heart as the innermost seat of man's spirituality (Rom. 8:16; Gal. 4:6) and instill very explicit emotions such as joy and peace (Rom. 15:13). Experiences of being gripped by God may accompany the saving work of the Holy Spirit (Rom. 14:17), such as, for example, speaking in

---

19 Elert, *Lord's Supper Today*, 11: "The proclaimed Word and the sacramental acts have in common that they, in relationship to faith, are external . . . They protect faith from doubt, just as though it were its own producer."

20 FC Ep II, 18 (Kolb-Wengert, 494); FC SD II 22, 89 (Kolb-Wengert, 548, 561).

21 See LC II 67–69 (Kolb-Wengert, 440).

tongues (1 Corinthians 14) or visions. But the latter experiences must be tested and interpreted against God's Word. Even if faith supposedly undergoes such experiences—as has been observed on the mission field in the conversion process and is claimed by the Charismatic and Neo-Pentecostal Movements—yet the Christian is still not dependent on them for salvation or preservation. Faith must place confidence outside itself in the atoning work of Christ and promises in the Word of God. Faith should move beyond the "visible" experiences and earthly expectations to the invisible (2 Cor. 4:18; Rom. 4:11–25; Heb. 11:17–19). Faith moves to the external Word in Scripture and clings to the Word made flesh as the faithful Christian endures hardship, feels forsaken by God, or undergoes other forms of suffering in this life (Rom. 5:3–5). As Pentecostal and Charismatic Movements focus on healing ministries, it becomes evident that in such contexts of healing, faith is presented as something into which one places confidence and trust for healing. That, however, establishes a false sense of security (*securitas*). For what if the manifestations of healing or tongues are not there? Such absence could lead to despair and feelings of guilt. Lutherans instead plead for a "confidence" or "certainty" (*certitudo*) that is not placed on faith itself but, as said, on the external promise of God through His Word.[22]

One important aspect of the Holy Spirit's mission is that it resists principalities and powers opposing God (John 8:44; Rev. 12:9; Eph. 2:1–3; 6:11–12), also those supposed "cosmic powers" used by individuals for selfish reasons (Acts 8:18–19). According to Scripture and the tradition of the Reformation, the "schemes of the devil" (Eph. 6:11) take hold of Enthusiasts (*Schwärmer*) or Ravers, who are demonically inspired since they claim to have the Spirit apart from the Word (2 Cor. 11:4). Luther's dictum remains true: "Everything that boasts of being from the Spirit apart from such a Word and sacrament is of the devil."[23] Christians are thus admonished to withstand such adversarial spirits (1 Pet. 5:9), to put on the whole armor of God (Eph. 6:11), and to train themselves in the ability to distinguish between spirits (διακρίσεις τῶν πνευμάτων, 1 Cor. 12:10; 1 John 4:1).

In a missionary setting, missionaries may encounter those who use magic and witchcraft very deceptively and persuasively as powers of God and the Holy Spirit. Missionaries should be quick to point out that such powers are not used in the name of God, but rather are of occultic, satanic origin that must be overthrown by the Gospel. In this connection, a common phenomenon discussed by anthropologists and missionaries is *shamanism*. An illustration of *shamanism* can be found in the Tswana and

---

22 See, e.g., LC IV 29, 30, 32 (Kolb-Wengert, 460). See also Lindberg, *Third Reformation*; Commission on Theology and Church Relations, *Charismatic Movement and Lutheran Theology*.

23 SA III VIII 10, 4–6 (Kolb-Wengert, 323, 322). See also LC I 18–21, 100–101 (Kolb-Wengert, 388, 400).

Zulu cultures of Southern Africa where the traditional tribal doctor, known among the Zulu as the *isangoma*, applies occult powers. This diviner is considered in his culture to be the real link, the communicator between the ancestors and those who are living. He is also the protector of society and so is consulted frequently in times of illness, when cattle are lost, or when inexplicable events occur. The *isangoma* will discover the cause of a disaster and then prescribe the steps necessary to set things right again, at times pointing out spirits who possess someone and then taking measures to "bar" the spirit. The *isangoma's* position is not hereditary but established usually by his own claim to possess spirits, which is then verified under the guidance of another doctor.[24]

As the Gospel takes root among indigenous people, it will be strongly opposed by the *isangoma*. One would think that modernity erases such traditional African customs, but the reality of evil spirits or their inferior servant, the dwarf (*Tokoloshe*), is still affirmed and has in fact experienced a resurgence in South African cultures as part of the re-Africanization process. It is still *en vogue* to consult a diviner, even for Christians, which displays the constant dangers of syncretism among Christians in Southern Africa.[25]

The above example of *shamanism* illustrates what is meant by furthering mission through "power encounters" as the Gospel meets with traditional power structures in cultures. It has become popular among Church Growth circles and Charismatic-Pentecostal Movements to flaunt such power encounters as part of the "power evangelism" that seeks to make advances with the Gospel through various means such as healing, victories (exorcisms) over evil forces, or overcoming poverty through "Prosperity Theology." For its promoters, such power evangelism today is hailed optimistically as a great awakening or outpouring of the Holy Spirit, even more than the first century experienced.[26]

Understandably, Lutherans oppose power evangelism for the obvious reasons that it undermines the central status of God's means of grace and substitutes instead a "theology of glory" (*theologia gloriae*) that preempts the coming kingdom of God in this interim period with false hopes and promises of personal achievement and gratification. On the basis of the

---

24 For a description of the Zulu religion, see Krige, *Social System of the Zulus*, 280–335.

25 See the personal testimony of a Dean Isashar Dube in the Lutheran Church in Southern Africa, *Mit den bösen Geistern unter dem Himmel.*

26 Wagner, *Spiritual Power and Church Growth*. In the third edition of McGavran, *Understanding Church Growth*, editor Peter Wagner inserted an additional chapter, which, because of frequent meetings with charismatic groups, deals with the significance of healing the sick for church growth. Later, Wagner developed this concept further into the idea of "power encounter." See also Wagner, *Church Growth*. It also includes the Korean pastor Dr. Paul Yonggi Cho, whose background included connections to Korean *shamanism*; see Cho, *Fourth Dimension*.

cross, Lutherans also dismiss the notion of displaying miracles as spectacle events. All miracles in Scripture clearly make the point that they must be seen in the light of Christ's resurrection. Christ's resurrection is a miracle of faith and not merely a show for public display. Such signs or wonders that the people demand are not always the signs and wonders that God wished to show (Matt. 12:38–42).

While Lutherans do not deny that God reigns over the natural order and that He is quite capable of the miraculous, they nevertheless point to the clear witness in Scripture that miracles do not point to God in His power, but rather to God in His mercy, specifically to Christ, the cross, and the resurrection (Matt. 12:39; John 2:19–21; 1 Cor. 1:18–25). Christ's resurrection, like our own, is a firm and unshakable reality that we nevertheless grasp as a miracle through faith and not through sight (1 Cor. 15:12–28). Similarly, we see that human sight can betray. As we see in Matt. 28:11–15, the reality of the empty tomb did not prove Christ's miraculous resurrection to the hard-hearted Pharisees; they would only believe that His body was stolen. Therefore, all miracles are perceived as miracles through faith and not through sight. Faith does not originate or flow from miracles as it does through the preaching of God's Word. This is so clearly presented in the Gospel of John (John 4:48; 20:29).

In terms of the continuation of miracles, it should be clear that the Lord gave powers to perform miracles directly to the disciples. By contrast, Christians today must beseech God's healing powers through prayer for those who are ill and where all medical resources and know-how have reached an end. Here, God's healing comes at a time when He sees fit or not at all. Thus Christians cannot use reputed quasidivine powers to perform miracles at their own behest and for this reason cannot use them as a means to convince or bring non-Christian bystanders to faith.[27] They must point to the cross and resurrection of Jesus as the foretaste of the resurrection that we desire above all earthly good and that will heal all earthly suffering (1 Cor. 15:29–58). For according to the apostle Paul, all creation in this world groans under "its bondage to decay" and lives in hope of future physical healing in a time to come (Rom. 8:21).

---

27 As Protestant mission emerged in the seventeenth century, the apostolate and the role of the apostles was greatly discussed by theologians at that time. Lutheran theologians such as Johann Gerhard pointed to the distinction between the apostles' direct possession of powers to perform miracles and the Christian Church today, which must rely on the Lord's work in prayer. See Größel, *Die Mission und die evangelische Kirche*, 80–81.

The Holy Spirit Gathers and Equips the Church for Mission

We emphasize the fact that the Holy Spirit must be connected to the doctrine of the Church. The Spirit calls the Church into being, and in her midst, He continually brings about and preserves faith in Jesus Christ. This puts the Church in the correct relation to God, as Vicedom states:

> There is danger that the church itself may become the point of departure, the purpose, the subject of the mission. This is not, however, in accord with Scripture, since it is always the Triune God who acts, who makes His believers members of His kingdom. Even the church is only an instrument in the hands of God. The church herself is only the outcome of the activity of God who sends and saves.[28]

Therefore, as we consider the work of the Holy Spirit, His means, and the Church, we may, from a missiological point of view, suggest the following sequence: God gathers His Church through the Holy Spirit where the Word is preached and Baptism administered. The Church cannot congregate first and then look around for the activity of preaching; she is the creation of the Word (*creatura verbi*) having been called together by the Gospel. Her existence is thus preceded by the coming of the Holy Spirit and the preaching of His Word.[29] The Church may not abstain from these activities if she wishes to ensure the work of the Holy Spirit for her own survival and for the world. She may not sit idle over the means through which the Holy Spirit chooses to build and increase His Church. She diligently proclaims and examines God's Word, engages in prayer and in fellowship, practices Baptism as the foundation of faith, and trusts in the strengthening powers of Holy Communion. From such activity flow fruits of service as good works (Matt. 5:16; Eph. 5:9; Gal. 5:22–23); manifold spiritual gifts, especially the gift of love (1 Corinthians 12; Rom. 12:3–8); the mutual conversation and consolation of the saints; and witness to the world.[30] But all the gifts that exist

---

28 Vicedom, *Mission of God*, 4–5.

29 The Augsburg Confession clearly presents this sequence in placing AC V before AC VII. See Kimme, "Die Kirche und ihre Sendung," 103. This sequence is also suggested in SC II 6 (Kolb-Wengert, 355); LC II 44–45, 51 (Kolb-Wengert, 436–37). That does not exclude the fact that the reading of Scripture also serves as a means, e.g., SD II 50 (Kolb-Wengert, 553), but the emphasis is on hearing. Georg Vicedom: "But where the Lord is, there a visible congregation comes into being and lives not only in the proclamation, but above all in the hearing, which is the prerequisite for the witnessing. The church also lives in the love which through Christ becomes effective in her precisely through the hearing" (*Mission of God*, 86). For testimony to the living voice of the Gospel (*viva vox evangelii*) in the Confessions, see Ap IV 257, 271 (Tappert, 144, 148); Ap VII 28 (Tappert, 173); Ap XI 2 (Tappert, 180); Ap XII 39 (Tappert, 187). Wiebe, "Missionsgedanken in den lutherischen Bekenntnisschriften," 25 n. 15, 53.

30 From the "mutual consolation" (SA III IV, Kolb-Wengert, 319) the argument can be made that "the keys were given to the church, not just to particular persons," as Melanchthon states in Tr 68

within the Church should be arranged in such a way that everything points to unity and the one Spirit (1 Cor. 12:12–30).[31]

Georg Vicedom notes that the Holy Spirit constantly renews and empowers the Church through justification and forgiveness so that it may participate in mission.[32] Thereby the Spirit's work *ad intra* strengthens and prepares the Church for her service in the world: "The church performs the *opera ad intra* in order that it may then perform the *opera ad extra*. It builds itself up in order that it may then extend its bounds. The *opera ad intra* are the means to the *opera ad extra* as the end."[33] Activities within the Church always carry a missionary focus to the world from which new members will enter the fellowship. In the interim period between the resurrection and ascension of our Lord, on the one side, and the return of the Lord, on the other, the Church serves as the instrument of God's mission. The Holy Spirit remains and continues His work with His Church to the final day.[34] But the Church in this age cannot be the place of origin, nor can it be the final goal of the Spirit's work. In light of the Holy Spirit's universal interest in gathering all believers to His glorious kingdom, His work in the Church will come to an end in earthly terms at the Last Day.[35] But until Christ comes in judgment, the goal of the Spirit is always to reach out beyond the boundaries of the Church to the ends of the earth. Parts of the world must still come to the full knowledge of the Lord. The Church is the realization of the kingdom of God and at the same time also an instrument of that kingdom. For this reason, the Church is not a static entity but one that offers herself to be a servant toward the realization of the kingdom.

Mission is thus more than a practical expression of the Church; it lies in the very nature of the Holy Spirit. The mission is not at the disposal of the Church; both are at the disposal of the Spirit. In this way, Church and mission belong together since the survival of the world as well as of

---

(Kolb-Wengert, 341) and where he provides proof for the priesthood of all believers from Matt. 18:18. Melanchthon substantiates his own position with 1 Pet. 2:9: "You are a royal priesthood." However, mutual consolation is not equal to public absolution. Melanchthon is willing to grant the latter only to a Christian in a case of emergency (*casus necessitatis*). Thus mutual consolation in normal circumstances is an activity in which each Christian forgives and consoles his neighbor with the Gospel.

31 For a discussion on charismatic gifts, see Commission on Theology and Church Relations, *Lutheran Church and the Charismatic Movement*. For the Lutheran Confessions, one may add, next to faith and hope, that the gift of love stands out the most; Ap IV 226 (Tappert, 138).

32 Vicedom, *Die Rechtfertigung als gestaltende Kraft der Mission*.

33 Recker, "Concept of the Missio Dei," 194. See also Schulz, "Die Bedeutung des Bekenntnisses der lutherischen Kirche," 3.

34 E.g., LC II 45, 53 (Kolb-Wengert, 436, 438).

35 All Protestants seem to agree on this point; see Berkhof, *Doctrine of the Holy Spirit*, 39. See here Andersen, *Towards a Theology of Mission*, 41. See also LC II 61–62 (Kolb-Wengert, 439); SD II 50 (Kolb-Wengert, 553); Brunstäd, *Theologie der lutherischen Bekenntnisschriften*, 127; Bosch, *Transforming Mission*, 201.

the Church herself is at stake: "The vocation of the Church as missionary Church belongs to its very essence, and that the Church lives only so long as it is engaged in missionary activity."[36] Such an understanding is frequently argued today in literature, and the term "missional" underscores the point.

For His universal mission, the Holy Spirit has thus called the Church to cooperate, or serve as *cooperatrix*.[37] To this end, the Church remains faithful to her missionary task by calling men into the ministry who will engage in the means of the Holy Spirit, that of proclaiming God's Word and celebrating the Sacraments. And in a broader sense, each Christian, as a member of the royal priesthood, assumes special missionary responsibility in God's mission according to his or her own abilities. In this way, the Church becomes the instrument of the ongoing movement of the Holy Spirit through which He speaks and does His work.

Affirming the Holy Spirit as the subject of mission from the cross frees Lutheran mission from seeking ambitious goals of expansion. Rather, the Church concentrates on one major activity: the proclamation of the Gospel, from which the Church as community emerges and lives. The full extent of the Church's mission is the correct preaching of God's Word, and just this constitutes God's mission. For what goes on beyond our preaching activities lies in the hands of the Holy Spirit, including the growth and expansion of the Church. This understanding summarizes the Lutheran contribution to missiology.[38] The Church participates in the mission of the Holy Spirit, but she does not become "co-redeemer" (*co-redemptrix*) in the strict sense. To put it simply: the Church's proclamation of the Word only reaches the ears; she cannot penetrate the heart to bring saving faith, as conversant and as knowledgeable as her preachers may be in the language and culture of the people to whom they minister.

---

36 Andersen, *Towards a Theology of Mission*, 48. See also Brunner, "'Rechtfertigung' heute," 128; Meyer-Roscher, "Die Bedeutung der lutherischen Bekenntnisschriften," 24; Vicedom, *Mission of God*, 130.

37 Peters, *Kommentar zu Luthers Katechismen*, 2:239.

38 This point is repeatedly made in Lutheran contributions to missiology, see Kimme, "Die Kirche und ihre Sendung," 97. Gensichen, *Glaube für die Welt*, 75; *Toward a Theological Basis*, 14; Koester, *Law and Gospel*. This explains Lutheranism's reservation toward the Church Growth Movement, as promoted by McGavran, *Understanding Church Growth*, 24, 93, 147, 159.

CHAPTER TEN

THE PROJECTION OF GOD'S MISSION

THE UNIVERSAL AND SALVIFIC WILL

SEEKING OUT THE TRUE WILL OF GOD

From the sixteenth to the eighteenth century, Protestantism could have backed the doctrine of election or the universal call of the Gospel with a concerted summons to mission. For among the many reasons raised against foreign mission at that time, the doctrine of election, too, was subject to false interpretations that stripped Protestantism of a desire to share the Gospel with unbelievers.

As early Protestantism progressed in years, a battle ensued between private, self-appointed entrepreneurship and the "established church," the politically sanctioned territorial churches. For example, the Austrian nobleman Justinian von Welz (1621–68) promoted overseas mission through his own mission society, the "Jesus-Loving Society." The Lutheran Heinrich Ursinus of Regensburg (1608–67) doubted the sincerity of Welz's argument that this was an opportune time for mission.[1] To be sure, Ursinus and Orthodox Lutherans affirmed the universal claim of the Gospel and the central role of the Church in proclaiming it. The question, however, was whether God had given the Church the important sign of going ahead with that task. Until then, the Church waited.[2] She also entertained a kind of universal theism, which was common during the medieval period. Theism claimed that all nations should know about God the Creator through the revelation in their hearts. Instead, they had turned against God and thus had wasted their chance to hear the Gospel a second time.

---

1 "The *Corpus Evangelicorum* was a loose assembly of state counselors representing the interests of some thirty-nine Protestant kingdoms and territories within the Holy Roman Empire" (Scherer, *Justinian Welz*, 17).

2 Melanchthon, for example, had pointed out that the heathen nations since the time of Adam and Noah had repeatedly received the universal promises of the Gospel. One may read Maurer, "Die Lutherische Kirche und ihre Mission," 197–98; Raupp, *Mission in Quellentexten*, 26–27.

Such complacency seems all the more ironic in view of the possibility that Welz's efforts could have been a sign from God for Ursinus and the others to open the doors for foreign mission.[3] But this episode seems larger than that. It reveals that at various times in her history, segments of the Church have avoided the challenge of reaching out to others. It is undeniably true that God has had prior dealings with the world and that certain events or occasions may avail themselves as opportunities for mission. The Church may then use such moments to respond appropriately. Let us take, for example, the civil war that ravaged Liberia in the 1990s. That event, as gruesome as it was, turned out to be profitable for mission and may from that perspective be seen as a door opened by God for Christians to enter and do mission. When refugees fled to the neighboring countries of Sierra Leone, Ivory Coast, and Ghana, many were trained as preachers. Once peace was restored, the new preachers returned to begin missionary work. Another occasion for growth was the Korean War in the 1950s, during which many Christian U.S. soldiers made important contacts with the indigenous population. When the war was over, missionaries were invited back to that country to begin fruitful work.

Many events in the world have turned out to hold a blessing in disguise. Therefore, the Church in the world must be alert and learn to listen to the events of the times, lest she miss important opportunities to share the Gospel with others.[4] For even in such adverse times, God has not turned His back on His people in this world. He has elected them from eternity and called them in time through His means of grace, in which Gospel certainty resides.[5] He is a God who does not forsake those who have rejected Him, and He points His Church to reach out to the most hardened unbelievers.

THE PROBLEMS WITH DOUBLE PREDESTINATION[6]

The doctrine of election presents undeniable problems for mission. Although it may seem evident that God's salvific will extends to the populations of the entire world, particularistic notions of predestination may prevent Christians from engaging in mission. Such had been the case in England, where mission was greatly contested by what we may call hyper-Calvinism. By the year 1792, William Carey faced Christians who had turned a

---

3   Raupp, *Mission in Quellentexten*, 90; Größel, *Die Mission und die evangelische Kirche*, 89–91; Scherer, *Justinian Welz*, 20.

4   Being a realist, Luther was thankful to God for letting the Germans hear the Gospel that some day may leave them again. Stolle, *Church Comes from All Nations*, 62.

5   FC Ep XI (Kolb-Wengert, 517–20).

6   The remaining portion of this chapter was published in an edited form as the essay "Universalism: The Urgency of Christian Witness," *Missio Apostolica* 14.2 (November 2006): 86–96. Used with permission.

cold shoulder to mission because they had drawn their own conclusions from the doctrine of double predestination. They thought that God had already made up His mind whom He would include in His salvation plan and whom He would not. In this way of thinking, the Church was utterly powerless to effect conversion over against God's sovereign will. If God had made up His mind about the fate of people before the creation of the world, then the Church had no reason to interfere with mission by preaching the Gospel. Carey encountered this attitude and describes it in *An Enquiry into the Obligation of Christians to Use Means for the Conversion of the Heathens*: "It seems as if many thought . . . that if God intends the salvation of the heathen, he will some way or other bring them to the gospel, or the gospel to them. It is thus that multitudes sit at ease, and give themselves no concern about the far greater part of their fellow-sinners, who to this day, are lost in ignorance and idolatry."[7] According to Carey, the Church should broaden her scope for the world at large since the kingdom of Christ and the Gospel are there for all people. Even if the Lord has allotted a specific time for the fulfillment of His own purpose, it does not excuse Christians from proclaiming this kingdom to the world.[8]

Thankfully, not all theologians shared the sense of complacency and lack of initiative toward mission. Even John Calvin (1509–64), the father of double predestination, entertained the need for mission to the heathen.[9] Calvin's justification for mission may be summarized as follows: Since nobody knows who does and who does not belong to the number of the elect (*numerus praedestinatorum*), the Church is to take on the attitude of desiring that all be saved. And so Christians should diligently assume the task of sharing the salutary Gospel, even if it must finally be left to God to bring the Gospel to fruition among those whom He has chosen and predestined.[10]

The doctrine of double predestination in the Calvinist sense presents a real problem for mission. Indeed, Christians could complacently leave everything to God since it is impossible to change what God has decided already from eternity.[11] Strict Calvinism cannot supply the confidence or motivation for evangelism. As one scholar noted: "If they [the Calvinists] are consistent with their theology, they cannot say to every person they

---

7 Winter and Hawthorne, *Perspectives on the World Christian Movement*, 228.

8 Neill, *History of Christian Missions*, 222.

9 *Institutio Christianae Religiones*, vol. 2/III, 21, 5 (p. 133): "Non enim pari conditione creantur omnes; sed aliis vita aeterna, aliis damnatio aeterna praeordinatur."

10 *Institutio Religionis*, 1559, Book III, 711.

11 Bosch, *Transforming Mission*, 258.

meet, 'God loves you' or 'Jesus died for you,' because the person they are talking to may not be one of God's elect."[12]

William Carey contested just this sort of mind-set that had paralyzed mission. In particular, he realized that there is an important link between what we may call God's eternal decree and the believer's participation in that divine plan. Thus Carey exhorted: "Expect great things from God; attempt great things for God." God elects, and the Church lets herself be used as an instrument for mission, instead of speculating on who are the elect or when the time will be for God to intervene for His chosen to hear the Gospel. Christians should actively proclaim the Gospel of God, who truly intends to have all come to the knowledge of the truth in Jesus Christ.

One question still demands theological clarification: Why should the Church even take on the task of proclamation when the Lord from eternity has already passed His decree of election? Although Lutherans do not accept double predestination, no one among them would deny that God's election has already taken place. However, as we affirm the existence of God's election, we should avoid two errors. First, we should not look at the proclamation of the Gospel as a mere incidental action that in no way is associated with election since the fate of all humans has already been sealed before creation. Such thinking is inimical to mission, for it fails to accept the Word of God as the vehicle of God's grace. Second, we should not place all our confidence in our own ability and think that somehow our efforts influence God's will. In that case, we would believe that God makes a decision over whom He saves not on the basis of His sovereignty but on what we seek to accomplish.

Double predestination can generate two basic approaches: the affirmative and the emphatically negative. Both are skewed against the biblical witness as it is given in FC XI. One is a rigid doctrine of election to salvation for some and a corresponding rejection of others, while the other is a synergistic mind-set that holds the effectiveness of mission to be due completely to the Church's efforts. As we shall see below, neither of these positions gives full justice to the true nature of the mission of the Church. The answer lies somewhere in the middle, between the two extremes.

BRINGING CHRIST INTO THE EQUATION

Jesus Christ is the answer to the questions presented by predestination. God elects people from eternity, yes, but only through the person and work of Christ. Lesslie Newbigin observes: "We surely go far astray if we begin from a doctrine of divine decrees based on an abstract concept of divine

---

12 Boyd and Eddy, *Across the Spectrum*, 143.

omnipotence. We have to take as our starting point, and as the controlling reality for all our thinking on this as on every theological topic, what God has actually done in Jesus Christ."[13] To be sure, salvation for the children of God rests very much in His eternal decree before the foundation of the world. But, by bringing Christ into consideration and making Him the one through whom God elects, much light is shed on the very nature of God, who does the electing: "He predestined us for adoption through Jesus Christ, according to the purpose of His will" (Eph. 1:5). Scripture reveals that the divine election is one of grace and goodwill through Christ toward all men, not one of divine secrecy and capriciousness to benefit only a few. Thus it would be foolish to draw egotistical conclusions and thereby consider others who are currently in unbelief to be outside the benefits of divine election. Scripture testifies throughout that all people should come to Christ and that He will never thrust them away from Himself (John 6:37). Because of Christ, eternal election gives us all the more reason not to speculate on the secret and eternal counsels of God and to concentrate instead on getting the Gospel out to as many unbelievers as possible. The Church should spend its energies emphasizing the love of God in Christ for all people and His desire for their salvation.

Complexity surfaces when one considers particularity in the doctrine of election. It is true that God's will is one of sheer grace by which He desires to save all, but He has decided to elect before time, in Christ, a chosen people. That is to say, God did not merely prepare His salvation plan in general, but He did graciously consider His elect before all time to be saved through Jesus Christ, and their names are written in the book of life (Rev. 20:15). So there is a measure of particularity in the doctrine of election. Christians ought not speculate on the question that has been reduced to the following formula: "Why some and not others?" This appears in Latin as *cur alii, non alii* and also as *cur alii, prae aliis* ("Why some in preference to others?"). By such speculation Christians seek to encounter the unknown or hidden mind of God, which humans will never be able to discover. This speculation has indeed led to numerous theories that try to go beyond what Christianity and humanity can answer about God. The Lutheran Confessions provide a much-needed corrective to such speculation:

> Therefore, if people wish to be saved, they should not concern themselves
> with thoughts about the secret counsel of God—whether they are chosen
> and preordained for eternal life—Rather, they should listen to Christ . . .
> For he testifies to all people without distinction that God wills all people

---

13 Newbigin, *Gospel in a Pluralist Society*, 86. One may also see the Confessions: FC Ep XI 13 and SD XI 87 (Kolb-Wengert, 518, 654).

who are burdened and weighed down with sins to come to him, so that they may be given rest and be saved [Matt. 11:28].[14]

Turning to God's Call through the Gospel

The Lutheran Confessions admonish us not to engage in abstract speculation but to find assurance of our salvation by turning to the revealed Word of God, to our Baptism, and to the visible means of grace. In these places sinners receive the assurance that they have been called by the Gospel and so purchased and won by the atoning sacrifice. Indeed, the Word of God not only assures us of our salvation but actually brings about our election from eternity into time. God's Word, then, does the electing, and this fact has great consequence for every Christian. Every Christian, yes, every human being in this world, is invited to listen to the words of Christ and take comfort and pleasure in the Shepherd's voice calling him or her to salvation. Here is a glorious affirmation, a universal motive for mission. The Church may declare the love of God to all so that every human being will hear the inviting words of Christ and trust them.

All people in this world must hear the Gospel so that each person may equally believe that this call is meant for him or her. It is true that Christians may see themselves as the *beati possidentes* ("blessed possessors"), but not as those who selfishly guard the gift by denying others the possibility of hearing the Gospel.[15] This universal and salvific will of God, as revealed in the proclamation of the Gospel (Eph. 1:9–10; Rom. 8:29–30), thus embraces the dominical command to proclaim repentance and the promise of the Gospel to all people (Luke 24:47).[16]

The Universal Call, Not Universalism

By now it should be evident that the doctrine of election connects the thought of an eternal adoption of God's children in Christ before time with the universal salvific will of God that is made manifest in time through a conscious proclamation of the Gospel. Although God knows and has determined for every believer the time and hour of his calling and conversion,

---

14 SD XI 65 (Kolb-Wengert, 650); SD XI 66 (Kolb-Wengert, 651); SD XI 33–37 (Kolb-Wengert, 646).

15 "To be chosen, to be elect in Christ Jesus, and there is no other election, means to be incorporated into his mission to the world, to be the bearer of God's saving purpose for this whole world, to the sign and the agent and the first fruit of his blessed kingdom which is for all" (Newbigin, *Gospel in a Pluralist Society*, 87).

16 SD XI 28, 70 (Kolb-Wengert, 645, 651).

Scripture and the Lutheran Confessions lay out the divine salvation plan within history (Ezek. 33:11; John 3:16; 1 Cor. 1:21).[17]

In this regard, however, we must avoid one dangerous fallacy that has repeatedly plagued the Church. We could conclude that if God wills all to be saved, then all will in the end be infallibly saved. In this way, the universal and salvific will of God is made a *fait accompli* for all mankind, which all too readily dismisses the thought that there will be a negative outcome for those who reject God's Word. Such thinking provides another impediment to mission, at least the activity of proclaiming the Gospel to all.

Universalism bases its speculation upon the final outcome of Christ's second coming (eschatology). Some have speculated that there will be a "time for restoring all things" (known as ἀποκαταστάσεως πάντων, Acts 3:21).[18] Known supporters of this position have been the Alexandrinian theologian Origen and the twentieth-century theologian from Basel, Karl Barth. The idea of a general pardon is not entirely alien to Scripture—that is, at first glance. Supporters of the universal pardon typically point to the many places in Scripture where that word "all" occurs. In Romans 5, for example, Paul states that Adam's trespass led to the condemnation of all, but the act of Jesus Christ brings acquittal and life to *all* men. The eleventh chapter of Romans (Rom. 11:32) apparently ends with the universal claim that "God has consigned all to disobedience, that He may have mercy on all." In Ephesians 2, Paul states that Christ was sacrificed on the cross to reconcile the world to Himself and restore peace between God and the world. Finally, in 1 Timothy 2, Paul points out that God desires "all people to be saved and to come to the knowledge of the truth" (v. 4).

Supporters of the universal restoration of all things use such scriptural evidence to conclude that whatever God desires, He will also seek to accomplish. All pain and suffering will come to an end through the person of Jesus Christ. To say anything contrary would limit His almighty power and the universal implication of Christ's death and resurrection. Obviously, this

---

17 Here consider the Formula of Concord: "It is not God's will that any are damned but that all turn to him and be saved . . . Therefore, in his immeasurable goodness and mercy God provides for the public proclamation of his divine, eternal law and the wondrous counsel of our redemption, the holy gospel of his eternal Son, our only Savior Jesus Christ, which alone can save. By means of this proclamation he gathers an everlasting church from humankind, and he effects in human hearts true repentance and knowledge of sin and true faith in the Son of God, Jesus Christ. God wants to call human beings to eternal salvation, to draw them to himself, to convert them, to give them new birth, and to sanctify them through these means, and in no other way than through his holy Word (which people hear proclaimed or read) and though the sacraments" (SD II 49–50 [Kolb-Wengert, 553]; SD XI 23, 56 [Kolb-Wengert, 644, 649]).

18 This term occurs only once in Scripture, in Acts 3:21. But whether Peter is actually including in his statement the restoration of all things in God as a general pardon for all people is questionable. Those theologians who think it does have added this meaning to the text. The Augsburg Confession, however, explicitly rejects this position: AC XVII 4 (Kolb-Wengert, 51).

position, as Karl Barth holds it, completely restructures the Reformed doctrine of election. What had been an "either/or" has now become a "both/
and." Christ returned to His Father, but one day He will unite all humanity
in His person. This "all" includes not only those who have come to true
faith but also those who have no knowledge of the truth or have rejected it
because of their sinfulness. The final triumph will be the general pardon of
all humanity, regardless of who they are.

In a way, it seems as if universalism of this kind is more logical then
double predestination because it takes the consequences of Christ's work to
its fullest potential. But this version of universalism has troubled Lutheran
theologians. In fact, it concerned Adolf Köberle so much that he and others
decided to visit the aging Karl Barth at his home in Basel to confront him
with their concern over his doctrine. They rightly argued that Barth's universalism was a denial of conversion and of rebirth brought about by the
mission of the Church. Unfortunately, the outcome of Köberle's visit has not
been disclosed.[19] In his *Dogmatics*, however, Karl Barth answers the question by making mission merely an activity that announces or affirms one's
pre-Christian state rather than actually calling one out of sin to repentance
and conversion.[20]

There is a further strain of universalism that may be considered more
radical than the one just discussed, since it omits Christ entirely in the argument. Such Christless universalism takes a theocentric or theistic approach
and thereby emphasizes a universal salvific will of God that ignores the
cross of Christ. Proponents of this view assert the salvific will of God as
universal, but they reject the thought that the effects of this divine will
can be certified only through Jesus Christ. The Roman Catholic theologian Paul Knitter has pushed to their extreme the statements of Vatican II
concerning this matter, which were influenced by Karl Rahner.[21] Knitter
represents a plethora of scholars who have abandoned the uniqueness of
Christ in the scheme of divine salvation:

> Can we be so certain that God's salvific will, as expressed in Jesus Christ,
> will never make use of such pre-Christian forms of mediation? And if we

---

19 Köberle, *Universalismus der Christlichen Botschaft*, 81.

20 "We must first maintain that even mission to the heathen, and they particularly, can be pursued
    meaningfully only on the presupposition of the clear promise and firm belief that everything
    which was needed for the salvation of all . . . has already taken place . . . Thus the task of mission
    can consist only in announcing this to them" (Barth, *Church Dogmatics* 4, 3/2, p. 874). See also
    Scott, *Barth's Theology of Mission*, 30.

21 The encyclicals *Lumen Gentium* and *Nostra Aetate* of Vatican II state that there is a spark of
    knowledge among people in the world that attains truth and salvation outside Christ. It seems
    that this version has been somewhat corrected, if not partially withdrawn, by the papal encycli-
    cal *Dominus Jesus* (2000). But it is doubtful whether Roman Catholic theology can close its
    doors entirely to the possibility of salvation outside the church, particularly in view of its moral
    theology. One may see here Schulz, "Lutheran Response," 5–8.

do deny this, are we not only denying what, humanly speaking, seems to be a "logical" expression of this will but also the freedom and omnipotence of God?—To avoid misunderstanding: by this we are not arguing that the religions must be or always are "ways of salvation" but only that we cannot exclude the possibility—or the probability of them being instruments of God's salvific will.[22]

Those who speculate about the final destiny of the unevangelized debate the probability or possibility of salvation outside Christ. In many circles these speculations over the destiny of the unevangelized have led to a full endorsement of salvation outside of Christ and a complete equation of all belief systems with that of Christianity.[23] Aside from their lack of support for mission, these assertions have abandoned Scripture. The Scriptures maintain that there is no salvation apart from Christ (John 14:6; Mark 1:15; John 6:40; John 3:16). God the Father has decreed "in his eternal counsel that he would save no one except those who acknowledge his Son and truly believe in him" (Rom. 11:32; 1 Tim. 2:4; Ezek. 33:11; 18:23).[24] The natural desire of man to save himself outside of Christ by his own merits is entirely dismissed. God's election is an act of grace through Christ, and God in Christ alone is given full credit for it. For nineteenth-century Lutheranism in North America, the dismissal of synergism in election also included faith itself insofar as an individual's faith is not part of the basis upon which God elects (*intuitu fidei*). Rather, faith is the result, not the basis, of election. So much did Lutherans fear that faith itself could otherwise be argued as a "work"—as was and is indeed the case in the context of American Arminianism.[25]

AFFIRMING MISSION

Mission is thus the activity by which God puts His salvific intentions into practice. That is, God intentionally uses His Word and Sacraments as signs and testimonies of His will toward man, "intended to awaken and confirm faith in those who use them."[26] Thus God does not forego these means but uses them to bring about His work of salvation.

---

22 Knitter, *Towards a Protestant Theology of Religions*, 222.

23 Consider the survey in Sanders, *No Other Name*.

24 FC Ep XI 13 (Kolb-Wengert, 518).

25 Boyd and Eddy, *Across the Spectrum*, 143. One may verify the above with the statements in SD XI 5, 23, 23, 43 (Kolb-Wengert, 644, 648).

26 AC XIII 1 (Kolb-Wengert, 47); Ap XIII 1 (Kolb-Wengert, 219). "God permits His will to be carried out through the sacraments. They are not human acts of confession, or symbols of something that once took place; they are faith-creating divine means" (Fagerberg, *New Look at the Lutheran Confessions*, 170). See also SD XI 27 (and 29) (Kolb-Wengert, 645).

We affirm that mission is a kerygmatic activity of the Church. For God effects faith through the Gospel, not beyond or apart from it (Rom. 10:14). Here again, scholars often question whether God can and will also save those who have not yet encountered Christ through the means of grace. The same scholars present such figures as Job or Cornelius with whom God apparently worked outside of His normal ways.[27] Yet even Job knows of a Redeemer (Job 19:25), and Cornelius received the Spirit when Peter preached the Gospel, not when the angel appeared (Acts 10:3, 44). Such examples are admittedly rare and thus are a testimony to God's direct special revelation to man. Due to such rarity and to the fact that the Gospel proclamation gives context to such events, Lutheran theology insists on the normal arrangement by which God calls believers to faith, and it dismisses circumstances outside of such normal arrangements. To suggest otherwise would mean that God would contradict Himself and would undermine and destroy the assurance and promise He has given with His Word.[28]

THE NEGATIVE OUTCOME

We should add one additional aspect in our treatment of election, since it still remains unresolved. In view of God's unrestricted intent to save mankind, how should we then categorize the traditional concept of eternal damnation and punishment? If we attribute it to God, does that contradict our understanding of Him as loving and gracious?

The answer to that question lies not so much with God but with anthropology. At the beginning of this chapter, I explained how Lutheran Orthodoxy dismissed any plea of innocence for the nations outside of Christ. Lutherans argued that the nations had all become guilty before God for having hardened themselves to the promises of Christ. Indeed, the hamartological motive places all people alike under the curse of sin. A proper missiology cannot abandon this sinful self-hardening, and it is clear

---

27 See for example, Smith, "Religions and the Bible," 9–29.

28 SD XI 39 (Kolb-Wengert, 647). The passage in SD IX 76 (Kolb-Wengert, 652) observes that the means of grace constitute the "normal arrangement": "But the Father does not intend to draw us apart from means. Instead, he has preordained his Word and sacraments as the regular means and instruments for drawing people to himself. It is not the will of either the Father or the Son that people not hear the proclamation of his Word or have contempt for it, nor should they expect to be drawn by the Father apart from Word and sacrament. According to his normal arrangement, the Father draws people by the power of His Holy Spirit through the hearing of his holy, divine Word." The text does not specify the situation that would fall outside of the "normal arrangement." It could most likely be the thought of a direct calling from God—the triune God, nonetheless—apart from the means, as Scripture rarely illustrates. The occurrences of such an extraordinary arrangement are rare, however, and give no cause to abandon the "normal arrangement" for any kind of universalism. Any other opinion on this matter would constitute an accusation against God for contradicting Himself: "For this would be to ascribe to God contradictory wills" (SD XI 35, Kolb-Wengert, 646).

that Scripture places on all people apart from Christ a personal guilt for despising or rejecting the saving intentions of the Lord (Rom. 3:24).

Consider, for example, the parable of the great banquet (Luke 14:15–24): "Come, for everything is now ready." Sadly, many guests turn down the king's invitation. Each presents a different excuse for not coming. Thus the parable ends with these harsh words: "For I tell you, none of those men who were invited shall taste my banquet" (Luke 14:24).

A similar point is made in the parable of the ten virgins (Matt. 25:1–14). While all ten virgins plan to participate at the wedding feast, not all are permitted to enter with the bridegroom. Remaining behind closed doors, they beg in vain for admission. In the same chapter, Matthew describes the coming of the Son of Man, who sits on a glorious throne with all nations gathered before Him (Matt. 25:31–46). Just as a shepherd would separate sheep from goats, so also all people are placed to the left and right hand of Christ, the almighty Ruler. To those on His right Christ says: "Come, you who are blessed by My Father, inherit the kingdom prepared for you from the foundation of the world" (Matt. 25:34), and to those on the left He passes the crushing sentence: "Depart from Me, you cursed, into the eternal fire prepared for the devil and his angels" (Matt. 25:41).

The rich man described in Luke 16 eventually ends up in the place of torment. He does not find himself in that place because he was wealthy; instead, he had wasted his life, forgetting to take time to help the poor man who lay in front of the door of his house. Now the wealthy man suffers great pain in the flame and begs that the poor man may cool his tongue. Unfortunately, he cannot cross the rift that divides him from the water of life.

The negative outcomes are a result of what we are told in Matt. 12:31, that "every sin and blasphemy will be forgiven people, but the blasphemy against the Spirit will not be forgiven." The sin against the Holy Spirit is not a moral transgression but entails a conscious decision on the part of man not to have anything to do with the salvation found in Jesus Christ. The blasphemy against the Spirit represents, therefore, the hardened and persistent rejection of the Gospel.

Against universalism, the Lutheran Church has always affirmed the doctrine of damnation against unbelief. Thus the Augsburg Confession in both Articles II and XVII affirms an eternal punishment, the eternal wrath of God, that will pass over all "who are not born again through baptism and the Holy Spirit."[29] But the negative outcome is hardly the result of God decreeing from eternity who will and who will not be saved (double predestination). The blame for damnation rests squarely on the shoulders of

---

29 AC II 3 (Kolb-Wengert, 39).

unbelieving man for his decision against God.[30] In a way, the doctrine of election is structured asymmetrically: God only elects to salvation, whereas man himself assumes responsibility for damnation. It is thus evident that the Lutheran doctrine of election does not follow the concept of double predestination, for that would turn God into an unpredictable and capricious being. Instead, Lutheranism affirms both the scriptural statements on universal grace and that God's nature is love.[31]

The practical result of this teaching is that man can reject Christ's offer to be reconciled in Him out of his free will. Nobody is irresistibly coaxed into turning against God. On the other hand, nobody can earn his salvation; he can only lose it. This explains the Lord's tears over Jerusalem: "O Jerusalem, Jerusalem, the city that kills the prophets and stones those who are sent to it! How often would I have gathered your children together as a hen gathers her brood under her wings, and you would not!" (Luke 13:34). Even the hardening of Pharaoh's heart is not attributed to the sole action of God. In Exodus 7–9, God commands Moses to proclaim repeatedly to Pharaoh; only after Pharaoh's repeated rejection of that proclamation does God proceed from the fact that He hardened Pharaoh's heart (Exodus 10). God's hardening was not the ultimate goal; Pharaoh had legitimate opportunities to avoid that. The actions of God to send His Word to one person and to harden someone else are explicable only in light of man's refusal to hear the Word. This refusal to hear the Gospel explains God's withdrawal of His intent to save, leaving only the alternative of damnation.[32]

In this discussion on election, I have maintained an eschatological orientation vis-à-vis mission. Lutherans do not preach a final pardon of all, nor do they speak of life in only secular terms. A proper mission is set upon bringing the Gospel to those who must inevitably be gathered before the throne of the Lord. Mission calls all to repentance with the appeal, "We implore you on behalf of Christ, be reconciled to God" (1 Cor. 5:20). Such a

---

30 Schlink, *Theology of the Lutheran Confessions*, 290: "Not God's election but the sin of men is the cause of their damnation." Thereby the Confessions do not follow the strong deterministic tones of Luther's *Bondage of the Will* (see, e.g., AE 33:140), as Friedrich Mildenberger claims in *Theologie der lutherischen Bekenntnisschriften*, 157.

31 SD XI 67 (Kolb-Wengert, 651); Pöhlmann, *Abriß der Dogmatik*, 260. In maintaining this asymmetry and infralapsarian aspect of the doctrine of predestination, the Confessions reject in content but not by name Calvin's double predestination, e.g., Ep 19 (Kolb-Wengert, 519). The example in AC XIX (Kolb-Wengert, 52–53) shows that the phrase "*non adiuvante Deo*" (German: "As soon as God withdrew his hand . . ." Latin: "Since it was not assisted by God . . .") was omitted by Melanchthon in Ap XIX 1 (Kolb-Wengert, 235) to avoid a possible misinterpretation, namely, making God responsible for the cause of sin. See Schlink, *Theology of the Lutheran Confessions*, 290.

32 SD XI 57 (Kolb-Wengert, 649); Ep XI 12 (Kolb-Wengert, 516). In this connection, we may point out that God does not only base His rejection on original sin in general, but to the actual offenses against the Gospel that they hear and against the Holy Spirit's working through the Gospel, e.g., SD XI 40–42, 58–62 (Kolb-Wengert, 647, 649–50).

perspective imbues mission with an evangelistic zeal. Donald McGavran's famous question "Will Uppsala Betray the Two Billion (Unbelievers)?" reflects his concern that the motive and, with it, the evangelistic cutting edge has been abandoned by major parts of Christianity.[33]

UNIVERSAL MOTIVE

The doctrine of election taxes man's intellectual abilities. On account of the theological complexities of election, we can only bow in obedience to Christ's authority by engaging in mission; mission represents the activity of the Church that best affirms God's universal and salvific will.[34] We have already pointed out that Christianity comprises only 34 percent of the world's population, and that by the year 2050 it will most likely remain at that level. Such statistics, coupled with the doctrine of election, brings about a sense of divine urgency and intention. All missionary endeavor should be seen not merely as an extended arm of the Church, but as an instrument of God's saving and loving desire to embrace the whole world. As God's positive will for fellowship and union with man motivated Him to send His Son to the cross, so, too, God's salvific will motivates Him to take the Church into His service. Through the activities of His preached and sacramental Word, God wishes to bring the entire world into His loving fellowship.

---

33 Yates, *Christian Mission in the Twentieth Century*, 197.

34 Kähler, "Evangelisation der Welt—Gottes Wille," 101.

PART III

The Church, Her Task and Context

CHAPTER ELEVEN

MISSION AND THE WORD OF GOD

EVANGELISM AND MISSION

An important component of the Church's mission is her evangelistic activity. The Church commits herself to proclaiming the Gospel to an audience that has not yet come into contact with the biblical message of salvation. In fact, this evangelistic activity comprises the core of mission itself. Many scholars, however, would point out that mission deals with a far broader spectrum of activities than mere evangelism.[1] Examples of activities allied to evangelism in mission include social responsibilities through diaconal ministry and supporting the translation of the Bible and other Christian literature. In fact, the reason for keeping the term "mission" is that we wish to incorporate a far greater list of activities than evangelism itself. But evangelism should be considered the essence of mission according to the scriptural evidence already noted in the second chapter. Evangelism refers to the activity presented by the Greek term εὐαγγέλιον ("Gospel, Good News"), and the verb εὐαγγελίζειν ("to declare the Good News") denotes the activity of sharing the Gospel with others. The additional terms κήρυγμα ("proclamation") or μαρτυρία ("testimony, witness") likewise indicate the task of sharing the Gospel with people outside of Christianity. Scripture thus repeatedly draws attention to a cluster of similar expressions such as εὐαγγελίζειν, κηρύσσειν, or μαρτύρειν, which together have to do with the activity of sharing the Gospel.

The evangelistic or kerygmatic activity of the Church is designed to bring the Good News of Jesus Christ to those who have not yet come into contact with it. The missiologist Hans-Werner Gensichen states that mission has as its essential purpose and aim "to bring all people the message of universal reconciliation."[2] In staking our claim on this core aspect of mission,

---

1   For the role of evangelism in mission, see Bosch, *Transforming Mission*, 411–20, and Scherer, *Gospel, Church and Kingdom*, 182–84.

2   Gensichen, *Glaube für die Welt*, 75. Kirk, *What Is Mission?* 56.

we align ourselves with the divine intention of Scripture, which is to seek out the lost and offer salvation (John 3:17).

Quite a few have argued, however, that evangelism and mission target two distinct groups. Those involved in mission seek to convert and baptize the unbeliever, whereas evangelism addresses the already baptized person who may have become an apostate or a nominal Christian. Such apostate or nominal Christians have encountered the message of the Gospel before, and the preacher may expect to find extant knowledge about the Church and her doctrine as he engages in proclaiming the Gospel. That cannot be said for the unbaptized hearers that missionaries have traditionally encountered. Both audiences, however, are distant from the Church, and for that reason mission and evangelism share the common goal of assimilating or re-assimilating them into the Church. In view of the goal, there is no distinction between mission and evangelism. All of the unchurched and the lapsed must come to faith in Jesus Christ, even if one would expect the preacher to adjust the content of the proclamation in view of the audience.

THE MESSAGE AS METANARRATIVE

What exactly does it mean when a preacher has to "adjust the message" to an audience? Part of that meaning involves the source of the message in Scripture and part of it involves the context of the hearers. Would it imply, however, that a message could change so much that after a while its content hardly resembles the message from the original source? To use an illustration, a judge pronounces an imprisoned thief who is absent free. The thief hears that message through a series of intermediate messengers a few hours later, but something like the children's game of "telephone" or its German version, "*stille Post*," the message hardly resembles the original pardon of the judge.

The Gospel, too, is transmitted from one generation to the next through the preaching and witnessing activities of Christians. Fortunately, however, what they say is measured against Scripture where the content of the Gospel is written down. Scripture presents the Gospel as a kind of metanarrative, a comprehensive explanation of historical experience or knowledge that transcends time and geographic space and presents all people the same message that Christ is their Savior. To put it differently, the Second Article of the Apostles' Creed, which contains the life and ministry of Christ, is inextricably linked to the Third Article, which presents the Church and her proclamation. The Second Article about Jesus Christ, which speaks of our pardon in Jesus Christ, serves as the backbone to all preaching; it must reach the hearer through a clear and unchanged delivery system of proclamation and witness. In this way, three elements relate to missionary proclamation: the event of the cross, the proclamation of the cross, and the ear and faith of the believer.[3] Luther combines the three elements: "Neither you nor I could ever know anything about Christ, or believe in him and receive him as Lord, unless these were offered to us and bestowed on our hearts through the preaching of the gospel by the Holy Spirit."[4]

Theologians, however, have never shied away from discussing the relation of these three elements in missionary proclamation. In other words, how the content of the message relates to its source on the one side and to the audience on the other are important components of the mission enterprise. Neo-orthodoxy centralized theology around the proclamation (*kerygma*) of Jesus Christ (Rom. 16:25). Influential theologians such as Karl Barth (1886–1968) and Rudolf Bultmann (1884–1976) stand as formative figures for that movement. Such missiologists as Hendrik Kraemer[5] and Walter Holsten stood under the influence of Barth and Bultmann and fashioned their missiology around the *kerygma*.[6] Between the two world wars, Kraemer, siding mostly with Barth, highlighted the uniqueness of the Christian message against what is taught and believed in other religions. In true Barthian fashion, Kraemer dismissed all preexistent notions about God apart from the preaching of the cross. Kraemer supposed that all non-Christians stand outside of the revelation in Christ and practice their beliefs under false pretenses. For this reason, God holds them accountable for their wrongdoing. Kraemer still wanted to leave room for an experience of God and His revelation in the non-Christian world, but he declined any thoughts that the Gospel was merely a "fulfillment" of such erroneous conceptions. Christ is so "antagonistic to all human religious aspirations" that only through the Gospel and the acts of conversion and regeneration does God bring about His fulfillment of human aspirations.[7]

Holsten, on the other hand, followed Bultmann's kerygmatic theology more closely and in so doing divorced the content of the Gospel from the source, the historic event of the cross.[8] The danger of Bultmann's kerygmatic theology all along was that the historic events of the cross and the

---

3   Brunner, "Das Heil und das Amt," 296. Beyerhaus, "Christi Heilsangebot durch seine Gesandten," 62. Thomasius, *Das Bekenntnis der evangelisch-lutherischen Kirche*, 10–11.

4   LC II 38 (Kolb-Wengert, 436).

5   Kraemer, *Christian Message in a Non-Christian World*. A German contribution sharing similar views and still a valuable source for discussion is Wyder, *Die Heidenpredigt*.

6   Holsten, *Das Kerygma und der Mensch*, 44.

7   Kraemer, *Christian Message in a Non-Christian World*, 123–24; Yates, *Christian Mission in the Twentieth Century*, 113.

8   Holsten would thus state: "Das Kerygma [hat] das entscheidende Handeln Gottes in Christus zum Gegenstand und zur Ursache" (*Das Kerygma und der Mensch*, 44). See Andersen, "Die kerygmatische Begründung," 29–37. Also Althaus, *Fact and Faith in the Kerygma of Today*, 47–55.

resurrection become mythic and legendary expressions of the later post-Easter community. The hermeneutic of stripping the Christian message from its historic source and making all such accounts legendary and mythic expressions is called *demythologizing*. Thus Bultmann argued: "The world-view of the Scripture is mythological and is therefore unacceptable to modern man whose thinking has been shaped by science and is therefore no longer mythical . . . [Today] nobody reckons with direct intervention by transcendent powers."[9] As a result, all attention shifted to the proclaimed word, the *kerygma*, and to the existential reality of the believer. For what really matters is that the *kerygma* is preached in such a way that it makes sense to those who hear it, even if what it says corresponds little to the actual historic facts of crucifixion and resurrection. The modern world-view becomes the criterion, and the Christian message should not say anything that is in contradiction with it.

Much of theology and missiology still suffers from various forms of the modern deconstruction of Scripture. Yet the events of Christ's life cannot stand or fall simply because someone's faith or unbelief holds them to be true or not. The event of Christ's death and resurrection transcends every subjective approach and should be seen independently as realities in and by themselves.

We may be inclined to dismiss such radical existentialism as a passing scholarly fad of yesteryear that occupied generations of theologians before us. But today, decades later, these discussions still continue in various guises in the era of postmodernism.[10] Now, however, the interest has shifted slightly. It is not so much the denial of Jesus' death and resurrection as figments to the critical mind, but rather whether they should qualify as a metanarrative that transcends locality and subjectivity.[11] The postmodern trend argues against the objectivity of Scripture and a meaning in discourse that lets Scripture speak plainly for itself. Postmodernism argues instead that Scripture's value depends greatly on a reader's own subjective opinion.

---

9 Bultmann, *Jesus Christ and Mythology*, 36. Bultmann also made this well-known observation: "It is impossible to use electric light and the wireless and to avail ourselves of modern medical and surgical discoveries, and at the same time to believe in the New Testament world of spirits and miracles" ("New Testament and Mythology," 5). This debate has returned with the recent discussion between William Lane and Gerd Lüdemann. One may see Copan and Tacelli, *Jesus' Resurrection*.

10 Keegan, *Interpreting the Bible*, 81. There is renewed interest among reader-response critics for the existential philosophy of Martin Heidegger (and in part also Hans-Georg Gadamer), who significantly influenced Rudolf Bultmann. Bultmann himself had already preempted all discussions about the question of objectivity with the influential essay "Ist voraussetzungslose Exegese möglich?" ("Is Objective Exegesis Possible?"); see Bibliography for publication information.

11 This does not mean that it has been totally abandoned, as can be seen from a recent debate between the controversial theologian Gerd Lüdemann, a professor at the University of Göttingen, and William Lane, a professor at Talbot School of Theology. That debate is recorded in Copan and Tacelli, *Jesus' Resurrection*.

Unsurprisingly, the existential dimension of Bultmann's theology and hermeneutic has not lost its appeal. It has found its way into contemporary debates on the principles of biblical interpretation, that is, the question of semantics and the task of establishing the true meaning of Scripture. Some scholars promoting reader-response criticism claim that the full meaning of literature, including that of the Bible, is uncovered by the reader, and what it says bears little universal meaning beyond the reader's world. For them, God's sacred text contains a multiplicity of meanings, and it is up to the reader to choose from among them.[12] Grenz argues, for example, that there is indeed a danger in postmodernism of compromising God as the normative author of Scripture when postmodernism asserts that Scripture does not provide a single grand narrative that encompasses all peoples and all times.

We are dealing here with a complex field of biblical interpretation and can only say this much for Lutheran hermeneutics: Lutherans guard themselves against a random interpretation and localization of Scripture by affirming the biblical record as a grand and unchanging narrative for all people, whether they live in the fifth or the twenty-first century. But, in order that Scripture may speak that narrative for all people equally, it is necessary to read the text of Scripture with great care in an attempt to understand the historical context and the grammar of the text. The reader must at least attempt to come as close as possible to the actual intention of the author and what he meant.[13] Any method of contextualization or accommodation should not abandon the clear message of Scripture. Scripture and what it says may not be changed to such a degree that it cannot be recognized by anyone standing outside the culture.

THE PRESENCE OF CHRIST
IN THE CHRISTIAN MESSAGE

One important concern of all Christian proclamation is that it connects to the person of Jesus Christ and to the accomplishments of His earthly ministry. We cannot suppose that Christ, after He had commissioned His disciples to "go into the all the world and proclaim the gospel to the whole creation" (Mark 16:15), then parted completely from the very act of preaching the Gospel. To the contrary, we have His own promise: "I am with you always" (Matt. 28:20). He assures the Church of His presence wherever she preaches, teaches, and baptizes. To this day, Christ's person and deeds become the central content of the Gospel wherever preaching takes place.

---

12 Grenz, *Primer on Postmodernism*, 164.
13 Voelz, *What Does This Mean?* 351ff.

The Gospel, as it is preached and heard, is not separated from its foundation, the historic event of Christ's incarnation, death on the cross, and resurrection. These unique events are proclaimed as having brought about the righteousness offered in the Gospel. Such has been the concern of the Lutheran Confessions all along. The Augsburg Confession, for example, highlights in Article III the person of Jesus Christ and what He has done through the historic events of His virgin birth, His crucifixion, death, burial, and resurrection. Only then does the Augustana proceed to Articles IV and V to describe our justification and the means through which our saving faith comes about. Christ and His benefits are not a rationalized idea floating about somewhere, but they are joined to the preaching of the Gospel and must remain inviolate in every message the Church brings to the world.[14]

The Formula of Concord dealt with similar concerns when the theologian Andrew Osiander, a professor at the University of Königsberg, falsely claimed that the Christ brought to the believer is the risen, divine, and exalted Christ; he established no connection to the earthly ministry of Christ as part of the content of the Gospel message as well. In response, the Formula of Concord joins the Gospel and our justification to the historic ministry of Christ and states that our justification hinges on the total Christ (*totus Christus*), the human and divine Christ, and especially on everything He did in His earthly ministry, all that He endured obediently, both passively and actively on earth.[15]

So far, I have argued in favor of a missionary proclamation that preaches the entire Christ and that neither robs the Gospel of its substance nor fails to link it to the actual historic ministry of Christ on earth. Missionary proclamation is a faithful testimony to what Scripture teaches about Christ; it is a doctrinal commitment to Him. If the Church in mission were to withhold any truth from her listeners or "water down" the Gospel message, she would have to deal later on with the disastrous effects of that deficiency when the newly converted attempt to replace that deficiency with traditional or self-constructed tenets. In part, that very situation has led to syncretistic belief systems, an amalgam of Christian and traditional pagan beliefs. No church and no community is immune to that danger. Preachers who are afraid of bringing the whole Christ and the entire Gospel message to their audience

---

14 For example, SD III 57 (Kolb-Wengert, 572): ". . . and is revealed in the gospel." The theologian Edmund Schlink makes the following comment on this point: "The whole Gospel, the divine promise of the forgiveness of sins, and the whole Christ dare not be torn apart. Through the Gospel the sinner is made contemporaneous with the death of Jesus Christ on the cross. By the Gospel he is reconciled, even though the work of reconciliation was already finished in Christ's death on the cross. The reconciliation is not only the basis of justification laid long ago in the historical event, but justification is reconciliation for Christ's sake" (*Theology of the Lutheran Confessions*, 103).

15 For example SD III 15–16 (Kolb-Wengert, 564). Martens, *Die Rechtfertigung des Sünders*, 92.

for whatever reason are held accountable to the Lord Himself, who wants to reach the hearts and minds with the fullness of His words.

At the same time, the total grand narrative of Christ's story should be brought to hearers in their context, language, and mind-set. Here, every proclamation is challenged by context and culture, as we shall discuss below. Where the Christian message is presented either incompletely, that is, not in its fullness, or remains alien to people, then, sadly, listeners will appropriate substitutions from traditional pagan belief systems.[16]

Defining the Kerygmatic Motive

Although the Gospel proclamation is challenged by context and culture, we are not merely left to our own devices in facing that challenge. We can find guidance for it directly in God's Word. Scripture already distinguishes among hearers. Preaching in Acts targets those outside of the Church, the Gentiles (Acts 17:16–21; cf. Gal. 1:16; 2:2). This preaching activity to the Gentiles in particular should stand in the forefront of all mission activities. It addresses all those people who have not yet heard about the living God and Jesus Christ. In contrast to the catechumenate, the preaching to Gentiles is not yet a regular ministry of teaching the basics of the Christian faith. It is the ministry that precedes it—namely, the first encounter between missionary and the Gentiles, where through a short message, the Gentiles hear for the first time the Good News of Jesus Christ and salvation. Such preaching to the Gentiles should be seen as a continuation of Jesus' and the apostles' preaching ministry, and this stands apart from the instruction provided by the Church to those who have already heard the message and have come to faith. Missionary proclamation to the Gentiles ought to consist of a short, concise message containing statements on God's kingdom and salvation in Jesus Christ with the goal to awaken faith in the hearer so that he may turn from his false belief to Jesus Christ. Once this preaching has borne fruit, the missionary will proceed to deeper instruction (*didaskalia*; Matt. 28:20)—namely, into parts of Christian belief such as Baptism and following Christ. This short yet concise proclamation to the Gentiles is truly a specific genre of its own.

We must argue for such a form of onetime and unique missionary proclamation, since we encounter it in Scripture and since it makes sense, theologically speaking, even if today's missionary is predominantly engaged in a teaching ministry to those already committed to the Gospel. Preaching to the Gentiles should remain to this day a form of proclamation that engages people at every level in the Church as she finds herself in situations where

---

16 Nida, *Message and Mission*, 184–88.

people may live next door, yet they live far from the Christian Church and have in fact never heard anything before about Christ. Since Christianity comprises only 33 to 34 percent of the world's population, as noted previously, the task of missionary proclamation should take precedence over other activities of the Church.

Even if missionaries, evangelists, or other workers are involved in tasks such as expressing Christian love through works of mercy, the Church is obligated to pursue missionary proclamation from Scripture and Lutheran theology. This *kerygmatic motive* obligates her to the task of finding ways to seek out the unbelievers in the world.

COMMUNICATION

It has become customary to use the broader term "communication" to describe the total activity of bringing the Gospel message to the world. Communication embraces all kinds of activities of bringing the Word to others, be it proclamation, witness, or nonoral forms of communication. Communication represents a complex linguistic affair that requires one to study the mechanism of encoding and decoding a set of signs between two or three parties: the messenger, the biblical text, and the hearer.

As important as this technical side of proclaiming the Gospel is, one must stress the divine character of such communication; otherwise, the emphasis may fall upon the mere technicality of proclaiming the Gospel. Communication should include or make provision for the fact that God, too, is involved in the communication. Communication has to do with divine address. It is God who speaks to the unbeliever by stepping into his life and completely transforming him from what he has been before. Proclaiming the Gospel is thus more than a cross-cultural event or a mutual dialogue between two individuals from two different religious backgrounds. God looks beyond these particulars and sees a human being standing before Him, irrespective as to whether he is in Beijing or Nairobi. Scripture presents a generic anthropology that all unbelievers share in common despite their own distinctive contexts. Although God uses human agents who speak the Gospel in a multitude of languages to people in many contexts, it is the same God who speaks through the agents with the same goal of reconciliation. It is God Himself who wants to speak and have His voice heard so that those who hear Him may come to faith and serve Him (John 10:16).

Communication as proclamation includes the important theological notion of divine address that questions man's condition and dispenses forgiveness. In a sermon preached at the dedication of the Castle Church in Torgau on October 5, 1544, Luther presents us with the clearest evangelical definition of proclamation and our response to it. He begins his sermon by saying that in worship no one else than "our dear Lord himself may speak to us through his holy Word and we respond to him through prayer and praise."[17] Here, Luther defines proclamation as address and response. God Himself speaks the Word to people, and the appropriate reaction elicited from that divine address is prayer and praise. In fact, God communicates the Gospel to people categorically, that is, there are only two ways the hearer responds: either he or she believes and acknowledges, or he or she refuses and rejects the truth about Jesus Christ (John 14:6). There is no third zone, a grey or an intermediate one, in which listeners finds themselves.

We need to emphasize, however, that the kerygmatic communication does not exclude other activities in sharing the Gospel. The preaching activity of the clergy and ordained missionaries is one among many forms of witness. For these reasons, the terms "communication" and "dialogue" are helpful in pointing to the informal exchanges people have with each other in conveying the Gospel. The famous and much-venerated missionary Ludwig Nommenson (1834–1918) adopted what may be called a kenotic (dialogical) approach to evangelizing. He chose to share the Gospel with the Batak people of Sumatra not only from the confines of the pulpit but also amid the people by posing questions on hope, eternal life, and obedience to the triune God. He coupled such dialogical activity with a personal lifestyle modeled after the life of Christ (Phil. 2:5–11). The underlying principle guiding Nommenson was of understanding the Batak people and they him.[18]

Unfortunately, "dialogue" has become for many a technical term for postmodernism. Today, dialogue pleads often for an open mutual exchange between a Christian and someone of another religion, where both learn from each other without either pursuing the goal of conversion. In other words, Christians must be prepared to relinquish some of their own beliefs and convictions as they dialogue with others. Clearly, today's concept of dialogue follows different principles than those once pursued by Nommenson.

The Church commits herself to the very particular activity of proclamation by requesting ordained pastors and missionaries to step out on behalf of all Christians. But then also all Christians commit themselves to the task of mission by actively and intentionally witnessing to Christ. In a later chapter, we shall discuss the motivation of a Christian to share Christ with others. Here, we say that each Christian ideally becomes so overjoyed at his own salvation that he becomes consciously and intentionally involved in the task of letting the world know Christ. The apostle Paul knew this joy

---

17 AE 51:333.

18 Schreiner, "Legacy of Ingwer Ludwig Nommenson," 81–84.

so much so that it pained him as a burden: "Woe to me if I do not preach the gospel!" (1 Cor. 9:16).

The Goal and Purpose of God's Word

The reformers, Luther especially, placed an extraordinary confidence in the power of the Word of God. If one were to ask Luther and others why the Reformation was successful, such would attribute success to the Word of God and not to human activity. It almost seems as if the reformers supposed that the Word needed no human agent. The preaching of the Word would continue automatically, and there is no stopping its course. Even as one rests at home from all the labors of the day, that Word proceeds outwardly into the world—as Luther would preach in a sermon on Ascension Sunday 1523: "With this message or preaching, it is just as if one throws a stone into the water. It makes waves and circles or wheels around itself, and the waves roll always farther outward. One drives the other until they reach the shore. Even though it is still in the middle, the waves do not rest; instead, the waves continue forward. So it is with the preaching."[19] David Bosch singled out Rom. 1:16 as the biblical text to which the reformers of the sixteenth century gave greatest prominence.[20] But in making the Word of God the means, the reformers received also great opposition, especially from those of the radical Reformation (Spiritualists or Enthusiasts). The Enthusiasts supposed that in binding God to the Word, God's sovereignty is diminished or inhibited. Luther passionately defended his position against such a notion; his unyielding and critical words are applicable today also in view of Pentecostalism, a fast emerging "third force" behind Roman Catholicism and Protestantism.[21] Luther maintains: "In these matters which concern the spoken, external Word, it must be firmly maintained that God gives no one his Spirit or grace apart from the external Word which goes before. We say this to protect ourselves from the enthusiasts, that is, the 'spirits,' who boast that they have the Spirit apart from and before contact with the Word."[22] The Lutheran confidence placed in the Gospel has everything to do with its function and purpose. Faith understands that the Gospel does the work of God as He intended it for this world: "All who want to be saved should listen to this proclamation. For the proclamation and the hearing of God's Word

---

19 Stolle, *Church Comes from All Nations*, 24. That same confidence is also expressed in the Confessions, for example, SD II 55–56 (Kolb-Wengert, 554).

20 Bosch, *Transforming Mission*, 240.

21 David Hesselgrave identifies at least four streams of Pentecostalism: (1) Classical Pentecostalism, (2) Neo-Pentecostalism or Charismatic Pentecostalism, (3) Catholic Charismatics (often designated as Renewal), and (4) the Pentecostal movement within nonwhite indigenous churches throughout the Third World; see Hesselgrave, *Today's Choices for Tomorrow's Mission*, 117.

22 SA III VIII 3 (Kolb-Wengert, 322).

are the Holy Spirit's tools, in, with, and through which he wills to work effectively and convert people to God and within whom he wants to effect both the desire for and the completion of the conversion."[23] We thus preach the Gospel not merely to deliver abstract information to tease the intellectual mind or simply to affirm people in who they are and what they do.[24] God's Word rather becomes a useful and beneficial doctrine or message for all listeners by bringing faith and consolation to consciences plagued by sin and guilt or to those troubled by disturbing events in their life. In short, it is designed—as the two quotations from the Lutheran Confessions above highlight—to bring about conversion. Ultimately, there is no other goal for missionary proclamation than to call all listeners to Jesus Christ. We thus say in reference to Rom. 10:11–13, 17 that the goal of proclamation to the Gentiles is to awaken the justifying faith, in which the believer calls upon the name of His Lord and so is saved. The goal of conversion transcends all other goals of a religious and psychological nature.

Moreover, the Lutheran theology of the Word leaves little room to speculate on the details of just how God awakens faith in hearers. It is enough to know that the Word is comprised of Law and Gospel, and so God is at work in this world through the terrors of the Law and the consolation of the Gospel. Frequently, Law and Gospel are called the "two chief works of God in men."[25] In its chief use, the Law "will terrify the hearts of unrepentant people and bring them to a knowledge of their sins and to repentance." The Gospel is designed to counter the function of the Law by strengthening and comforting those who hear it: "This gospel proclaims that through Christ God forgives all the sins of those who believe the gospel, accepts them for Christ's sake as his children out of sheer grace without any merit of their own, and makes them righteous and saves them."[26] With this division of God's Word into two forms of proclamation, the reformers found a key to interpret Scripture and to unravel the complexity of God's dealing with humanity. Since the Law represents God's righteous and immutable will of what He desires from us, it serves as the norm against which our

---

23 SD II 52 (Kolb-Wengert, 554).

24 "Attentive listening" (*attenti auditores*) and not just an "acute intellect" (*acuti intellectores*) (Ap IV 33, Kolb-Wengert, 125); Brunner, "'Rechtfertigung' heute," 131: "The Gospel is not merely a word of information, instruction, news. The Gospel is a word of authority, a word with the power of performance . . . a giving, creating, saving, decision granting word."

25 Ap XII 53 (Kolb-Wengert, 195). The overriding interest on them being preached, for example, in SD V passim (Kolb-Wengert, 581ff.), does not diminish the fact that Law and Gospel are also used as two hermeneutical principles (SD V 1, Kolb-Wengert, 581) and that reading the Bible is also a means through which the Holy Spirit works faith (e.g., SD II 52, Kolb-Wengert, 554).

26 SD V 24, 25 (Kolb-Wengert, 586); also SD V 20 (Kolb-Wengert, 585). The emphasis on the dialectical relationship between Law and Gospel is particularly evident in Werner Elert's theology; see Elert, *Christian Faith*, 69–100. Content and function should not be separated, see Forde, "Forensic Justification and the Law," 293–94.

inadequate actions are measured: "It shows how man ought to be disposed in his nature, thoughts, words and deeds in order to be pleasing and acceptable to God."[27] For this reason, it is absolutely imperative that the missionary preaches the Law in all its clarity. As he does so, the Law uncovers the failures of every person and pronounces over him God's wrath and judgment. The Law provides listeners with the prospect that Christ will return on the Last Day as judge.

As the proclamation of the Law exposes a hearer's total depravity before God, it is met with stiff opposition. For the Law reproves a person not only for what he does, that is, his actual sins, but it goes far deeper by uncovering a person's being as totally corrupted and deprived of any goodness. All men are conceived and born in sin and they all stand equally under the accusation of the Law (Psalm 51; Rom. 3:23).[28] This inherent corruption since conception can be described by various terms: original, hereditary, or personal sin. Each term expresses the sad reality that through the first sin of Adam, a person lacks the ability to approach God in a positive way and instead possesses the inherent inclination to sin. In the traditional language of the Church, that inclination is called concupiscence (concupiscentia). It is a force or desire that drives man against God and leads him to not "fear, love and trust in God above all things." In fact, Luther realized that the real underlying cause for not keeping every commandment is precisely this lack of being able to "fear, love and trust God."[29]

The cause of a person's contempt for God is his unwillingness to accept the news about his own corrupted state and his inability to comprehend it. Luther states that "hereditary sin is so deep a corruption of nature that reason cannot understand it."[30] Thus upon hearing the Law, the human heart

---

27 SD V 17 (Kolb-Wengert, 584). "The proclamation of the law will terrify the hearts of the unrepentant and bring them to a knowledge of their sin and to repentance" (SD V 24, Kolb-Wengert, 586); Ap IV 9 (Kolb-Wengert, 121): "God's wrath or judgment." Luther describes the Law as a "thunderbolt" that, upon revealing the judgment and wrath of God, will condemn and kill (SA III III 2, Kolb-Wengert, 312).

28 SA III II 4 (Kolb-Wengert, 312): "The foremost office or power of the law is that it reveals inherited sin and its fruits. It shows human beings into what utter depths their nature has fallen and how completely corrupt it is." SD VI 14 (Kolb-Wengert, 589): "the proper function of the law;" see also SD II 17 (Kolb-Wengert, 547); SD V 12, 20, 22 (Kolb-Wengert, 583, 585). All human beings are addressed without any exception, AC II 1 (Kolb-Wengert, 37): "all human beings"; SA III III 1 (Kolb-Wengert, 312): "the whole world," "no human being."

29 Luther makes this point by opening each explanation to the Ten Commandments with the phrase: "We are to fear and love God" (SC I 2, Kolb-Wengert, 350). In the explanation to the First Commandment in the Large Catechism, the root of all religions is precisely the failure of the heart to cling to the true God; LC I 2–3 (Kolb-Wengert, 386). Melanchthon picks up this thought in the Apology: Ap IV 7–8 (Kolb-Wengert, 121).

30 SA III I 3 (Kolb-Wengert, 311).

without the Spirit "either despises the judgment of God in its complacency or in the face of punishment flees and hates God who judges them." [31]

Only God can remove this opposition or rebellion. Through the Gospel, the Holy Spirit creates faith in man to give him that peace with God. Moreover, the Gospel moves a person to do good works and to fulfill the First Commandment.[32] The Gospel must therefore complement the function of the Law as mirror. It removes contrition and despair with the assurance that forgiveness is at hand and bestowed graciously by God for Christ's sake.[33] This is a forensic and eschatological act of God. Just as the judgment passed by the Law already prefigures the Day of Judgment, so, too, the Gospel's gift of faith grants eternal salvation undiminished: "The forgiveness of sin is an eschatological reality."[34]

A failure to draw a proper distinction between Law and Gospel in proclamation and witness has disastrous consequences in the life of the Church and her mission. In a domino effect, the confusion of Law and Gospel topples one thing after the other. It diminishes all honor and glory to Christ for what He has done for us. Once the Word is ineffective, a dangerous anthropocentrism emerges that hails our accomplishments and our part in the scheme of salvation. It would truly be a grave pastoral mistake to raise our contribution or efforts in light of what Christ did for us. In the end, anthropocentricism robs a troubled conscience of the true comfort in Christ. Theological language identifies this problem as a wrongful mingling of justification with sanctification when our works are "drawn into and mingled with the article of justification and salvation."[35]

LANGUAGE AND TRANSLATION

To this point, we have discussed the theological side of proclamation itself and accentuated some of the more prominent theological nuances. As indicated above, prominent missiologists have turned to linguistics and have begun to highlight the technicalities and pragmatics of communication in mission. In the latter half of the twentieth century, missiology took a technical turn, due mostly to the influential publication of Eugene Nida's *Message*

---

31 Ap IV 34–38 (Kolb-Wengert, 125–26). See also SD II 17 (Kolb-Wengert, 547).

32 AC XVI 4 (Kolb-Wengert, 49); AC XX 29, 36–37 (Kolb-Wengert, 57); LC II 10 (Kolb-Wengert, 432).

33 SD V 21 (Kolb-Wengert, 585); Ap XII 79 (Kolb-Wengert, 200–201). Werner Elert relates to this dialectical function of the Word as follows: "Wrath and grace become revealed in God, sin and faith in man" (*Christian Faith*, 87).

34 Prenter, *Spiritus Creator*, 244. See Ap IV 305 (Tappert, 154); Ap IV 41 (Kolb-Wengert, 126–27).

35 SD IV 22 (Kolb-Wengert, 578); SD III 28 (Kolb-Wengert, 566). See also SD V 1 (Kolb-Wengert, 581) and the condemnations in AC II 3 (Kolb-Wengert, 39).

and Mission.[36] As a result, cultural anthropology together with linguistics and philology have established themselves as important branches of missiology. According to Harvey Conn, contemporary missiology should assume a trialogue structure. Next to the traditional pillars of theology and mission stands the field of linguistics, which focuses on the local interpretation and contextualization of Scripture.[37] Hence, linguistics takes a closer look at the dynamic relationship between the areas of the biblical world or text, the sending or communicating context, and the culture targeted.[38] Obviously, learning and speaking the language of the targeted group of people is a standard prerequisite of any missionary endeavor. To that end, missiology has always explored the area of linguistics. Today, however, many consider anthropologists and linguists who have earned degrees in the area of social sciences to be especially well suited for mission. Yet as mission borrows insights from cultural anthropology and from the broader field of social studies, it must still maintain the overall theological character in view of its task: "Reflection on mission through the social sciences must demonstrate that such approaches are truly complementary, for they can in no sense be allowed to become substitutional."[39]

Obviously, the study of languages, especially learning the vernacular of a specific group of people, was always an important component of training missionaries and much of their success on the field hinged on a thorough knowledge of the customs and language of a target people. A mark of success is for a missionary to preach the Gospel in a foreign language without having to rely on translators. Protestant mission has always adopted an open attitude to embrace other languages for worship and proclamation. Luther was one of the first successful modern adherents to that approach. But before him, the missionary Ulfilas (ca. 311–383) developed an alphabet for the Gothic language and translated the Bible into it. This East Germanic language, now extinct, was the first time a northern European language became a literary language.[40]

In contrast, Roman Catholic mission rigidly clung to Latin as the liturgical language and suppressed vernacular languages until Vatican II (1962–65), with the only exceptions granted to the two great missionaries to the Slavs, Constantine (later Cyril, 826–829) and Methodius (ca. 815–885).

---

36 See Bibliography for publication information. Since then, contributions abound; see, for example, Kraft, *Christianity in Culture*, 131–46, 392–94, and Van Rheenen, *Missions*, 113–33.

37 Conn, *Eternal Word and Changing Worlds*. Although Hesselgrave, a linguist himself, considers that trialogue to be of great potential, he also looks upon the heavy leanings toward anthropology with caution in view of its dangers of compromising biblical authority: Hesselgrave, *Today's Choices for Tomorrow's Mission*, 145.

38 Nida, *Message and Mission*. 46.

39 Scherer and Bevans, *New Directions in Mission and Evangelization*, 2:182.

40 Neill, *History of Christian Missions*, 48–49.

Coming from the East, Cyril and Methodius applied and were granted legal permission for their work by the Roman see. They created an alphabet, the so-called Glagolitic Script, and provided a translation of Scripture and liturgy in what we know today as Old Church Slavonic, the forerunner of modern Slavic languages. In general, however, Rome regarded such practices to be revolutionary and an abrogation of the use of Latin as the sole liturgical language of the West. Rome considered the language of the barbarians to be unfit for the dignity of liturgy, even if worshipers understood little of what was going on in the service.[41]

Luther himself diligently pursued the translation of the Bible into German and in so doing followed the rule of watching closely the "mouths of the people."[42] In other words, Luther noted carefully people's ways of expressing themselves as they pursued their daily chores and duties. This principle laid down by the reformer has become an inspiration for all Protestant missionaries. The nineteenth century, hailed as the "Great Century" for pioneer mission all over the world, had its greatest accomplishments also in the translation of Scripture into the many languages of the world. That task continues undiminished to this day with organizations devoted solely to the task of biblical translation.

The effort of bringing the message of the Bible into the vernacular was truly an admirable feat of pioneer missionaries despite their tarnished image of allegedly complying at times with colonial expansionary interests and displaying overall cultural insensitivity to other people. From the start, missionaries made the translation of the Bible their priority. The first German Protestant pioneer missionary to India, Bartholomäus Ziegenbalg (1682–1719), translated the New Testament and much of the Old Testament for the Tamil-speaking Indians. The pioneer missionary and linguist Robert Moffat (1795–1883), when sent to South Africa in 1817 by the London Missionary Society (LMS), immediately plunged into rendering the Bible into the Setswana language. Of the many translation projects undertaken all over the world, some have been a success, and others, such as William Carey's efforts in Calcutta, lost significance when better linguists such as Alexander Duff stepped forward and provided greatly improved translations. The task of translation is far from completed. In addition to Scripture, the translation of important literature for deepening the faith of people is now in the hands of qualified scholars and organizations, and it continues undiminished all over the world.[43]

---

41 Neill, *History of Christian Missions*, 73.

42 *On Translating: An Open Letter* (1530), AE 35:189). Sanneh, *Translating the Message*, 78–79.

43 The initial setbacks of William Carey's efforts in translation come to mind when in 1812 his priceless manuscripts went up in flames in a warehouse. But the quality of much of his voluminous translation of the whole Bible into Bengali, Sanscrit, and Marathi was really in want of

Protestant missionaries' contributions toward the translation of Scripture and other materials were formidable efforts given the fact that such tasks were mostly done in addition to regular missionary duties. The missionaries must have burned midnight oil to compile and write such foundational works as grammars, dictionaries, catechetical helps, commentaries, and guides of pastoral theology. This literature actually served the purpose of training and raising up indigenous churches and pastors so that the Christian message could be preached and heard in native languages. In fact, missionaries could have published far more had it not been for the lack of time, finances, and strains upon their personal health and family life.[44]

CONTEXTUAL CHALLENGES

The translation of the Christian message is bound to context. However, the task of contextualizing the Gospel is a challenging endeavor and the measures taken are so different that they can hardly account for every situation. In other words, the attempt of conveying the meaning of the biblical truth to a given context as effectively as possible becomes an incredibly difficult and challenging one. Yet there is one telling, classic piece of advice on contextualization given in a letter by Pope Gregory the Great in 610 to Augustine, his dispatched missionary to Canterbury in Kent, England. Augustine had supposed that Christian mission consisted of a careful study and gradual replacement of heathen practices with Christian ones. The pope replied:

> The heathen temples of these people need not be destroyed, only the idols which are to be found in them . . . If the temples are well built, it is a good idea to detach them from the service of the devil, and to adapt them for the worship of the true God . . . And since the people are accustomed, when they assemble for sacrifice, to kill many oxen in sacrifice to the devils, it seems reasonable to appoint a festival for the people by way of exchange. The people must learn to slay their cattle not in honor of the devil, but in honor of God and their own food; when they have eaten and are full, then they must render thanks to the giver of all good things. If we allow them these outward joys, they are more likely to find their way to the true inner joy . . . It is doubtless impossible to cut off all abuses at once from rough hearts, just as the man who sets out to climb a high mountain does not advance by leaps and bounds, but goes upward step by step and pace by pace.[45]

---

improvement, as the skilled linguist and helper to Carey, Alexander Duff, later admitted. See Tucker, *From Jerusalem to Irian Jaya*, 118–20.

44 Fortunately, new advances are being made to uncover the literary contribution of past missionaries. One should credit the Lutheran Heritage Foundation (LHF), founded a decade ago, for its efforts in translating crucial theological and instructional literature.

45 Thomas, *Classic Texts in Mission and World Christianity*, 22.

The quote vividly portrays how important it is that the Gospel change outward practices, behaviors, and artifacts. A mere removal of them without a deeper transformation of the people's belief system and worldview simply will not produce long-term sustenance for Christianity.

LITERAL AND DYNAMIC EQUIVALENCE

The Gospel comes through the proclamation of words understandable in human speech. Although the message may be affected by context, there is also a debate on the character of the language itself. Two groups of linguists stand divided over the issue of language: the so-called purists (or literalists) and those who argue for dynamic equivalence. While the purists wish to remain faithful to the literal meaning of a word or text of Scripture, there are those who would prefer a dynamic equivalence over the literal approach to translation. Both parties make an important point. If nothing else, the debate illustrates that proclaiming the Christian message is indeed a complex affair. Communicators of the Gospel often need to tinker with the structure of a language and its symbols in an effort to be as truthful as possible to both the text and the listeners.

Indeed, there is hardly an acceptable solution to this issue when the Gospel contacts a specific culture and context. One example, however, may illustrate the value of the discussion. In 2 Cor. 5:18–20, the Greek word καταλλαγή (traditionally translated as "reconciliation") implies God's activity of reconciling a hostile world to Himself. Scripture and theology explain this as a one-sided affair, as God's doing alone, apart from any human achievements. In order to meet a changing audience, one translation has rendered the meaning of the word καταλλαγή as "making friends."[46] Such a translation, however, destroys the divine monergism and places God on equal par with man.

In this example, the literal meaning of a biblical term cautions against dynamic equivalency. An important step to take here is to trace the meaning of a word back to original context (etymology), but then also to follow the meaning over time (diachronic approach) to contemporary understanding (synchronic approach). This procedure might reveal the fact that a certain meaning is indispensable to the overall Gospel message. In this case, the missionary would be required to use the indispensable meaning, even if that concept is foreign. The idea of indispensable meaning explains why missionaries in areas such as Papua New Guinea or among the Inuit in Alaska have continued to teach the biblical theme of shepherding sheep, even though that concept is foreign to the natives. The same can be said of

---

46 See Beck, *Holy Bible: An American Translation.*

the Kalanga people in northern Botswana and southern Zimbabwe who, though not familiar with the biblical concept of wine, vineyard, and fruits of the vine, were nonetheless familiarized with them. Thus if the missionary considers the literal meaning of the biblical message indispensable, he may have to import its meaning and complement that with proper catechetical instruction.

APOLOGETICS, APOSTOLIC INCARNATION, AND POINTS OF CONTACT

Not only does missionary proclamation involve the translation and proclamation of Scripture, but it also engages in missionary apologetics. Christians should not underestimate the value of arguing persuasively and reasonably against common misconceptions and criticisms of Christianity. The missiologist Olav Myklebust highlights the need for apologetics as follows: "The confrontation of Christianity with non-Christian faiths and ways of life is not only an academic question, but a matter of life and death to the church. What is at stake is the nature and the purpose of the Gospel."[47]

Obviously, apologetics is an ancillary discipline to the Church's witness; it cannot replace the role of Law and Gospel or the Sacraments. The Gospel is by nature self-authenticating and has no need of proof.[48] But as an important handmaiden to the Christian witness, apologetics addresses popular factual errors and mistakes about Christianity among the media, literature, and in popular opinion. The apostle Paul, too, in the Book of Acts, argued and reasoned with those people who opposed his message, work, and belief (Acts 26:2). Moreover, he did not approach his opponents from a bird's-eye perspective or in a triumphalistic manner, but voluntarily chose to lower himself to them (1 Corinthians 9). It is evident that the apostle Paul brought his entire person into the communicative process and adopted a nonverbal approach to his witness as well as a theological approach. His missionary lifestyle was flexible enough in clothing, behavior, and dietary habits without compromising his Christian faith.[49] As a person, Paul truly exhibited and practiced a freedom from certain laws by being entirely devoted to winning others over to Christ. Missiologists have seized upon Paul's manner and coined the phrase "apostolic incarnation" to encourage an incarnational witness. This incarnational approach to mission follows

---

47 Myklebust, *Study of Missions*, 1:29; Jongeneel, *Philosophy, Science, and Theology of Mission*, 2:343–45.

48 Valleskey, *We Believe—Therefore We Speak*, 111.

49 Braaten, *Apostolic Imperative*, 77–78.

the first principles laid down in the life and ministry of Jesus Christ and in the apostle Paul.[50]

The bottom line is that the lives of all involved in mission must reflect the claims of their message. This was a principle the Moravian missionaries followed closely. For example, in the early 1730s, when the Moravian missionaries Leonhard Dober and Tobias Leupold were sent to do mission work among the slaves on St. Thomas, they planned to become slaves themselves.[51]

In his instructions to his missionaries (1738), Zinzendorf clearly affirmed his radical Christocentric approach, stating that all unbelievers have no understanding either of the cross of Christ or of the God of creation in Scripture. Most will agree with the former, that the cross is foolishness to Gentiles (1 Cor. 1:23), but would be hesitant to consent to the latter position, since the audience on the basis of general revelation might to a certain extent share common sentiments with the way God is portrayed in Scripture as Creator.[52] Should missionary proclamation be set on building bridges or establishing linkage points (*Anknüpfungspunkte*)? Should a preacher accommodate his audience in the message or let the Gospel find its own ways to the hearts of the people? It is true that Lutheran theology has never rejected the thought, at least theoretically, of building bridges to other religions' general knowledge of God. And, as stated before, proclamation does not imply solely a linguistic affair; it involves the entire person of the preacher who is willing to lower himself to the partner in the conversation—a method, as we stated, the apostle Paul himself employed (1 Corinthians 9).

The answer given on this issue depends much on the type of audience a missionary encounters. In other words, the missionary must carefully distinguish his audience—as also the apostles did. Paul spoke to his Gentile audience differently than to the Jews. Among the Jews, Paul discussed the Law and the prophets and demanded obedience to them. He also ensured that they heard clearly that God had become manifest in Christ. The case with heathens was different; they were not accustomed to hear about a single God but more so about gods and a mythological description of them, as the incident in Lystra illustrates (Acts 14:8–18). The Christian apologists sought to dismiss false analogies of all kinds among audiences, particularly those in Gnosticism and Greek philosophy. In many post-Christian situations today, the preacher may expect to find certain ideas circulating about God and Christianity in his audience. However, as he seeks to find ways

---

50 Guder, *Incarnation and the Church's Witness*, xii.

51 Roy, *Zinzendorfs Anweisungen*, 13.

52 Don Richardson has gone so far as to argue in favor of features that he calls "redemptive analogies," which he illustrates in *Peace Child*.

of building a common bridge to the audience, he may come dangerously close to compromising the full character of proclamation. The sermons in Scripture always fully disclose the life and person of Jesus Christ, so that even if common contacts were sought, proclamation never withheld anything of the revealed truth about Jesus Christ. The apostle Paul demonstrated this fact when he pointed to the resurrected Christ (Acts 17:31). The art of studying the audience and seeking them out with a message about God should thus serve the ultimate purpose of fully revealing Christ to them so that the Gospel may transform them to a new life in Christ. Thus our Christian witness does not merely "align" or draw parallels and comparisons between the Christian message and the non-Christian religion. Instead, the goal is that of transforming and correcting a hearer's preconceived notions in order to lead a sinner to repentance and faith (justification). For justification corrects, rebukes, and smites a person in order to resurrect him again through the Gospel. Since general revelation cannot provide the correct worship of God, but only provides, negatively speaking, a misleading knowledge and worship that ultimately denies Him (LC II 66), we would be hard-pressed to affirm a positive approach to build on a preexistent knowledge of the triune God.

Obviously, building bridges with the Gospel can ultimately only come about through the Holy Spirit.[53] Anthropological insights cannot adequately explain how missionary proclamation brings about faith, for though a human being is a created being of God, he does not posses the innate ability to communicate with God.[54] Christian witness must point to the work carried out by the Holy Spirit. The Spirit alone has power in bringing about faith and the relationship with God. The role of the Spirit in communication also dismisses any kind of force, dishonesty, enticement, or persuasion with which one may desire to elicit a relationship between man and God.

The role of the Spirit also explains the failures in our witness. Samuel Zwemer (1867–1952) toiled in Arabia and Egypt for almost thirty-eight years and saw only a few Muslims profess their Christian faith. Robert Moffat waited fifteen years before a member of the Bathlapeng tribe converted. What accounts for this "failure"? Failure to lead people to faith and Baptism is not necessarily a fault of the missionary's limited communication skills.

---

53 LC II 31–33, 44–45 (Kolb-Wengert, 434–35, 436); Ap II 10 (Tappert, 102); Ap IV 298 (Tappert, 153); Ap XII 50–52 (Tappert, 189). See Holsten, *Das Kerygma und der Mensch*, 61–65; Strasser, "Das Wesen der Mission nach lutherischem Verständnis," 11.

54 Blauw, *Goden en Mensen*, 163: "Man spreke dus niet van een in den mens liggende mogelijkheid, maar slechts van een in Gods genade gegeven werkelijkheid."

Apparent failure can be explained theologically as man's rejection of God. In the final analysis, failure is an inexplicable phenomenon that belongs to the hidden God with whom the mission of the Church will always have to contend.[55]

---

55 SD XI 40 (Kolb-Wengert, 647). For a discussion on result-oriented communication that looks into the effectiveness or ineffective nature of communication, see Kane, "Work of Evangelism," 564–68.

CHAPTER TWELVE

THE MISSIONARY GOAL

THE GOAL AS SEQUENCE

We engaged the "how" of mission as the Holy Spirit working through the Word in the context of communication; we now turn to the "why," that is, the goal of mission. However, the discussion surrounding the goal of mission may be more involved than the reader may initially anticipate. A persisting challenge for missiologists is to define just what the goal of mission should be.[1] Yet clarity on the goal of mission has huge ramifications: it will impact also the strategy, task, and role of those who will be involved in mission. We have already pointed to the all-important goal of bringing the Gospel to the nations so that all may believe in Jesus Christ. We thus affirm once again the doctrine of justification as the central article in the theology of mission and as the core missionary goal of mission (Rom. 10:14–17). Preachers call sinners to repent and believe in Jesus Christ. This was the quintessential task of John the Baptist at the river Jordan (Mark 1:4; Matt. 3:2). It was also part of the preaching ministry of Jesus Christ on earth (Matt. 5:17; 11:20–21; 12:41; Luke 5:32), as well as that of apostles such as Peter (Acts 2:38; 3:19) and Paul (Acts 17:30; 26:20).

However, we need to place the goal of creating faith and conversion within the broader context of the Church. For the individual's faith is nourished and maintained in the Church after he or she has been placed into that community through Baptism (Acts 2:41; Rom. 12:4.5; 1 Cor. 12:13). Baptism is therefore the visible beginning of the believer's spiritual life and his incorporation into the Body of Christ (Mark 1:4; Luke 3:3; Acts 2: 38; 13:24; 19:4–5). The goal of mission is thus that all nations be converted and baptized, with the result that the Church be planted in this world. Scripture often points to the furthering of the kingdom of God (Mark 1:15) and the community of believers through the act of preaching, conversion,

---

1 For a discussion of various models, see Müller and Sundermeier, *Dictionary of Mission*, 431–32.

and Baptism. A study of the Book of Acts alone would underscore that observation.[2]

To make matters even more complicated, the mission of the Church integrates a number of mundane yet important matters that pertain to the overall goal of mission as well. Alhough Scripture has little to say on this, the goal of planting a church body generally includes also the three-selfs: that a new church body may be self-supporting, self-propagating, and self-governing. After some time, the planted church body must demonstrate the ability to stand on her own feet in terms of providing support, governance, and growth. These three-self principles also offer a helpful measure by which one may gauge the relationship of the new church body to its parent—that is, those original missionaries who brought the Gospel to the new Christians in the first place.

From the above introduction, it is apparent that the goal of mission includes a number of issues. The goal presents a sequence in which one event leads to another. In the next two chapters, we shall explore and illuminate the sequence of mission.

CONVERSION AS PASSING FROM THE DEVIL'S KINGDOM TO CHRIST'S KINGDOM

We shall begin with conversion. Conversion is the work of the Holy Spirit, who through the Word of God brings faith. It is a divine miracle, and through it occurs a switch in dominion: the believer is placed under the rule of Jesus Christ. We may thereby consider the discussion closed. However, conversion has found its place in Christian anthropology and has become of interest for missiologists, particularly those who engage in inductive studies and look at the context in which individuals encounter the preaching of the Word.

In terms of anthropology, the Word of God addresses the conscience, will, and mind of man. As the hearer listens to the Word, he stands accused as a sinner before God. In his conscience (συνείδησις), the hearer learns to distinguish between what God considers right and wrong and the judgment (Acts 23:1; 24:16; Rom. 2:15; 13:5; 1 Cor. 8:7; 10:25, 27–29; 2 Cor. 1:12; 4:2; 5:11). The Word of God functions in both its uses, Law and Gospel. The Law of God sheds light on a person and reveals his true sinfulness. As a result, the one exposed to the Word endures a conflict and is stricken by fear and terror. At the same time, however, the Gospel of Jesus Christ consoles the hearer with the news that his sins are forgiven and that he has

---

2   This chapter deals with a number of passages in Acts. One may consider Acts 2:41–42, 47; 4:4; 6:7; 8:12, 36, 38; 9:31; 10:44, 48; 11:21; 12:24; 14:1; 16:5; 16:14–15; 19:20.

been reconciled with God. The Gospel thus brings about a breakthrough or victory over a death-struggle engulfed in fear and terror (1 Cor. 15:57), and it now motivates the will to do what is God-pleasing.[3] Faith becomes active; its fruits are visible through good works that also include missionary activity of confessing and witnessing faith and leading a Christian lifestyle. Indeed, there is an ethical dimension to mission.

Through his conversion, the believer passes from the devil's kingdom to Christ's kingdom (*Herrschaftswechsel*). Formerly, he was ruled by the kingdom of darkness but now has become a child of God and is ruled by the Lord Jesus Christ. Here, the Sacrament of Baptism plays a significant role. Luther maintains that as Baptism is administered in the name of the triune God, it becomes God's own act and ushers in a switch in dominion (*Herrschaftswechsel*) when the Holy Spirit "snatches" someone "from the jaws of the devil." In other words, Baptism is salvation, which is nothing else than to be delivered from sin, death, and the devil, to enter into Christ's kingdom, and to live with Him forever.[4] On this occasion, the baptismal candidate intentionally renounces the devil and his works. Often, the adult may underscore that event even further by requesting a new name, still a common custom in many churches of Africa, or he may choose a change of dress to indicate a new outward beginning that commences with conversion and the Sacrament of Baptism.[5]

ANTHROPOLOGICAL STUDIES AND CONVERSION

Conversion thus stands for a change in a person's life that shifts from rebellion against God to a joyous Christian service to God and neighbor through the Holy Spirit. Some theologians and missiologists have engaged in inductive and empirical studies in an attempt to trace the internal struggles a person undergoes as he passes from the devil's kingdom to Christ's kingdom. The late Walter Freytag (1899–1959) is the leading missiologist in this area. On his mission excursion to Asia, Freytag recorded in two important essays his observations on conversion and its intermediate influences on an adult when he is confronted with the missionary proclamation. Freytag's descriptions of inner struggles, accompanied with visions, provide important evidence to the "otherness" of the Gospel message as it

---

3   This sequence is described in FC SD III 41, 70–71 (Kolb-Wengert, 569, 557). For a statement of Law and Gospel, see Ap XII 53 (Tappert, 189).

4   See LC IV 10, 83, 24–25 (Kolb-Wengert, 457, 466, 459). Franz Wiebe attests to this *Herrschaftswechsel* in Baptism as the "radical change of frontiers in baptism" ("Missionsgedanken in den lutherischen Bekenntnisschriften," 37). Georg Vicedom similarly states: "This is precisely what baptism among the heathens is concerned about: to let oneself be placed on the side of Christ and be divorced from the godless world" (*Taufe unter den Heiden*, 19).

5   Vicedom, *Taufe unter den Heiden*, 37.

reaches the hearer. Indeed, becoming a Christian impacts the entire life of the believer amid his surroundings.[6]

There are, however, certain dangers that accompany such anthropological studies, since these could detract from seeing conversion as a divine and spiritual phenomenon. In other words, what matters is that conversion is God's doing. Otherwise, one might perceive conversion in synergistic terms as a kind of cooperation between man and God or a condition in which someone begins to listen more to his heart and internal state than trusting the Word. For this reason, a theology of conversion must pay close attention to the *modus agendi*—namely, the mode of becoming a Christian.

First, conversion is a *monergistic* or *transitive event* so that the person's role in it is described in purely passive terms.[7] God is the subject in this whole affair. Gensichen affirms the divine monergism: "Conversion is not something that man can perform for himself or on behalf of someone else. It is God's doing on man."[8] The Lutheran Confessions speak of only two efficient causes of a believer's spiritual renewal: the divine Word and the Spirit.[9] One should, therefore, not attempt to describe conversion as though a person can assume an active role. Pelagianism was a type of synergism that diminished the divine activity and so stole the honor and glory of Jesus Christ. Wilhelm Maurer elaborates upon the Word of God and the Holy Spirit as the sole means of conversion: "Conversion is therefore a work of the faith produced by the Spirit. This decisive shift in the event of conversion is not accomplished by our human will affirming the forgiveness of sins. The Spirit, rather, working in the Word brings about the change by opening ear and heart so that God's inviting call is heard."[10]

Second, conversion is a crucial event associated with the *coming about of faith*. Although conversion, broadly speaking, often embraces more than justification by including the preceding event of repentance and the subsequent renewal through good works, both conversion and justification have

---

6 See Freytag's essays "Wie Heiden Christen werden" and "Zur Psychologie der Bekehrung bei Primitiven." See also the study devoted to Freytag's missiology: Triebel, *Bekehrung als Ziel der missionarischen Verkündigung*.

7 The following point should thus be made: though the Confessions provide limited anthropological, that is psychological, observations on conversion and the coming about of faith, their reliability in such matters underscores the divine monergism in conversion by describing how God is at work and that He coerces no one to conversion (e.g., SD II 64–65, 83, 89, Kolb-Wengert, 556, 560–61). Schlink is thus correct: "By using apparently psychological terms all accomplishments are in fact excluded" (*Theology of the Lutheran Confessions*, 97). The explicit reference to a passive capacity (*capacitas passiva*) underscores this aspect also (SD II 23, Kolb-Wengert, 548).

8 Gensichen, *Glaube für die Welt*, 112.

9 This is argued against Melanchthon's attempt to add a third cause—namely, the human will (SD II 90, Kolb-Wengert, 561).

10 See also Maurer, *Historical Commentary of the Augsburg Confession*, 312.

this in common: as soon as the righteousness of Christ is imputed, or, when the hearer is pronounced forgiven, he is saved.[11] There is no third stage or grey zone in which a person can find himself; he is either in the state of unbelief or belief. Thus justification as divine imputation or the declaration of forgiveness is embedded in the center of conversion, making conversion, strictly speaking, a momentous event. We have a perfect illustration of this in Scripture in Cornelius (Acts 10), where conversion may include a series of events without sacrificing its important character. Although all the events prior to his hearing the salutary message of Peter are part of Cornelius's conversion, the momentous kindling of faith actually takes place in verse 44 where it is said that "while Peter was still saying these things, the Holy Spirit fell on all who heard the word." That hearing of Peter's words occasions the decisive event in Cornelius's spiritual life. It is the punctual or mathematical turning point.[12]

Third, conversion presents divine "intrusion" in a person's life that bestows nothing less than *salvation*. It is thus more than a mere deliverance from common human pains or a fulfillment of one's earthly needs. The Gospel is in view of its purpose far more than a "commercialized" tool to remedy peoples' needs or desires. Often, strategies are chosen that will "soften up" the audience for the Gospel message by considering their needs as "an opportunity for Christian response which stimulates within the person a receptivity to the gospel."[13] Such attempts actually belie the reality of natural man's state, how totally corrupted and spiritually deprived a person is who will "stubbornly persevere in resisting the Holy Spirit's activities and movement."[14] How such a rebellious person changes to become a willing and consenting person is entirely a miracle from God. The Gospel is clearly an answer to that spiritual plight. It is not a "user-friendly tool" for every aspect in life, a means to solutions, health, happiness, and wealth. Despite the "felt needs" approach to evangelism, the Gospel cannot offer an answer to everything. Paul Tillich also saw the Gospel as a means of correlating to existential questions and answering their specific concern.[15] We cannot entirely dismiss the concern for the human situation. But the Gospel

---

11 Here, conversion is not a process, as Beißer, *Hoffnung und Vollendung*, 34, points out, but actually an event (*Ereignis* or *Urteil*), which means, according to the Confessions, "to make unrighteous men righteous or to regenerate them" (*ex iniustis iustos pronuntiari seu regenerari*) and "to be pronounced and accounted righteous" (*iustos pronuntiari seu reputari*). We should note the passive infinitives (Ap IV 71, Tappert, 117)! Compare also SD III 20, 41 (Kolb-Wengert, 565, 569).

12 Luther uses this example in SA III VIII 7–8 (Kolb-Wengert, 322–23). Another example may be that of Zacchaeus in Luke 19:1–10. Elert, *Structure of Lutheranism*, 1:90–106.

13 Wagner, *Church Growth*, 290.

14 SD II 83 (Kolb-Wengert, 560).

15 Tillich, *Systematic Theology*, 1:59–66.

cannot be turned into a superficial remedy for all concerns. By contrast, Luther's breakthrough and his discovery of a merciful God was more than a mere answer to personal needs. Luther experienced a breakthrough from deep spiritual desperation, from a wrestling with an angry and judging God. He tried to escape this God by probing into the divine Word in search of answers.[16] And as a Christian continues to be stricken by temptation and affliction throughout his life, he may continue to find comfort and assurance, which Luther defined as certitude (certitudo), in contrast to a false security (securitas), in the soothing words of the Gospel.[17]

Thus classical missiologists rightly affirm that conversion is more than merely a fulfillment of preexisting spiritual notions and needs. Conversion represents the decisive spiritual change or transformation in a believer's life. It leads to the "crossing of frontiers"[18] and the liberation of man from the perils of the devil and death through justification. The Gospel presents the hearer with Christ, who placated God's wrath through His satisfaction on the cross and who thereby opened the way to God the Father. The believer is declared righteous, given peace and access to God as the gift of forgiveness of sins is apprehended through faith (Rom. 5:1–2; Eph. 3:12).[19] Through Christ, God restores the "image of God" to His fallen creation and adopts the believer as His child (Col. 3:10; 2 Cor. 3:18).[20] The fundamental result is that the believer now invokes God as Father through Christ and confesses Christ as Lord through the Holy Spirit. The missiologist Peter Beyerhaus calls this the doxological aim of mission and underscores it by saying that "it is extremely important to emphasize the priority of this doxological aim that comes before all other aims of mission."[21]

---

16 Some have called the attempts to use the Gospel for all felt needs a "hedonistic" soteriology. Instead, justification wishes to promote the assurance of faith (Glaubensgewißheit) rather than just to affirm our existence (Daseinsgewißheit). Martens, "Glaubensgewißheit oder Daseinsgewißheit?" 171–79. One may see the critical survey on precisely this question by Harrison, Righteous Riches.

17 Kurz, Heilsgewißheit bei Luther, 197.

18 A term used in LWF, "'Two Kingdoms' and the Lordship of Christ," 79–88.

19 Romans 5:1–2 is a text frequently cited in the Confessions; see Ap IV 81, 195 (Tappert, 118, 134).

20 In the Formula of Concord, "pronounced righteous," "remission of sins," and "adoption" are often mentioned together; see SD III 9, 19 (Kolb-Wengert, 563, 565); Ap IV 196, 351, 354 (Tappert, 134, 161); Ap XII 47 (Tappert, 188); SD XI 49 (Kolb-Wengert, 648). See Vicedom, Mission of God, 15, and Johnson, "Justification according to the Apology," 193.

21 Beyerhaus, Shaken Foundations, 42. This doxological goal is repeatedly found in Lutheran theology, e.g., AC XX 24–25 (Kolb-Wengert, 56): "All who know that in Christ they have a gracious God call upon him and are not, like the heathen, without God." Faith responds with invocation and doxology; see Ap IV 59–60, 205, 385 (Tappert, 115, 135, 166); Ap XXI 10, 13 (Tappert, 230); SC II 2, 4 (Kolb-Wengert, 355). Albrecht Peters discusses this aspect in his explanation of Luther's catechisms; see "Vaterunser-Auslegung in Luthers Katechismen," 75. See also Trillhaas, "Regnum Christi," 42, and Goppelt, "Lordship of Christ," 15–39.

Looking at Faith More Closely

Paul explains how "proclamation" and "faith" are correlative terms. In Rom. 10:8–9, he lists together the preaching of the Gospel, faith, and the confession of Christ as Lord. He then adds that if you "believe in your heart that God raised Him from the dead, you will be saved" (see also 1 Cor. 2:5; Phil. 1:27; 1 Thess. 2:15; Eph. 1:13). Seen from the perspective of a believer, faith is the only correlation to the external Word through which God justifies. The Lutheran Confessions state that faith "alone and absolutely nothing else is the means or instrument by and through which God's grace and the merit of Christ which is promised in the gospel are received, laid hold of, accepted, applied to us, and appropriated."[22] Faith therefore is the only means of apprehending Christ's righteousness, the forgiveness of sins, offered in the Gospel.

In view of theological schemes plaguing the Church throughout the centuries that give human freedom a role in the salvation process, one would have to explain the exact nature of faith.[23] If any perception of freedom should enter soteriology, then faith could be understood as a virtue or a work. Contrary to such misperceptions, faith is rightly understood as a gift (*donum*) of the Holy Spirit. It is also more than knowledge (*notitia*) of the history of Christ's suffering and His resurrection from the dead. It is a special faith that is called trust (*fiducia*). This faith not only holds to be true all the historic facts of Christ's earthly existence, but it also entrusts itself to them. Faith is also personal, so that the believer passively appropriates for himself (*pro me*) the promise of the forgiveness of sins in the Word.[24]

---

22 SD III 38 (Kolb-Wengert, 569). Faith and Christ are inseparable (SA III III 20, Kolb-Wengert, 315); SC II 6 (Kolb-Wengert, 355). Schlink thus concludes: "Christ and faith are so intimately united that *propter fidem* may be said for *propter Christum*, and *per Christum* for *per fidem*" (*Theology of the Lutheran Confessions*, 100). Faith also shares in the person of Christ. In this way, the righteousness is a righteousness in us yet always imputed (e.g., Ap IV 140, 351, Tappert, 126, 161; Ap X 3, Tappert, 179). But the Christ *in nobis* still remains *aliena iustitia* (Ap IV 305, Tappert, 154).

23 Most blatantly, this position was taken by the fifth-century British monk Pelagius. But it seems to continue in Arminianism started by Jacob Arminius, an early seventeenth-century theologian. It would also pertain to the Anabaptists and to Revivalism represented by John Wesley and Charles Finney. In more recent years, C. S. Lewis and Clark Pinnock are known to promote human freedom in the salvation process. One may see Boyd and Eddy, *Across the Spectrum*, 134.

24 See the discussion on faith in these passages, SD III 10–13, 31 (Kolb-Wengert, 564, 567). The Confessions would call *notitia*: "that general faith, which the demons also have" (e.g., Ap XII 45, Tappert, 546). Of the salutary faith or personal faith, the Confessions say: "It signifies faith which believes not only the history but also the effect of the history, namely the article of the forgiveness of sins" (AC XX 23, Kolb-Wengert, 57); see also Ap IV 45 (Tappert, 113) and AC XX 26 (Kolb-Wengert, 57). Mildenberger, *Theologie der Bekenntnisschriften*, 40–41; Schlink, *Theology of the Lutheran Confessions*, 96.

Although passive regarding justification and the forgiveness of sins, this special faith is also described as being active to "want and to accept the promised offer," of being "a strong powerful work of the Holy Ghost, which changes hearts" and which produces such good dispositions as love and works.[25] Luther's statement in the preface to his commentary on Romans defines what faith is: "O, it is a living, busy, active, mighty thing, this faith. It is impossible for it not to be doing good works incessantly."[26] Here, justifying faith becomes the vehicle of sanctification or regeneration that shifts gears from being a passive faith to an active faith. It is important to note this transition of faith and to see that it acts as the means for both justification and sanctification. By linking faith to both important events, Lutheranism rejects the position that faith is only the beginning of a Christian life and that good works are produced apart from faith in some other way. Moreover, without faith no works are considered God pleasing. For if God's favor is extended to a Christian because of his merits, then he could either fall into despair and sadness for not having done enough works or into a false sense of security that he has already done all the works necessary to earn God's favor. Both errors are even common among Christians and need to be corrected by the proper distinction of God's Word in Law and Gospel.

In summary, everything is attributed to faith not only as the "access to grace but also the basis for our standing in grace."[27] Because of faith, "good works are pleasing and acceptable to God."[28] Love and works, however, have no part in providing access to grace or of providing a guarantee of remaining in it; they are only a consequence of faith.[29]

Speaking to the situation of mission, it would be helpful to remind ourselves that when considered from the perspective of sanctification, faith does in fact contribute toward mission through confession and conduct. Faith leads to a witness and missionary lifestyle in the world for which the Thessalonians were praised by Paul (1 Thess. 1:8; compare Matt. 5:16; 1 Pet. 2:12; Rom. 10:9).

---

25 For the respective quotes and references, see Ap IV 48 (Tappert, 114) and Ap IV 125, 250 (Tappert, 124, 143). After clarifying justification as a forensic act that alone saves, the Confessions would not shy from explaining sanctification in terms of justification being also an effective act insofar as it becomes the experience of a *mutatio*, a change of affects (effectual change) that brings forth good works. See AC XX 29–31 (Tappert, 45) and Ap IV 72 (Tappert, 117).

26 AE 35:370–71, and quoted in SD III 10 (Kolb-Wengert, 576).

27 SD IV 34 (Kolb-Wengert, 579–80).

28 SD IV 8 (Kolb-Wengert, 575).

29 Ap IV 64–68, 74 (Tappert, 115, 117); Fagerberg, *New Look at the Lutheran Confessions*, 159.

Baptism, the Missionary Sacrament

We stated earlier that the obligation to preach the Gospel also includes the duty and the goal to baptize. Although conversion comes about through the preaching of God's Word, it is anchored and made visibly manifest in Baptism.[30] From Scripture, we also know that Baptism is the means whereby one is added to the communion of believers (Acts 2:38, 41; 8:12; 18:8). In view of the fact that the Great Commission speaks so clearly of preaching coupled with Baptism (Matt. 28:19; Mark 16:16), it seems odd that so little attention is given the Sacrament of Baptism in missiological literature. One notices primarily a minimalist version that focuses on witness, isolated from Baptism.[31] Peter Brunner's insights on Baptism seem instructive: "The Gospel seeks the faith of the hearers. Once it comes to faith, then baptism follows by necessity. Therefore the Great Commission embraces immediately also baptism. It cannot come to a faith in the Gospel through the Holy Spirit, that does not desire and lead to baptism. The place where baptism takes place is where church has come about."[32] The conspicuous lack of references to Baptism in current missiological literature in the United States points to a Reformed coloring that fails to see Baptism as the visible Word through which God expands His kingdom. To do full justice to the Great Commission, the Church should call for a strategy that includes the act of Baptism. This would in turn motivate the Church to pay attention to those regions where the unbaptized predominantly live and to implement and emphasize adult Baptism. *The Evangelizing Church* thus correctly calls for a renewed focus on adult Baptism and catechesis. Indeed, this Sacrament should become part of our mission spirituality and identity in a greater and more conscientious way.[33]

The value and necessity of Baptism for mission is based on nothing else than on the Lord's mandate to do so. It is performed in His authority and in the name of the triune God. There can be no higher stamp of approval for its practice than that. To baptize is thus not an arbitrary or optional act that could be postponed for an indefinite time in the mission

---

30 "After God has made his beginning through his Holy Spirit in baptism" (SD II 16, Kolb-Wengert, 546).

31 A perusal through missiological literature demonstrates that Baptism is given marginal or no treatment at all. See, for example, Van Rheenen, *Missions*, 25–26; Van Engen, *Mission on the Way*, contains no references; and even David Bosch hardly offers insights except for a scant reference (*Transforming Mission*, 167–68, 219). A valiant theological attempt is made in Guder, *Missional Church*, 159–62, though it, too, does not attribute to Baptism the attention it deserves.

32 Brunner, "Heil und das Amt," 304. See also Vicedom, *Taufe unter den Heiden*, 34.

33 Bliese and Van Gelder, *Evangelizing Church*, 47.

of the Church.[34] If it is God's intention to use Baptism for His salutary purposes, then urgency to perform it is the best approach. The Church would inadequately represent the mission of the Lord if she were to refrain from the activities of proclamation *and* baptizing. That is a scriptural and theological principle. It stands even if reality today shows otherwise, namely, when missionaries are deployed as teachers and when many countries, such as parts of Sri Lanka and Southern India, marginalize or persecute those who baptize or have been baptized. Some even question the necessity of Baptism. Herb Hoefer, for example, debates the need for Baptism in *Churchless Christianity*. The Church, he argues, should accept the fact that many so-called Jesus followers (*Jesu bhakta*) who live in regions such as rural Tamil Nadu and urban Chennai, India, avoid Baptism and membership in the Church, lest they suffer rejection in society, especially since many of these devotees also come from higher castes, including the Brahmans.[35] For some the idea of belonging to a Christian Church may bring in negative connotations of Western imperialism or colonialism. By refraining from Baptism and church membership, the Hindu *bhakti* movement can choose to worship Jesus, even exclusively, and still maintain their cultural and social particularities as Hindus.

Such suggestions, however, have not found wide acceptance in missiological circles, not only because they stand against the clear testimony of Scripture and theological evidence but also because they cast doubt upon the cause of Christian martyrs who dearly paid for their membership and Baptism.[36] For the relationship to God cannot be better expressed than through one's membership in the Church by receiving Baptism. No other event embodies visibly the divine intervention in the life of a convert as does this Sacrament. Whatever happened before one's Baptism or after it, a convert's life in Christ marks its visible beginning with it and is continually shaped by it. Baptism is thus no loose antecedent of the Gospel. It is part of the divine mission to reach out to all of mankind and to build the

---

34   The Roman Catholic Rite of Christian Initiation for Adults (RCIA) envisages a year of baptismal instruction that is divided in five phases and extends until Easter. From a Lutheran perspective, it is of little help to have Baptism delayed, for that would undermine Baptism's salutary efficacy and the urgency of it.

35   Hoefer, *Churchless Christianity*. The necessity of Baptism and church membership is briefly raised in LWF, *Mission in Context*, 28.

36   Timothy C. Tennent challenges the notion of a churchless Christianity for the following reasons: "We worship a triune God who is, by nature, a relational God. He made his relational nature fully public in the incarnation of his Son, which is reflected in the life of the church, which in turn is called his body. Our very doctrine of Christ demands that all believers, in all times, in all parts of the globe must seek—whenever possible—to form themselves into visible communities of faith. The visible communities may have to meet in catacombs or suffer great persecution or undergo cultural misunderstanding, as did the primitive church, but the early church did not forsake the assembling of themselves together. They understand that biblical conversion, by definition, implies community" ("Challenge of Churchless Christianity," 176).

THE MISSIONARY GOAL 193

Church through it. In his explanation to the Third Article of the Creed, Luther extols Baptism as that act "through which we are first received into the Christian community."[37] Baptism stands as the visible sign for the coming of God's reign in the life of the baptized, and it draws a visible divide between Christians and non-Christians.[38]

In view of the multifaceted visible sign presented by Baptism, missionary activities and their goal are shaped by the signs of the Church (*notae ecclesiae*): "The church is the assembly of saints in which the gospel is taught purely and the sacraments are administered rightly."[39] Although these signs are connected to the preposition "in which," suggesting that they take place within an established community, the Church in her outward orientation and work actively engages these signs as well. Mission of the Church is part of the *notae ecclesiae* in that God's Word is dynamic in character. The Word itself never rests but pushes out beyond the community of faith to the unbelieving world.[40] Indeed, as she performs the task of preaching Christ, Baptism is the missionary Sacrament of incorporating newcomers, both adults and infants, into the community. For the Baptism of infants is implied in the term "all nations" (Matt. 28:19) and elsewhere encouraged in Scripture (Acts 2:38–39; 10:48; 16:15). Obviously, as the first generation in the Early Church and in new mission fields initially become Christian, adult Baptism predominates. But with the second generation and so on, the Baptism of children becomes more prevalent. The Lutheran Confessions pick up this concern and call infant Baptism a necessity, particularly in view of being born with original guilt:

> Therefore it is necessary to baptize children so that the promise of salvation might be applied to them according to Christ's command (Matt. 28:19), "Baptize all nations." Just as there salvation is offered to all, so Baptism is offered to all—men, women, children, and infants. Therefore it clearly follows that infants should be baptized because salvation is offered with Baptism.[41]

---

37 LC IV 2 (Kolb-Wengert, 456). Luther also says the same of the Gospel: ". . . the Holy Spirit has called me through the Gospel" (SC II 6, Kolb-Wengert, 355; LC II 52, Kolb-Wengert, 438). This shows how much the Sacrament of Baptism is seen as nothing but the "Gospel." Vicedom, *Taufe unter den Heiden*, 32.

38 Schlink, *Doctrine of Baptism*, 150.

39 AC VII 1 (Kolb-Wengert, 43).

40 Brandt, "Über den Beitrag lutherischer Mission zum Gemeindeaufbau," 19–44.

41 Ap IX 2 (Tappert, 178). The Augsburg Confession argues likewise: "Concerning baptism they teach that it is necessary for salvation, that the grace of God is offered through baptism, and that children should be baptized. They are received into the grace of God when they are offered to God through baptism" (AC IX 1–2, Kolb-Wengert, 43). Obviously, the motivation to baptize all nations comes not alone from the divine mandate (*mandatum/Gottes Gebot* or *Befehl*) but also particularly from the divine promise (*Verheißung/promissio*) in Baptism. See here Fagerberg, *New Look at the Lutheran Confessions*, 185–88; SC IV 1–2 (Kolb-Wengert, 359); LC IV 39–41 (Kolb-Wengert, 461); Ap XIII 3, 15–16 (Tappert, 211, 213).

But the preposition "in which" provides the important principle that infant and adult Baptism is not just conducted on anybody, but only to those who promise they will grow up in the context of the Church.[42] Baptism should be performed in the context of a faith community, where there is a high probability that the baptized will be reared with proper spiritual supervision and guidance. The practice of forcing it upon people without their consent and without the benefit of a faith community has no scriptural warrant.

As the desire of the Ethiopian eunuch illustrates, the Church should not ignore the request of an adult to be baptized, nor should the Church in such a case unnecessarily delay Baptism.[43] Yet such a request has no basis in Scripture as the sole determinant, as the account of Naaman suggests (1 Kings 5:1–19). His decision to bathe was nevertheless fraught with an inner, spiritual struggle. The ability of an adult to make a decision and even the question of an infant's faith are thus subsidiary to the vertical and theocentric dimension of Baptism, even as God's work was the central fact of Naaman's cleansing in the Jordan. Basing Baptism solely on human decision-making would indeed diminish its characteristic of being willed by God as an instrument for salvation.

In keeping with Baptism as one of the signs of the Church and an instrument of salvation, theologians often call Baptism the Sacrament of visible justification.[44] Consider Acts 2:38, for example: "Repent and be baptized every one of you in the name of Jesus Christ for the forgiveness of your sins, and you will receive the gift of the Holy Spirit." Consider also Titus 3:5: "He saved us, not because of works done by us in righteousness, but according to His own mercy, by the washing of regeneration and renewal of the Holy Spirit." Paul reminds his readers in Rom. 6:1–14 that they are "baptized into Christ Jesus." They are buried with Him by Baptism and raised from the dead as Christ was to walk in a newness of life. Baptism takes us into the life of Jesus Christ, into a communion with Him: "For as many of you as were baptized into Christ have put on Christ" (Gal. 3:27).

A further significant aspect of this Sacrament is its intrinsic connection to water. Water combined with the divine Word of the Lord makes

---

42 Schlink, *Doctrine of Baptism*, 130. See also Schlink's arguments in favor of infant Baptism, 157–60.

43 Fagerberg, *New Look at the Lutheran Confessions*, 183–84; Vicedom, *Taufe unter den Heiden*, 20.

44 See Brunner, "'Rechtfertigung' heute," 132. Justification and Baptism coincide in that Baptism receives a believer into grace and the Church just as justification does coming through the Gospel (LC IV 2, Kolb-Wengert, 456); compare to LC II 45 (Kolb-Wengert, 436). Thus the phrase "they are received into grace" applies to Baptism also. Compare the statements made in AC IV 2 (Kolb-Wengert, 41) and AC V 3 (Kolb-Wengert, 41) with AC IX 1–2 (Kolb-Wengert, 43).

Baptism "a grace-filled water of life" (*gnadenreich Wasser*) and a "bath of the new birth in the Holy Spirit."[45] Through the Word coming to the water, Baptism awakens and strengthens faith: "The water in Baptism is gracious and salutary like the Word in Baptism. For in the sacrament the Word and the Water can no longer be separate . . . In the definition of the sacrament either the Word or the Water can be the predicate noun. Faith can cling both to the Word and the water."[46] Throughout their lives, believers may put their trust in this visible act as the manifestation and assurance of their own salvation. This is truly the purpose of Baptism, in that it provides an objective reality of one's salvation and takes one out of any attempts to secure salvation apart from this event, be they the day of "accepting Christ," fetishes, or other rituals.[47]

The use of an earthly element such as water in the Sacrament of Baptism contributes visibly and, with the Word, audibly to the bestowal and affirmation of salvation. This leads to Baptism's wide acceptance in Africa (and India), a culture that deals so much with ritualism and the use of water, such as in obligatory ritual washing of hands and pouring libations to ancestors. Obviously, once the motives become Christian through Baptism, ritual washings are of the past. However, in such contexts in which ritual washing plays such an important role, Baptism builds a valuable contextual bridge.

BAPTISM IN THE POST-CHRISTIAN CONTEXT

The post-Christian situation today raises a new perspective on the meaning of Baptism for mission. What we mean by post-Christian is that Western countries have a population among which many nonpracticing Christians, unbaptized and baptized, live. Often, these nonpracticing Christians are people who may be described as nominal Christians. Such nominal Christians might identify themselves with a denomination such as Lutheranism or Roman Catholicism, yet they show no personal commitment to Christ or to the Christian faith. Then there are those who intentionally abstain from any church membership. Many scholars believe that this post-Christian situation started as early as the fourth century, when

---

45 SC IV 10 (Kolb-Wengert, 359). In the Confessions, this rebirth (and illumination) is linked to Baptism, the Holy Spirit, and eternal life or salvation from eternal death: SD II 15 (Kolb-Wengert, 546); Ap IV 352 (Tappert, 161); AC II 2 (Kolb-Wengert, 29).

46 Schlink, *Theology of the Lutheran Confessions*, 184. See also SA III V 1 (Kolb-Wengert, 320); LC IV 36, 52–54 (Kolb-Wengert, 461, 443). Obviously, this would apply also to the Word and the elements in the Holy Communion. See Schlink, *Theology of the Lutheran Confessions*, 155–56.

47 The aspect of *Heilsgewißheit* for those justified through Baptism is important in the Confessions, e.g., SA III XIII 1–2 (Kolb-Wengert, 325); Ap IV 345 (Tappert, 160). Luther argues it at great length in LC IV 54–63 (Kolb-Wengert, 463–64). See Krispin, "Baptism and *Heilsgewißheit* in Luther's Theology," 113–15.

Christianity became a legitimate religion under Emperor Constantine. The Church emerged from persecution to become an accepted, even favored, institution and thus began to practice infant Baptism publicly. A downside of that practice was that as baptized infants grew up, in many instances they lost their conscious allegiance to the Christian Church.[48] In this case, the usual distinction for mission between the baptized and unbaptized is not helpful. Nominal Christians, too, are part of the lost to whom the Church must bring the Gospel. The evangelistic preaching in this post-Christian context must not summon an audience to Baptism, which is the usual strategy in the mission field, but rather call them back to the treasure of the baptismal grace that God once conferred to them and has never removed.[49]

A post-Christian context bears similar characteristics to the reality of the Church during the time of the Reformation in the sixteenth century. Luther included in his intentions to reform the Church also the attempt to restore an appreciation for Baptism among those who had already been baptized.[50] He achieved this primarily through his Small Catechism, which promoted a proper elementary instruction in the basic truths of the Christian faith, including a part on the Sacrament of Baptism. Similarly today, a sound instruction in the theology of Baptism affirms Christians in their divine calling through this Sacrament. Christian education on Baptism also reminds the Church of her ongoing missionary obligation to bring the reality of Baptism to all without exception, be it to an unbelieving world, the nominally baptized, or to active churchgoers.

The loss of membership in Christian congregations is a reality that has accompanied the Church since its inception. However, the Church should not become despondent in her resolve to reach out, nor should she be too idealistic in the thought that she may keep all the baptized within her. For Christians are constantly tested in their faith throughout their lives, and, unfortunately, many succumb to temptations and trials. In the case of a willful rejection of a commitment to Christ, the baptized lose the salutary benefits of the Sacrament of Baptism by falling away from the salvific trajectory of Baptism. Without faith, the Sacrament remains an "unfruitful sign."[51] This does not imply, however, that God withdraws His divine

---

48 Vicedom, *Taufe unter den Heiden*, 33.

49 One may consult Gensichen, *Taufproblem in der Mission*. In German missiology, the term *mission* generally implies outreach to the unbaptized and *outreach* to nominal Christians. That distinction is helpful but is no longer that much in use. In English-speaking missiology, that distinction is not made at all. Mission and evangelization are mostly seen as activities that address the same groups.

50 The Confessions show this reality full well, SD II 67–69 (Kolb-Wengert, 557).

51 LC IV 73 (Kolb-Wengert, 465): "Where faith is present with its fruits, there baptism is no empty symbol, but the effect accompanies it; but where faith is lacking, it remains a mere unfruitful sign." Luther's statements of Christians being "halfway pure and holy" in LC II 58 (Kolb-

promise of grace extended through Baptism. The problem rests with the unbeliever who has rejected that very gift. There is thus the danger that the Church preaches a false sense of security by promulgating and trusting in the idea that Baptism magically dispenses its gift apart from faith. At the same time, the Church may not diminish or destroy the comfort and assurance of salvation that Baptism brings to the believer and from which the Christian takes strength and comfort: "Misuse of the sacrament does not destroy the substance but confirms its existence."[52]

The Kyriological Motive

The idea of expanding the kingdom of God (Matt 12:28) or of Christ (Matt. 13:41; 16:28; Luke 1:33) is crucial to the goal of mission. As we have stated earlier, the kingdom of God theology may not be isolated from the missionary goals of conversion, Baptism, and the Church. For through proclamation, conversion, and Baptism, believers are added to the Body of Christ, the Church, and ruled by their Lord Jesus Christ. We thus argue for a model of conversion and church-planting that includes the reign of Christ over all believers. In the next chapter, we shall discuss the ecclesiological ramifications of such a model. Therefore, wherever the preaching in this world continues, the Holy Spirit grants the gift of faith and thereby also the reign of Christ over all believers. Luther's famous prayer to the petition "Thy kingdom come" comes to mind:

> Dear Father, we ask you first to give us your Word, so that the gospel may be properly preached throughout the world and then that it may also be received in faith and may work and dwell in us, so that your kingdom may pervade among us through the Word and the power of the Holy Spirit and the devil's kingdom may be destroyed so that he may have no right or power over us until finally his kingdom is utterly eradicated and sin, death, and hell wiped out, that we may live forever in perfect righteousness and blessedness.[53]

Luther associates the coming of God's kingdom with the preaching of God's Word. He also indicates that the kingdom is a gift from God that can neither be hastened nor forcefully imposed on people through human

---

Wengert, 438) or "both sinner and saint" (*simul*) would often be complemented by him calling Christians "half heathens" or *christliche Heiden* ("Christian heathen"). In view of this reality, Luther would even define all preaching *Heidenpredigt* ("alle Predigt ist Missionspredigt!"). Yet this "deepened" definition of the term "heathen" ultimately made him not lose sight of those outside the communion of the baptized. One may see Dörries, "Luther und die Heidenpredigt," 327–46; Wiebe, "Missionsgedanken in den lutherischen Bekenntnisschriften," 34–35; Peters, *Kommentar zu Luthers Katechismen*, 2:227.

52 LC IV 59 (Kolb-Wengert, 464).

53 LC III 52, 54 (Kolb-Wengert, 447).

efforts.[54] While the Church prays for its coming, she always understands it as God's gift to every believer, received through faith (Matt. 10:15; Luke 18:17). Moreover, as much as the kingdom is present among those who believe, it also points to the future. In other words, Christ's kingdom has an eschatological reality that means it will be fully vindicated only at the second coming of Christ. Then, finally, the struggle with the kingdom of evil will end and the blessed state in which all those ruled by Christ through faith find themselves will become visible. Now already the kingdom embodies the gift of salvation. One day, however, it will be made fully manifest upon the Lord's return.

For this reason, the missionary goal ought always to consider the kingdom of God. The Church is motivated for mission so that the kingdom may be brought to all those who do not yet confess Christ as their Lord and also that they do not fall away but remain with those who are in God's kingdom. The German theologian Paul Althaus calls this motivation the "kyriological motive" of God's mission: "The goal of mission can be expressed twofold: That every knee may bow before Jesus Christ and confess him as Lord (Phil. 2:10), or that salvation may come to the Gentiles (Rom. 1:14). The motive of mission is kyriological and soteriological at the same time . . . The kyriological-theological and the soteriological motive— both are also not separate but one and the same."[55]

It is important that we affirm the eschatological reality of the kingdom of God. As long as the world exists, Christ's lordship holds sway only among those believers over whom He actually rules through His Word. Theologically, it would thus be legitimate to speak of the kingdom as one embracing only true believers.[56] Granted, Christ also shares in the full power of His Father, and in our confession we state that the Son sits at the "right hand of God." This includes the understanding that He shares in the powers and cosmic rule of God the Father. The Son is the Lord of creation without exception. That *regnum potentiae*, or *regnum universale*, as it is called, extends over the universal world, believers and unbelievers alike. But this mode of ruling is complemented by Christ's rule that relates to His Word of grace as it is preached and extends only over those who are converted and baptized. This kingdom is called a kingdom of grace (*regnum gratiae*), and in it, Christ displays His ordained power (*potesta ordinata*), which is bound to the Word, through which He exercises His rule over the hearts of all His believers.

---

54   Vicedom, *Mission of God*, 26.

55   Althaus, "Um die Reinheit der Mission," 49–50.

56   Melanchthon does so in the article on the Church (Ap VII–VIII 16, Tappert, 171), and so does Luther (LC II 31, Kolb-Wengert, 435); LC III 51 (Kolb-Wengert, 437); Vikstrom, "Mission und Reich Gottes," 64. Beißer, *Hoffnung und Vollendung*, 20.

Unfortunately, missionaries disagree among themselves about this issue. When the reign or kingdom of God is invoked in many circles, missionaries call for the full manifestation of God's kingdom and Christ's universal rule, rather than the kingdom of grace. The great theologian Jürgen Moltmann (theology of liberation) places much of the glory that belongs to the coming kingdom already as a proposed reality today. From Moltmann's perspective, our present behaviors and that of the Church's mission is to make the invisible future as visible as possible. The future-oriented perspective would have the Church commit herself to the task of relieving the abject conditions of the creation that groans in this world, of identifying with the socially marginalized and oppressed. In short, the Church's goal would be to make the future visible today.[57]

For Lutherans, however, the expansion of the kingdom of God occurs through the proclamation of the Word and the coming to faith. Talking about justice and peace submits to a rule of Christ in the present world that is associated with the rule of the Word, faith, and Church, not the hidden God. Under the influences of Moltmann, however, numerous scholars contend that the reign of God should already take on a far more glorious display of its absolute powers because modern human reason cannot accept waiting for the Last Day. Concepts and ideals such as peace (often spoken of as *shalom*) and justice become terms divorced from preaching, the Church, and the individual's faith (Luke 8:11–15; John 18:36).[58] Here, the traditional distinctions of the two kingdoms and the eschatological reality of Christ's kingdom in this world are helpful. Certainly, the mission of the Church should be concerned for the physical state of its audience. To give it priority, however, would diminish or compromise the spiritual and eschatological reality of Christ's reign. The coming of Christ's kingdom is a personal encounter with Christ through the preached Word, which brings forgiveness from personal guilt and sin. We must concur here with Werner Elert's opinion: "There can be no other than this soteriological conception of Christ's dominion."[59]

---

57 This is incongruent with the doctrine of justification, as Mark Mattes points out in his incisive study *Role of Justification in Contemporary Theology*, 86.

58 This could be seen from the 1980 WWC conference on Mission and Evangelism in Melbourne. Although the conference was held under the Second Petition of the Lord's Prayer, "Thy kingdom come," it avowed the kingdom as one that brings justice, love, peace, joy, and freedom from the grasp of principalities and powers, but failed to relate that to conversion and the kingdom of God as an eschatological reality. Scherer and Bevans, *New Directions in Mission and Evangelization*, 1:27–35.

59 Elert, *Christian Faith*, 241. Other Lutheran scholars affirm the same: Brunner, "Herrlichkeit des gekreuzigten Messias," 61; Brunstäd, *Theologie der lutherischen Bekenntnisschriften*, 37–38; Terray, "Mission und Reich Gottes," 69–70; Beißer, "Mission und Reich Gottes," 46.

CHAPTER THIRTEEN
BUILDING A NEW COMMUNITY

AFFIRMING AN ECCLESIAL REALITY FOR MISSION

Any discussion of the goal of mission would be incomplete without the inclusion of ecclesiology. So far, I have spoken of the goal of mission in individualistic terms: through conversion and Baptism, the believer enters the kingdom of God. That appropriation of salvation, however, points also to an ecclesial reality. In other words, where mission takes place, there should also be the concern that the believer can find a spiritual community where his faith is nurtured throughout his earthly life.[1] In *The Logic of Evangelism*, William Abraham points out that various streams in Protestantism have never really broadened their goal beyond the individual basis to include an ecclesiology:

> Pietists, Methodists, and Revivalists over the years have given the distinct impression that the heart of evangelism has nothing to do with the rites and ceremonies of the classical liturgies of the church. For them evangelism is centered on new birth and conversion; the individual stands alone before God in need of personal regeneration, which no church can supply; only God through the action of the Holy Spirit can meet this need. The church, rather than helping in this arena, has been best indifferent and at worst thoroughly hostile. This is the impression one receives from reviewing the history of modern evangelism within the Protestant tradition. What in earlier generations was a mere impression has now become a matter of fixed and absolute principle with the arrival of the television evangelist. The contrast is clear. On the one side is the church with its dead formalism, boring liturgy, and moralistic sermons, which are unlikely to convert anyone. On the other side is the individual soul, stricken in conscience over sin and desperately hoping to find relief in the gospel when called to repentance and faith. The two are set against each other in a relation of mutual hostility.[2]

---

1 See Aagaard, "Missionary Theology," 207–8.
2 Abraham, *Logic of Evangelism*, 118.

202 MISSION FROM THE CROSS

While Abraham's observation is certainly accurate in many situations, there is within Evangelicalism also the Emergent Church Movement that posits an ecclesiology and worship to offset such overt individualism. The emergent church addresses postmodern culture critically yet constructively by finding ways of reclaiming the tradition in hopes of remaining missional to younger generations:

> We call Evangelicals to turn away from an individualism that makes the Church a mere addendum to God's redemptive plan. Individualistic Evangelicalism has contributed to the current problems of churchless Christianity, redefinitions of the Church according to business models, separatist ecclesiologies and judgmental attitudes toward the Church. Therefore, we call Evangelicals to recover their place in the community of the Church catholic.[3]

We, too, must argue for a missionary goal that takes the Church as its focal point. In fact, it would be a misrepresentation of the Gospel if we were to exclude the existence of the Church, which, one might add, actually precedes the faith of the believer. Here is a mission goal that attempts to connect the preaching of the Gospel to ecclesial reality:

> The Gospel does not fulfill its purpose by making individuals who live in a heathen environment Christian. No, the Gospel proclaims that it is necessary to form Christian communities in which individuals may be led on their path of salvation by being in communal fellowship with the triune God and with believers through the preached and sacramental fellowship of the Word.

Personal experiences of salvation do not necessarily generate a conscious connection between faith and the Church. However, Scripture and the Confessions do establish a powerful link between saving faith in Christ and incorporation into the Church. Such thinking often runs counter to the popular perception of what the Church is, where Christians look at the Church as an option only after they have come to faith. This explains the common usage of phrases such as "church hopping" or perceptions that see the Church as "a place where something happens." Sadly, making the Church merely a vendor of religious services and goods suggests that a Christian, after coming to faith, may or may not decide on its services and a fellowship with other Christians. That would make ecclesial life only incidental to a Christian's existence. However, ecclesiology is central to the Christian's life of faith from the start. As a believer is taken into the fellowship with

---

3   Taken from the movement's document "The Call" (Thesis 2); see www.ancientfutureworship. com. A recent conference on November 7–9, 2006, at Northern Baptist Seminary, Chicago, Illinois, was held under the theme "Towards an Ancient Evangelical Future," at which the important document "The Call" was closely studied. For a description of the movement, see Gibbs and Bolger, *Emerging Churches*.

the triune God, he simultaneously also belongs to the Body of Christ, the fellowship of believers. In fact, as Karl Barth once rightly pointed out, it should be self-evident already from the fact that "to be wakened to faith and to be 'added' to the community are one and the same thing. Those who believe *are in* the church, and they *are the* church."[4] Barth's thinking resonates with such passages as Acts 2:41, 47. There, we are told that new believers "were added" to those who were already saved, the Church. Still other passages reference the communal or ecclesiological dimension (1 Cor. 1:2–9; 12:12–31; Eph. 1:21–23; 2:11–21). Martin Luther makes much of his personal incorporation into the Church: "I was brought into it [the Church] by the Holy Spirit and incorporated into it through the fact that I have heard and still hear God's Word, which is the beginning point for entering it. Before we had come into this community, we were entirely of the devil, knowing nothing of God and of Christ."[5]

Luther knew the value of that community precisely as the place into which a believer is brought and receives therein the gift of his salvation, which cannot be obtained anywhere else: "For where Christ is not preached, there is no Holy Spirit to create, call, and gather the Christian church, apart from which no one can come to the Lord Christ."[6]

THE CHURCH AS *HEILSANSTALT*

The above should impress on missiologists an appreciation for the Church as God's creation. The Church is not fashioned by man, even though such issues as budgeting, building material, and contractors will necessarily factor into the mind of a church planter. No, the Church derives her existence from God and continues to exist solely in view of God (*coram Deo*). Christians know that without God they would remain in sin.[7] In this sense, the existence and survival of the Church depend on the missionary work of the triune God. More precisely, the Church is the outcome of God's salvific will in Jesus Christ. She leads a life in Christ as His Body (Romans 10; 1 Corinthians 12), a life that has been founded on His death on the cross and His resurrection.[8] Thereby, Jesus Christ has made the Church His own property and He exercises His lordship over her. Founded on the objective

---

4   Gensichen, *Living Mission*, 58. For further discussions on this topic, see Guder, *Missional Church*, 77–85, as well as Schulz, "Towards a Missionary Church for the City," 4–13.

5   LC II 52 (Kolb-Wengert, 438).

6   LC II 45 (Kolb-Wengert, 436); Ap IV 138–39 (Tappert, 126).

7   SA III III 5 (Kolb-Wengert, 313); Ap VII 15 (Tappert, 170).

8   E.g., Ap VII 29 (Tappert, 173); SA II I 1–5 (Kolb-Wengert, 300–301). Two essays discuss the relation of justification and ecclesiology: Schwarzwäller, "Rechtfertigung und Ekklesiologie," 85–86, and von Loewenich, "Die Kirche in lutherischer Sicht," 200.

fact of the Christ event, the Church now receives her righteousness and salvation through the Word by faith.[9]

For this reason, the Church never attributes her existence to any subjective notions. People might choose their congregation for very personal reasons and longstanding members might place a sense of ownership on the church body, but ultimately Christ is Lord of the Church. There should not be any kind of intrusions that form a wedge between Christ and His Church. Such happened in pre-Reformation times when the elaborate hierarchical system of the Romanists, particularly papal jurisdiction and infallibility, built more on tradition than Scripture. In contrast, the reformers turned the Church over to Christ, and, most important, understood her to be a product of His Gospel. The Word alone became the mediating means between Christ and His Church. A third, meaning the papacy as it was advanced and defended during their time, was thus not allowed to be possible: "*tertium non datur!*"[10]

Today, activism rules in the Church. It still remains the case, however, that the Church is on the receiving end of God's gifts. Luther, on his deathbed, used the term *beggar* to describe the correct posture and attitude for himself and all Christians. Christians always receive from Christ the gifts He bestows. The doctrine of justification is the best description of that passive attitude. As believers adopt a receptive frame of mind, they attribute their existence to the Lord's activity through His Word. For this reason, Luther's definition of the Church makes a lot of sense when he describes her as "holy believers and sheep who hear the voice of their Shepherd," whose holiness solely "consists of the Word of God and true faith."[11] Luther's argument is simply this: if everything depends on Christ, then *everything* comes from Him through Word and Sacrament, which are the gifts upon which the Church lives.[12]

Christ is Lord over the congregation of saints. The Church is *the* community in which salvation is mediated, a *Heilsanstalt* ("institution of salvation"). Such exclusivity is evident in the following passage from Luther's Large Catechism: "All who are outside of this Christian people (*extra christianitatem*), whether heathen, Turks, Jews, or false Christians and hypo-

---

9 The salvific implications of Christ's lordship are described in LC II 30 (Kolb-Wengert, 414). Compare Peter Brunner's description of that relationship: "'Rechtfertigung' heute," 127–28.

10 SA II IV 9–13 (Kolb-Wengert, 308). Luther's rejection of the papacy is an obvious consequence for having placed itself illegitimately in a mediatory position between Christ and the believers.

11 SA III XII 2–3 (Kolb-Wengert, 325). See von Loewenich, "Die Kirche in lutherischer Sicht," 200.

12 Schwarzwäller, "Rechtfertigung und Ekklesiologie," 89. How the article on Christ ties in with the Sacraments and the life of the Church can be seen from the Smalcald Articles, where the article on the Mass (SA II II 1, Kolb-Wengert, 301) follows the article on the office and work of Christ.

crites . . . remain in eternal wrath and damnation. For they do not have the Lord Christ, and, besides, they are not illuminated and blessed by the gifts of the Holy Spirit."[13]

That exclusivity is further supported by Luther's imagery of the Church as the mother who nurtures and brings up her children through the Word.[14] Naturally, against the backdrop of this Lutheran ecclesiology, the classical saying *extra ecclesiam nulla salus est* ("outside the Church there is no salvation") still holds. We therefore question those proposals that wish to accommodate all outsiders who have no affiliation to the Church. Paul Tillich, for example, prompted notions of a "latent church" among other religions,[15] and Karl Rahner has exerted a similar influence in his suggestion that there are "anonymous Christians" interspersed among other religions in the world. Such efforts, however, destroy the belief that the Church takes central place in salvation history. The cord that connects Christ with the Holy Spirit is severed, and its place is taken by a scheme wherein God's salvific activity occurs apart from the Holy Spirit, the means of grace, and the Christian community.[16]

WHAT KIND OF A CHURCH SHOULD BE PLANTED?

Our discussion on the nature of the Church sheds valuable information on the concept of church planting (*plantatio ecclesiae*).[17] Church planting is a useful concept once we know what exactly the Church is. A basic definition would be to call the Church a spiritual entity, an assembly of saints

---

13 LC II 66 (Kolb-Wengert, 440). Exclusive claims are interspersed throughout the Confessions, e.g., Ap IX 2 (Tappert, 178); LC II 56 (Kolb-Wengert, 438); LC IV 69 (Kolb-Wengert, 465).

14 LC II 42 (Kolb-Wengert, 436). Because of her possession of the Word, Brunner calls the Church the "Arche des Heils" ("'Rechtfertigung' heute," 128–29).

15 See Tillich, "Missions and World History," 281–89, and Amstutz, *Kirche der Völker*, 104.

16 This, I believe, is apparent in numerous statements of Vatican II. To be sure, the encyclical *Dominus Iesus* (2000) has placed greater emphasis on the ecclesiological dimension. Vatican II, in its declaration *Nostra Aetate*, speaks of a "ray of truth which enlightens all men." See also *Lumen Gentium*: "Those also can attain everlasting salvation who through no fault of their own do not know the gospel of Christ or His Church, yet sincerely seek God and, moved by grace, strive by their deeds to do His will as it is known to them through the dictates of conscience. Nor does divine Providence deny the help necessary for salvation to those who, without blame on their part, have not yet arrived at an explicit knowledge of God." These statements are available in Abbott, *Documents of Vatican II*, 662, 35.

17 From a Protestant point of view, the term *plantatio ecclesiae* is theologically permissible only if the term implies the Church of "true believers" and a "congregation of saints" gathered around the "signs of the church," the preached and sacramental Word (AC VII 1, Kolb-Wengert, 43). In Roman Catholic circles, however, the theory "church plantation" includes the organization of the Church from the simple formation of the community to the establishment of the full hierarchy. See Müller, *Mission Theology*, 37–38. Such Protestant missiologists as Gustav Warneck broadened the plantation concept to the raising of a church that permeates and civilizes the broader community. See Warneck, *Evangelische Missionslehre*, 1:5.

or communion of believers consisting of all those who have been justified. Some scholars point out that this definition should include Baptism. This would identify the believers even more closely—namely, as those who are baptized (*coetus baptizatorum*), since Baptism is the "most unmistakable mark of membership in the Christian church."[18] This is most certainly true, despite the fact that there are those who, though baptized, no longer identify themselves with the Church. We may add also that identifying the Church as the baptized does not exclude those who have come to faith through hearing the Gospel but have not yet had the opportunity to be baptized. Using Baptism as the margin or border of the Church in distinction to those outside of her is still the most helpful means of distinguishing the Church, since it calls attention to the specific target group.

We also know that a church body cannot be sustained in faith apart from the Word. The Augsburg Confession, which provides the first Protestant definition of the Church, added to its definition of the Church as the *congregatio sanctorum*, the relative clause "among whom" or "in which" the Gospel is taught purely and the Sacraments are administered rightly.[19] Looking thus at the Church as those believers who are gathered around the Word and Sacraments, the classical distinction of invisibility and visibility is less helpful if it leads to an understanding of the Church being solely a Platonic entity of the mind.[20] The Church on earth is visible, shaped and normed by its signs, *the activities* of preaching and the administration of the means of grace.

The visible signs of the Church, around which believers gather, form the spiritual life of a Christian community. Particularly in the context of a dominant heathen culture, the Sacraments ultimately serve as a barricade against the perpetual onslaught of non-Christian elements on the believers. The gifts that began to shape the life of the community in Baptism continue to strengthen the fellowship through the Sacrament of the Altar. The Church is a sacramental community living in alien and hostile situations, and the Sacrament of the Lord's Supper affirms her as that. The Church of Christ thus lives in and from the Sacraments. The missiologist Walter Freytag observes correctly: "A church without Sacraments will die."[21]

---

18 Elert, *Christian Faith*, 252.

19 AC VII 1 (Kolb-Wengert, 43). Karl-Hermann Kandler thus points out that all emphasis should be placed on the relative clause: "Der Relativsatz ist also das Entscheidende . . . CA VII definiert Kirche von den Gnadenmittel her" (Kandler, "CA VII," 74).

20 Melanchthon clearly dismisses the attempt to posit the Church as a Platonic community since it is made up of "true believers and righteous men scattered throughout the world. And we add its marks, the pure teaching of the Gospel and the sacraments" (Ap VII 20, Tappert, 171). See also Ap XVI 13 (Tappert, 224).

21 Freytag, *Reden und Aufsätze*, 1:219–28, therein page 228. This can be corroborated from AC XIII 1–2 (Kolb-Wengert, 47).

If, as argued, the Christian community knows that it is brought together by outside means and not by self-initiated actions or interests, then it will also understand that it is much different from any other meeting and gathering in society. The Church is defined in the indicative, for what she *is*, rather than by what she *does*. To be sure, Christians are inclined to understand themselves by what they are doing, by purposes established in their life, and as such they think in terms of ethics and activism. For example, some Christians affirm their Christian calling by getting involved in mission. However, such activism (even mission activism!) should not be confused with the true definition of what the Church is. Any ethical dimension of the Church is only a consequence of what it is: the community of faith.

What does all this have to do with the goal of mission? Church planting efforts should focus on establishing communities that identify themselves with the objective realities of the Word and Sacraments. If the Church is able to guarantee those activities as they are set in the definition of the Church, then the missionary goal of church planting has in essence been accomplished. It is thus ultimately irrelevant whether an expatriate church planter or an indigenous leader is given the task of spiritual leader. The distribution and continuation of God's Word is paramount and that should be guaranteed first in every church planting project.

Planting a Church: What Matters

Church planting efforts need to distinguish between the dispensable and the indispensable issues. No longer should church planting efforts focus on creating replicas of the church body back home or on that entity which sponsors the project. Take South Africa, for example: large buildings and the use of pipe organs and brass instruments are indicative of foreign missionary import among the Zulu and the Tswana people. The lack of funds and skills needed to repair peripherals once the majority of missionaries had returned to their home countries have left such structures and instruments dilapidated and in disuse. What is indispensable, however, is the community raised on essential elements of the Christian faith. Church planting includes an obligation to the proclamation and teaching of all essential elements of the Lutheran faith as found in Scripture and as they are expounded in the Confessions.

Church planting efforts also include the goal of raising up an indigenous, independent church body. This might have to be an absolute necessity. Roman Catholicism more readily disperses its personnel all over the world than Protestantism does. Ideally, however, the regional church body should raise up her own indigenous clergy to continue and sustain the proclamation of the Gospel and the administration of the Sacraments. A regional church should be able to address her own financial needs and find leadership at all levels. To the three-selfs (self-propagation, self-governing, and self-supporting) should be added self-theologizing so that the church plant may teach herself the Gospel and Sacraments wherever her location may be. Sometimes, however, a church body may never reach the levels suggested by the three-selfs. Church planting strategies should thus entertain a certain degree of latitude that leaves time for development and growth. For example, for the welfare of a young church, Rufus Anderson (1796–1880) and Henry Venn (1796–1873) pleaded incessantly for the avoidance of a paternalistic approach to church planting that rigorously and legalistically imposes foreign structures upon indigenous Christians.

It makes sense to provide church planters with guidelines as they plan to lead a young church on her path to a responsible maturity.[22] A rigorous imposition of these guidelines, however, may result in disastrous consequences. A premature withdrawal of support, for instance, may disrupt the missionary and pastoral activities of a congregation and so offset the work of the Gospel. For example, when a partner church in South Africa sought to cut its own support from German and U.S. partner churches, the unfortunate result was that many pastors had to abandon their parishes for lack of salary and basic means to support their families. Wherever the three-self goals are implemented, partner churches should evaluate carefully any thought of terminating their support, in view of the grave consequences of such a decision.

CHURCH STRUCTURE
AND PASSING ON THE BATON

We suggest that church planting projects should return to the basic definition of what a church is and recognize the difference between primary goals based on that definition and secondary goals that engage ancillary issues. Such definition allows church bodies to seek out their own structure in freedom. The Reformation has taught us that the Church is not defined by a hierarchy or by foreign traditions foisted upon a congregation. Church polity and structure are variable. We cannot identify the progress of the Gospel with the extension of this or that institutional church.[23] Whether a church body adopts an episcopal or synodical structure, or a synthesis of the two, should be negotiable rather than a fixed rule.

---

22 Stolle, "Über die Zielsetzung organisierter Missionsarbeit," 134. See in contrast Smalley, "Cultural Implications of an Indigenous Church," 494–502.

23 The issue of church structure and tradition is discussed in Ap VII 23-42 (Tappert, 172–77). Gensichen, "Were the Reformers Indifferent to Missions?" 121

In the 1990s and obviously well before, the goal of planting indigenous churches became a point of discussion. Steffen[24] asserts that the
self-propagating and self-governing principles should include not only
the Gospel that is taught and preached in the language of the people but
also self-chosen structures of leadership that govern indigenous churches.
Mission should implement ways and means that would diminish the domi-
nating presence of foreign missionaries and allow the indigenous church
to assume its own structure of preference. For example, in the early 1990s,
the Lutheran Church of Southern Africa (LCSA) changed the status of
missionaries from official voters at pastors' conventions to advisors. Such
changes and many others were made in church bodies worldwide, and
even today as the foreign missionary presence continues, churches address
these issues. Sadly, very often, as a church initiates these transition phases,
tensions between missionary personnel and church leadership arise. Such
strife has a demoralizing effect on missionaries, and many choose to return
home. Unfortunately, the call of an indigenous church to readjust her relations with foreign missionaries often casts a shadow over the valuable contributions and services pioneer missionaries had made on her behalf as the
church transitions from a formative stage to a mature stage.

A further quandary is the appropriate length of stay for a missionary
in a partner church or in the mission field. Should churches and societies opt for the shortest time possible, as the trend seems to indicate? Are
planners motivated by the fear that the expatriate missionaries might overstay their welcome, plant roots, and so establish paternalistic structures
that could damage an emerging church? The passing on of the baton too
quickly to an indigenous leadership creates its own problems, one of which
is the danger of syncretism. Such a hybrid Christianity, where the Word of
God is merged with traditionally held beliefs, can be the result of a situation in which national leadership is raised in the shortest possible time
and with minimal education. Africa is an example where one of the side
effects of Christianity's rapid growth is the emergence of thousands of syncretistic communities. One lesson learned is that church planting efforts
cannot ignore the global and, properly understood, ecumenical claims of
the Gospel, and that these must be taught worldwide, no matter what, in
every context.

Thus the push of finding ways and means of adapting the Gospel to
the cultural and indigenous contexts bears its own dangers. As necessary
as such concerns are, I maintain that the task of raising homegrown, indigenous churches must not lose sight of the universal or catholic character

24 Steffen, *Passing the Baton.*

of Christianity and the Gospel. The following statement points to the commitment of striking a balance between universality and locality:

As local congregations endeavor to engage in mission, they must seek a balance between locality and universality, for universality and particularity are inseparably connected with each other. Without the universal communion of faith, each local church is unable to find a genuine self-understanding in the local context. For the church in mission, therefore, catholicity or universality without contextuality leads to imperialism, and contextuality without catholicity leads to provincialism.[25]

ETHNIC IDENTITY AND SOCIAL STRATIFICATION

The "homogeneous unit" principle is the idea that church bodies identify with a particular group or ethnicity of people. It has found widespread support within Church Growth circles.[26] This identification raises interesting questions about the true biblical and missional nature of ecclesiology. The homogeneous approach has found its way into missiological discussions and practices through Donald McGavran, who made this trenchant observation: "People like to become Christians without crossing racial, linguistic, or class barriers."[27] Elsewhere he observes:

The goal is not one single conglomerate church in a city or a region. They may only get that, but that must never be their goal. That must be a cluster of growing, indigenous congregations every member of which remains in close contact with his kindred. This cluster grows best if it is in one people, one caste, one tribe, one segment of society.[28]

McGavran's interest for homogeneous groups grew out of his experience with the caste system in India, where he saw the limited numerical growth in churches of India. Yet most may not know that McGavran drew his observations from two important Lutheran missionaries, Bruno Gutmann and Christian Keysser. Gutmann (1876–1966) devoted his attention to the Chagga tribe in Tanzania and Keysser (1877–1961) to the small clan system in the highlands of Papua New Guinea.[29] Both missionaries had adopted unique ways of accommodating the Gospel to the specific people group to whom they reached out. They combined the Gospel and

---

25 LWF, *Mission in Context*, 29–30.

26 Engle and McIntosh, *Evaluating the Church Growth Movement*, 140, 197.

27 McGavran, *Understanding Church Growth*, 163.

28 See McGavran, "Church in Every People," 624; McGavran and Arn, *How to Grow a Church*.

29 For a closer description of the practices of Bruno Gutmann and Christian Keyser, see Bürkle, *Missionstheologie*, 67–73; Yates, *Christian Mission in the Twentieth Century*, 34–56; Jaeschke, *Bruno Gutmann*. McGavran saw to it that Keysser's *Eine Papuagemeinde* was published in English as Keysser, *People Reborn*.

First Article issues relating to creation by arguing that the Gospel should preserve the natural practices and structures of a tribe, which Gutmann called "primordial structures" (urtümliche Bindungen).

Obviously, ethnic and tribal situations have always affected church planting efforts, and for missionaries it is hard to ignore a particular people group with its own ethnic and cultural identity. But if these principles are applied indiscriminately, the Church becomes focused on herself and protective of her interests. That was the Dutch theologian Johannes Christiaan Hoekendijk's (1912–75) criticism of Gutmann and Keysser in his 1948 work *Kerk en Volk in de Duitse Zendingswetenskap* (*Church and Nation in German Missiology*). Hoekendijk's criticism of Gutmann and Keysser seems unfair since they certainly did not promote their strategy in a way that nurtured a people's selfish interests against others. Hoekendijk's concern is considered today to be far too radical, particularly since he hardly thought along ecclesiological lines. Nonetheless, his concern should at least call every church body to reflect seriously about social and racial configurations and possible negative outgrowths. Such extreme results in which church bodies model themselves after specific interests existed during the apartheid regime in South Africa. Churches became so protective of their own tribal and national identity that they lost sight of the Gospel's integrative nature.[30] Previously, a similar problem had emerged in the German Church during the Third Reich, when she was founded along the Germanic ideals of *Volk, Blut, und Boden* ("nation, bloodline, and country").

Applying the homogeneous principle to the context of the United States would mean that the Church would have to appeal to every group of people according to private, social, and cultural dispositions. One church body focuses on the young adults in their early twenties, another congregation concentrates on reaching out to parents with young children, and still another church seeks out heavily tattooed motorcycle riders. Today, the principle of homogeneity has evolved into various ideas and approaches. For example, it is replicated among those who promote outreach to small groups. This strategy seeks to bring people together around preexisting interests such as golf or embroidery classes, then shares the Gospel with them.

Indeed and undeniably almost every church body identifies itself with a specific group of people. Certainly, mission should be genuinely concerned for a people group's needs, such as language and cultural characteristics,

---

30 One may see the South African debate with Donald McGavran in Fung, *Evangelistically Yours*, 147–50. Critical theologians in South Africa such as Fung have generally been dismissive of the homogenous principle "because the gospel must always be a crisis in the life and culture of a people; the Christian must always be called forth by the gospel from old life relations to enter into a new community."

as it brings the Gospel to a specific context.[31] There is always the danger, however, that where a church is planted with these principles in mind, she becomes so focused on the "felt needs" of the target group that she ends up identifying herself with things other than the Gospel or compromises parts of it. All popular forms of Church Growth, such as the market-driven and seeker-oriented approaches, are prone to such mistakes, namely, of determining ministry from the "felt needs" of the people and then formulating the Gospel to meet those needs.[32]

Social and cultural distinctions should not find their way into the Church. The reason lies in the theological claim and integrative power of the Gospel. The Gospel wishes to tear down human boundaries and walls erected between people for selfish reasons. The Gospel integrates socially and does not divide people into groups. It breaks apart the barriers of class, race, and culture and calls out a new community through the Holy Spirit. Ideally, every church should attempt to reflect the Gospel by becoming multicultural, even transcultural, in its life and service, even as Peter (Acts 11:4–18) and Paul (Gal. 3:28) both proclaimed. Where places of demographic homogeneity exist, God may some day place other groups of people and oblige Christians to take on a new perspective. Perhaps if a congregation were to concentrate on the traditional classic characteristics of the Church—one, holy, catholic, and apostolic—she would become fuller and more biblically grounded in outlook and configuration. In Scripture, we see a church that integrates people of all social and racial backgrounds. Only God's Word can bring everyone together and correct human-centered desires and egotistical interests, such as those of preserving one's own ethnic identity (e.g., Ephesians 2; Gal. 3:28). It took an apostolic council (Acts 15) to break the gridlock of ethnic rules and traditions to let the freedom of the Gospel prevail (Rom. 1:16–17).

Although it is necessary to take seriously the widespread cultural mosaic resulting from the tower of Babel, church bodies must visibly embody reconciliation across racial, ethnic, social, and linguistic divides. What comes to mind is Luther's caution that we should not understand the church as just any other social gathering that congregates around specific human desires and interests.[33] The Evangelical Lutheran Church in Kenya (ELCK), for example, consists of tribes, including the Luo, Kisi, and Kikuyu. The LCSA also has a membership from various tribes: the Batswana, Zulu, Xhosa, and

---

31 The so-called "church for the poor or homeless" reflects a true Christian concern, but that, too, can be a one-sided concern, as the WCC has shown. See here the ecumenical proposal in Section I of *Your Kingdom Come*, 171–78.

32 Engle and McIntosh, *Evaluating the Church Growth Movement*, 51.

33 This explains Luther's choice of *Gemeine* for "church" over *Gemeinschaft* (LC II 47–50, Kolb-Wengert, 436).

Sotho. As these church bodies look at the biblical term τὰ ἔθνη ("nations") of Matthew 28, they see that they embrace a multitude of nations who come and worship together. Such church bodies should seek to avoid preferential treatment for one tribe over others, especially with respect to leadership structures.

THE ETHICAL CHURCH

For a long time ethics has had a role in church planting strategies. Bernhard of Clairvaux (1090–1153), Francis of Assisi (1182–1226), and Raimund Lull (1235–1316) were ascetic divines who followed the ideals of Matt. 10:7–10 in the hope of winning Christians to a peaceful mission to the Muslims rather than the ongoing crusade movement. The era of pietism saw many pursue mission through a committed core within the larger Church (*ecclesiolae in ecclesia*). Both monasticism and pietism thought that mission demanded a special form of piety that went beyond that of ordinary Christians. Schleiermacher defined the Church in ethical terms that were not governed by doctrine: "Now the general concept of 'Church,' if there really is to be such a concept, must be derived principally from Ethics, since in every case the 'Church' is a society which originates only through free human action and which can only through such continue to exist."[34]

More recent missiological thinking has tended to portray the Church as an activist organization. For many, the Church is not a congregation of true believers, but a "reproductive fellowship" that is comprised of disciplers rather than disciples.[35] Supporters of this definition of the Church indicate that that they are unsatisfied with descriptions that portray the Church statically, as one that *is*, rather than dynamically, as what it *does*. The focus here is not on the indicative but on the imperative, the call for action. The concern this raises is that it potentially ignores the indicative, that the Church is one that must receive before she can engage in activity.

Those who focus upon the ethical shape and formation of a church body's existence often comment disparagingly on church bodies in which mission activity is lacking: "Any church that spends all its time huddling in worship without ever getting into the game of evangelism and social action is not worthy to be called a 'church.'"[36] Such criticisms exchange ethics for

---

34 Schleiermacher, *Christian Faith*, 1:3. See Holsten, "Die Lutherische Kirche als Träger der Sendung," 12–14.

35 Van Rheenen, *Missions*, 148. In chapter 9, the biblical evidence to prove his point of a reproductive fellowship is scant and unconvincing. See Guder, *Missional Church*, 110, 183–220, where the traditional sign "apostolic" is solely identified with sentness and the goal of "equipping God's people for mission."

36 Seamands, *Harvest of Humanity*, 16. Rick Warren's thinking is similar. See Warren, *Purpose Driven Church*, and Warren, *Purpose Driven Life*.

the marks of the Church. They are motivated by pietism and hence target the inactivity of a congregation. By so doing, these approaches also impugn the Lutheran definition of the Church. Certainly, those in a congregation who respond to the Gospel with a missionary interest are most desirable and, theologically speaking, are an important part of a church body's existence; faith never exists without good works. Nor should congregations take an inward orientation and forget missionary obligations. On the other hand, we should not presume that members are disqualified from the Body of Christ because of their slowness or failure to seek the lost. Drawing that conclusion would compromise the essence of the Church that points to the Holy Spirit and God's Word as what builds all Christian life and the community.[37]

Those who call the Church to activism and ethics should return to the simplicity with which the Reformation encountered the world and shared the Gospel. The social sciences, technology, programs, and media cannot replace the Gospel.[38] To be sure, mission has become a complicated and sophisticated endeavor, and there is still much truth in Werner Elert's remark that much of what we learn as mission theorists today in reality "belongs in the technical high schools, where the science of business is taught."[39] As we add ancillary methods and additional means to mission, we must avoid the danger of drawing mission further away from a Gospel- and Sacrament-focused ministry.

MISSION AND WORSHIP

Luther remarks that the Holy Spirit has "appointed a community on earth, through which he speaks and does all his work."[40] God continues His

---

37 See the LCMS statement *Toward a Theological Basis*, 10: "We do not mean to say that our slowness or failure to seek the lost has disqualified us from the body of Christ." See also Kandler, "CA VII," 76: "Sicher ist jede Kirche Zeugnis- und Dienstgemeinschaft . . . Aber das ist doch nur die Folge, nicht das, was Kirche zur Kirche macht." Vicedom also dismisses all ethical descriptions from the Church: "Da die Gemeinde von dem Worte Gottes lebt, muß sie in erster Linie eine hörende Gemeinde sein. Sie kann nur das in einem gemeinsamen Leben umsetzen und bezeugen, was sie gehört hat" (*Die Missionarische Dimension der Gemeinde*, 29.

38 For supporters of the Church Growth Movement, social sciences are crucial, as Peter Wagner clearly affirms: "Church growth looks to social science as a cognate discipline" (*Church Growth*, 33). See also Engle and McIntosh, *Evaluating the Church Growth Movement*, 45–48. Other scholars in turn warn against placing one's confidence in human observations, for in doing so the identification and synthesis of mission with contemporary culture seems to be more evident. Thus Gerhard O. Forde argues how justification creates a discontinuity with former social and psychological bindings, how the Gospel calls us out of our past sociological bindings and frees us for service to the world ("Forensic Justification and the Law," 283).

39 Elert, *Structure of Lutheranism*, 1:390.

40 LC II 61 (Kolb-Wengert, 439). The ecclesiology in the individual books of the Confessions varies somewhat. Although the Church is the medium in and through which God performs

mission in the world through the Church so that the Church takes the role of becoming an instrument in the mission of God. God authorized it for that activity. The Church finds herself in an interim lodged between two events. The starting point (*terminus a quo*) is the cross of Christ; the goal (*terminus ad quem*) is the full manifestation of Christ's rule on the Last Day. During this period, the Christian community is the seat where God is at work and through which God reaches out to the world.[41] It is impossible to see God's mission continuing without the Church. God desires that the Church preach the Gospel—though, strictly speaking, the success of God's mission depends on the Word and Spirit alone, not on the proclaimer.[42] Gensichen calls these two sides of God's mission the *divine intention* and the *missionary dimension*. God intends the salvation of mankind, and He translates His desire into calling the Church to mission. Both aspects are interlocked. This does not compromise the divine aspect of mission since all human activity goes back to God, who does the calling to salvation.[43]

In fact, the definition of the Church already bears a missionary dimension particularly in view of the relative clause: "*in which the Gospel is purely preached and the sacraments rightly administered.*" The relative clause "in which" uses the preposition "in," and it refers to an activity within the communion of believers that must be done in order to sustain them in the salutary faith. We are willing to call this inwardly focused liturgical aspect of the Church missional, insofar as believers receive the gifts of the triune God through it. The worship and liturgical rites of the Church allow the members to understand that they are recipients of the gift of salvation that the world has yet to receive.[44] Such an understanding of worship shares its roots, for example, in the traditional intercessory prayer service of the Church for those outside the Church:

> Almighty and everlasting God, You desire not the death of a sinner but that all would repent and live. Hear our prayers for those outside the Church. Take away their iniquity, and turn them from their false gods

---

His mission, Luther focuses in the catechisms largely on the congregation (*Gemeinde*), whereas Melanchthon thinks more in universal dimensions (*Kirche*).

41 The following is a short list of scholars who affirm the central role of the Church: Öberg, "Mission und Heilsgeschichte," 32–33; Beißer, "Mission und Reich Gottes," 51; Amstutz, *Kirche der Völker*, 47, 68–74; Vicedom, *Die missionarische Dimension der Gemeinde*, 52; Freytag, "Sendung und Verheißung," 217–23; Wiebe, "Missionsgedanken in den lutherischen Bekenntnisschriften," 41; Müller, *Mission Theology: An Introduction*, 24–25.

42 Dörries, "Luther und die Heidenpredigt," 340 (and 333), brings out this twofold aspect in Luther's theology: "Mission ist nicht Menschen-Sache, sondern allein Gottes Sache," but "Mission ist Sache aller Christen."

43 Gensichen, *Glaube für die Welt*, 90.

44 For a discussion on the relationship of worship, liturgy, and mission, see Schattauer, *Inside Out*.

to You, the living and true God. Gather them into Your holy Church to the glory of Your name; through Jesus Christ, our Lord.[45]

In the Early Church, after the proselytes and catechumens were released and the doors shut, the members brought the concerns of church and world before God prior to the Service of the Eucharist. As only they can do, the people of God pray to Him on the world's behalf in the end times.[46]

Thus the inwardly focused definition of the Church bears a missionary character, even if it is not yet that intentional, outward-oriented activity. But that shift is merely one of *focus and not of function*. As the Church shifts her attention to the world, the activities of preaching and teaching to outsiders remain the same. Here, Wilhelm Andersen's thinking informs us that "there is one thing which cannot be doubted—missionary activity belongs to the *esse*, to the nature, to the existence of the Church." One should be careful to qualify Andersen's statement by remembering that the Church is "that which has the Holy Spirit" (Ap VII 22), and thus missionary "activity" should be seen in the light of the Spirit working through the means of grace.[47] This working of the Spirit through Word and Sacrament in worship to bring about the existence and unity of the Church does have a missionary dimension. On the other hand, it is not the case that "the church is simply the mission."[48] While the extrinsic or outward missionary focus flows from the intrinsic missionary existence of the Church, both aspects are not identical. A congregation worships for other reasons than simply to reach out to outsiders. Peter Brunner observes:

> Whoever beholds in worship only an agency for the completion of an incompletely executed missionary undertaking is undermining worship instead of establishing it. The reasons adduced for the need of worship must prove their validity by the very fact that this need also exists when the missionary task may be regarded as basically solved. It must be shown why worship is an inner, spiritual necessity especially for the true believers, for those who earnestly desire to be Christians. Only when the function of worship for the true believers is recognized and this is made the

---

45 Commission on Worship, *Lutheran Service Book*, 305.

46 See Sasse, "*Ecclesia Orans*," 3–4.

47 Kolb-Wengert, 177.

48 See Andersen, *Towards a Theology of Mission*, 54. Also Hartenstein, "Theologische Besinnung," 63. Strasser, "Das Wesen der Mission nach lutherischem Verständnis," 7, equates the functional understanding of the Church with her mission: "Die *Kirche des wirkenden Wortes* hat weiter darin ihr Wesen, daß ihr Bestand davon abhängig ist, daß das Wort von und in ihr verkündet wird. . . . Sofern von und in ihr das Evangelium gepredigt wird, ist sie da, hat sie ihren Bestand, wirkt sie und lebt sie. Diese Lebensäußerung ist aber nichts anderes als *Mission*." See also Meyer-Roscher, "Die Bedeutung der lutherischen Bekenntnisschriften," 24: "Kirche ist erst da, wo wirklich gelehrt und gepredigt wird, wo die Sakramente wirklich gereicht werden. Kirche gibt es nur im Blick auf das Zeugnis an die Welt . . . Kirche und Mission gehören zusammen, und zwar so, daß das missionarische Zeugnis zum Wesen der Kirche gehört."

standard of its essence and its realization only then may this worship, without any change in its essence, also assume missionary interests, even though these interests at present undoubtedly demand special programs of the church for the indifferent, the estranged, and near-apostates, programs which do not coincide with the worship of the congregation or cannot be absorbed into it.[49]

We could elaborate on the preceding quotation at great length. Let it suffice to add that the Church must strike an important balance between reaching out as the instrument in God's mission to the world while serving and strengthening members for that role through the means of grace proffered at worship. Welcoming newcomers to worship should not imply that worship is now intended for newcomers instead of for the regular members who have been initiated and taught the liturgical practices. For this reason, David Valleskey, though willing to entertain the thought of an alternate worship form such as a *Friendship Sunday* for visitors, dismisses the use of so-called *Seeker Services* on the basis of their character being alien to the traditional understanding of worship.[50] Many in Evangelical circles would concur with the concern Valleskey raises:

> Thus, we call Evangelicals to turn away from forms of worship that focus on God as a mere object of the intellect or that assert the self as the source of worship. Such worship has resulted in lecture-oriented, music-driven, performance-centered and program-controlled models that do not adequately proclaim God's cosmic redemption.[51]

GOALS IN LIGHT OF ESCHATOLOGY

Often, the Church underscores her missionary purpose and intent with a solemn pledge to do so. Such pledges may include numerical goals. Yet, as Barrett points out, the history of mission reveals that the goals of such pledges have not been achieved, be it Edinburgh's pledge in 1910 to evangelize the world in the contemporary generation[52] or during the so-called "missionary decade" (1990s) when denominations across the board vowed to intensify their outreach in order to expand Christianity throughout the world.[53] Numerous reasons may account for the unaccomplished missionary goals. Perhaps it is because the Gospel has to contend with immense

---

49 Brunner, *Worship in the Name of Jesus*, 110–11.

50 Valleskey, *We Believe—Therefore We Speak*, 197–204.

51 To be found in "The Call" (Thesis 4), www.ancientfutureworship.com.

52 Scholars conclude that the tone of the conference was motivated by an apocalyptic enthusiasm. See Bosch, *Transforming Mission*, 336–39. See also Gäbler, "Der eschatologische Neuansatz in der Mission," 42–43.

53 Barrett and Johnson, *World Christian Trends*, xiii.

powers and forces outside of human control. We have spoken already of the eschatological character of the Church. We need to reiterate the point that the Church on earth is a militant church and so her triumph is often hidden by signs of apparent failure. She struggles against a hostile world. As she preaches the Gospel, she faces rejection, retaliation, and martyrdom. The Gospel comes and goes, Luther said, like a rain cloud dropping at a certain location the blessings of the Gospel before moving on.[54] The Church will not be victorious in this world, but rather she anxiously awaits the day of victory at the final coming of the Lord. That does not mean the Church is despondent and inactive. But her attitude includes the posture of humbly praying to the Lord that He may provide her with endurance and resilience to address those who withstand the preaching of the Gospel.[55]

A proper focus on the end includes an attitude that lets the Church know of her limited powers and her inability to "hold up" or hasten the coming of the end. The Church has no control over the Gospel, since the labors of mission are rewards of the Gospel and not of the Church's efforts.[56] She sees herself merely as an agent, a *cooperatix* as it were, and not as co-redeemer, a *co-redemptrix*.[57] However, as the Church faithfully performs her divinely given activities to the world, the proclamation of the Word and the administration of the Sacraments, she may be confident that the Holy Spirit adds members to the community. The Lord truly is sovereign, but He has bound His work of bringing salvation to the Word.[58]

Perhaps the Church Militant will never strike a perfect synthesis between the divine intention and her own missionary involvement, so that she is continuously called upon to purify her own missionary motives. Paul Althaus suggested that the Church is never free from the constant task of reviewing her activity in this world.[59] Althaus made his point against the backdrop of a decade of dubious compliances between the German Church

---

54 Stolle, *Church Comes from All Nations*, 82; Maurer, "Reformation und Mission," 31. See also Blöchle, "Die Missionarische Dimension in der Theologie Luthers," 362.

55 Luther expresses his hope in a final vindication, SA II IV 15 (Kolb-Wengert, 310): "We must rely upon the hope that Christ our Lord has attacked his enemies and will carry the day, both by his Spirit and at his return. Amen." See also LC II 31, 58 (Kolb-Wengert, 434–35). Freytag, "Mission im Blick aufs Ende," 186–98, points out a threefold consequence of an eschatological orientation in mission. It gives mission its validity (*Begründung*), it makes up an important aspect of her proclamation (*Verkündigung*), and it defines her goal (*Zielsetzung*).

56 Luther lists the enemies of the Church as being "the devil," "sin or our flesh," and the "world" (LC III 62–64, Kolb-Wengert, 448).

57 See here Gensichen, *Glaube für die Welt*, 114.

58 See here *Toward a Theological Basis*, 16.

59 Althaus, "Um die Reinheit der Mission," 48–60; Gensichen, *Living Mission*, 20–21.

and the state and between mission and colonial imperialism for which Christians still have to apologize to non-Christians.[60]

THE RELATION OF CHURCH
AND MISSION SOCIETIES

Let us assume one important principle as the Church pursues her missionary obligation—namely, that all believers assume a role in mission. We will discuss this principle in the next chapter. In the past, where church bodies responded to mission, it became the task of a few committed members within the Church. After the Reformation, the natural movement or expansion of the Church was soon complemented by the services of the great Lutheran Societies of Hermannsburg, Neuendettelsau, and Leipzig, which took on the difficult task of addressing overseas mission. As the nineteenth century progressed, parachurch organizations emerged that took on the task of mission, often without the support and consent of the church bodies. That lack of support was painfully evident when church leadership often refused to ordain and commission missionaries.

In light of mission becoming a concern of the whole Church, the idea of making the missionary obligation part of the congregations and not just a board or society representing these congregations makes a lot of sense. Wilhelm Maurer concludes that in the early days of the Church and during the Reformation, a *proprium* in mission was the congregation (*Gemeindemission*) and not the organized work of a society (*Gesellschaftsmission*). He concludes from an overview of the history of mission "that congregational mission was the more original and appropriate form."[61] And when Luther encourages mission, he thinks of the winsome powers that emanated from Protestant congregations and individuals into their unbelieving surroundings. Hans-Werner Gensichen draws the same conclusion from a comparison between the present and the time of the Reformation: "Here perhaps lies the main difference between the theology of mission as developed by the Reformers and the various modern attempts to define mission as one activity of the Church among others, an additional enterprise which need not concern too much the Church as a whole but can be left to some specialists or little groups of enthusiasts."[62]

Already early Christianity, at least since postapostolic times, carried out mission through the life of entire congregations that penetrated their surroundings. Today, mission has become a project at multiple levels in the

---

60 This impacts in particular the Christian-Muslim dialogue; see Huff, "Crusades and Colonial Imperialism," 141–48.

61 Maurer, "Der lutherische Beitrag zur Weltmission," 181.

62 Gensichen, "Were the Reformers Indifferent to Missions?" 124.

Church: from being organized at a denominational or synodical level, to one that is initiated also by district-synods and local circuits or diocesan counterparts, and finally pursued also by a congregation and all its members. Mission is an issue for all Christians today, and so it will no longer simply involve donations and tithing but members actually going to those who do not know the Christian faith.[63] But as one looks at such operations and the numerous activities overseas, the question should be asked whether overseas mission in particular should not remain an important concerted and organized effort of the entire church body. Thus placing the obligation on a board or society would imply that it is doing it on behalf of and as a joint effort of all congregations. Overseas mission could easily fall into a chaotic enterprise when no organized and clear strategic focus is provided. In addition, so that the resources for foreign mission are used efficiently, it would be logical and prudent to have an administrative body such as a board or society, rather than every congregation, create its own oversight committee. Finally, mission does operate with an *authorized* sending. Lutheranism has never taken the radical faith mission approach in which individual Christians choose to go of their own accord, without the authorized commissioning of the church body through the board or society.

The relationship of Church and mission society is even more evident when we look at the ecumenical, world-embracing character of mission. Since mission represents the task of preaching the Gospel, it needs to ensure that it does so in accordance with what Scripture teaches. This concern is reflected already in the Augsburg Confession: "The church is the assembly of saints in which the Gospel is taught purely and the sacraments are administered rightly."[64] The adverbs "purely" and "rightly" mean that missionaries bring the unadulterated scriptural message of salvation to the people. Mission is all about bringing the Gospel to those held in unbelief, but this activity is built on a serious concern that the Gospel is brought to people true to the biblical message. This is where the Lutheran Confessions, as the proper explanation of Scripture, assist the Church in keeping her message to the world biblically sound.

Often, however, this confessional concern for the content of the Gospel is contested and decried as "ecclesiastical propaganda" or "patriarchial pedagogy."[65] Some call it a selfish interest of missionaries who foist an ecclesiology on others and push a standard of purity that stands in the way of getting the message out to the people who are in need of it. This assessment

---

63   Bliese and Van Gelder, *Evangelizing Church*, 28.

64   AC VII 1 (Kolb-Wengert, 43).

65   Scherer, *Mission and Unity in Lutheranism*, 41. Peter Beyerhaus also faults it in *Die Selbständigkeit der jungen Kirchen*, 313. See also the critical notes made by Stolle, *Wer seine Hand an den Pflug legt*, 97–100.

sets up false alternatives. There should be no conflict between getting the message out and doing so in accordance with the teachings of Scripture and the Church. The apostle Paul shared both concerns. Indeed, his goal was to bring the Gospel to all nations, but he clearly mandated that it must be kept inviolate (Gal. 1:6–9). The Epistle to the Romans demonstrates well both interests. Paul shares with the Romans the depth and heart of his theology and puts it between the bookends of his opening and closing chapters. By using such a framing technique, he joins his theology with his missionary interest, the desire to bring it to all nations (Rom. 15:28). Too often, this missionary framework of Romans is sidelined in exegetical treatments. The fact stands, however, that Paul was a missionary at heart, and he wanted to proclaim the Gospel with integrity.

It is thus questionable whether Roland Allen adequately captures Paul's interest in preserving the proper content of the Gospel. Allen warns missionaries and church planters that they should not be too guarded and rigid in their preaching and teaching of the message, for this will get in the way of the Spirit's work. Allen points out that we are generally motivated by fear and concern: "[T]he terrible fears that beset us, fears for our doctrine, our moral standards, our civilized Christianity, our organization . . . Spontaneous expansion must be free: it cannot be under our control."[66] Concern for the content of the Gospel or doctrine cannot be placed among the variables of church planting, as Allen claims. The history of mission is replete with examples of syncretism, a result of superficial preaching where the Church was not built on a proper theological foundation.

THE GOAL OF MISSION: ECUMENICAL YET AUTHENTICALLY LUTHERAN

Perhaps the answer on whose behalf mission is done may help to clarify some of the questions above. No mission would ever claim to further a particular denomination. Every preaching activity occurs on behalf of the Church of Christ, the Church catholic or *una sancta ecclesiae*, comprised of believers all over the world. The mandate for mission is a universal one, and it represents the service for the one Church on earth across all denominational lines. To affirm this unity of the Church is an article of faith; Christians believe in such unity despite divisions and the great multitudes of the wicked within the Church. And through mission, God collects His redeemed community across all denominations far beyond the borders of what we may believe to be the particular righteous and true

---

66 Allen, *Spontaneous Expansion of the Church*, 5.

visible Church. Missionaries work for the one Lord Jesus Christ and for His catholic Church.

At the same time, the missionary also represents his own denomination. Lutheran mission must serve the one true Church, and it exists for the very reason of upholding the purity of the Gospel throughout the world. Lutheran mission is thus not selfishly arguing for its own validity apart from the Church catholic. Lutheran mission exists because it harbors a deep soteriological concern for the salvation of the world and the truth being preached in its true biblical form. As missionaries seek to speak the truth, they are concerned that nothing be placed in the way of the Spirit's work. They also wish that new believers would learn to distinguish the Gospel from doctrinal aberrations and not repeat mistakes that have already been addressed. The great founder of the Lutheran mission society at Hermannsburg in Germany, Ludwig Harms, presented the following motivation and goal of mission:

> For we cannot bring them [the heathen] anything else but that what we possess. Since we belong to the Lutheran Church we should and want to bring to the heathens no other church than the Lutheran Church, whose members we are. For we teach in the Lutheran Church the Word of God in pure, unadulterated form and administer in our church baptism and Holy Communion purely and in accordance with the Lord's institution.[67]

Here come to mind also the three programmatic statements that capture the tradition of Lutheran mission. These were articulated by the Lutheran Church Mission (Bleckmar Mission), founded in 1892. Its executive director, Friedrich Wilhelm Hopf, reaffirmed them in 1953. These three principles set down the important strategic rules for the relationship between mother Church, mission society, and the goal:

Principle 1: "The Lutheran church can pursue only Lutheran mission";

Principle 2: "Lutheran mission work can only be pursued by the Lutheran church";

Principle 3: "Lutheran mission work must lead to a Lutheran church."[68]

These principles also establish significant ecclesiological guidelines for all Lutheran missionary efforts, particularly for mission societies as they seek support and pursue their goals on behalf of the Lutheran Church. The

---

67 Harms's interest was also supported by numerous other theologians representing their own mission societies such as Eduard Huschke of the Silesian Lutherans, Johann Gottfried Scheibel and Karl Graul of the Dresden (later Leipzig) mission, and Ludwig Adolf Petri and Wilhelm Löhe of the Neuendettelsau Society for Home and Foreign Mission. See Maurer, "Der Lutherische Beitrag zur Weltmission," 177–79.

68 Hopf, "Lutherische Kirche treibt Lutherische Mission," 13–47.

following case study of David and Mary (though hypothetical) illustrates their validity:

> David and Mary have started their own mission project across the border in Mexico, and as Lutherans, they work out of a Lutheran congregation in Texas. On a weekly basis, they visit a village in Mexico where they have planted a church and erected a church building for services that both David and Mary lead. David and Mary, however, have chosen not to baptize children, but true to their former past as Baptists still believe only those should be baptized who can account for their faith around the age of twelve or older. They choose to baptize by immersion. In addition, they are also uncertain whether the Lord's Supper actually contains Christ's bodily presence and thus leave that an open question. Moreover, as they stage servant events, they seek the support of all denominations, rather than just from those who are Lutheran.

It is evident that David and Mary would not concur with the three principles articulated above. Their congregation out of which they work also seems to be content with the non-Lutheran character of David and Mary's witness and mission, in violation of principle 1. David and Mary see no reason why their mission society should be supported and backed theologically by a Lutheran congregation. They keep their witness deliberately broad to accommodate a larger donor base. Their nondenominational character accommodates many supporters who would otherwise not be willing to cooperate. This clearly speaks against principle 2. In terms of the goal or the end product, they have produced a church body and worship life that seems to reflect little of the Lutheran home church in Texas and its belief, a violation of principle 3.

The One Church of Christ (the *una sancta*)

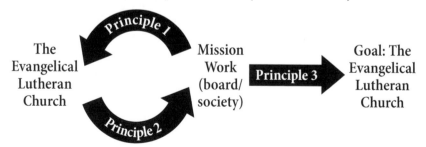

Principle 1: The Lutheran Church can pursue only Lutheran mission.
Principle 2: Lutheran mission work can be pursued only by the Lutheran Church.
Principle 3: Lutheran mission work must lead to a Lutheran Church.

Fig. 3: The Relationship of Church, Mission Work, and Goal

The Lutheran missionary and church planter represents a church body that claims to stand for the content of the Gospel. As he conveys this content of the Gospel in a church planting context, the new community's faith and practice will reflect the missionary's preaching and confession. Every preacher knows how much his preaching and teaching shapes also the life of a Christian community. In his role as preacher and teacher, the church planter shares scriptural truths with specific people who interpret Scripture as they have learned it from him. Important truths such as who Christ is, how one is justified, the proper distinction of faith and works, the two kingdoms, and the real presence of Christ in the Lord's Supper are all elements of a missionary's preaching. Thus every church planter assumes responsibility in two ways: he is accountable to the faith of the church body to which he belongs and he is responsible for the theological outlook of the members of his congregation. For in terms of the latter, preaching and teaching the Gospel with integrity becomes a visible mark of a particular church at a specific locality and time. The true mark of a young church's indigenous aspect is to appropriate the correct preaching of the Gospel and right administration of the Sacraments in her people's language so that it will penetrate the world and all sections of society around her. To bring this goal to reality is testimony to a church planter's legitimate spiritual concern. It is not, I submit, an expression of theological paternalism.

This discussion points to a question often asked: with whom may the missionary join to further the church planting and evangelizing project? Here, the principle for pulpit and altar fellowship is applicable—or, as it is often called, the communion in sacred things (*communio in sacris*). This principle allows joint preaching and church planting efforts only among those who stand in the same faith in Christ, such as partner church bodies and their congregations and mission projects. Thus Lutheran preaching will partner only with other mission projects in which a common consensus on the Gospel and its doctrines exist.[69] On the other hand, human care and other services addressing physical concerns need not abide by the same standard since such represent external concerns and do not pertain directly to the preached and sacramental Word. Thus the well-known rule of cooperation in externals (*cooperatio in externis*) applies here and allows

---

69 The nature and content of this consensus in doctrine is crucial insofar as it preserves and promotes saving faith. For example, Christians do not only believe that they are saved in Christ, but they should also know who their Savior is (Matt. 16:16). The Lutheran Confessions themselves support the idea of a consensus, e.g., SD X 5–8, 16 (Kolb-Wengert, 636, 638), but the concept of such a consensus must not be presented as a complex theological system. Rather, it must find its promotion in the context of the life of the Church, in the activities of the preached and administered Word (AC VII). See Meyer-Roscher, "Die Bedeutung der lutherischen Bekenntnisschriften für die gegenwärtige ökumenische Diskussion," 31. See also Sasse, "Über die Einheit der Lutherischen Kirche," 244–58; Sasse, "Die Frage nach der Einheit der Kirche," 216–27.

a partnership of cooperation in efforts such as establishing clinics or relief programs between two denominations that do not stand in full theological agreement.

The Lutheran Confessions are a tool that assist church planters in bringing the Gospel with integrity to their members. This point lies in the claim of the Confessions themselves as being nothing but an explanation of what Scripture says. Also, as they are appropriated by new believers and especially by a new church body, it may cross their mind to formulate their own confession. In fact, scholars such as Edmund Schlink are willing to entertain the thought of new confessions: "No Confession of the Church," he argues, "may be regarded as definitive in the sense of precluding the possibility of further Confessions."[70] Schlink's proposition is certainly interesting. At first, it may seem true that new theological problems arise in different contexts. After a moment's reflection, however, one realizes that most so-called "new" problems are nothing but old wine in new skins. Moreover, what prevents a new confession from being established is precisely the ecumenical concern that must find agreement among a broader body of churches than just the one particular church body that has formulated it. An important provision for unity among church bodies is not that of promoting diversity in confession but rather a unity underscored by *common confessional documents*.[71]

THE DOXOLOGICAL GOAL: PLANTING A WORSHIPING COMMUNITY

Ultimately, what is the goal of mission? The goal of mission has reached its apex when the baptized gather around the preached and administered Word and praise Christ as their Lord. This is what occurred when the church in Jerusalem was formed (Acts 2:42). The Christians gathered together, praised Christ through hymns and prayer, and shared the Lord's Supper. The doxological moment coincides with the kyriological goal. In terms of the former, the worship service leads newcomers and Christians into the presence of Christ, and they praise Him as their Lord.[72] The community hails Christ as the Lord who was crucified and risen, and it looks

---

70 Schlink, *Theology of the Lutheran Confessions*, 31.

71 This was a clear concern for the authors and subscribers of the Formula of Concord; see SD Summary 1 (Kolb-Wengert, 526). See Schlink, *Theology of the Lutheran Confessions*, 207 n. 13, and Sasse, "Über die Einheit der Lutherischen Kirche," 245.

72 The doxological dimension is the "Ziel und Gipfel dieses Gottesdienstes" (Brunner, "Theologie des Gottesdienstes?" 114). See Cullmann, *Salvation in History*, 116. Note, therefore, the sequence in LC I 70 (Kolb-Wengert, 395) as suggested also in Rom. 10:9: "First the heart honors God by faith and then the lips by confession." Beyerhaus, "Die Predigt als Ruf zur Mission," 27, makes the doxological aspect the first priority of the *missio ecclesiae*.

upon Christ as the Lord who will eventually return as Judge. In terms of the latter, the Christian worship service becomes the seat where the Lord Himself rules. He is present to bestow His gifts of eternal life, to which the community then responds in prayer, praise, thanksgiving, and service.[73]

Every missionary effort should lead to a worshiping community. The outsiders who were first addressed through the missionary proclamation come together and continue to receive the gift of salvation in their joint celebration. Like the missionary proclamation, the worship service of the Church, starting from Baptism to the celebration of the Lord's Supper, carries a common soteriological motive. For the worship service primarily has to do with every Christian's salvation before God and his preservation in that salvation so that eternal damnation does not await him at his death.[74] Church planters and pastors are aware that there are many reasons why newcomers are brought to the service or why believers come together. But worship takes place as a public event in order that salvation is imparted from the pulpit and altar through the absolution of sins to all gathered. Consequently, forgiveness of sins and justification represent not just abstract doctrine, but they are also realized within the concrete structure of the actual hearing of the believers in the worship service.

We know that, for Luther, the key criterion for addressing false elements in the traditional service, the Mass, was the doctrine of justification. Today, we should think no differently. The doctrine of justification still remains the crucial element for evaluating the correct worship service in terms of what must be preached, in counseling (*Seelsorge*), and in the proper administration of confession and Absolution.[75] The central doctrine on which the Church stands and falls takes its critical seat in the worship service and sheds light on all false worship and idolatrous practices. There is only one true Christian worship, and it stands as a wall opposing all false expressions of worship.

What, then, is true worship? Fundamentally, true worship is the proper trust and faith of the heart that acknowledges and gives full credit to God for who He truly is. Luther observes: "It is the trust and the faith of the heart alone that make both God and an idol. If your faith and trust are

73 Ap IV 309–10 (Tappert, 155). Brunner, "Theologie des Gottesdienstes?" 315.

74 Brunner, "Theologie des Gottesdienstes?" 109.

75 Martens, *Die Rechtfertigung des Sünders*, 23: " 'Rechtfertigung' bezeichnet in den Bekenntnissen als doctrina das Geschehen, das sich in den Wesenskonstitutiva der Kirche, Wort und Sakrament, vollzieht, sowie deren Inhalt." See here the respective passages in the Lutheran Confessions where justification relates to the ecclesial acts in preaching: AC XX 8 (Kolb-Wengert, 55); Ap XII 88 (Tappert, 195); Ap XV 42–43 (Tappert, 220–21); FC SD V 1 (Kolb-Wengert, 581); and in penance and the Mass: AC XXV 5 (Kolb-Wengert, 73); AC XXVI 7 (Kolb-Wengert, 75); Ap IV 300 (Tappert, 153); Ap XII 91–92 (Tappert, 195–96).

right, then your God is the true one."[76] Proper worship takes place where faith places trust in God alone and in no one else. The righteous or correct faith in Christ sets the standard that defines religious action that pleases God or that obscures the honor and glory of Jesus Christ. By contrast, false worship does not give full honor to Christ and what He achieved. Rather, it is focused on oneself with the interest of earning the forgiveness of sins and righteousness.[77]

It is true that proper Christian worship is argued from Luther's perspective, at least on an individualistic basis, namely, from the faith and proper relation of a Christian to God. We may speak of this as worship in the "broad sense," as the immediate existential relationship of a Christian's faith in God. We should point out, however, that this individual nature also defines the corporate nature of worship, or what we may call worship in the "narrow sense." Both reflect the relation of God to man and that of man to God, even if one brings out the corporate and the individual aspect. In this sense, both should be discussed together.[78] Believers come to worship as individuals and find value in its public and corporate character. There, every believer finds the assurance that he does not exist on his own as a Christian and that he receives the same gift of salvation as do all the others. Worship is also where the public liturgical life provides an ecumenical perspective. What the local community does in terms of practice reflects its understanding of what the catholic Church teaches, which in turn reminds it to take a guarded approach to innovation, even when it means providing inculturated and contextualized worship forms.[79] Public worship is thus crucial for the support and preservation of a Christian's faith.

---

76 LC I 2 (Kolb-Wengert, 386). For Luther's and Melanchthon's discussion of true and false worship, see Ap XV 13–21 (Tappert, 216–18), with the frequent connection of justification or faith and worship (*cultus*). For it shows how Melanchthon wishes to draw out the radical difference between Christian and heathen worship (*cultus*) in using the doctrine of justification in relation to faith and works. Luther sees a united block set against Christianity in his Large Catechism within the frame of the First Commandment and the Creed, e.g., LC I 3, 13, 17 (Kolb-Wengert, 386–87); LC II 66 (Kolb-Wengert, 440); SA III VIII 9 (Kolb-Wengert, 323).

77 See, for example, Ap XV 14, 17, 20 (Tappert, 216–18).

78 Brunner, "Theologie des Gottesdienstes?" 97.

79 The Augsburg Confession makes this programmatic statement: "It is enough (*satis est*) for the true unity of the church to agree concerning the teaching of the gospel and the administration of the sacraments. It is not necessary that human traditions, rites, or ceremonies instituted by human beings are alike everywhere" (AC VII 2–3, Kolb-Wengert, 43); Ap VII 30 (Tappert, 174); SD X 9 (Kolb-Wengert, 637). The statement is also made that adamant demand for a certain rite or tradition should not convey the impression that they are useful or necessary for salvation (Ap XV 20, Kolb-Wengert, 218). For a recent study on the topic, see Waddell, *Struggle to Reclaim the Liturgy*; Brunner, "Theologie des Gottesdienstes?" 109; Martens, *Die Rechtfertigung des Sünders*, 25.

THE BORDERLINE OF FAITH AND UNBELIEF

One should not expect communal worship to represent perfection in every sense. Luther, as we said, speaks of a uniform and idolatrous array of worldly and diabolical powers that stand outside and against the true worshiping community. But he is also mindful that as long as the Church exists on earth, she represents a mixed body of people among whom there are also false Christians and hypocrites (Matt. 13:24–30). These false Christians might worship the one, true God with others, but they do not know, as Luther would argue, God's attitude toward them.[80] No Christian who participates in worship with others will automatically be immune to idolatrous and pagan influences. In fact, all Christians, even those who consider themselves perfectly versed in Scripture, who believe they have mastered most of what the Church teaches, and who abstain from pagan practices, are still exposed to the dominion of the devil. In Luther's words, the evil one relaxes neither day nor night, stealing upon Christians unawares and kindling in their heart unbelief and wicked thoughts. Every Christian must therefore be vigilant throughout his entire life and remain continually in God's Word and in the supportive structure of a worship life. There, the Word of God is preached and does its power publicly; it sees to it that the devil does not do his damage;[81] and it awakens a new understanding of and devotion to Scripture, as well as a renewed pleasure and desire to do God's will.

The proclamation of God's Word in worship assumes a missionary role. Even if most worship services presuppose a mature audience, for them, too, the sermon becomes a missionary proclamation.[82] Believers are reminded of their sinfulness, and God redeems them of it regularly as they participate in the preached and sacramental Word. The worshiping community is built on the reality of salvation, which has entered their lives through Baptism. Even if the worship of Christians will never attain a direct missionary function, all Christians gathered remain thankful for God's protective mission against spiritual onslaughts.[83]

---

80 LC II 66 (Kolb-Wengert, 440).

81 See Luther's discussions on the Third Commandment and worship: LC I 91, 94, 100–102 (Kolb-Wengert, 399–400). Wiebe, "Missionsgedanken in den lutherischen Bekenntnisschriften," 33: "Man bricht also weder durch Gottesglauben noch durch christkirchliche Zugehörigkeit ohne weiteres aus der Einheitsfront des 'Heidentums' aus!"

82 Hermann Dörries concludes this from Luther's theology: that "alle Predigt ist Missionspredigt!" ("Luther und die Heidenpredigt," 328).

83 See here Brunner, "Theologie des Gottesdienstes?" 115.

THE LORD'S SUPPER

The Sacrament of the Lord's Supper plays an important and ongoing role in creating a bond among believers in their common faith in the presence of the Lord. Moreover, it plays a part in the spiritual formation of believers and strengthens the worshiping community for spiritual battle in the world. Although the Lord's Supper is not a "missionary" sacrament as Baptism is, it gives a public testimony to the world that something special is taking place amid the believers. There is an exclusivity experienced with the celebration of the Eucharist that cannot permit all newcomers indiscriminately to the table without ascertaining who they are and from what background they come.[84] For the Eucharist is a sacrament reserved for those who are baptized and instructed. In this sense, being admitted to the Lord's Supper is a consequence of proper Christian education (*didache*) and, as such, an application of Matt. 28:19 that they all may be "taught" in what Christ Himself has taught.[85]

The foregoing considerations emphasize the missiological importance of the worship service in a mission setting. The Divine Service provides the basis and prerequisite for mission that cell groups or "small group"-oriented church planting projects, given their lack of the full preached and sacramental Word, cannot provide.[86] The community finds strength and preparation for her missionary service to the world (*ad extra*) through worship. Worship edifies and builds up the Body of Christ and strengthens it for activity and for the confrontation with the non-Christian world. Stanley Hauerwas and William H. Willimon suggest that the worship life molds and shapes Christians as aliens in a hostile world.[87] The designations

---

84 This is where Bliese and Van Gelder, *Evangelizing Church*, 46–47, is disappointing, since it pleads for Eucharistic hospitality toward believers and nonbelievers alike. In contrast, the exclusive character of the Lord's Supper is affirmed by the Lutheran Confessions: AC XXIV 6 (Kolb-Wengert, 69): "For people are admitted only if they first had an opportunity to be examined and heard." See also LC V 2 (Kolb-Wengert, 467). A number of missiologists concur: Kandler, "Kirche als Exodusgemeinde," 256: "Das Abendmahl ist nie Missionsmittel in der Kirche gewesen!" See also Vicedom, *Die missionarische Dimension der Gemeinde*, 40; *Toward a Theological Basis*, 8.

85 The "intensive" instruction and "extensive" proclamation are generally known as "didache" and "kerygma," respectively. The "didache," however, ties into the missionary proclamation, since it connects with the prebaptismal catechemunate instruction. "Didache" is therefore nothing else than the logical continuation of the Great Commission "to teach" and the attempt to fulfill the Great Commission's command. These observations can also be made from the preface to SC 1–3 (Kolb-Wengert, 347). See Caemmerer, "Kerygma and Didache in Christian Education," 197–208; Weber, "Die lutherische Tradition in Gottesdienst," 177.

86 Vicedom, *Die missionarische Dimension der Gemeinde*, 30. The understanding of cell groups or small groups has been modified over the years.

87 Hauerwas and Willimon, *Resident Aliens*, 12: "We believe that the designations of the church as a colony and Christians as resident aliens are not too strong for the modern American church—indeed, we believe it is the nature of the church, at any time and in any situation, to be a colony. Perhaps it sounds a bit overly dramatic to describe the actual churches you know as colonies in

"colony" and "alien resident" indicate that Christians must sharpen their wits about what it means to be committed to Christ in an alien culture. But this does not mean that Christians choose a life of seclusion. Lutherans are devoted to their secular vocations, and they would see that the faith and sanctification that they receive from God in corporate worship life flows outward in God-pleasing ways into their daily lives.[88] As a part of the clash between the powers of darkness in the world with the Lord and His people, Christians are hated by the world (see John 15:18) for leading a holy life in distinction to the world outside (Colossians 3). Christians practice their love for their neighbor in this world through vocation and witness (Matt. 22:37–40).

---

the middle of an alien culture. But we believe that things have changed for the church residing in America and that faithfulness to Christ demands that we either change or else go the way of all compromised forms of the Christian faith."

88 One may see, e.g., AC XVI 1–2 (Kolb-Wengert, 49).

CHAPTER FOURTEEN

Mission as Ethics

Mission: A Common Concern

The most important role for all Christians is participation in the mission of God and the Church. There may be divergent views on defining exactly what that missionary obligation entails. However, the underlying premise should be that the Church's mission engages all Christians, not just a few. When the opportunity arises for a Christian to witness about Christ to those who are without Christ as their Savior, he or she should have no second thoughts about doing so. As Lutherans, however, we have difficulty in promoting mission in precisely this way. As I have said before, by and large, church bodies still make mission a complicated enterprise that enlists a chosen group of people for a specific program or project. True, to a certain degree, there is always a need to engage a few specific individuals in organized mission. Overseas and congregation-based projects, such as church planting or outreach activities to another ethnic group, require individuals called to do so. In many ways, such an approach to mission looks for an authorized sending. In the next chapter ("The Missionary Office"), we shall draw attention to what "authorized sending" means. Underlying that narrowly defined task, however, is the understanding that all Christians are involved in mission.

Christians contribute toward furthering God's kingdom through their witness, which speaks to their cultural situation yet flows from Word and Sacrament into their lives and their Christian vocation. The arena of mission is precisely where Christians are placed at home in the family, at work, and in their daily activities. This is a fundamental Lutheran doctrine. Unlike the monastic life, the Lutheran doctrine of vocation points Christians to a life in the world where they are asked to follow the will of the Lord.[1] The faith that saves leads to a life that bears fruit in this world. Speratus's hymn "Salvation Unto Us Has Come" intimates what we need

---

1   See, for example, Afflerbach, *Handbuch Christliche Ethik*, 55.

to elaborate on in this chapter, namely, that there is an ethical component of mission that flows from faith and is evident through the love of serving one's neighbor.

> Faith clings to Jesus' cross alone
> And rests in Him unceasing;
> And by its fruits true faith is known,
> With love and hope increasing.
> For faith alone can justify;
> Works serve our neighbor and supply
> The proof that faith is living.[2]

NURTURING A MISSIONARY CULTURE OR MIND-SET IN CHURCH

Most circles today would agree that promoting mission and evangelism in a programmatic way, where evangelism programs are either put in place or adopted by principles borrowed from other denominations, does not adequately cover the missionary potential of a church body.[3] As the Church pursues her mission, the divine gifts and new life in the Gospel that she receives penetrates all aspects of her public life—on Sundays as well as in the private lives of her members.

For the missionary dimension of the Church to take effect, it is important that a bridge be built between the context of the Church in her corporate role, such as in worship, and the private lives of her members. They are not two separate realities; one leads to the other. Word and Sacrament in worship are those divinely instituted means through which a Christian is renewed for life in the world. Christians are reaffirmed in their baptismal grace in worship and from it are nourished to resume an active Christian life in the world. The Lord shapes a baptismal community through worship and provides the strength and energy for the longevity of service in the vocation through His means.

The congregation should actively nurture a particular "missionary" culture or mind-set so that the thought of outreach conceptually and intentionally permeates every Christian's life. By missionary culture in the Church, I mean "the total body of belief, behaviors, knowledge, sanctions, values, goals that mark the way of life of a people."[4] Such a culture prevails in the Church if the pastor and members share a common interest and nurture it in various ways through proper instruction at Bible class and

---

2 Commission on Worship, *Lutheran Service Book*, 555:9.
3 Bliese and Van Gelder, *Evangelizing Church*, 2.
4 Bliese and Van Gelder, *Evangelizing Church*, 114.

through sermons, through literature, through the invitation of missionaries, through particular visual reminders in worship, and by the example of the pastor himself. A pastor's active contribution is vital in shaping a missionary mind-set at church! In his *Pastoral Theology*, John Fritz demonstrates how pastors should set an example for mission:

> A Christian pastor is in duty bound to instruct his congregation and to persuade it to be active in the mission-work of the Church by prayer, by personal testimony and efforts in winning the unchurched, and by supporting the work of the Church at large (colleges, seminaries, mission) by their liberal contributions. The pastor himself ought to be a missionary leader; he ought to have a passion for souls.[5]

Moreover, the pastor preaches and teaches his sheep to prepare them in the mission of the Lord. In his sermons, the particulars of a Christian vocation should be frequently impressed on the minds of all believers, as Melanchthon attests:

> In our churches all the sermons deal with topics like these: repentance, fear of God, faith in Christ, the righteousness of faith, consolation of consciences through faith, the exercise of faith, prayer ... the cross, respect for the magistrates and all civil orders, the distinction between the kingdom of Christ (the spiritual kingdom) and political affairs, marriage, the education and instruction of children, chastity, and all the works of love. From this description of the state of our churches it is possible to determine that we diligently maintain churchly discipline, godly ceremonies, and good ecclesiastical customs.[6]

Catechetical instruction, too, contributes to the role of missionary formation. David Valleskey observes that Christians often are reluctant to witness and relate their faith to others out of fear and lack of confidence. That could be overcome through proper instruction at various levels.[7] The Small Catechism, too, has included a biblical "Household Chart," commonly known as the Table of Duties, which lays out what Christians ought to do in a life devoted to vocation.[8] The "Household Chart" serves as the foundation for an exemplary and, at the same time, missionary lifestyle. It also shows that no Christian (if he truly regards himself as a Christian) may evade the ethical consequences of faith. The fruit of faith need to become evident. All Christians are also able to confide in each other through

---

5   Fritz, *Pastoral Theology*, 283. Fritz also spent time providing concrete advice to the pastor in the promotion of mission, such as celebrating annual mission festivals, offering monthly mission lectures, and disseminating information and encouragement concerning mission opportunities at the local level (*Pastoral Theology*, 268–69).

6   Ap XV 43–44 (Kolb-Wengert, 229).

7   Valleskey, *We Believe—Therefore We Speak*, 168.

8   Kolb-Wengert, 365–67.

"mutual conversation and consolation." As they comfort each other with the Gospel message, they encourage each other to take on a missionary orientation toward those who are without the Gospel message and in need of the comfort it extends.[9]

Members may undertake specific tasks to bring about the Church's mission. Since pastors are limited in their capacities to assume the entire missionary obligation of the congregation, they may enlist Christians to assist them in the task of visiting delinquent members and canvassing out-siders. In Scripture, the apostle Paul himself had chosen from the Christian community individuals such as Priscilla and Aquila. After the service in the synagogue, they took Apollos aside and privately instructed (ἐξέθεντο) him. The Church, together with the pastoral ministry, may establish spe-cific auxiliary services or co-workers (διάκονοι, e.g., Eph. 6:21; Col. 1:7; 4:7; 1 Thess. 3:2; or συνεργοί, e.g., Rom. 16:3, 9, 21; 1 Cor. 16:16; 2 Cor. 8:23; Phil. 2:25; 4:3; Col. 4:11), be they called evangelists, catechists, or deacons.[10] Such practice is found today in many Lutheran church bodies worldwide. Specific roles and duties are handed to auxiliary offices, particularly with the purpose of furthering the mission of the Church. (See Fig. 6.)

Scripture reveals that every Christian has a service. Christians should see themselves as salt that permeates the world and a light to all people that shines forth through exemplary conduct so that as others observe them, they may give glory to God in heaven (Matt. 5:13–16). This doxological and ethical motive, which calls for a mission lifestyle, is affirmed also in 1 Pet. 2:12. Christians should maintain good conduct (ἡ ἀναστροφή) among the Gentiles (τὰ ἔθνη) so that these may see their "good deeds and glorify God." In 1 Pet.2:9 and 3:15, that lifestyle or nonverbal communication is joined with a verbal sharing of the faith, such as through a good confession, defense (ἀπολογία), or proclamation (ἐξαγγέλλω) to unbelievers regard-ing what the Lord has done. In 1 Thess. 1:8–10, we are given a glimpse into the practical dimension of that very missionary obligation as the Christians of Thessalonica are praised by the apostle Paul for communicating their Christian faith in nonverbal and verbal ways in an alien environment that rejects faith in the triune God. A Christian's missionary lifestyle in the world offers little reward. In John 15:18–16:4, a Christian earns scorn, hatred, and ultimately persecution. The term for witness is none other than μαρτυρέω (15:26–27), the origin for the word *martyrdom*. In the Book of Acts, we catch a glimpse of persecution. Christians fled the city of Jerusalem, and as they scattered into neighboring regions, they actively preached the Gospel

---

9 SA III IV (*BSLK*, 449; Tappert, 310).
10 See Commission on Theology and Church Relations, "Ministry," 12.

(Acts 8:1, 4; 11:19–20). This example was born from an emergency set off by a persecution.[11]

In an explicit way, Hans-Werner Gensichen lists five helpful points that would encourage a missionary mind-set in the Church:

- Outsiders are welcome in the Church and made to feel at home.

- The congregation offers pastoral care and other services through her members without the pastor enjoying the monopoly.

- The members are equipped for involvement in society and are in fact involved in it.

- The congregation is structurally supple and able to meet new needs and challenges.

- The congregation does not defend the privileges of its members as a select group but remains focused on the world, the locus of the *missio Dei*.[12]

Without going into great detail on every point, we should empha-size that as much as one might desire to bring the Gospel to the world, that desire is incomplete unless it is backed up by the goal of invitation, incorporation, and participation in the Christian community. This convic-tion is based on the understanding that the fullness of God's Word must become manifest in the Christian community.[13] To be sure, Christian vocation places a believer in the world where he finds his own niche in the mission of God through a voluntary and unselfish witness of Christ in his surroundings. Valleskey points to a Christian's own mission field with reference to the FRAN network, a helpful acronym to remind a Christian that he has **F**riends, **R**elatives, **A**ssociates, and **N**eighbors who are without Christ.[14] However, after having identified such individuals, Christians should invite them into a worshiping and serving community. Andrew brought his brother Simon to Jesus (John 1:40–42), and Philip did the same with Nathanael (John 1:45–46). And those called to faith by Peter's message found their way into a fellowship of believers (Acts 2:42–47).

Simply put, each Christian should support the Church's missionary orientation. The role that befalls every Christian equally is that of inviting

11 For example, nineteenth-century theologian Wilhelm Löhe argued for an ordained pastoral ministry under regular conditions. One may see his *Aphorismen* printed in *GW* V, I, 315–17; Pragman, *Traditions of Ministry*, 134.

12 Gensichen, *Glaube für die Welt*, 168–73; Bosch, "Theological Education in Missionary Perspective," 26.

13 Hoffmann, "Gedanken zum Problem der Integration," 207; Vicedom, *Die Rechtfertigung als gestaltende Kraft der Mission*, 15. According to Freytag, *Reden und Aufsätze*, 1:228: "A Church without sacraments will thus perish." Manecke, *Mission als Zeugendienst*, 86; Holsten, "Reformation und Mission," 27.

14 Valleskey, *We Believe—Therefore We Speak*, 171.

and welcoming outsiders into their community. Here, the missiologist David Bosch makes an important exegetical observation from the apostle Paul's ministry and how the apostle viewed the missionary role of ordinary Christians. It bears little of that overt activism that seems to prevail in so many church bodies today. Speaking of Christians, Bosch observes:

> Their "exemplary existence" is a powerful magnet that draws outsiders toward the church . . . The missionary dimension of the conduct of the Pauline Christians remains implicit rather than explicit. They are, to employ a distinction introduced by Hans-Werner Gensichen, "missionary" ("*missionarisch*") rather than "missionizing" ("*missionierend*"). References to specific cases of direct missionary involvement by the churches are rare in Paul's letters. However, this is not just to be seen as a deficiency. Rather, Paul's whole argument is that the attractive lifestyle of the small Christian communities gives credibility to the missionary outreach in which he and his fellow-workers are involved. The primary responsibility of "ordinary" Christians is not to go out and preach, but to support the mission project through their appealing conduct and making "outsiders" feel welcome in their midst.[15]

The Florescence of the Community

By making mission a communal affair and a significant reality in the broader context, the four traditional activities or expressions of the Church come to mind. It is crucial for the Church to practice the following four roles: human care (*diakonia*), witness (*martyria*), fellowship (*koinonia*), and worship (*leitourgia*). As the figure on the next page indicates, only when these four activities are in place will a congregation fulfill a balanced and biblical role in this world and serve, figuratively speaking, as a flower whose sweet and inviting smell penetrates the world. The Church thus looks like a flower, blossoms like a flower, smells like a flower, and attracts like a flower.

---

15 Bosch, *Transforming Mission*, 137–38. Elsewhere in his book, he states with respect to Paul's congregations in Corinth, Rome, and Thessalonica that they are not so much involved in direct missionary outreach, but rather that they are "missionary by their very nature, through their unity, mutual love, exemplary conduct and radiant joy" (*Transforming Mission*, 168).

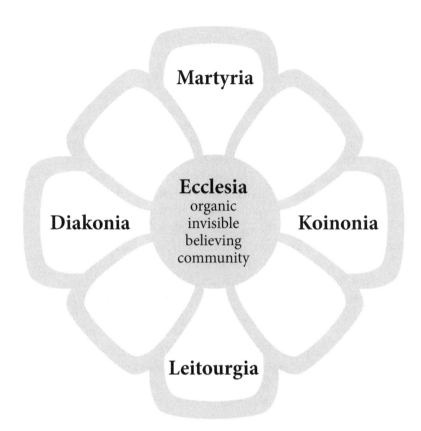

Fig. 4: The Florescence of a Missionary and Contextual Church

EPHESIANS 4:12

As the Church enlists the service of laity for mission, she rightly underscores their cooperation with references to Scripture. A text frequently used in this context is Eph. 4:12. However, the complicated syntax of v. 12 has created quite a debate among scholars over its correct translation and interpretation. Two positions have emerged from that discussion, and we shall now briefly trace them. The first option translates the original Greek text of Eph. 4:12 as: ". . . to prepare God's people *for works of service*, so that the body of Christ may be built up . . ." (NIV). According to this translation, which most contemporary texts follow, the phrase "for works of service [or ministry] (*diakonia*)" is referenced to God's people or the saints, that is, all Christians. They are prepared to perform the "works of service" by the "gifts" in v. 11, that is, the apostles and other specific ministries. Thus the question is what kind of "service" or "ministry" is implied here for the saints? The Epistle to the Ephesians does not offer an exact list of works of service. However, the general direction of the letter gives the sense that this is a wider service of love toward one another for the upkeep of unity in the Body of Christ. Such a service of love would not stand in tension with the specific ministry (also *diakonia*) the apostle Paul describes for himself in Eph. 3:7–8; 6:19–20.[16] Such a work of service would also include the task of sharing the Gospel with non-Christians.[17] Elsewhere in Scripture, we find examples of works of service. Mary offered a special service to the Lord when He visited her house (Luke 10:40); also the person who bears the sword over the wrongdoer is a servant of God (Rom. 13:4). These works of service performed by Christians as they pertain to fellow believers and to the world around them also point to Eph. 4:1, which brings in the "calling" or "vocation" urged upon them by the apostle Paul: "I urge you to live a life worthy of the calling you have received" (NIV; see also 1 Cor. 7:20).

The second, alternative, translation of Eph. 4:11–12 is offered by the King James Version (KJV): "And he gave some, apostles; and some, prophets; and some, evangelists; and some, pastors and teachers; for the perfecting of the saints, for the work of the ministry, for the edifying of the body of Christ." The KJV also agrees with Melanchthon's interpretation of the text in the Treatise, which the Lutheran Church has adopted as one of its confessional documents. Melanchthon states that "among those gifts belonging to the Church, he lists pastors and teachers and adds that such are given *for serving and building up the body of Christ*."[18] According to this second translation, the specific ministries in v. 11 are given to the Church for serving and for building up the Body of Christ. A reader notices that the KJV has a comma placed after "saints" and before the prepositional phrase "for the work of the ministry," though the comma is not found in the Greek text.[19] With the help of the comma in this second translation, Paul implies that the "work of the ministry" is done by the apostles, pastors, evangelists, and teachers (v. 11), and it is the service of their preaching and teaching through which the saints are "perfected" (καταρτισμός). We may assume that this "perfection" applies to both the inward and outward life of the

---

16 A recent and widely acclaimed commentary points this out: Schnackenburg, *Der Brief an die Epheser*, 186: "Since there is in the entire passage no mention of services other than those of preaching, leadership and teaching, one must connect the aforementioned 'diakonia' to the evangelists, shepherds and teachers" ["Da aber von Tätigkeiten anderer Art als Verkündigung, Leitung und Lehre im ganzen Abschnitt nicht die Rede ist, wird man die genannte Diakonia doch auf den 'Dienst' der Evangelisten, Hirten und Lehrer beziehen müssen"].

17 A book that popularized this view is Feucht, *Everyone a Minister*.

18 Tr 67 (Kolb-Wengert, 341, *emphasis added*).

19 One may see the arguments in support of this translation made by Hammann, "Translation of Ephesians 4:12," 42–49.

saints. Their faith, knowledge, and love for one another is increased as they approach the coming of the Lord (cf. Rom. 12:4–8; 1 Pet. 4:10).

Both translations provide valuable observations. Whatever text the reader should choose, it would be important to reference the point made by the other translation: the Church needs the important work of the laity, which includes witness, just as much as she desires the essential preaching and teaching of pastors, which keeps and strengthens Christians in faith and love. Both follow Scripture and the will of God in the best manner when they each maintain their appropriate roles and gifts.

THE PRIESTHOOD OF ALL BELIEVERS

Our discussion on the contribution of the laity in mission will be incomplete if we do not bring in the doctrine of the priesthood of all believers. For that, we need to go back to Luther, who provided the framework for what we call the "spiritual priesthood of all believers."

So much has been written on this doctrine. Unfortunately, many of its interpreters use this doctrine in ways that affirm a scope of ministry for the laity that runs contrary to pastoral ministry in the Church. This radicalization is an unfair treatment of Luther's intentions. Never would he have suggested that we idealize or romanticize the spiritual priesthood to the degree that we should minimize the pastoral ministry in the Church. Luther was far too careful in his choice of terms. He expounded this doctrine in a number of treatises, including the *The Babylonian Captivity of the Church*[20] and the *The Freedom of a Christian*.[21] Next to the understanding of Scripture alone and the doctrine of justification, Luther argued early in his career for the third principle of the Reformation—namely, the spiritual priesthood of all believers. As he did so, he chose the term *sacerdotium* for the spiritual priesthood and the word *ministerium* for the pastoral ministry of the Church. In English, these distinctions have been confused with the generic term "ministry," which implies any activity performed by either laity or clergy. In the New Testament, *ministerium* is rendered with the word *diakonia*. Luther chose to translate *ministerium* consistently as *Amt* ("office") to indicate that the term specifically refers to the pastoral ministry, not to the spiritual priesthood.[22]

How do the two relate to each other, the *sacerdotium* and *ministerium*? Not all Christians are the perfect true believers (*vere credentes*); instead,

---

20 AE 36:11–126.

21 AE 31:333–77. See also "Open Letter to the Christian Nobility in Works of Martin Luther" (PE 2:69), "Answer to the Superchristian, Superspiritual, and Superlearned Book of Goat Emser of Leipzig (1521)," (PE 3:31–401), and *Misuse of the Mass* (AE 36:127–230) (see esp., p. 12 n. 4).

22 See Brunotte, *Das Amt der Verkündigung*, 21–22. For an example of equating *diakonia* with *ministerium* or *Amt* in the Lutheran Confessions, see Tr 26–31 (Kolb-Wengert, 334–35).

the Lutheran doctrine of sinner and saint reminds every Christian of the daily failures in his or her service in the Lord's mission. In fact, the Church enlists the services of those who are redeemed, yet answerable to the second use of the Law. For this reason, the congregation must rely on the gracious institution of the office of proclamation, which in God's name delivers the Word of God to all believers. A Christian congregation will only mature spiritually if she first is a listening congregation, knowing that her faith is received through hearing (*fides ex auditu*). After that and only then will she become a believing and witnessing community and find appropriate structures for outreach.[23] Pastoral ministry is thus not just a dispensable function organized by the congregation, but rather it is a divine prerequisite given to the Church by God and through which the means of grace must be administered. The office of the Church (*ministerium*) and priesthood of all believers (*sacerdotium omnium*) are not mutually exclusive, and, at the same time, they are not identical. With this premise in place, we may now move on to discuss a number of characteristics of the spiritual priesthood from Luther's perspective.

Already in 1519–20, Luther came to the realization that there is no difference in the spiritual quality between believers and priest. Luther's approach was indeed radical. It opposes a practice and hierarchy in the Roman Church that centered on those who were consecrated as priests, bishops, and pope. Some in the church had committed themselves by oath to certain commandments of God known as the evangelical counsels (*consilia evangelica*).[24] Ordinary Christians did not take such oaths and were excluded from following those counsels and vows. Based on their consecration, the clergy believed that they had not simply a different dignity (*dignitas*) but also a special quality (*qualitas*). Spiritually speaking, the clergy were thus higher and closer to God. Indeed, priests guaranteed salvation for the laity through their acts of sacrifice, soul keeping, and jurisdiction. Luther rejected this construction, as well as monastic vows in 1521, because such distinctions split Christianity into at least two *spiritual* groups: into the holders of churchly office and monastic orders, on one hand, and the

---

23 As Jobst Schöne points out in *Christological Character*, 1: "The royal priesthood means to serve just as Christ served us. The royal priesthood serves through prayer, by comforting and encouraging, and by giving spiritual and material help to others. This service is rendered in the place and situation where the Lord has placed you as father or mother to your children, as husband and wife to each other, as members of the congregation mutually to each other, and so on. *It is a service that continues after the divine service where we receive what Christ gives—namely, the gospel in all its forms—and we are to spread this gospel in word and deed. This is not identical to what the minister in the divine service does when he handles the sacraments and preaches the gospel. Rather, the royal priesthood echoes it. The royal priesthood passes on to others what it has received in the divine service*" (emphasis added).

24 Those freely chosen means to achieve perfection: virginity (chastity), poverty, obedience (Matt. 19:12, 21; 16:24), the classic oaths taken by the monks.

laity, on the other. Luther saw only one spiritual equality, which is attained by all through Baptism. Luther now applied the term "priesthood" that the Roman Catholic Church had monopolized for one specific group to all believing Christians: all were *priests* in the sense of the New Testament.[25] In support of his position, Luther carefully studied texts such as Matt. 16:18–20; John 20:21–22; 21:17; Rev. 1:6; 5:10; 20:6. His main scriptural support, however, was 1 Pet. 2:5, 9. This passage points to all believers as the people of God, not just a select few.

Luther did not intend to introduce modern democratic equality into the Church; such ideas did not exist in his context or in the context of Scripture. That came later with the introduction of political theories developed by philosophers such as Locke, Montesquieu, and Voltaire. Christians did not understand equal rights as a kind of social contract, neither in the political realm nor in the Church. Thus Luther chose to use a Christian ruler as the supreme overseer of the Church. Luther saw in the ruler the foremost Christian above all others, who would bring order to a church that was in disarray. Luther was unwilling to promote an equality that erased all distinctions among Christians by referring to the First Article concerning creation. In caste systems in India, nineteenth-century Lutherans such as Karl Graul (1814–64), leader of the Leipzig Mission, and missionaries of that society thought much the same way. These cultural distinctions, they maintained, are a form of created order arranged by God. Yet despite these distinctions, Luther affirmed the important spiritual principle that all *believers* are united equally through faith in Christ. Christ has graciously redeemed them and bound them together in Himself through faith. This fundamental insight set the stage for a number of individual components, which may be seen as characteristic of the priesthood of all believers.

The *first* is that all who are baptized are *equal* in the eyes of God despite the physical, psychological, and intellectual conditions, gifts, social standing, or misfortunes. Complete equality of man and wife, master and slave, Jew and non-Jew, such as is spoken of in Gal. 3:28, comes into being through faith in Christ. Indeed, God looks beyond any differences as described above because the greatest position one may hold is that of being a child of God. All true believers are justified sinners and belong to the "spiritual standing," the priesthood of all believers.[26]

The *second* characteristic of the priesthood of all believers is that every Christian has immediate access to God, the Judge and Father. A believer has immediate access to God the Father in prayer. The means of grace

---

25 *Babylonian Captivity* (1520), AE 36:112–13; Brunotte, *Das Amt der Verkündigung*, 18.

26 *To the Christian Nobility of the German Nation Concerning the Reform of the Christian Estate* (1520), AE 44:127. Also *Babylonian Captivity*, AE 36:112–13; Brunotte, *Das Amt der Verkündigung*, 20 n. 20.

are immediately accessible. A Christian can read and interpret Scripture. He can even apply God's Word from Scripture to himself, respond to its demands, and find consolation therein. This immediate relation to God was a special characteristic of the Old Testament's priestly order. Only the priest was allowed to stand immediately before God in the realm of the holy. To Luther, every believer stands immediately before God. Access to the Word makes every Christian a priest.[27]

The *third* characteristic of the priesthood of all believers relates to the second. Actually, both are two sides of the same coin. A consequence of the immediacy to God is that the true believer does not have an earthly mediator such as a consecrated priest, but only one mediator whom God has given Himself: Christ. Again, one may misunderstand this principle and suppose that Luther rejects the ecclesiastical office. However, he does not dismiss the need for special preachers of the Gospel in the Church. As the years progressed, especially as Luther faced the radical reformers (*Schwärmer*), he became increasingly aware of the value in ordered structures and the visible side of the Church, of which pastoral ministry was one. For Luther, its incumbents are, in the words of the apostle Paul, "assistants for their joy" (2 Cor. 1:24). By offering the Word of God and distributing the Sacraments, they assist Christians to remain in the faith. Luther only rejects the false claim of priests who argue for some quality within themselves that contributes to their salvation. The consecrated priesthood is rejected if its incumbents refuse to see themselves, spiritually speaking, as a part of the spiritual priesthood.[28]

The *fourth* characteristic of the priesthood of all believers holds that every Christian offers his life as *sacrifice*. Thereby, Luther does not impose a pagan or Jewish sacrificial cult on Christians. He spiritualizes the idea of sacrifice by saying that the true believer sacrifices himself in the praise of God, in obedience in life, and in the suffering of the cross. This sacrifice bears itself out in service to the neighbor. Such sacrifice has missionary implications (Ps. 51:17; Rom. 12:1; Phil. 2:17; 4:18; 1 Pet. 2:5).[29]

The *fifth* and final characteristic of the priesthood of all believers applies most aptly to the mission of the Church. Luther emphasizes that every Christian has the right and obligation to pass on and *witness* God's Word in his personal sphere of life. In fact, Luther may at times even use the term "preach" (*predigen*) for this act, implying that the incumbents of the priesthood of all believers are actually given a certain task to proclaim the Gospel wherever they may be. The context of this private preaching

---

27 *Freedom of a Christian* (1520), AE 31:354. Brunotte *Das Amt der Verkündigung*, 20 n. 21.

28 *Misuse of the Mass* (1521), AE 36:138. Brunotte, *Das Amt der Verkündigung*, 20 n. 22.

29 *Treatise on the New Testament, That Is, the Holy Mass* (1520), AE 35:98. Brunotte, *Das Amt der Verkündigung*, 20.

does not stand in conflict with the pastoral ministry of preaching and administration of the Sacraments publicly affirmed through the proper rite of vocation (*rite vocatus*). Nonetheless, Luther positively promotes every Christian's standing in this world through the role of confessing, giving testimony, and witnessing to Christ. A Christian's faith cannot be silent and is bound by duty to give missionary witness, a sincere confession, as Paul states: "For with the heart one believes and is justified, and with the mouth one confesses and is saved" (Rom. 10:10).[30] The right and duty of each individual Christian to proclaim the Gospel extends to the private realm, which is mainly the family, the neighborhood, and the workplace. Very often, Luther connects the prepositional phrase *in privato* ("privately") to the individual Christian's confirmation of the Gospel. In Luther's day, "private" meant something totally different from today's understanding. Today, a person will claim his privacy as a legal right to keep things to himself without having the obligation to share information with anyone. Christians may thus draw the conclusion that their religious life and belief is a private matter. To Luther, on the other hand, private meant the personal sphere of one's home that connects a Christian with the people he frequents on a daily basis. Christians are obliged to share God's Word *in privato*— that is, educate and instruct all those around them.[31] Unfortunately, the family structures have changed over the years. In Western countries, families have shrunk in size. Other countries encourage couples to have only one child to curb overpopulation. Single parenting of only one or two children is thus a common reality for many Christians. From a missiological perspective, however, Luther's understanding of "private" certainly offers great potential. In South American countries, for example, in the city of Fortaleza, Brazil, the family and the extended kinship is an important tool for evangelism.[32]

EMERGENCY SITUATIONS

God has given Word and Sacrament as the means to establish His Church. Where they are absent, the Church suffers. Therefore, the ability to alleviate that suffering and restore the proper ministry of Word and Sacrament amid God's people is important. As one looks at such occasions with respect to the service of individual Christians, one encounters the argument of "emergency." No one should seek to deprive the Church of Word and Sacrament merely to protect an ecclesiastical order; AC XXVIII and

---

30   *Right and Power of a Christian Congregation or Community* (1523), AE 39:309–10. Brunotte, *Das Amt der Verkündigung*, 21 n. 24. Stolle, *Church Comes from All Nations*, 21.

31   Brunotte, *Das Amt der Verkündigung*, 20–21.

32   Neitzel, *Mission Outreach*.

the Treatise speak clearly against that, as I have already shown. Yet the definition and understanding of "emergency" situations, especially since the
Second World War, have caused seismic changes in some church bodies
regarding the understanding of the diaconate, the entry of women into the
ministry, and the basic understanding of the public ministry.[33] We need
balance and definition in this context.

Some differences arise regarding the definition of an emergency. Is
an emergency situation an occasion in the Church where normal circumstances have collapsed? Is an emergency something that requires more
than a mere inconvenience? Does an emergency imply imminent danger
of death and spiritual anguish combined with the inaccessibility of an
ordained minister?[34] The definition of "emergency" speaks significantly to
the understanding of lay ministers.[35] While one can appreciate that conditions which disrupt the normal operation of the pastoral ministry in a
given parish can be traumatic and should be an important concern of the
Church, nevertheless, seeking a well-defined definition of "emergency"
based on Scripture and the Lutheran Confessions is important in establishing an understanding of the issue.

The overriding principle in such situations is that the Church needs to
guarantee that those in need do not lose access to God's Word. AC V and
AC XIV, themselves based on the scriptural mandate of Matt. 28:19–20 and
John 20:21–23, as previously shown, establish the proper attributes of the
ministry as the divinely established order by which God provides for the
public teaching of the Word and the administration of the Sacraments on
behalf of the congregation. In keeping with Scripture, one must weigh and
define one's options carefully and not enter lightly into the declaration of
an "emergency" situation.

In such an emergency, the Church may enlist the services of laity who,
for a limited period, take the place of regularly called and ordained servants.[36] A situation like this arose, for example, in the Communist era of
the Soviet Union, when most ordained pastors had been forcefully removed
from the Church. Churches had to adjust by falling back on the services of
nonordained elders for pastoral care, individuals whose only theological
education had been confirmation classes. For decades, particularly from

---

33 Olson, *Deacons and Deaconesses through the Centuries*, 353, 357–60.

34 Marquart, *Church and Her Fellowship*, 163–64.

35 The argument based on emergency arises twice in Resolution 3-05B in LCMS, *Convention
    Proceedings*, 111–12. The specific criteria on p. 112 includes the lack of a pastor due to illness,
    transportation issues, or some other circumstances. We respect the fact that the Missouri Synod
    has resolved this position and that it has not been revoked. No one is suggesting that the provi-
    sion for lay ministers runs immediately contrary to Scripture. Rather, here the concern is the
    understanding of proper definition and context.

36 See also Fritz, *Pastoral Theology*, 126–27.

the 1940s to the late 1980s, the emergency situation prevailed and the life of the Church changed substantially as a result. Liturgical life, instruction, and pastoral care could not be maintained at the same level that had existed with university- and seminary-trained pastors. Thankfully, since the political change in the late 1980s, full pastoral care is now slowly being restored.

Augustine offers a classic description of a case of emergency. Two Christians find themselves in a boat; the catechumen baptizes the other, who in turn is then absolved by the one who is baptized.[37] This illustrates a layperson absolving someone of his sins, a role under normal conditions assumed by the pastor. Yet emergency does not apply to Baptism and Absolution alone; it also embraces Holy Communion and preaching. If a Christian should find himself near death without a pastor available and desires the Lord's Supper, or if Christians in remote regions of Alaska are in desperate need of God's preached Word, there may be a special dispensation granted to a layman to dispense God's Word by reading a sermon or administering the Lord's Supper. In both cases, there should be no doubt in the validity of the act and in the efficacy of God's Word. C. F. W. Walther held that, in such situations, the layperson officiating does so not as a layperson but as a legitimate incumbent of the office, as one temporarily called as a servant of the Church for a limited period of time.[38]

The duration of this solution is limited in time and only applies if the criteria of an emergency are met, namely, the dire need for God's Word. Luther offers an example in which a Christian finds himself in a missionary situation by landing as a prisoner among the non-Christian Turks. Here, the Christian prisoner has the obligation to preach and teach, being driven by a love for them. Such an emergency was not far removed from reality, since the Turkish threat to the Germans was imminent in Luther's time. Luther thus explains in his own words what the two situations, both regular and emergency, entail:

> Second, if he is at a place where there are Christians who have the same power and right as he, he should not draw attention to himself. Instead, he should let himself be called and chosen to preach and to teach in the place of and by the command of the others. Indeed, a Christian has so much power that he may and even should make an appearance and teach among Christians—without a call from men—when he becomes aware that there is a lack of teachers, provided he does it in a decent and

---

37 Recorded by Melanchthon in Tr 67 (Kolb-Wengert, 341).

38 "Dass die Verwaltung des heiligen Abendmahls von einem im Nothfalle von einer ganzen Gemeinde zeitweilig berufenen, obgleich nicht ordinierten, Laien *giltig* und *rechtmäßig* sei, bezweifelt niemand . . . Auf dieser Weise aber spendet der Laie nicht als Laie aus, sondern als ein *wahrhaftig* und *für eine Zeitlang berufener Diener*" (Walther, *Americanisch-Lutherische Pastoraltheologie*, 180–81, *emphasis added*]).

becoming manner. This was clearly described by St. Paul in I Corinthians 14 [: 30], when he says, "If something is revealed to someone else sitting by, let the first be silent." Do you see what St. Paul does here? He tells the teacher to be silent and withdraw from the midst of the Christians; and he lets the listener appear, even without a call. All this is done because need knows no command.[39]

While Luther was aware of the need for God's Word in a true emergency, he did not allow a temporary emergency situation to displace the regular practice of the Church. For example, Luther would not grant the father of the household (*Hausvater*) permission to celebrate Communion with his household as if it were his congregation. He was reluctant to dismiss the distinction between the role of the housefather and the public role of the pastor, and he argued further that the Christians in the Book of Acts came together to celebrate as a congregation in a house.[40] In another case, Luther would not grant emergency status to Lutherans in Augsburg who found themselves in a eucharistic emergency (*eucharistischen Notstand*). Living in a city controlled by followers of Zwingli, they were forbidden by law to celebrate Holy Communion according to the Lutheran doctrine. Kaspar Huberinus thus wrote to Luther and requested permission to have a private house Communion administered by a layperson. Luther again was unwilling to grant such permission. Without the proper pastoral office, they should regard themselves as Jews living in the Babylonian captivity, being without a church and proper worship service. In place of the Holy Communion, Luther suggests they use spiritual communion (*geistliche Kommunion*) by enduring these afflictions and finding consolation in prayer, reading, and the teaching of God's Word.[41] These incidents show how Luther maintained a consistent position in the particular case of the Lord's Supper. Peter Manns thus concludes that Luther never thought that an emergency applied for Holy Communion.[42]

---

39 AE 39:309–10. Luther comes to speak of emergencies in his tracts *The Right and Power of a Christian Congregation or Community* (1523) and *Campaign Sermon against the Turks* (1529); in Stolle, *Church Comes from All Nations*, 21–22, 71–73.

40 In the case of Siegmund Hangreuther, a Christian *Hausvater* requesting to celebrate the Lord's Supper at home, Luther advises Pastor Wolfgang Brauer in a December 30, 1536, letter: "That, however, a father of the household teaches his next of kin God's Word is right and proper, since God has commanded that we should teach and educate our children and house. For the Word applies to everyone. But the Sacrament is a public confession und demands public administrators . . . For what pertains to the public office of the church and to a housefather over his servants are two different things. For this reason they should not be mingled or separated . . ." (WA Br 7:339, 18–22, 339, 29–31; Erlangen edition, 55:160–61). For the above, see Manns, "Amt und Eucharistie in der Theologie Martin Luthers," 82, 92, and n. 129.

41 See WA Br 6:244–45.1–21; Manns, "Amt und Eucharistie in der Theologie Martin Luthers," 72 and n. 17.

42 Peter Manns corroborates his observation with other examples; see "Amt und Eucharistie in der Theologie Martin Luthers," 68–173 passim.

It is important that the Church immediately correct emergencies by addressing the need and reinstating normal circumstances. Otherwise, the impression is given that emergencies take precedence over the normal circumstances. Given modern infrastructure, technology, and seminaries, it seems difficult that emergencies, defined as situations in which a properly arranged order is absent, arise with considerable frequency. It may be true that wartime situations and other cases demand special exceptions. Overall, however, the Church should be thankful that cases of true necessity are quite rare.

Throughout its history, Lutheranism generally has refrained from the practice of licensing lay preachers where there is no emergency situation.[43] The Missouri Synod followed this position at least during the nineteenth century.[44] The *Saxon Parochial Order* of 1839–40, for example, called for lay elders to be ordained in order to function with the pastor in the oversight of the congregation.[45] As the founding fathers of the LCMS encountered the spiritual need of the scattered immigrant Germans, they raised and ordained a limited number of traveling missionaries (*Reiseprediger*) or colporteurs of Lutheran literature.[46] Where the need could not be met, they called for additional pastors from Germany, as the famous letter of distress (*Notruf*) to German Lutheran churches from Friedrich Wyneken (1810–76) indicates.[47] As stated before, one must use the greatest care in defining an emergency, and one must exercise the greatest effort to bring back the normal state envisaged by AC V and AC XIV.

MOTIVATION, OBEDIENCE AND THE MISSIONARY MANDATE

Having affirmed the need to embrace the duty of all Christians for mission, we need to move on to an important question: What motivates Christians and the Church to pursue mission? It could be argued that Christians *should* tell the truth about Christ to all people; that is, they *ought* to do so. If they fail, they put their salvation at risk. Obviously, we cannot draw the latter conclusion, as if a Christian's salvation is contingent on personal missionary outreach. No, a Christian's salvation remains unconditional. To

---

43 See Walther, *Americanisch-Lutherische Pastoraltheologie*, 64–65.

44 See *Thesen für die Lehrverhandlungen der Missouri-Synode*, 11–15, 64–65.

45 See *Fünfter Synodal-Brief von der Synode der aus Preußen ausgewanderten evangelisch-lutherischen Kirche, versammelt zu Buffalo, N.Y., von 23. Juni bis zum 5. Juli 1856* (Buffalo: Friedrich Reinecke, 1856), 49–52.

46 See also *Thesen für die Lehrverhandlungen der Missouri-Synode*, 12–14.

47 Meyer, *Moving Frontiers*, 90–97, 202–8. See also Walther, *Americanisch-Lutherische Pastoraltheologie*, 64.

turn the matter into a condition that is based on one's sharing of the Gospel with others would destroy all comfort that the Gospel brings. But, in fact, many pastors and church leaders often summon laypeople to mission as if it were the Protestant version of *satisfactio*, where salvation and forgiveness may be pronounced conditionally in view of someone's good works. We should avoid this misperception at all costs.

At the same time, we cannot entirely dismiss our obligation for mission. It *ought* to be done. The missionary mandates in Scripture are clear. At first, we should explain that Luther's example of the prisoner-of-war situation[48] underscores that Christians are motivated out of love to speak to others about Christ. To be sure, this still places the mission of the Church in the realm of ethics, but it demands a careful investigation into the distinction of justification and sanctification. Since the motivation toward mission is not one of compulsion but only out of love, the argument of making mission a legal or coerced response to the divine command simply misses the point. True, obedience to God's own intention that His Word should be preached and shared is not an optional activity or debatable point in the life of the Church. The missionary mandates in Matthew 28 and Luke 24 are not optional activities but are—albeit in specific ways—given to all Christians. Mission is certainly a mandated work (*opera mandata*) by God and demands an obedience as any other law of God does. But if its obedience were to be borne out of terror as servile fear rather than filial fear, then it would lack the inner motivation and natural outflow from justifying faith. The important point to make is that mission as the obedience of faith is intrinsically and inseparably connected to faith and love.

> There has been the long tradition which sees the mission of the church primarily as obedience to a command . . . It tends to make mission a burden rather than a joy, to make it part of the law rather than part of the gospel. If one looks at the New Testament evidence one gets another impression. Mission begins with a kind of explosion of joy. The news that the rejected and crucified Jesus is alive is something that cannot possibly be suppressed. It must be told. Who could be silent about such a fact?[49]

For this reason, we are called to pay close attention to the missionary mandates. Since the call to preach and baptize is paired with the promise (*promissio*) of salvation (Mark 16:16), they cannot be categorized merely as legal mandates. The *promissio* diminishes the legal brunt of the missionary mandate, for it sheds light on a God who passes the command on to the

---

48   *Campaign Sermon against the Turks* (1529), see Stolle, *Church Comes from All Nations*, 71.

49   Newbigin, *Gospel in a Pluralist Society*, 116.

Church not as the hidden and wrathful Lawgiver, but as One who is gracious and compassionate.[50]

All believers who seek to fulfill the mandate thus respond to a loving and forgiving God who has brought sinners to faith personally. Mission, like any other Christian work, is an act performed by a Christian who has become the subject of God's redemptive work. Mission can be seen as a response from a Christian already *fully* justified, an obedience from a faith that has received the forgiveness of sins. Thus mission is a "fruit of faith."[51] Likewise, Karl Barth calls mission a "work of faith,"[52] and the missiologist Walter Freytag, "a response [*Antwort*] to the message of God," a "self-offering [*Hingabe*] of the will," or an "obedience of faith." [53]

An important Lutheran principle applies here—namely, that all good works, particularly our response to mission, become an obedience of faith in the Lord driven by joy and love. That principle needs to underlie all missionary mandates. Consequently, a Christian looks at the missionary mandates as the conclusion of what he already knows of Christ and His will:

> There would be a mission even if we did not have a missionary command. For God always grants to His disciples through the working of the Holy Ghost a faith that is not passive, dumb, simply contemplative, or selfish, but a faith which produces in the Christian a restless concern for the salvation of others, a "living and active thing," a faith which lifts the believer out of his own self-edification and makes him a building stone and a builder.[54]

Luther especially pleaded for the inseparable link between faith and good works, implying that the latter, if flowing from faith, become an expression of sheer joy and pleasure. In his famous preface to the Epistle to the Romans, Luther describes how faith gives birth to works:

> O it is a living, busy, active, mighty thing, this faith. It is impossible for it not to be doing good works incessantly. It does not ask whether good works are to be done, but before the question is asked, it has already done them, and is constantly doing them . . . For through faith a man becomes free from sin and comes to take pleasure in God's commandments.[55]

---

50 Fagerberg, *New Look at the Lutheran Confessions*, 178. A striking feature in how the Lutheran Confessions use the missionary mandates is that they are quoted to support the universal mandate to baptize (Ap IX 2, Kolb-Wengert, 184; SC IV 4, Kolb-Wengert, 359; LC IV 4, Kolb-Wengert, 457).

51 Vicedom, *Die Rechtfertigung als gestaltende Kraft der Mission*, 5: "Frucht des Glaubens." See also Schwarz, "Der missiologische Aspekt der Rechtfertigungslehre," 210–11.

52 Barth, "Theologie und Mission in der Gegenwart," 105.

53 Freytag, "Das Ziel der Missionsarbeit," 183.

54 Vicedom, *Mission of God*, 83.

55 *Preface to Romans*, AE 35:370–71.

Melanchthon, too, sees faith not as "an idle thought" but as "a new light, life, and force in the heart as to renew our heart, mind and spirit, [which] makes new men of us and new creatures" and "as long as it is present, produces good fruits."[56] Since this faith is "living" (*fides viva*)[57] and "firm and active," witness and confession are never far from it.[58]

If obedience to mission is a product of faith worked through the Word, then every preacher would want to motivate Christians for mission through preaching the Gospel and not the Law. It is the Gospel, the words of forgiveness, that produces faith and motivation. In the first instance, the believer is passive by listening to the Lord's Gospel. Only then, in the secondary sense, does he proceed to become active and supportive of mission. The missionary mandate as an imperative stands on the foundation of God's redeeming act in Christ "for you."[59] Every Christian is a recipient of that indicative "for you" and, ideally, understands the universal direction of the Gospel toward the world: "I cannot believe in redemption only for myself. I receive divine love as 'the man,' as 'Adam,' who is part of all others. If I do not believe in salvation for all, then I won't believe for myself either . . . Laxity in mission is always a sign of an individualistically reduced and thereby disfigured faith."[60] An important contribution to mission is that a Christian understands the Gospel as universal in its dimension and purpose, that the message of the cross is meant for all sinners to enter God's kingdom.[61] Moreover, the Christian takes on the role of service before God (*coram Deo*) in worship to Him, and before man (*coram homnibus*), of witnessing and helping him in every need.[62] The Gospel reorientates natural man from being inwardly focused on himself (*homo incurvatus in se est*) to

---

56   Ap IV 64 (Tappert, 116): "Faith . . . is not an idle thought." Ap IV 64 (see German text and its translation in *Triglotta*, 139). SD IV 12 (Kolb-Wengert, 576) compares the extricable connection of faith and works to heat and light.

57   Ap IV 248 (Tappert, 142). Vicedom, *Die Rechtfertigung als gestaltende Kraft der Mission*, 14, calls it the living faith (*fides viva*) that witnesses (*die Zeugnis gibt*).

58   Ap IV 384 (Tappert, 165): "No faith is firm that does not show itself in confession."

59   Kirk, *What Is Mission?* 61; Hoffmann, "Gedanken zum Problem der Integration," 206. See also Schlink, *Theology of the Lutheran Confessions*, 112–13.

60   Althaus, "Um die Reinheit der Mission," 51. See also Karl Barth's observations in Manecke, *Mission als Zeugendienst*, 174.

61   The severity of sin and damnation and the universal implication of God's judgment serve as an important motivating factor for mission; Vicedom, *Die Rechtfertigung als gestaltende Kraft der Mission*, 6–7, 35; Schwarz, "Der Missiologische Aspekt der Rechtfertigungslehre," 211.

62   Vicedom, *Die Rechtfertigung als gestaltende Kraft der Mission*, 13. McGrath, *Justification by Faith*, 80–81. Ap IV 125 (Tappert, 124) lists next to the lip-service of giving thanks to God as one of the spiritual impulses of a renewed heart also the act of *praedicare* ("praising Him," or, in German, *preisen*). This close relation between faith and lip-service is expressed by the act of confessing (Ap IV 384, Tappert, 166) and prayer and holy living (LC IV 52, Kolb-Wengert, 447). All actions added comprise the true worship (*Gottesdienst*) of faith (Ap IV 49, 57, Tappert, 114).

becoming "ex-centric," as it were, in his outlook. One could even say that a Christian exists solely in his outlook to God and his neighbor.

THE DANGERS OF ANTHROPOCENTRICISM

When we explain the ethical dimension of mission as a human activity, we should not lose sight of the author of that very activity itself, namely, the Holy Spirit. While probing conversion in a previous chapter, I affirmed divine monergism—namely, that conversion is the work of the Holy Spirit through His means of the preached and sacramental Word. One must maintain this theocentric perspective, even when it is true that a newly reborn man, who has come to faith, actively cooperates with the Holy Spirit. But that cooperation in the Spirit should be further qualified in the sense that the newly reborn's participation is only possible through the continual work of the Holy Spirit. This understanding avoids synergistic conclusions of various shades. If we attribute to the believer spiritual powers and a new will, they only remain with the believer insofar as he places himself under the continual guidance of the Holy Spirit who, in Word and Sacrament, increases faith and good works. The believer delights in his good works, but he should do so with the awareness that they are purely a gift from the Holy Spirit and that this remains so all his life.[63]

All who approach mission optimistically need to know that even Christians operate both at their best *and* their worst, as saint *and* sinner. Left on their own, Christians would not succeed in mission. They would spoil it with their own selfish inclinations. But through the Holy Spirit's work, they become willing participants and attribute all success in mission to God alone. Mission, as all good works, may often be done to reap rewards (utilitarianism). Mission is pure, however, when there is no reason for wanting to seek spiritual goodness and benefits from our participation in God's mission. The believer has received all benefits as a gift *already* through faith in Jesus Christ. Doing what God desires is an act that flows from justification; it does not lead to, nor earn, justification.[64]

---

63 The above observations are drawn from Article II of the Formula of Concord, SD II 64–66, 71, 77, 83 (Kolb-Wengert, 556–57, 559–60). The idea of improvement is implied in LC IV 67 (Kolb-Wengert, 465) and SD II 39 (Kolb-Wengert, 551): "Even do good deeds and grow in practicing them."

64 In this regard, Melanchthon cautions clearly in AC IV "that this incipient keeping the law does not justify, because it is accepted only on account of faith" (Tappert, 129). Although the Confessions underscore the close relation of faith and works, they take great care at keeping them apart when it comes to explaining salvation. See, for example, AC XX 9 (Kolb-Wengert, 54); Ap VII 36 (Tappert, 175): "The fruits please God because of faith and the mediator Christ but in themselves are not worthy of grace and eternal life." The Confessions also explain faith and good works in terms of sequence, namely, that faith comes "first": Ap IV 111–14 (Tappert,

Mission may fall subject to another kind of moralism: that others are disqualified from salvation if they fail to comply with mission. As certain Christians force their own particular brand of mission on fellow Christians, they may harshly judge those who refuse to comply with that understanding and even disqualify them from salvation. Moralism sees Christian activity in light of reward and punishment so that those Christians who fail to cooperate in mission in a very particular way should know the dangers of their failure.

One problem linked to such moralism is the tendency to define what mission actually means for the average member of the Church. If mission is approached in a programmatic way, then all those not involved in the program would immediately earn the harsh judgment of others. As programs are adopted in Christian communities, they may unsettle the life within. Judgments are imposed. But what is considered "healthy" and "worthy" for one Christian is not necessarily so for the other. Mission should be a joyful expression of faith trusting in the comfort of acquittal by Christ, and it should find an expression in a natural way that allows all Christians to participate in it equally.[65] The call to a general, yet intentional, act of witness through both word and deed should become an underlying principle operative in the life of the Church.

Unfortunately, the art of drawing conclusions from one's own conduct has always tempted Christianity. This type of moralism has sometimes been called the *syllogismus practicus,* the practical syllogism wherein one's own observations come to govern the perception of one's state with God. German Pietists such as the Lutheran Johann Rambach caught hold of such trends in the idea of the "heart" that drives truth in action.[66] The practical syllogism is generally made among Christians of Reformed background that draw their own logical conclusions from the success or fruit of their labors, namely, that God looks favorably on them and that He has not only blessed them but also has elected them.[67] What conclusion should a Christian make when he finds himself in a miserable state? Does a difficult situation imply God's disfavor or even condemnation? The example of Job and Luther's theology of the cross speak otherwise. Although the practical syllogism itself is rarely used, an implied yet clear sense of it emerges in U.S. society in many popularized forms. As Christians look upon their

---

123); Ap XII 76–87 (Tappert, 193). Then good works "follow": Ap IV 114 (Tappert, 123); Ap XII 38 (Tappert, 187); SA III XIII 3 (Kolb-Wengert, 325); Ap IV 222–23 (Tappert, 138).

65 Bliese and Van Gelder, *Evangelizing Church*, 2, thus dismiss the programmatic approach to evangelizing and mission.

66 See Rambach, *Christliche Sitten-Lehre*, 2–48.

67 For a discussion of the term, see Mildenberger, *Theologie der lutherischen Bekenntnisschriften*, 68, also 146–47.

own achievements or success in sport and business, in the fulfillment of so-called "purpose-driven" formulas, and in keeping missionary visions, they might not only draw Pelagian conclusions regarding their ability to contribute to their salvation but also affirmations of the practical syllogism in their Christian calling and salvation.

Lutherans have always been careful not to draw such theological conclusions. It is true that God blesses life, but whether such blessings should be argued theologically as signs of salvation go too far. Signs of our salvation rest solely with the Gospel and the Sacraments. To seek the signs of one's salvation or perseverance elsewhere in an anthropocentric way would discredit Christ's role as mediator and propitiator:[68]

> A Christian does not keep one eye on the work of Christ and the other on his good works. Such a slanted glance is alien to him. This divided vision contradicts the nature of faith. The Christian fixes both eyes on his crucified and resurrected Christ. He is thus free from the aching anxiety about his salvation. He is thus free from the concern for "meritorious" works . . . In this freedom he is liberated for a service to God and liberated for a God-sanctioned service to the neighbor.[69]

THE MISSIONARY MANDATE AND THE THIRD USE OF THE LAW

One wonders if perhaps Lutheran theology is far too ideal in its claim that a Christian faith should produce good works joyfully and willingly, particularly in view of a Christian's consistent inclination toward sin. But there is no indication that Luther ever retracted his statement made in the preface to Paul's Epistle to the Romans about faith being a living and active thing; and his successors did not do so either.[70] Yet optimism in this area has always been qualified with the understanding that Christians, because of their proclivity to sin (Rom. 7:22–23; 1 Cor. 9:27),[71] are still in need of being prompted and encouraged by the mandates of the Lord to produce the fruits. Indeed,

---

68 SD IV 1 (Kolb-Wengert, 574); Ap IV 157 (Tappert, 128). The Lutheran Confessions come close—but only in passing—to what the *practical syllogism* expresses: Good works are looked upon as an "indication of salvation" (SD IV 38, Kolb-Wengert, 580) and confirmation of one's call and election if correctly done to prevent sin (Ap XX 12–13, Tappert, 228; 2 Pet. 1:10). They are thus seen as a "testimony" of the Holy Spirit's presence and indwelling (Ep IV 15, Kolb-Wengert, 499). Ultimately, however, all such talk is governed by the overriding interest that the good works are done out of "gratitude to God" and not to be mingled with our justification (e.g., Ep V 18, Kolb-Wengert, 499); See Schlink, *Theology of the Lutheran Confessions*, 117–18, and Koester, *Law and Gospel*, 87–92.

69 Brunner, "'Rechtfertigung' heute," 39.

70 The authors of the Formula of Concord commit themselves to that principle (SD VI 6, Kolb-Wengert, 588).

71 SD IV 19–20 (Kolb-Wengert, 577); SD II 68 (Kolb-Wengert, 557).

Christians "ought" to pursue good works, and that also includes obedience to mission. The missionary mandates serve for us Christians as important roles to guide and direct our thoughts and minds toward mission, lest we forget it. The missionary mandate is thus an expression of God's immutable and universal will, a desire of the Lord that His mission may continue unhindered until His second coming. Mission is *necessary*; it *ought* to be done; it is not an optional activity.[72] Just as the mandate to love God and neighbor (Matt. 22:37–39) remains with Christianity, so also the missionary mandate summons us to action: "The missionary mandate has something in common with all the other commandments of God. It has been given to the lax whom he calls to repentance because of their resistance to God's saving work. To all believers, however, it is given as instruction and comfort that they may do his work in proper fashion, and to the church as a warning that mission is not at her random disposal."[73] Theologically speaking, the missionary mandate in its positive role functions for every Christian in the Law's "third use." Consider the following illustration, for example: Just as a driver learns from the signs of the road which direction he should take, so also the missionary mandate provides valuable information for the Christian Church to navigate in this world. Ideally, Christians do not neglect but obey the missionary mandate as the Law in its third use reminds and informs them.[74]

The reality may be even harsher for Christians. Failure and negligence are common in the Church, and so often the informative or guiding function of the divine Law switches to its second use, namely, that of being a

---

72 The Confessions speak here in various yet similar ways of "necessity" or the "will of God." SD V 17 (Kolb-Wengert, 584): "the righteous, unchanging will of God." LC Preface 10 (Kolb-Wengert, 381): "God's commandments and words." The "necessity of unchanging order" (Ap IV 11, Tappert, 108) or the "unchangeable will of God" to which all are bound but which does not mean coercion (SD IV 16, Kolb-Wengert, 577). Peter Brunner calls it "the necessity of pneumatic spontaneity" (*die Notwendigkeit der pneumatischen Spontaneität*), for from a true repentant heart and a justified faith, the spiritual rule must hold that improvement and good works will follow ("Die Notwendigkeit des neuen Gehorsams," 281).

73 Vicedom, *Die Rechtfertigung als gestaltende Kraft der Mission*, 16.

74 Because of sin, the third use has a place in a Christian's life to serve as a guide, according to which Christians can orientate and conduct their entire life (Ep VI 1, Kolb-Wengert, 502). We affirm this point, even if Christians, "insofar as they are reborn (*quatenus renatus est!*)," do everything from a "free and merry Spirit" (SD VI 17, Kolb-Wengert, 590). Thus, even if the regenerate has the Law written in his heart by the Holy Spirit and lives in the Law anyway (Ep VI 2, Kolb-Wengert, 502; SD VI 6, 17, Kolb-Wengert, 588, 590), he becomes the addressee of the third use of the Law because of his personal union with the old Adam who remains in the regenerate also after Baptism; e.g., SD VI 7, 18, 24 (Kolb-Wengert, 588, 590–91). The "third use" as described in SD VI serves as a source of information (SD VI 12, Kolb-Wengert, 589) for the regenerate, even if Article VI gravitates toward the Law in its function as a mirror, the *lex accusans*, through which the Holy Spirit reproves; see SD VI 4 (Kolb-Wengert, 588); SD VI 21 (Kolb-Wengert, 590); SD VI 13–14 (Kolb-Wengert, 589). See Elert, "Gesetz und Evangelium," 163–64. Also Martens, *Die Rechtfertigung des Sünders*, 107 n. 242, and Forde, "Forensic Justification and Law," 301–3.

mirror in which a Christian recognizes his fault, is accused, judged, and condemned. Lutherans are well aware that Christians will never attain the high degree of perfection that they wish. Thus the Christian is in potential danger of falling from the state of grace into the state of unrighteousness by losing the Holy Spirit.[75] Forgiveness of sins as a gift from the Holy Spirit becomes the basis for such renewal; a Christian cannot merely assume a blessing of renewal.[76]

As a Christian continually struggles against sin, the reality of Baptism becomes meaningful. That does not mean that rebaptism[77] has to be performed on those who have lapsed, but that acts of mortification of the old Adam (literally, putting to death, *mortificatio*) through contrition as well as resurrection (*vivificatio*) through renewed faith (Col. 2:1; Rom. 6:1–6) must be repeated daily throughout a Christian's life.[78] Repentance therefore belongs to the very essence of faith and Christian life. Through it, the believer continually returns to the promise of forgiveness offered to him in the Gospel.[79] This applies to the Church as well, as she pursues her mission. The Lutheran Church lives in a repentant state. The question of changing structurally in view of mission is fundamentally a question of penance. Nevertheless, that change builds on the strength of forgiveness. Through the act of her contrition, God forgives the Church for all her failures so that she can once again pursue her endeavor in God's mission with renewed strength.[80]

DISCIPLESHIP, THE CROSS OF CHRIST, AND THE MOTIVE OF LOVE

Discipleship contains all ethical and missiological components of Christian living. One becomes a disciple through the missionary activities of preaching and baptizing (Matt. 28:19–20). Discipleship involves a series of steps of actually going to worship, hearing the message of Christ for the first time, being baptized, breaking and continually struggling with unchristian

---

75 Those who believe that they may attain such perfection in this life, that they cannot sin, are expressly condemned in the Confessions: AC XII 7 (Kolb-Wengert, 44): "Rejected are those who teach that whoever has once become righteous cannot fall again." Similarly, SA III III 43 (Kolb-Wengert, 319); SD II 69 (Kolb-Wengert, 557).

76 AC XII 6 (Kolb-Wengert, 45); Brunner, "*Die Notwendigkeit des neuen Gehorsams*," 281.

77 SD II 69 (Kolb-Wengert, 557).

78 Both the Large and Small Catechism stress this point (SC IV 12 and LC IV 64–65, 74–86, Kolb-Wengert, 360, 464–67). In fact, *mortificatio* and *vivificatio* are both acts performed by God as the sinner undergoes contrition and comes to faith (AC XII 3–5, Kolb-Wengert, 45; Ap XII 46, Tappert, 188).

79 SD V 20 (Kolb-Wengert, 585).

80 Krusche, "Die Kirche für andere," 174.

behavior, deepening one's understanding of God's Word, and sharing it within and outside of the Christian community. More precisely, discipleship entails a spiritual journey for the individual: "After we have been justified and regenerated by faith, therefore, we begin to fear and love God, to pray and expect help from him, to thank and praise him, and to submit to him in our afflictions. Then also we begin to love our neighbor because our hearts have spiritual and holy impulses."[81] As the Christian participates in God's mission, he turns to the precepts God provides. In the New Testament, the dual commandment of love takes precedence. Loving God and one's neighbor are in fact the summary expressions of all obedience to God (Matt. 22:34–40). That love stands for the fulfillment of the First and Second Table of the Ten Commandments and focuses on God and the neighbor. It is through this love for the neighbor that a Christian is motivated for mission. Love expresses concern for the neighbor's welfare, both physically and spiritually, and thus points to the activities of service and verbal witness.

The Church's mission and that of every Christian is unselfish in nature; it focuses on the neighbor's welfare, regardless of his need and situation and without strings attached. Christians might not always be prepared to assist others unconditionally. Unfortunately, the Church and Christians often offer their assistance as a form of "self-help," to the end that those receiving assistance demonstrate a willingness to improve their own condition! If they fail to gain control over their own lives, they do not deserve to be helped any longer. Moreover, preachers often offer Christians the Gospel as a self-help tool so that if they truly believe and follow its principles, they will learn to be "rich, healthy, and trouble free." Those who do not show such improvement are blamed for their lack of faith. Alternatives to the unconditional help of one's neighbor stem from the secular and political sphere and have little to do with the cross of Christ. Whereas business ventures and other worldly expectations confidently base their strategies on self-attainable goals and make prognoses of future success, Christian spirituality cannot entertain such expectations. It alone can appreciate thankfully the rewards of earthly and spiritual life as a gift from God.

The commitment to help the neighbor's plight is rooted in Christ. This Christological basis is absolutely crucial for any discipleship worthy of the name. What a Christian should avoid at all cost is the so-called discipleship without Christ: "Discipleship without Jesus Christ is a way of our own

---

81 Ap IV 125 (Tappert, 124).

choosing. It may be the ideal way, it may even lead to martyrdom, but it is devoid of all promise. Jesus will certainly reject it."[82]

For Dietrich Bonhoeffer, discipleship is not one of self-choosing or achievable by one's own power. It is not one of human merit. Instead, Christ calls and takes a Christian into His fellowship with the consequence that such discipleship is devoted to every neighbor, and not just one of self-choosing. Bonhoeffer continues: "Every moment and every situation challenges us to action and to obedience. We have literally no time to sit down and ask ourselves whether so-and-so is our neighbor or not."[83]

A further consequence of such discipleship is bearing the cross because of allegiance to the suffering Christ. That does not mean we deliberately have to seek out suffering. Following Christ means a passive suffering, a cross that is laid on every Christian, bringing suffering and rejection to everyone according to his allotted share. Every Christian will go through a death of his old Adam at his Baptism and continue to encounter new temptations and suffering throughout his daily life for Jesus Christ's sake. Luther was thus willing to include suffering as one of the marks of the Church. A Christian's refusal to take up the cross and submit himself to suffering will disqualify him from the fellowship of Christ. Bonhoeffer's cross literally led him to the gallows: "If we lose our lives in his service and carry our cross, we shall find our lives again in the fellowship of the cross with Christ."[84]

There is a line of thought here that can be traced back to Luther, who also committed himself totally to Christ and derived from Him the motivation also to serve his neighbor. While it is true that only Christ bore the sufferings for our atonement, the sacrificial attitude of Christ is one that Christians also adopt.

> I will therefore give myself as a Christ to my neighbor, just as Christ offered himself to me; I will do nothing in this life except what I see is necessary, profitable, and salutary to my neighbor, since through faith I have an abundance of all good things in Christ . . . Behold, from faith thus flow forth love and joy in the Lord, and from love a joyful, willing, and free mind that serves one's neighbor willingly and takes no account of gratitude or ingratitude, of praise or blame, of gain or loss. For a man does not serve that he may put men under obligations. He does not distinguish between friends and enemies or anticipate their thankfulness

82 Reprinted with permission of Scribner, a Division of Simon & Schuster, Inc., from p. 50 of *The Cost of Discipleship* by Dietrich Bonhoeffer. Copyright © 1959 by SCM Press, Ltd. Used with permission.

83 Reprinted with permission of Scribner, a Division of Simon & Schuster, Inc., from p. 67 of *The Cost of Discipleship* by Dietrich Bonhoeffer. Copyright © 1959 by SCM Press, Ltd. Used with permission.

84 Reprinted with permission of Scribner, a Division of Simon & Schuster, Inc., from p. 80 of *The Cost of Discipleship* by Dietrich Bonhoeffer. Copyright © 1959 by SCM Press, Ltd. Used with permission.

or unthankfulness, but he most freely and most willingly spends himself and all that he has, whether he wastes all on the thankless or whether he gains a reward.[85]

There is thus a clear mandate for a particular understanding of discipleship in Lutheranism. It isdoes not end with the Commandments, but rather passes through the legality of things to become a Christologically based and motivated undertaking. True, "discipleship" is often an underused term in the Lutheran Church, as a recent study bemoans: "Lutherans seem to lack one essential requirement for fulfilling their missionary task. They lack the compulsive reason for sharing the good news of God's kingdom in Jesus Christ with others."[86] The fear is that once Christ is set up as an example, pietistic or synergistic conclusions may follow. All doctrines, however, are subject to misunderstandings, and that of discipleship is no exception. Properly understood, discipleship may never pass by the cross of Christ without asking the crucial question about personal commitment to Christ and neighbor through witness and lifestyle. Yet this need not violate the vicarious nature of Christ's work, as if our commitment aided salvation. In this way, a call to discipleship will not divorce itself from our justification by grace through Christ's death, nor will it threaten its substitutionary character.

The most compelling argument for discipleship exists in the reality of the cross itself. Therein we see the sacrificial love of God for us sinners. There is no other reason needed to underscore discipleship than that we give ourselves sacrificially for the spiritual and physical welfare of the neighbor (1 John 3:16; 4:11). From the beginning of his theology, Luther listed sacrifice as one aspect of the spiritual priesthood.

TWO KINDS OF RIGHTEOUSNESS

Luther makes the most compelling case for discipleship in his treatise *Two Kinds of Righteousness* (1519). Although written early in his career, there seems to be no reason to believe that he would later want to retract the gist of his arguments and the radical demands placed on a Christian. In fact, the Lutheran Confessions affirm the two kinds of righteousness as Luther previously had presented them. First, there is the righteousness of faith that is reckoned to believers. Second, there is the righteousness of new obedience or good works done by Christians. It is the first kind of righteousness (Christ's obedience, suffering, and death) that counts and saves sinners before God. The second kind of righteousness cannot be used to stand in

---

85 AE 31:367.
86 Bliese and Van Gelder, *Evangelizing Church*, 19.

front of God's throne but matters a great deal in our Christian lives as we engage in activities to our neighbor.[87]

Luther bases his arguments for the second type of righteousness on Phil. 2:5: "Have this mind among yourselves, which is yours in Christ Jesus." What follows is what we may call a "putting-on-of-the-mind-of-Christ" in a self-effacing or kenotic way. The second kind of righteousness flows from the righteousness that Christ earned on the cross and leads to total dedication or surrender of service in the example of Christ in Philippians 2:

> This righteousness is the product of the righteousness of the first type, actually its fruit and consequence . . . it hates itself and loves its neighbor; it does not seek its own good, but that of another, and in this its whole way of living consists. For in that it hates itself and does not seek its own, it crucifies the flesh. Because it seeks the good of another, it works love. Thus in each sphere it does God's will, living soberly with self, justly with neighbor, devoutly toward God.

> This righteousness follows the example of Christ in this respect (1 Pet. 2:21) and is transformed into his likeness (2 Cor. 3:18). It is precisely this that Christ requires. Just as he himself did all things for us, not seeking his own good but ours only—and in this he was most obedient to God the Father—so he desires that we also should set the same example for our neighbors.[88]

We cannot go any deeper than Luther does here in applying the Christological component to our mission. Although Lutherans are strong in arguing the first kind of righteousness (our justification), the second kind of righteousness is equally important and impresses on us the idea of our fruit of faith or obedience to the will of Christ. The second righteousness is of a sacrificial kind, willing to give itself up for the well-being of the neighbor. Although Luther does not specify exactly the details of our obligation to the neighbor, it clearly entails such concerns as the neighbor's spiritual well-being too.

What matters here above all else is the attitude of self-denial and sacrifice for the good of the neighbor. In modern Western society, that concern may be alien and may conflict with popular consumer-driven, self-oriented interests. In this way, the radical nature of the Lutheran doctrine of discipleship is crucial in shaping our Christian life in a missionary way.

TRIANGLE OF THREE RESPONSIBILITIES

A diagram shall close and frame this chapter on ethics. The diagram lists three important areas of Christian contribution to the mission of the Church and society, based on scriptural and theological evidence. I call it

---

87 SD III 32 (Kolb-Wengert, 567).

88 AE 31:299–300.

the triangle of three responsibilities in which a Christian may see himself at work in mission. The vertices point to three main foci: the secular vocation of the Christian, the proclamation of the Church, and the Church's works of Christian mercy. In the diagram, the Christian bears his responsibilities in these areas and is therefore active. The Scripture passages indicate the divine source of the activities and the courses in which they run. The unity of the triangle indicates that these areas also connect with one another, and it is in the context of such interconnection that the Christian lives his life.

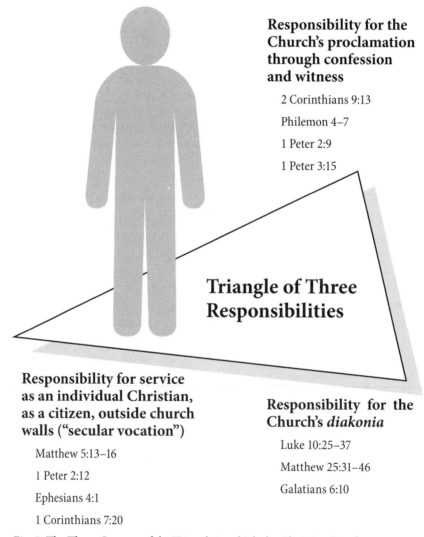

Responsibility for the Church's proclamation through confession and witness

2 Corinthians 9:13

Philemon 4–7

1 Peter 2:9

1 Peter 3:15

Triangle of Three Responsibilities

Responsibility for service as an individual Christian, as a citizen, outside church walls ("secular vocation")

Matthew 5:13–16

1 Peter 2:12

Ephesians 4:1

1 Corinthians 7:20

Responsibility for the Church's *diakonia*

Luke 10:25–37

Matthew 25:31–46

Galatians 6:10

Fig. 5: The Three Corners of the Triangle in which the Christian Stands

CHAPTER FIFTEEN
THE MISSIONARY OFFICE

EARLY MISSIONARY ATTEMPTS
IN PROTESTANTISM[1]

In a previous chapter, we pointed out that the lack of direct contact with heathen lands, the absence of colonies, and the lack of support of territorial rulers made overseas mission during the Reformation impossible. Luther's underlying premise had been that many of the foreign lands needed to be reached with preachers of the Gospel. There were, however, early valiant attempts to establish contact with foreign peoples. Primus Truber (1508– 86) and Hans von Ungnad (1493–1564) sought to translate and publish Bibles into the languages of the Croats and Wends. They followed up this work with a translation of Luther's catechism, the Augsburg Confession, the Apology, Melanchthon's *Loci*, the Wuertemberg Church Discipline, and a hymnbook. After instituting the first Protestant printing press, they helped to create a new written language, the Glagolithic script, for the Croats. Duke Christoph and the Church of Wuertemberg offered financial support for this project. The main goal for Truber and Ungnad was that their efforts would eventually open doors to the Turks and others living under the darkness of Islam.[2]

Despite the devastating consequences of the Thirty Years' War (1618– 48), Peter Heyling (1607/8–52), a German Lutheran from the Hanseatic city of Lübeck, became a missionary teacher, preacher, and doctor in Egypt and Ethiopia among the Coptic Christians and for King Fasilides (1632–67). Influenced by the great Dutch mission apologist Hugo Grotius (1583–1645),[3] Heyling's work led to an Amharic translation of the New Testament. He died probably as a martyr in the Sudan. To this day, traces

---

1 The most noted study on mission in Lutheran Orthodoxy is provided by Größel, *Die Mission und die evangelische Kirche*.

2 Raupp, *Mission in Quellentexten*, 49–51.

3 Grotius, *Truth of the Christian Religion*. Its original title is *De Veritate Religionis Christianae* (1627).

of his work are evident in the Coptic Church, and he is still much revered in the Ethiopian Evangelical Lutheran Mekane Yesus Church. Mention should also be made of John Calvin (1509–64), who supported efforts to create a Christian colony in Northern Brazil in 1557 by electing two missionaries, Pierre Richier and Guillaume Chartier, to accompany the French admiral Gaspard de Coligny (1519–72) and twelve other Huguenot settlers. Among this group was Jean de Léry (1534–1613), from whom we have the account of attempts to convert the cannibalistic Topinambu Indians. After two months of missionary efforts (October–December 1557), the project failed. A dogmatic dispute arose with Nicholas Durand de Villegaignon (1519–72), the owner of the colony, which led to the execution of the Calvinist missionaries.

Erasmus of Rotterdam (1467–1536) summoned missionaries to Asia and Africa to engage in the noble task of converting believers of Islam and other religions to Christianity. Another call for mission came from Martin Bucer (1491–1555), who not only pioneered the Lutheran cause in Alsace but also bemoaned the lack of interest for mission and the failure to resume it in his time. Mission was necessary, he claimed, in part because it would counter the negative consequences that resulted from the Spanish Catholic mission. Two noted voices among the pastors of Lutheran Orthodoxy were Balthasar Meisner (1587–1626) and Christian Scriver (1629–93). Both expressed concern over the lack of mission, and Scriver in particular hoped that God would again send apostles to the heathens.[4] In the Scandinavian countries, where Christians came into direct contact with the heathen Lapps, the royal house of Wasa—especially King Gustavus Vasa (1523–60) and later Gustavus Adolphus (1611–32)—sent pastors to plant congregations. One of these pastors appointed in 1559 was Michael Agricola. In 1611, Nicholas Andrea worked among the Lapps, preparing books in the Lapp language and establishing schools and a mission seminary. Although this project is insignificant in comparison to other worldwide efforts and did not last very long, it represents the first Protestant mission subsidized by a state. The Danish Halle mission to the colony called Tranquebar in India became a well-known representative of this model. Underlying such initial efforts, however, was a burning theological issue, namely, the debate whether the Church is allowed to engage in the divine mandate of authorizing and sending missionaries into the world, as Christ had done with His apostles. Can the Great Commission be passed on to the Church, or had it lapsed with the death of the apostles?[5] What follows is an account of how the debate was resolved.

---

4   Raupp, *Mission in Quellentexten*, 105, 109; Flachsmeier, *Geschichte der Evangelischen Mission*, 104–15.

5   Most recently, for example, Tucker, *From Jerusalem to Irian Jaya*, 67.

THE PAROCHIAL CAPTIVITY OF MINISTRY DURING THE PERIOD OF LUTHERAN ORTHODOXY[6]

The formative figures and institutions of Lutheran Orthodoxy who considered the missionary nature of the Church and what role the pastoral ministry played in it were primarily Philip Nicolai (1556–1608), the hymnologist and theologian at Hamburg; the great theologian Johann Gerhard (1582–1637); Johann Heinrich Ursinus (1608–67), the superintendent in Augsburg; and the Wittenberg faculty (1652). We now examine some of their fascinating arguments.

There were two outsiders who sparked debate among the Lutherans: the Jesuit Robert Bellarmine (1542–1621) and the Anglican Hadrian Saravia (1531–1613).[7] In his most famous book in which he discussed the controversies of the Christian faith (*Disputationes de controversiis christianae fidei*), Bellarmine had scoffed at the Lutheran Church, calling her a sectarian movement since the Lutherans had yet to convert an overseas heathen. Bellarmine saw this as evidence that the Lutheran Church was not in possession of the salutary Gospel.[8] Bellarmine also argued that the unrestricted continuation of the apostolic mission was continued by the Roman Catholic Church, particularly in its monastic form that legitimately pursued the apostolate by having individuals submit to poverty and celibacy. Instead, the German Lutheran pastors remained fixed in their parishes where they led a happy and contented family life.

Bellarmine's arguments certainly presented a quandary for the Lutherans by raising the question of what form the Christian Church was allowed in the role of continuing the apostolate? Philip Nicolai came forward with the tract *De Regno Christi* [*On the Kingdom of God*], in which he provided a missionary ecclesiology. With somewhat extraordinary geopolitical proof and Scripture verses, such as Mark 16:15; Rom. 10:18; Col. 1:6–23, Nicolai demonstrated that every region had encountered the preaching of the Gospel by way of the apostles. If the Gospel should be taken again to these regions, then God would provide the time and occasion. In

---

6   As I have discussed also in my article "The Lutheran Debate over a Missionary Office," which first appeared in *Lutheran Quarterly* 19.3 (Autumn 2005): 276–301, and is used here by permission of Lutheran Quarterly, Inc.

7   Besides Johann Gerhard, there were also other Lutheran theologians, such as Johann Fecht (1636–1716) and Johann Georg Neumann (1661–1709) who contested Saravia's naïve hermeneutics. Calvinism, too, felt the criticisms and was strongly defended by Calvin's successor, Theodor Beza (1516–1605). Größel, *Die Mission und die evangelische Kirche*, 8.

8   Jesuit compatriots of Bellarmine joined him in this invective, including Francisco de Suarez (1548–1619), Leonhard Lessius (1554–1623), and Jacob Keller (1568–1621). For Johann Gerhard's comments on Bellarmine's accusations, see *Loci Theologici*, 2:422–35.

other words, one waited for a "wink of God's finger" (*Fingerzeig Gottes*).[9] *De Regno Christi* was a seminal work; it not only shaped the ecclesiology of later Orthodox Lutheran theologians, but it also influenced Wilhelm Löhe in his *Three Books about the Church* almost 250 years later.[10]

The discussion on the apostolate was taken over by the Anglican theologian Hadrian Saravia (1531–1613), who in 1590 published a treatise entitled *De diversis ministrorum evangelii gradibus, sicut a Domino fuerunt instituti [Concerning the different orders of the ministry of the Gospel, as they were instituted by the Lord]*. He argued that the ministry of the apostles continued immediately in the episcopacy of the Church.[11] His arguments were refuted by leading theologians in Reformed and Lutheran circles. On the Reformed side, it was Calvin's successor, Theodor Beza (1519–1605), and on the Lutheran side, there were especially Johann Gerhard, Johann Fecht (1636–1716), and Johann Georg Neumann (1661–1709).

In a chapter on divine election in the *Loci Theologici*, Gerhard dismissed the accusations of Bellarmine by hailing Lutheranism as the true possessor of the universal Gospel. This Gospel calls all people to salvation (*vocatio est universalis*) because the Lord commissioned His disciples to preach the Gospel to all of creation. This the apostles did, as Gerhard would agree with Nicolai. However, because of the guilt of the people for rejecting the first preaching of the apostles, many people today are without the Gospel. Thus when people today exist without the Gospel, they should not blame God or question the universal character of the Gospel for their ignorance, but their forefathers.[12] Should the Gospel be preached to them again? Yes, Gerhard would argue, but the question is how. In his discussion on the ministry of the Church, Gerhard was very cautious not to promote an office like that of the apostles, for that had been uniquely bestowed on them directly or immediately by Christ. Nobody may replicate that apostolic office or claim to be in direct succession of it since there are clear distinctions between the apostles' ministry and the Church's ministry of preaching the Word. Although

---

9 Nicolai's innovative arguments are recorded in Holsten, "Die Bedeutung der altprotestantischen Dogmatik für die Mission," 148–66, and Größel, *Die Mission und die evangelische Kirche*, 992–96. Luther, in contrast, still argued that the preaching of the Gospel that was begun by the apostles must be continued around the world. Stolle, *Church Comes from All Nations*, 24–25. Wetter, *Der Missionsgedanke bei Martin Luther*, 323–24.

10 In his arguments on ecclesiology in *Three Books about the Church*, Löhe included portions of Nicolai's tract; Heß, *Das Missionsdenken bei Philip Nicolai*, 16–17.

11 Excerpts of the Latin text are published in Raupp, *Mission in Quellentexten*, 61–62, and in Größel, *Die Mission und die evangelische Kirche*, 71. The English text is quoted in Thomas, *Classic Texts in Mission and Evangelization*, 41–43. For further references, one may also see Smith, *Contribution of Hadrian Saravia*. Saravia's true motive was covered by his appeal for mission. His real argument was for an episcopal constitution—not an exclusively Roman one— understood as a nonbinding continuation of the missionary apostolate.

12 Gerhard, *Loci Theologici*, 2:58–59; Raupp, *Mission in Quellentexten*, 67.

the universal promise of the Gospel still applies, Gerhard was hesitant to endorse a continuation of the apostles' ministry through the bishops of the Church as the Calvinist Hadrian Saravia claimed. True, Gerhard would point out, the preaching of the Gospel may continue to those where the seed had once been sown but not through a specific group that believes it has all the same powers and authority as the apostles. In fact, just as the promise that Christ "will be with you always" applies to all Christians, so, too, the preaching of the Gospel goes on through all Christians as co-workers of the apostles (Greek: *synergia*). However, that does not mean that these co-workers may claim to possess that unique and exceptional authority of the apostles, which was manifest in their ability to speak in different languages, perform miracles, and be infallible in their preaching.[13] Unfortunately, Gerhard became so involved in his apologetic approach of defending the uniqueness of the apostolic ministry that he failed to raise an unequivocal concern for the unbelieving world and its need to hear the Gospel. His arguments that the forefathers had all heard the Gospel at an earlier time and that we are thus not dealing with a first-time proclamation sounds somewhat contrived. Gerhard's forceful and beautiful treatment on the universal will of God and the universal call through the proclamation of the Gospel does not carry over into a convincing summons or plea to preach the Gospel.[14] I will reflect more on Gerhard's arguments below.

The discussion on the apostolate continued unabated as Justinian von Welz (1621–68), an exiled Lutheran nobleman from Austria, appealed to the leadership in the Lutheran Church to support his newly formed mission society, the *Jesus Love-me Society*, as an institution for mission within Germany and beyond. Johann Heinrich Ursinus and the Evangelical alliance of territorial Lutheran churches (*Corpus evangelicorum*), meeting in Regensburg, withdrew its goodwill and support for that program out of fear that they might be sanctioning a spiritual-mystic movement that could revive those subversive elements within Lutheranism that the Reformation had so successfully dismissed in the sixteenth century. Obviously, Welz's association with the spiritualists Friedrich Breckling (1629–1711) and Johann Georg Gichtel (1638–1710) did not help his cause. Welz's strong attacks on the rulers and the pastors strengthened the opposition. Embittered, Welz left for Holland and in 1666 sailed to the colony Surinam in the northern part of South America, where, according to rumors, he died two years later, having been torn to pieces by wild animals.

On April 24, 1652, the Wittenberg faculty issued its famous opinion on the apostolate, reiterating most of Gerhard's arguments and adding also the

---

13 Gerhard, *Loci Theologici*, 2:145–46; Raupp, *Mission in Quellentexten*, 69.
14 Stolle, "Zur missionarischen Perspektive der lutherischen Theologie," 26

point that God had revealed Himself through the light of nature (Romans 1–2; Acts 17) and on many other occasions through the preaching of Adam, Noah, and His holy apostles. Since these nations rejected the Gospel, God punished them for their ignorance by taking the preaching from them. This response was submitted as an answer to the queries (scruples) of an Austrian, Reichsgraf Ehrhardt von Wetzhausen from Vienna, who wanted to know how the Orient, Meridian, and Occident could be converted to the salutary faith "when he sees no one of the Augsburg Confession go there to preach and to save as much as 100,000 people from damnation."[15]

Wilhelm Maurer argues in his essay that Lutheran Orthodoxy treated the question of the apostolate and mission in view of two important challenges:[16]

1. Saravia's argument, which had its supporters among the Roman Catholics, that the apostolate continued undiminished either in the form of monastic mission or in the episcopacy; and

2. Welz's mystic enthusiasm that infiltrated the church and threatened the standard interpretation of Scripture and the well-structured church order.[17]

The hermeneutical arguments presented by the Lutheran Orthodox theologians reflect the quandary over the validity of *rite vocatus* if the preaching office was set apart from its parochial setting. Could someone other than the apostles assume authority to wander from his congregation and become transient? The answer the Lutheran Orthodox theologians provided engaged the biblical evidence; they were unwilling to erase the clear distinctions between the life of the apostles and the pastoral ministry in their time. For them, it was evident that after the passing of the apostles, the Church lacked the clear mandate (*ite mundum universum*) to continue a transient ministry of the apostles that was detached from its parochial setting. The mission of the postles and of Paul in particular stood out as a unique phenomenon. Paul and the apostles were also given the unique ministry of teaching infallibly (*infallibilitas absoluta*) and the ability to perform miracles (*thaumaturgia miraculosa*). If the Church was actually

---

15 The text of the faculty's response is recorded in Größel, *Die Mission und die evangelische Kirche*, 84–85, and Raupp, *Mission in Quellentexten*, 70–71.

16 Maurer, "Die Lutherische Kirche und ihre Mission," 192.

17 The reasons for questioning Welz's proposals were legitimate when one reads his first tract: *De Vita Solitaria* (1663), subtitled *Hermit Life according to God's Word* (*De Vita Solitaria, das ist / Von dem Einsidler Leben / Wie es nach Gottes Wort / und der Alten Heiligen Einsidler Leben anzustellen seye*). Welz sought to revive a monastic holiness and evangelical asceticism for missionary purposes that were influenced by theologians such as Eusebius of Caesarea (260–339), Augustine of Hippo (354–430), the medieval mystic Thomas à Kempis (1379/80–1471), and Johann Arndt (1555–1621). Scherer, *Justinian Welz*, 15–17; Größel, *Die Mission und die evangelische Kirche*, 46–47.

in possession of such an extraordinary call (*vocatio extraordinaria*) that embraced these unique activities, why then did not all clergy become transient as well?[18]

It is evident that Lutheran Orthodoxy tied the ministry of the apostles to the pastoral functions within a congregational setting. Scripture, especially the Pastoral Letters (Acts 14:23; 20:28; Titus 1:5; 1 Pet. 5:2), proved that the apostles passed on their authority to teach, preach, and administer the Sacraments to qualified individuals by the laying on of hands in the context of a congregation.[19] Lutheran Orthodoxy traced the office of Word and Sacrament ministry back to the ministry of the apostles, but this origin was one that embraced the functions of preaching, teaching, and administering the means of grace. The apostolate was attached to a bound locality, the place of a shepherding ministry. This explains the insensitive and allergic reactions of leading church officials to Welz's proposal. He was unable to demonstrate persuasively that if they were to endorse his enterprise, he would be sent where an existing congregation would request and accommodate his ministry. The idea that one could send an individual with the task of planting a congregation in a region where no Christians lived escaped the notice of Lutheran Orthodoxy. Consequently, the Lutheran Church could no longer resort to an unrestricted sending into the world. That right was no longer applicable to the *ministerium* of the Church during Lutheran Orthodoxy.[20]

The reader may find it difficult to accept Lutheran Orthodoxy's view of the apostolate in such restricted form since the sending of missionaries has become such a part of contemporary mission. With the progression of time and situation, especially through the discovery of new heathen lands that fell into the possession of Lutheran territorial rulers, the constricted notions of Lutheran Orthodox theologians about mission had to be expanded. The theological progression over mission, however, came only as late as the mid-nineteenth century.

It is an interesting question to ask whether Lutheran Orthodoxy would have boycotted the kind of sending that is done today. One may conjecture that they would not have prohibited a sending as such, but they might have offered a legitimate concern. Since church bodies today exist all over the

---

18 Gerhard, *Loci Theologici*, 2:145–46; Größel, *Die Mission und die evangelische Kirche*, 16–17, 127–29.

19 Gerhard, *Loci Theologici*, 2:146. Similarly the Wittenberg faculty, in Größel, *Die Mission und die evangelische Kirche*, 87–88.

20 Gerhard, *Loci Theologici*, 6:48–55. Also Gerhard, *Loci Theologici*, 6:145–48, where he observes (p. 145): "respectu primi omnes veri et sinceri ecclesiae ministri, respectu secundi omnes episcopi apostolorum successores dicuntur ecclesiastica loquendi consuetudine . . . Respectu tertii, in quo etiam apostolatus proprie consistit, nullus fuit apostolorum successor, sed apostolatus fuit ordo temporarius et extraordinarius."

world, they would have encouraged that the sending of ordained clergy tie them into the existing life of a congregation, the parochial setting. In other words, the deployment of missionaries would prove to be legitimate only if they joined their missionary service to a Word and Sacrament ministry in a foreign congregation. For Lutheran Orthodoxy, today's missionary would in fact be understood as a translocated pastor in a foreign setting. We need to keep this concern in mind for a later moment.[21]

The Missionary Apostolate in the Early Church

The word for mission (*missio*) is a Latin rendering of the Greek word ἀπο-στέλλειν ("to send"). The implications of the word "apostolic" for a missionary apostolate in Protestantism are not that evident. Traditionally speaking, confessing the Church as "apostolic" had always meant an obligation to remain faithful to the message or teaching of the apostles and of upholding preaching and administering the means of grace. As such, it had little to do with copying the apostles in their transient mission. Ecumenical discussions today, however, point to the interest of capturing the "apostolic" character of "sentness."[22] "When the church in North America discards the Christendom mind-set, it can become truly apostolic. To be apostolic is, literally, to be sent out."[23] Since mission has become a reality in the Church, a renewed discussion of the full meaning of the term *apostolic* is certainly welcome. As one scholar has pointed out, the apostolic succession

---

21 An interpretation to this effect is made by Stolle, "Zur missionarischen Perspektive der lutherischen Theologie," 23.

22 Consider evidence provided by the WCC in Geneva, for example: "[B]ased on their [the commissioned apostles'] testimony which is preserved in the New Testament and in the life of the Church, the Church has one constitutive mark of its being apostolic, its being sent into the world" (Scherer and Bevans, *New Directions in Mission and Evangelization*, 38). For a discussion on the Church's mark as "apostolic," see Guder, *Missional Church*, 110–41, 255–56. See, for example, the Roman Catholic statement in Vatican II on the "Dogmatic Constitution of the Church" (*Lumen Gentium* 35) and the decree passed on the lay apostolate in November 1965 (*Apostolicam Actuositatem* 10). See Rahner and Vorgrimmler, *Kleines Konzils-Kompendium*, 165, 400–401. In both its statements, Vatican II affirms the missionary apostolate for the laity in the Church to the degree that the laity has a part in the salvific mission of the Church with the consecrated order of the Church. That right, we are told, is bestowed on them through Baptism and confirmation (*Apostolicam Actuositatem* 3, 391). The implication for Roman Catholic mission is that the laity no longer have to accompany a consecrated priest in order to be considered legitimate church planters. It may be argued that the reason for this change came about through the worldwide clergy shortage, forcing the Roman Catholic Church to recognize the valuable contribution of the lay apostolate in her mission.

23 Guder, *Missional Church*, 110. Witte, "Kirche als Ziel der Sendung," 20: "The office entrusted uniquely to Paul cannot be continued by another person. But there is a true continuation of the function of the mission-apostolic office wherever the church sends—namely, her preachers of the Gospel to nations, heathen, Jews and Muslims. The *successio apostolica* is mission."

is mission (*successio apostolica est missio*). But from a historic perspective, this statement is problematic, at least for the period of Lutheran Orthodoxy and, as we shall briefly note, also for the Early Church.

Einar Molland asks whether the Early Church intentionally followed a specific missionary method. Thereby, he raises the important issue: in what way the apostolic transient ministry continued after the passing of the apostles. On one occasion, of course, the Church experienced an extraordinary event of persecution, and, through it, a transient ministry in remote areas ensued, which soon led to the founding of new churches (Acts 8:1–8; 11:19). Next to the apostles' ministry, there is the infrequent mentioning of the evangelist (Acts 8:40; Eph. 4:11; 2 Tim. 4:5). This could imply that evangelists continued the mission of the apostles among Jews, God-fearers (those who were not full Jewish proselytes but who believed in one God and respected the moral teachings of the Jews, e.g., Acts 10:2), and heathens. In the New Testament context, the evangelists were still closely associated with the mission of the apostles and assisted the apostles in the ministry of proclamation. But the office of an evangelist soon disappeared as well.[24] Although Eusebius in his *History* mentions a postapostolic activity of evangelists, they, too, seemed to be have had a role that passed away in the Church.[25] One hundred years before Eusebius, Origen describes such transient activity of individuals who were traveling from village to village to win others to faith in Christ.[26] Where, however, do we have the explicit office of missionary? Unlike the apostles and the evangelists as mentioned in Eph. 4:11, the missionary office was not part of the hierarchy of the Church. By the year 252 in Rome, the hierarchy of spiritual office in the Church included a bishop, forty-six presbyters, seven subdeacons, forty-two acolytes, fifty-two exorcists, lectors, and doorkeepers. None of these titles indicate or reveal the task of bringing the Word to those outside of the Church, except if one were to include in some way the instruction of the catechumens. Catechesis, however, focused on those who were already within the Church.

To whom was the missionary task in the Early Church assigned? In part, apologists took it on.[27] Yet the apparent lack of persuasive reflection on missionary activity in the Early Church is striking, and it suggests the belief that the apostles had brought the Christian message to all parts of

---

24 Wilhelm Löhe, "Aphorismen," in *GW* 5/1:282. See also Ratke, *Confession and Mission*, 88.

25 Molland, "Besaß die Alte Kirche ein Missionsprogramm und bewußte Missionsmethoden?" 59.

26 Molland, "Besaß die Alte Kirche ein Missionsprogramm und bewußte Missionsmethoden?" 59; *Contra Celsum* 3.9.

27 Molland, "Besaß die Alte Kirche ein Missionsprogramm und bewußte Missionsmethoden?" 59–60; Foster, *After the Apostles*.

the known world. For both the Greek and the Latin fathers, it was not self-understood that the words of Matt. 28:18–20 should also be applied as a commission to them and their times, a view we saw still held in the sixteenth and seventeenth centuries.[28] The growth of Christendom in the Early Church, therefore, may not be attributed to a deliberate pursuit of an "apostolic" strategy. Rather, it embraced numerous contributions: the role of the apologists, the persecution of the martyrs (to which Tertullian added the epithet "*Semen est sanguis christianorum*" ("The seed [of the Church] is the blood of the Christians") and the everyday witness of Christians to one another. These all were effective means of spreading Christianity.[29]

We should note also that after the mission of the apostle Paul, the Church underwent a period of consolidation. It was a significant transitional phase in which the ministry of the apostles was handed down to individuals who assumed the pastoral functions in the context of congregations (e.g., Acts 14:13; 20:28; 2 Tim. 2:2). Individuals were properly installed through the laying on of hands and were advised to continue faithfully in the ministry of the Gospel (e.g., 1 Tim. 5:22; 6:11–16; Titus 1:5). This biblical insight was shared by Johann Gerhard and the faculty of Wittenberg, and it cannot be dismissed as an arbitrary or odd exegetical position. The calls of Justinian von Welz and Saravia were countered with quite plausible concerns from biblical observations that ordained clergy should remain where they have been placed. However, as soon as fertile territories were found in all corners of the world during the Age of Discovery, it became evident that these could not be reached by such a parochial-oriented concept of outreach. The universal call of the Gospel had to backed with an intentional ministry to the unbelieving world. The motive of relieving people from their sin through the preaching of the salutary Gospel indeed necessitated a strategy of instituting a missionary office that would allow for the sending of individuals who would preach and teach beyond the boundaries of already existing church bodies.

The Ordained Ministry in Lutheran Mission

If, however, the Lutheran Church would adopt such a missionary office, it would have to introduce something that would expand the otherwise constricted understanding of ministry. Could one link a universal ministry of properly called servants to the missionary apostolate and still leave the apostolic ministry unique and inviolate? That was an important quandary

---

28 Molland, "Besaß die Alte Kirche ein Missionsprogramm und bewußte Missionsmethoden?" 62–63.

29 Tertullian, *Apologeticum* 50, 13; Molland, "Besaß die Alte Kirche ein Missionsprogramm und bewußte Missionsmethoden?" 65.

in the nineteenth century. Lutheran theologians such as Adolf von Harless (1806–79) and Ludwig Harms (1808–65)—and, in the twentieth century, the systematic theologian Peter Brunner—stepped up to the plate with important and groundbreaking reasoning. Before them, nineteenth-century theologians such as Ludwig Adolf Petri (1803–73), Wilhelm Löhe (1808–72), and Karl Graul (1814–64) had attempted to bypass the sending and ordaining of missionaries. All three thought that the missionary was in many ways a volunteer who went (German: *Gehlinge*, i.e., "go-lings," rather than *Sendlinge*, i.e., "sendlings") on his own accord, not as one authorized by the sending Church. Wilhelm Löhe, for example, who began the important work of supplying American Lutherans with candidates for the pastoral ministry, considered those whom he trained for such foreign work as volunteers, who had to seek legitimization and ordination for their ministry not from a German congregation but from the American congregation to which they were going. Löhe also chose a strategy to establish Christian communities of settlers in Michigan. Among them, the pastoral office was placed, and under it, Christians worked and witnessed to a foreign world.[30] Colonist mission, in which a number of settlers accompanied the pastors in their efforts to bring the Gospel to outsiders, also became the initial strategy of Ludwig Harms of Hermannsburg, who was intrigued by the Celtic mission through monastic communities. His colonist mission to the Zulu tribe in Africa soon disintegrated into individual farm holders, so Harms chose to have missionaries ordained and sent by the Evangelical Lutheran Church of Hannover through his mission society of Hermannsburg.

Within this critical period of Lutheran mission formation, a theological progression took place that would add a universal dimension to the pastoral ministry. The ministry of the Church has universal implications, and though this was not evident in Lutheranism throughout history, it merely had to be brought to light. As Hans-Werner Gensichen points out:

> There is no differentiation of ministries but of situations. The Reformers distinguish between those where there is a Christian congregation in non-Christian surroundings, and those where there is none. In the first case, it is the duty of the congregation to call a minister, and thus to exercise its authority, privilege, and responsibility to preach the gospel in its surroundings, to Christians and non-Christians alike.[31]

Soon, the connection between the missionary's ministry and Articles V and XIV of the Augsburg Confession, which speak of the office of the Church,

---

30 One may see here Wilhelm Löhe's helpful exposition on what apostolic means for the Church in *Three Books about the Church*. See also Ratke, *Confession and Mission*, 42–43; Schulz, "Lutheran Debate over a Missionary Office," 276–301.

31 Gensichen, "Were the Reformers Indifferent to Missions?" 124.

was made. In these articles, Harless argued, the called office of missionary finds its theologically legitimate place, just as the office of the pastor.

> As far as their [the missionaries'] status is concerned, it would be difficult to dismiss the fact that it bears all marks of a proper, Christian and apostolic call. They are placed in the call of the Lord to the Apostles: Go ye to the world. They did not go on their own accord, but have been found fit for their office and have been placed into it by those who in the Evangelical Lutheran Church have the right to do so. The church is the community of believers, that keep themselves to the pure Word and Sacrament and such a community has sent them out with a loyal pledge to their confession . . . We cannot find anything amiss here that would prevent us from considering them *rite vocatus* in the sense of the Fourteenth Article of the Augsburg Confession.[32]

From then on, Lutheran mission societies were legitimized agencies of the Church, since the Church now selected, ordained, and commissioned missionaries on behalf of the societies. This external ecclesial support given to the missionary is important becaise it bars any individual's claim to the missionary office on the basis of an internal call, as is in particular a trait of the Faith Mission. The missiologist Walter Holsten observes:

> The missionary must be *rite vocatus*; an individual's call experience does not warrant sufficient legitimization. Essentially, the right to serve as a "free" standing missionary is rejected and the status of a society's missionary is only insofar legitimate as his call or commission is not extended from a society that stands in deliberate isolation from the church, which (the church) has no other signs (*notae*) to show forth than the right proclamation of the Gospel and the administration of the Sacraments.[33]

The principle of ordaining a man into the preaching office (*rite vocatus*) of the Church still continues to be the practice for Lutheran mission. On an important day in 1894 at a convention in St. Charles, Missouri, the LCMS officially commissioned its first foreign missionaries, Theodor Naether and Franz Mohn, who were sent to India. Having been sent by the Church, they were accountable to the Church as well, and when Mohn returned, he was repatriated into the Missouri Synod as a pastor.

This ecclesial backing of the missionary office is in accord with the interpretation of the Great Commission as a mandate the Lord gave to the Church. The mandate points to a ministry of preaching and baptizing that the Lord gave to the apostles, yet it is continued still today through the Church. One often talks here of the office given to the Church in the abstract (*in abstracto*), that is, broader than the historic office of pastor but

---

32 Aagaard, *Mission, Konfession, Kirche*, 2:718.
33 Holsten, "Die lutherische Kirche als Träger der Sendung," 14.

in continuity with it. This more abstract understanding of the office antici-
pates not only the concrete activity of ordained pastors but also of missionaries, whom the Church also assigns the functions of the office.[34] The
original form of ministry of the apostles suggested in the mandate now
finds its full application and explication in the life of the Church through
the work of pastor and missionary. Wilhelm Maurer thus concludes: "It is
certain: Also the missionary office is *rite vocatus* and it is in that respect
not different to that of the pastor."[35] But the Church does not understand
the missionary office as one of circumstance—namely, in such a way that
she chooses to place an individual in the ministry to the Gospel simply
because someone needs to be found who can do it on behalf of all those
who can't; rather, she responds to a divine necessity and prerogative. The
Lutheran Confessions thus clearly remind the Church that what applies
to the pastoral office also applies to the missionary.[36] The Church has the
command to appoint ministers, and through these appointed men, God
will preach and work. The incumbents of that ministry are thus acting not
solely in the name of the Church, but because it is Christ's mandate—"they
do so in Christ's place and stead," yes, as representatives of "the person of
Christ"—so that those who hear them are assured of the fact that they also
hear the voice of Christ (Luke 10:16).[37]

There is thus imprinted on the Church an obligation for mission
through an ordered, structured ministry that cannot be replaced but only
complemented by the services of the laity. In *Together in God's Mission,*
its statement on mission formulated in 1988, the LWF gives tribute to this
concern by sketching an indelible structure regarding the mission of the
Church: "Among all the ministries of the church, the ministry of Word
and Sacrament occupies, however, a special place because of its responsibility for the means of grace. The Augsburg Confession states that the

---

34 I concur here with Schulz, "Das geistliche Amt nach lutherischem Verständnis in der missionarischen Situation," 164–65, and Kimme, "Die Kirche und ihre Sendung," 100. Robert Preus
argues for a concrete aspect of AC V in that it "not only implies, but already entails the actual
preaching of a concrete minister" (Preus, *Doctrine of the Call in the Confessions and Lutheran
Orthodoxy,* 3 n. 3). The debate on the correct interpretation of the office in AC V is worth following. Wilhelm Maurer, in *Historical Commentary on the Augsburg Confession,* 355, is willing
to broaden it to the degree that AC V also includes the priesthood of all believers. That applies
to Wilfried Joest as well in "Amt und Ordination," 77, 80. Fagerberg, *New Look at the Lutheran
Confessions,* 226–38, argues instead for a special office in AC V; so does the latest contributor,
Gunther Wenz, in *Theologie der Bekenntnisschriften der evangelisch-lutherischen Kirche,* 2:321–
28: "Der Schluß liegt daher nahe, daß es sich bei dem ministerium ecclesiasticum von CA V um
kein anderes Amt handelt als um das ordinationsgebundene Amt von XIV" (325).

35 Maurer, "Der lutherische Beitrag zur Weltmission," 185: "Fest steht: Auch der Missionar ist ein
rite vocatus und unterscheidet sich insofern nicht vom Gemeindepfarrer."

36 Elfers, "Amt und Ämter in der Mission," 36.

37 Ap VII 28 (*BSLK,* 240; Tappert, 173). See also Ap XIII 12 (Tappert, 212); Tr 24, 67 (Tappert, 324, 331).

ministry of Word and Sacrament is given in order that people may come to faith."[38] In the context of the United States in particular, Lutheranism is challenged to maintain that structure in view of frequent hermeneutical arguments that deny to the Church a *rite vocatus* ministry for mission. In fact, where Scripture clearly points to the need for a pastoral ministry in the Church (Acts 14:13; 20:18, 28; 1 Tim. 5:2; 2 Tim. 2:2; 6:11–16; Titus 1:5), critical voices claim quite the opposite.[39] Lutheranism is thus challenged to abide by scriptural and confessional evidence with integrity, and in order to underscore that concern, let us briefly examine the helpful arguments provided by Lutheran theologian Peter Brunner (1900–1982).

From Missionary to Pastor

In his two essays on the subject, "Vom Amt des Bischofs" (1955) ["On the Office of a Bishop"] and "Das Heil und das Amt" (1959) ["Salvation and the Office"],[40] Brunner affirms that the Church is still in possession of an apostolic missionary office. The Church of God has the "apostolate" in the sense that it is a Church "sent" into the world to preach the apostolic and universal Gospel. The Church is thus in possession of two forms of ministry involving the Gospel. First, the Gospel is preached to the world through which new members are added to the Body of Christ. Second, this Gospel ministry nurtures all those who regularly gather around the preached Word and the Sacrament of the Altar. Both these activities, the outward or missionary-oriented Gospel ministry and the one committed "inwardly" as a service to all believers through Word and Sacrament, are given to the Church and belong to its very essence. If the Church neglects her missionary task by not sending individuals to preach and teach, she violates or negates the divine mandate given to her and thus rejects her own nature and essence. Thus, for Brunner, the Church may not remain content with the general missionary task of witness and lifestyle assumed by all believers, to which they are obliged by virtue of their Baptism and confirmation. All Christians may follow the dominical command, but in a derived way that does not have the specific confirmation of the Church. For

---

38 LWF, *Together in God's Mission*, 14 (see also p. 12 n. 24).

39 Evangelical missiologists have been very vocal in their dismissal of any clerical paradigm. One may see, for example, the remarks of George Hunter III, a professor at Asbury Theological Seminary in Kentucky, a distinguished center for Church Growth and evangelism, who rejects any thoughts of a "two-tiered" Great Commission between the ordained and the laity in a chapter on the "apostolic ministry through an empowered laity": "The New Testament did not inflict upon us the artificial and tragic split between the clergy and the laity, the professionals and the amateurs, the players and the spectators; that came later [in the post canonical development of the church]" (*Radical Outreach*, 100). Similar comments are also made by Van Engen, *Mission on the Way*, 247–48, and Van Rheenen, *Missions*, 164–74.

40 Brunner, *Pro Ecclesia*, 1:235–92, 293–309.

Brunner, the mandate of the Lord is truly fulfilled when certain individuals are actually visibly set apart as missionaries. The Church thus performs the universal mandate of the Lord not only by placing individuals as shepherds in congregations gathered around Word and Sacrament but also by sending messengers into the world. The call to two different localities for individuals is part of the essence and structure of the Church.

Those who have been set apart for that missionary task are, according to Brunner, legitimate representatives of the Church and of Jesus Christ Himself and are acting in the authority of both.[41] Since Christ wants such sending to take place, the Church is authorized to do so by divine right (*de iure divino*; German: *kraft göttlichen Rechtes*), and because of that call, the missionary finds himself in a divinely instituted and legitimate office in which the Church has placed him (*rite vocatus*), just as she does with pastors.[42]

One noticeable feature in his essay "Das Heil und das Amt" is that Brunner places the missionary office within a divinely approved scheme of salvation (*Heilsplan*). It deals with the fourfold character of the Gospel: the oral Word of proclamation, Baptism, Holy Communion, and Absolution. All four forms are not arbitrarily arranged; rather, they represent a scheme or logical sequence: It begins with the preaching of the Gospel among the nations. Once people hear the Gospel, they believe and are baptized. They then congregate and celebrate Communion together. Throughout their Christian lives, they repent and are absolved of their sins.[43]

In other words, Brunner presents the Gospel in a soteriological sequence. Most important, this Gospel in all its forms is connected to the ministry given to the Church. However, Brunner will not identify this divinely instituted office solely with the parochial office of the pastor.[44] Just as the Gospel has a universal dimension so, too, does the ministry of the Church. There are thus two sides to the ministry: both the missionary and shepherding function. Together they find their roots in the one call, authorization, and commissioning of the risen Lord. In distinction from the apostles, however, the Lord does not immediately place missionaries and shepherds into office. He does so through the mediation of a gathered church body.[45] And despite that mediation, there is still an "immediate" dimension to the ministry of the Church in that it fulfills what is commanded and instituted by Christ. This implies that the call and sending of

---

41 Brunner, *Pro Ecclesia*, 1:280–81.

42 Brunner, *Pro Ecclesia*, 1:281, 304. Hellmut Lieberg argues also that both the immediate and mediated calls are equally divine calls; *Amt und Ordination*, 144.

43 Brunner, *Pro Ecclesia*, 1:297.

44 Brunner, *Pro Ecclesia*, 1:304.

45 Brunner, *Pro Ecclesia*, 1:306.

missionaries is not dependent on the whims of the Church; the Church is obliged to send missionaries for all times. It may also not be relinquished in view of every Christian's role to fulfill that mandate; one cannot replace the other. Instead, they complement each other.[46]

Since the ministry of the Church has a missionary dimension, mission is part of the essence of the Church. In fact, the preaching of God's Word to the world, the task "of preaching the Gospel and teaching God's Word to the outside," leads to the pastoral or shepherding activity, that which "works towards the inside within the congregation."[47] Thus, though both the missionary side and the shepherding role of the office are different, they cannot be separated. Only temporarily will the missionary pursue his initial task and goal of creating faith through the Gospel among its hearers and gathering them together.[48] Once faith comes about and Baptism follows, then the congregation consolidates and the shepherding role ensues. The baptized community joins for worship, celebrates the Lord's Supper, and requires further spiritual oversight and care.[49]

Brunner now raises the important question: when in the above sequence does the missionary cease being a missionary? Brunner believes that as long as the missionary remains with his newly baptized members, he will also have to assume the shepherding role. In fact, the office of a missionary inevitably evolves into that of a shepherd; one leads to the other. The shepherding functions in a local community evolve from a missionary who has decided to stay put. At that juncture, however, the missionary-turned-shepherd would not lose his missionary obligation. New duties certainly emerge, but the call to proclaim to the world still implicitly remains with the pastoral office as it builds up and shepherds the Body of Christ. For in that context, it should still be incumbent upon the shepherd to witness to the unbaptized in the immediate surroundings of his flock. The obligation and connection to a missionary task for a shepherd has its roots in the office of the apostles who, as shepherds of congregations, served on occasion as missionaries among the heathen.[50]

Finally, Brunner sees the pastoral office complemented with the missionary obligation of all members. All Christians should assume the role as witnesses to the salvific deeds of the Lord. And as long as the missionary remains with his newly formed congregation, he leads it with the apostolic

---

46 Brunner, *Pro Ecclesia*, 1:303.

47 Brunner, *Pro Ecclesia*, 1:252, 306.

48 Brunner, *Pro Ecclesia*, 1:302.

49 Brunner, *Pro Ecclesia*, 1:304.

50 Brunner, *Pro Ecclesia*, 1:306, 283. These twofold functionary explications of the *ministerium verbi* can already be seen in the duties performed by the apostles Peter and Paul (Witte, "Kirche als Ziel der Sendung," 20).

Word and sees to it that his members truthfully witness it to others. Thus, ultimately, the ministry or office given to the Church, whether occupied by missionary or shepherd, assumes a leading role in guarding and professing the Gospel for all generations.[51]

CHANGES IN THE PRESENT ROLE AND DUTY OF A MISSIONARY

The above discussion highlights the important service of those in the ministry of the Church and in the salvation scheme of the Lord. The Church should affirm, rather than denigrate, the value of pastoral ministry in the life of the Church and her mission. Lutheranism has the particular advantage to affirm in theology and practice a corporate understanding of mission that pays its dues to the services of both clergy and laity.[52]

It should also be clear that a missionary's duty involves an active ministry, one that preaches, teaches, and baptizes. Although the following definition does not explicitly mention these specific components, it focuses on the sending and church planting component of such a ministry to the Gospel. "The missionary is a sent servant of the church, who leaves his own context for a time to proclaim the Gospel in partnership with the church if already present or with the intention to plant a church where it has not been planted before."[53]

Today, there is no agreement in the discussion of who and what missionaries are and should do. Unlike the past pioneer model, missionaries today are not so much engaged in the tasks of planting churches through Baptism, preaching, and other pastoral functions. Rather, they are educators who raise up local leadership, who in turn assume the pastoral functions of building the Body of Christ. What explains that shift? Mistakes from missionaries have necessitated some of these changes, as well as the emergence of young partner churches in areas where missionaries were previously on their own. The transition stage in which leadership had to be handed over to indigenous pastors often led to tensions. Missionaries generally overstayed their welcome on the mission field and unwillingly relinquished their privileged status as leaders in the young church. That

---

51 Brunner, *Pro Ecclesia*, 1:304–5.

52 It is inexplicable why pastoral ministry or the service of clergy is so curtly and negatively dismissed in the ELCA's contribution by Bliese and Van Gelder, *Evangelizing Church*, 43.

53 The Evangelical Lutheran missiologist Peter Beyerhaus provides this definition in his article "Missionar I (Evangelisch)," 278. The conspicuous absence of his article in the English translation of this dictionary (Müller and Sundermeier, *Dictionary of Mission*) truly serves as an example of the controversy over the missionary office as Beyerhaus defines it here.

278 MISSION FROM THE CROSS

problem needed correction. This partly explains the shift of the missionary
task to teaching.

THE INFLUENCE OF EVANGELICALISM

A further reason for this shift has to do with the desire for rapid growth. The
interest for strategies that promote growth has been part of Protestantism
ever since the founder of the Church Growth Movement, Donald McGavran,
pleaded for it.[54] In the past, missionaries had their ministry tied to one or
two single congregations with little focus on achieving fast growth or a
rapid multiplication of local congregations. To remedy that situation, the
strategic and theological concept of "leadership formation" was intro-
duced, which would oblige the missionaries to become teachers and to raise
up local leadership. Their task is specifically geared to training and equipping such local leaders for a ministry that they themselves would have been
involved in decades earlier during the age of pioneer mission. Evangelical
Gailyn Van Rheenen is an avid promoter of this program and believes that
missionaries in the past have been negligent of this task. They had not been
"training their converts to become reproductive; they have not been training leaders to plant other churches."[55]

This approach has generally also decentralized education from a traditional formation of pastoral leadership at seminaries to local congregations. Strategies such as "Theological Education by Extension" (TEE) raise
indigenous leadership on site at the congregational level where such leaders
may live and sustain themselves and their family through a bi-vocational
ministry. In many ways these new education models focus on "learning
by doing." They promote an "in" ministry ideal that does not immediately
select and extract a few individuals for a seminary track to ordination;
rather, it broadens its base group to include as many students as possible.

It seems that most denominations in the United States promote this
new paradigm with great conviction. It thus impacts mission strategies
worldwide, not merely questioning the role of the ordained missionary but

---

54 McGavran, *Understanding Church Growth.* James Scherer succinctly captures the movement's
underlying philosophy: "God wills the numerical growth of Christians . . . Factors that assist
or hinder church growth can be analyzed through interdisciplinary methods. Churches should
normally show a minimal growth of 50 % in one decade. Mission agencies should concentrate
their resources on rapidly growing churches, avoiding entrapment in other causes" (*Gospel,
Church and Kingdom*, 178). Obviously, it would be unfair to place all Evangelicals in the same
camp as the supporters of the Church Growth Movement. For example, the European organization *Arbeitskreis für Evangelikale Missiologie e.V. (AfeM)*, known for its journal *Evangelikale
Missiologie*, repeatedly offers critical observations on that movement. The Emergent Church
Movement must be acknowledged for its direction in recapturing the nature of the Gospel and
tradition of the Church, rather than concentrating on numbers alone.

55 Van Rheenen, *Missions*, 148.

also the nature of education at tertiary institutions.[56] Entry into the ministry often no longer requires an advanced degree at an institutionalized center and a subsequent approval by the Church through ordination; the standards have been lowered or even abandoned entirely. One of the promoters of the new inclusive ministry paradigm is Evangelical Charles Van Engen:

> The purpose of the . . . paradigm is to form leaders who can lead the church. The focus is not on ordination, function, profession, legitimization, or any other of a host of issues that sometimes cloud our perspectives of theological education . . . And ordination, rather than serving as a prerequisite doorway to a position or function in the church, involves a corporate recognition by the church of giftedness in ministry.[57]

The approach chosen by Evangelicals may appeal to some Lutherans as well; but to adopt it unguarded would destroy the structure of Lutheran mission that differentiates the ministry of the ordained from that of the laity.[58] Lutherans cannot easily dismiss that structure, since it is bound to a confessional subscription that supports what Article XIV of the Augsburg Confession stipulates: "No one should teach publicly in the church or administer the sacraments unless properly called [*rite vocatus*]."[59] Lutheran mission must heed a strategy that pays close attention to that distinction.

Proposing a Solution

As we review past mistakes of missionaries and strategies, one may wonder why we still need qualified and trained missionaries. One of the apparent downsides of the leadership formation paradigm is that it divorces the missionary from the context of a local congregation and places him in a classroom environment in which he assumes responsibility as the trainer of leaders. Obviously, a critical review of the past contributions of missionaries has revealed a tendency for missionaries to overstay and create paternalistic structures that stifle the life of the community and its path toward independence—a legitimate fear the new paradigm hopes to correct. However, how many adjustments can be made to the missionary office until it no longer resembles those activities called for by the Lord in the missionary

---

56 See also Lienemann-Perrin, "Theological Education," 428; Guder, *Missional Church*, 217.

57 Van Engen, *Mission on the Way*, 250–52.

58 Lutheran Kent R. Hunter provides this challenging statement in *Foundations for Church Growth*, 65: "The pastor is the called shepherd of the royal priesthood, but he is not there to do the ministry for the sheep. Shepherds don't reproduce sheep, anyway. Sheep reproduce sheep! Mission and ministry belong to the people. The pastor is there to be the trainer, the equipper of the people. The pastor is like a playing coach. He does ministry himself, but his primary responsibility is to train Christians to do this ministry."

59 AC XIV (Kolb-Wengert, 47).

mandates—namely, the call to preach repentance for the forgiveness of sins (John 20:23), to catechize all newly won converts, and to baptize (Luke 24:45–49; Matt. 28:18–20)? Obviously, theological education and raising indigenous clergy is a pivotal task in mission, and the nature of education of candidates for the ministry might be negotiable in view of the context. But there is no persuasive argument from Scripture that proposes a purely teaching ministry for missionaries. In addition, Scripture calls for local leadership that is placed in the role of pastoral leadership through ordination (Acts 14:21–23; 1 Tim. 4:14). This ordination follows a careful selection process in which the spiritual maturity and the abilities of candidates are carefully ascertained (1 Tim. 5:22). Roland Allen encourages missionaries to speed the process toward planting indigenous church bodies, but cautions them not to leave without a properly ordained leadership in place that is equipped for pastoral ministry: "The importance of the ordination of elders lay in this, that when a church was equipped with elders, it possessed not merely leaders, but men properly appointed to see that the Sacraments, without which it would have been starved in its spiritual life and crippled in the work of expansion, were duly performed."[60] One senses that the pendulum has swung too far to the opposite side of the scale. The wholesale rush to turn missionaries into teachers has resulted in missionaries abandoning the classical tasks of preaching and baptizing others, as well as a lowering— if not a total abandonment—of the standards for selecting candidates for ministry, particularly in view of their education and ordination.

A treatment of past faults should be fair and also acknowledge positive contributions of earlier missionaries. Once Henry Venn and Rufus Anderson had set the standards of self-governing, self-supporting, and self-propagation in the latter half of the nineteenth century, it became evident even then that foreign missionary presence would have to pursue the goal of raising indigenous leadership. As the latter half of the twentieth century started to limit the terms for missionaries, exit strategies became more important and necessary. The question in mission strategy has thus never been the denial of establishing local leadership, but rather how it can be done in such a way that it accommodates the other activities of preaching, translation, Baptism, and catechesis. These, too, are undeniably constants in mission and thus demand attention. When the missionary remains with a local church, he is by necessity responsible for the right administration of the apostolic Word, since he is the one who brought it to where it had never been before. When the time comes for him to transfer his leadership, it should only be assigned to those called and ordained to ministry.

---

60 Allen, *Missionary Methods*, 103.

Obviously, the changing situation worldwide has had a profound impact on the understanding of the missionary's role. In other words, with newly founded church bodies on all continents, pioneer mission involvement for foreign missionaries no longer seems necessary when local and indigenous leadership may assume that role. Thus missionaries are generally contracted by the mission board or by the supervising sending agency and hired to the partner church for whatever foreign service project it requests. Thus, in many ways, the missionary has become a jack-of-all-trades, versatile enough to cover a wide range of duties, if necessary. But would it not be possible to see in his service in a partner church precisely the role of a missionary pastor, with the important missionary dimension still pursued in the context of a congregation? This seat for missionary service in the context of worshiping and witnessing communities makes strategic sense. As one scholar argues: "Fundamentally, the theological place for the ministry of the missionary is with the congregation and the church, where he serves her with the means of grace."[61]

The emergence of short-term volunteer mission service in recent years has also changed the practice of mission. These projects have had an impact on the recruitment and support of career missionaries. For many years, the assumption had been that people who go on short-term assignments would eventually return as career missionaries. That assumption has not yet materialized, as recent studies have shown.[62] To be sure, the short-term movement fills an important niche in the mission of the Church, but it cannot replace the role of long-term, career missionaries, as John Stott (1921–), the leader of the worldwide Evangelical Movement, has strongly asserted in *Christianity Today*. Stott states that to become an effective crosscultural missionary, one who is viewed "as a national," requires at least ten years simply to learn the language and culture.[63] While he argues for the length of a missionary's service from a cultural perspective, the theological nature of a missionary's ministry also defines his length of service. Missionaries who stand in the authorized call serve the Church as active guardians over God's Word and as builders of the Body of Christ. That type of ministry could take place, if properly negotiated by all partners involved, for an indeterminate time in a non-Christian context apart or in relation to a congregation of a partner church.

The following chart illustrates the continuation of the apostolic ministry in the missionary efforts of the modern Church. It begins on top with

61 Stolle, "Über die Zielsetzung organisierter Missionsarbeit," 135: "Grundsätzlich ist deshalb der theologische Ort des Amtes des Missionars bei der Gemeinde und Kirche, denen er mit den Gnadenmittel dient."

62 See Priest, et al., "Researching the Short-Term Mission Movement," 431–50.

63 Stott, "Evangelism Plus," 94–99.

the office of the apostles. Then it points to the office of preaching that is given to the Church by God, and thus to a continuation of the apostles' preaching without the same direct calling from Christ and the authority manifest in the gifts of healing and speaking infallibly. Pastors and missionaries are the incumbents of this preaching office because they have been placed into it through the proper call and ordination. They may enlist auxiliary services such as catechists and evangelists. Moreover, the witness of the laity also permeates the world and serves an indispensable role in God's mission as well.

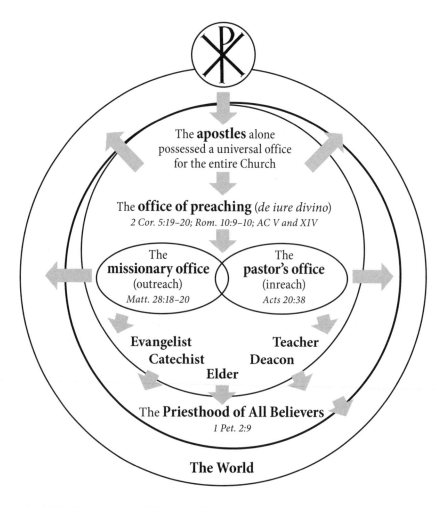

Fig. 6: The Continuation of the Apostolic Ministry in the Church

CHAPTER SIXTEEN

THE CHRISTIAN WITNESS
IN THE INTERRELIGIOUS CONTEXT

WITNESS AND PERSONAL COMMITMENT

One is struck by many a missionary's resolve and relentless drive to share the Gospel. Two examples come to mind. First, the American Board of Commissioners for Foreign Mission (ABCFM) sent Adoniram Judson to Burma on February 5, 1812. Judson's experiences are reminiscent of what the apostle Paul went through on his journeys (2 Cor. 11:16–33): hard labor, imprisonment, flogging, and exposure to death. Not long after the Judsons landed in Burma, the Burmese officials imprisoned Judson, thinking he was a British spy. He soon lost his beloved wife, Nancy, to fever, and his child died shortly thereafter. For a while, Judson lived as a recluse in the jungle, shaken by a mental breakdown. He married a second time, to Sarah Boardman, a widow. She gave birth to eight children in the first ten years of their marriage. In 1845, after having been away from home for thirty-three years, Judson returned to the United States for the first time. En route, Sarah died. In June 1846, during his stay in America, Judson met and married Emily Chubbock, with whom he returned to Burma.[1] Sadly, he left behind three children who would never again see their father. Two of three other children he and Sarah had left behind in Burma awaited him on his return. These children had never known their mother Sarah, except as infants.

Adoniram and Emily Judson served together for three years in Burma. Frequent illness was always part of their work. Emily gave birth to two

---

1   Emily Chubbock, a former journalist, wrote about her everyday life as a missionary's wife. "We are blessed," she writes, "with our full share of cockroaches, beetles, lizards, rats, ants, mosquitoes, and bed bugs. With the last the woodwork is all alive, and the ants troop over the house in great droves . . . Perhaps twenty have crossed my paper since I have been writing. Only one cockroach has paid me a visit, but the neglect of these gentlemen has been fully made up by a company of black bugs about the size of the end of your finger—nameless adventurers" (Tucker, *From Jerusalem to Irian Jaya*, 131).

children, but the last child was stillborn. In the spring of 1850, Judson became seriously ill, so he left on a sea voyage in the hope of recovering. He died aboard ship. Emily did not hear about her husband's death until August. In January of the following year, Emily; her young daughter, Emily; and two sons from Judson's previous marriage sailed for Boston. She died three years later at the age of thirty-six.

On Sunday, October 14, 1894, the Judson scenario repeated itself in the life of Theodor Naether, one of the first two foreign missionaries in the Missouri Synod. He was sent by the LCMS to Krishnagiri, India. In 1899, within the span of four days, he buried two of his dear children who had died of diarrhea. After nine years of seemingly fruitless labor, Naether died of bubonic plague in 1904 at the age of thirty-seven. Naether's death was the result of contracting the plague when he had buried a young boy in the mission compound. To avoid contaminating others, Naether dressed himself in a clean white suit and placed himself in the coffin so that he would die without anyone touching him.[2]

The stories of Adoniram Judson and Theodor Naether are moving tales of individuals who were willing to sacrifice their lives for service to the Gospel. They went to serve ministries that would last a lifetime, had no health insurance, and enjoyed few amenities that are provided to our missionaries today. Most notably, however, they had an uncompromising stance on the Gospel as the only answer for those who seek a complete life with God.

CHRISTIAN WITNESS AND CHRISTIANITY'S PAST

These formidable contributions on the part of missionaries cannot erase the tarnished image Christianity has accumulated because of her past. The average person outside the Christian faith will be quick to point out that Christianity has not always met its claim of being a religion of peace. One could cite many instances in which Christianity failed to excel and, as a result, was subject to prejudices and false accusations. For example, in discussions with Muslims, the Crusades will arise as a particular hurdle. Muslims typically hold Protestants responsible for abuses that were actually perpetrated by the Roman Catholic Church. Looking back in history, we find that Martin Luther vehemently opposed Christianity's violent measures of conversion and of conquering Turkish Muslims through military crusades. Instead, Luther made every effort to get to know the non-Christian religions he encountered in his time, Islam and Judaism. In his treatise *On War Against the Turk* (1529), which he wrote soon after the

---

2 Naether's life is recorded in Kirsten and Näther, *Unsere lutherische Mission in Indien*, 13–17.

THE CHRISTIAN WITNESS IN THE INTERRELIGIOUS CONTEXT 285

Turks had besieged Vienna, he rejected the thought of launching crusades against the Muslim people. He saw in these military ventures a violation of the Church's powers and yet another expression of the pope's greed for power and money. In other words, the Crusades had nothing to do with the Gospel and the Church's witness to other religions.[3] And Luther's position on the Jewish people, often touted as setting the stage for the anti-Semitic atrocities of the Third Reich, was in fact no attack on Jews as a race or a plea for an extermination of their bloodline, but rather it was an expression of extreme disappointment for their rejection of Jesus Christ.

We clearly should state that the Roman Catholic Church has come forward to apologize for Christianity's past. In her "Declaration on the Relationship of the Church to Non-Christian Religions" (*Nostra Aetate*) the second Vatican Council spoke conciliatory words to Muslims and dismissed a wholesale accusation of the Jewish people for having crucified Christ.[4]

On October 18–19, 1945, the Alliance of Protestant Churches in Germany expressed in the Stuttgart Declaration their regret for having collaborated or silently complied with the atrocities of the Third Reich. Likewise, in 1994, when a regime change took place in South Africa, church leaders stepped forward to heal a hurt nation by setting up a committee called the "Truth and Reconciliation Commission," which offered a pardoning of guilt. This set the stage for peaceful negotiations between victims and violators of human rights during the Apartheid regime. Those found guilty of compliance were given the opportunity to recall their past crimes and recant them before those who had suffered under their acts. Finally, for many years, Christianity bore the weight of Christian divisions in Northern Ireland as militant rivalry between Protestants and Roman Catholics marred Christianity's image among non-Christian nations.

As Christians engage in witness with others, references to the past may cause the Christian witness to shift to apology. It should be evident, however, that the Christian God as revealed in Scripture is a different God than the one we reflect through our frail actions because of our own sinfulness. Ultimately, though, even those most unappreciative of Christianity's past cannot disregard the huge responses to human need worldwide and the incredible help Christian churches have offered and continually offer to

---

3 Stolle, *Church Comes from All Nations*, 68–69. See also Miller, *Muslims and the Gospel*, 206–11; Rosenkranz, *Der christliche Glaube*, 158–59.

4 Abbott, *Documents of Vatican II*, 663–64.

the plight of non-Christians. This is a clear testimony to the unselfish love Christianity has for those who do not share the same faith in Christ.[5]

THE UNFINISHED TASK

It may be helpful to reiterate the urgency and need for our Christian witness in this world. In the first chapter, we opened with references to statistics that offer the prognosis that by mid-2025 the Christian population in the world will be 2,616,670,052 (33.4 percent) and by mid-2050, 3,051,564,342 (34.3 percent) in 238 countries.[6] Statistics suggest that Christianity will not make substantial inroads into the non-Christian population. That, however, should not diminish our resolve to share our faith with others in the context and vocation in which God has placed us. Indeed, a commitment to mission such as that offered by Adoniram Judson or Theodor Naether is just what the twenty-first century needs. And it will be necessary for the Western church to reaffirm a strategy that addresses the need for the Gospel among non-Christian nations of this world.

Scripture indicates that the Church proclaimed the Gospel to adherents of other religions from its earliest days. Greek terms identified with the task of sharing the Gospel are εὐαγγέλιον ("good news") and εὐαγγελίζειν ("to proclaim the good news"). Two other terms for the good news are κήρυγμα ("proclamation") and μαρτυρία ("testimony"). Such terms indicate that the task of sharing the Gospel with people outside of Christianity was key for apostolic times. This evangelistic or kerygmatic activity is one that the Church of today must pursue with similar zeal and discipline.[7]

To highlight the kerygmatic intention to those outside the Christian faith, the Christian Church has often spoken of mission and kept that activity separate from evangelism. Those involved in mission would seek to convert and baptize the unbeliever, whereas evangelism addresses previously baptized persons who have become apostate or nominal Christians. Since the apostate or nominal Christian has encountered the message of the Gospel before, one may expect to find a preexistent knowledge about the Church and her beliefs. That cannot be said for the unbaptized audience that Christian missionaries encounter.[8] Nonetheless, both the term

---

5   For example, after World War II, Christians, including members of the LCMS, immediately rushed to help war-ravaged Germany. By August 1945, the LCMS had raised approximately $6 million. *The Lutheran Standard* (August 4, 1945): 15.

6   Barrett and Johnson, *World Christian Trends*, 4.

7   The missiologist Hans-Werner Gensichen states that mission must be done with no other purpose and aim than "to bring all people the message of universal reconciliation" (*Glaube für die Welt*, 75). Kirk, *What Is Mission?* 56.

8   Now both terms come together in that both audiences are distant from the Church and, for that reason, mission and evangelism share the common goal of assimilating or re-assimilating all of

mission and evangelism have in common the reality of unbelief. Both the unbaptized outside of Christianity and those who are apostate are in need of hearing the Gospel. In this regard, both the terms *mission* and *evangelism* may be treated as synonyms, as seems to be the case today.

At the same time, we should still highlight a particular biblical genre of proclamation to the heathen (German: *Heidenpredigt*); such *Heidenpredigt* is preaching that specifically targets those outside of the Church, the Gentiles (Gal. 1:16; 2:2; Acts 17). This preaching is different than presenting the Gospel to the proselytes or the catechumens who already find themselves in the narthex. *Heidenpredigt* addresses all those people who have never heard about the living God and Jesus Christ. In contrast to the catechumenate, the preaching to Gentiles is not yet a teaching ministry in the basics of Christian faith. It is that ministry which precedes it. It is the first encounter between the Christian and the Gentile, where the Gentile hears for the first time the Good News of Jesus Christ and salvation. Such a witness should be seen as a continuation of the preaching ministry of Jesus and the apostles. Missionary proclamation to the Gentiles is thus a concise message containing statements on God's kingdom and salvation in Jesus Christ with the goal of awakening faith in the hearer so that he may turn from his false belief to Jesus Christ. Once this preaching has borne fruit, the missionary will proceed to deeper instruction (*didaskalia*)—namely, into parts of Christian belief such as Baptism and following Christ.

We have to argue for the form of a onetime and unique missionary proclamation because we encounter it in Scripture. It should remain to this day a form of proclamation and witness that engages people at every level in the Church as she finds herself in such situations where populations live that stand far from the Christian Church and have, in fact, never heard anything about Christ. The episode of Aquila and Priscilla (Acts 18:26) demonstrates that there are those people who, like Apollos, have heard the message for the first time and yet remain confused about its content. Instruction by Aquila and Priscilla alleviated Apollos's confusion. The same may be said of the Ethiopian eunuch who, after encountering the Christian message, was led by Philip into the meaning of what the prophet Isaiah says. Christians already immersed in the life of the Church may serve precisely as those who assist first-time hearers in deepening their knowledge of the Gospel.

---

them back into the Church. One might thus understand that the distinction in view of the goal at least falls away since all must come to faith in Jesus Christ, even if one would expect that the content of the proclamation will be adjusted differently.

288 MISSION FROM THE CROSS

CHRISTIAN ANTHROPOLOGY IN COMMUNICATION

In an interreligious context, Christians may need to study carefully the religious beliefs of the partner to whom they are witnessing. It is necessary to understand his religious background, his worldview, and his social and cultural context. Here, however, the amount of information provided in anthropology and social sciences can potentially obfuscate the simplicity of our Christian witness. For "communication" today has become a technical term that identifies Christian witness as a complex linguistic affair of studying mechanisms of encoding and decoding a set of signs. As important as this technical side of proclaiming the Gospel may be, it can distract from the important task of getting to know a person, then presenting the Gospel to the person's needs.

In our proclamation of the Gospel to others, we should thus take on the perspective of God and see human beings as He does. The fact is that God is involved in the witness of two people of different religious backgrounds. God looks beyond all particulars and sees a human being standing before Him, regardless of whether that individual is in Beijing or Nairobi. Scripture and theology presents a generic anthropology that all unbelievers share in common despite their distinctive contexts. God sees in everyone a sinner entrapped in his own selfish state of rebellion. God Himself wants to speak to him, let His voice be heard, so that he who hears Him may come to faith and serve Him (John 10:16). Such an anthropology should remain part of our understanding as we witness to others.

DIALOGUE AND POSTMODERN CHALLENGES

The bottom line for all Christian witness to non-Christians is that God seeks to instill faith through the Gospel that leads to Baptism. In mission resources and evangelism tools, not the least of which is *Dialog Evangelism II*, the Missouri Synod has sought ways to enter into intentional dialogue with people, with the goal of their salvation in mind. Such dialogue sees two parties finding common ground, sharing mutual points and experiences, and building a relationship that has the full intention of leading to conversion and Baptism. However, the influences of secularization and postmodernism on Christians have led many church bodies to abandon the traditional goals of conversion and Baptism and place in their stead the method of postmodern "dialogue" in the sense of a conversation that has no goal of salvation because such a goal would be viewed as an unfair exercise of power. Ultimately, this "dialogue" replaces Christian witness. It sees two people witnessing to each other without any preconceived intentions of converting the other. That is really a two-part monologue. This sort of "dialogue" cannot really happen between parties that have every intention of remaining static in their positions; it is not, as some have called that situation, a conversation between an elephant and a mouse.[9] Obviously, dialogue as an alternative form of witness proves to be a challenge for those who wish to further Christian faith among non-Christians. To be sure, Christians should learn to approach others with mutual respect, but the postmodern proposal for "dialogue" can only be seen as ancillary to missionary proclamation, rather than its substitute or an alternative to it.

Postmodernism is known for its defiance of modernism's quest for objectivity by pleading tolerance toward all expressions of faith. Christians regard postmodernism, therefore, with great skepticism since it seems to boycott Christian mission. However, in his recent study *Confessing Jesus Christ: Preaching in a Postmodern World*, David Lose argues that one need not give up the traditional belief in the Gospel as one engages with postmodernism relativism. Rather, what matters is how we approach the forthcoming generation with our witness. Lose suggests that the "confessional" approach is the appropriate and most genuine form of Christian witness to the postmodern generation. "By describing such preaching as 'confessional,' I seek to reclaim a Christian practice that rests not on empirical proof but on a living confession of faith, leads not to certainty but to conviction, and lives not in the domain of knowledge and proof but in the realm of faithful assertion."[10] It seems that Lose is affirming what Stanley Grenz highlights in *A Primer on Postmodernism*—namely, that we should commit ourselves in our witness to the whole person. In our witness, we should integrate the emotional-affective, as well as the bodily-sensual, with the intellectual-rational domain within the one human person. Grenz calls this a post-noeticentric Christian Gospel, for it locates our profession of the Gospel not just in the rational part of our being or as an accumulation of knowledge. Rather, the whole person exemplifies the Christian witness:

> A post-noeticentric Christian gospel emphasizes the relevance of faith for every dimension of life. It refuses to allow commitment to Christ to remain merely an intellectual endeavor, a matter solely of assent to orthodox propositions. Commitment to Christ must also take its lodging in the heart... The Christian gospel is concerned not only with the reformulation

---

9 Engaging in dialogue with the preconceived conviction of converting the non-Christian stands in the way of a two-way process, as Henry Maurier observes: "If Christianity (because of Christ) is the definitive truth, the absoluteness of God's revelation to mankind, it only remains for the other religions to convert to Christianity . . . What we have, in fact, is dialogue between the elephant and the mouse" ("Christian Theology of the Non-Christian Religions," 69–70). For a critical view on dialogue, see Etuk, "Theology of Contextualization in Africa," 221.

10 Lose, *Confessing Christ*, 3.

of our intellectual commitments but also with the transformation of our character and the renewal of our entire lives as believers.[11]

Christian witness need not give up its content and the truths of the Gospel. It should, however, reconsider the delivery of such knowledge. Christian knowledge cannot be wielded as a powerful weapon, striving to coerce someone to submission. Many things matter: life, context, emotions, and physical constitution.[12]

CONTEMPORARY STANCES TOWARD OTHER RELIGIONS

Numerous studies have investigated the subject of Christianity's relation to other religions by questioning the exclusive character of Christian mission. Alternative forms to that of exclusivism exist, for example, inclusivism (known as the wider hope theory) or universalism promoted as pluralism. In a seminal study on the topic entitled *No Other Name: A Critical Survey of Christian Attitude towards the World Religions*, Roman Catholic theologian Paul Knitter fleshes out three positions. He describes the first as that of claiming salvation only in Christ; the second (inclusivism) agrees that Christ is the center but also entertains a wider hope for those who did not have the opportunity to meet Christ in their lives. The third position (universalism) has abandoned the centrality of Christ entirely for a theocentric model that offers many ways to salvation.[13]

There is no unanimity among Christians on this topic. Disagreement as to Christianity's role vis-à-vis other religions has perhaps been with Christianity for as long as it has existed. The Evangelical scholar John Sanders demonstrates that renowned theologians of the Church including Augustine, Origen, John Calvin, R. C. Sproul, John A. T. Robinson, George Lindbeck, John Wesley, C. S. Lewis, and Clark Pinnock all differed in their definitions of the correct Christian attitude toward other religions.[14] In fact, what is apparent from Sanders's study is that the Evangelical Movement, otherwise known for a conservative, exclusivist approach in statements such as the Lausanne Covenant (1974), no longer represents a united front.[15]

---

11 Grenz, *Primer on Postmodernism*, 173.

12 Grenz, *Primer on Postmodernism*, 167–74.

13 With this study, in which he claims to be an universalist himself, Paul Knitter and a compatriot of his, John Hick, have paved the way for the discussions on Christianity's relations to other religions. See Knitter, *No Other Name?* and Hick and Knitter, *Myth of Christian Uniqueness*.

14 Sanders, *No Other Name*.

15 An indication of this struggle can be gleaned from the essay by Smith, "Religions and the Bible," 9–29. Donald McGavran (1897–1991), the leading founder of the Lausanne Movement, raised the famous question over the change in the direction of mission at the WCC Fourth Assembly

Some attribute this renewed discussion of Christianity's relationship to other religions to statements made by the Second Vatican Council. Indeed, we may say that Vatican II laid the conceptual groundwork for any talk on the topic. In a number of its statements, Vatican II approached the divine economy of salvation with a generous approval of natural man's religiosity by accepting the existence of truths of salvation in the midst of other religions apart from Christ. The document *Nostra Aetate* thus affirms in religions such as Hinduism, Buddhism, and Islam a "ray of truth which enlightens all men."[16] This statement affirms more than the traditional preparation for the Gospel (*preparatio evangelii*) among these religions; it actually posits a component in them that is considered salvific in and by itself. The same observation can be made from *Lumen Gentium* ("Light to the Nations"), which speaks of a salvific character among adherents of other faiths:

> Those also can attain everlasting salvation who through no fault of their own do not know the gospel of Christ or His Church, yet sincerely seek God and, moved by grace, strive by their deeds to do His will as it is known to them through the dictates of conscience. Nor does divine Providence deny the help necessary for salvation to those who, without blame on their part, have not yet arrived at an explicit knowledge of God.[17]

Among many theologians who influenced the theology of Vatican II was Karl Rahner. Already before the council, Rahner had advocated an "anonymous Christianity" among adherents of the Hindu religion, just as the Roman Catholic theologian Raimundo Panikkar had done before Rahner in a book entitled *The Unknown Christ of Hinduism* (1964). As receptive as the approach may at first seem to be to adherents of other religions, it actually proved to be patronizing to those who thought themselves legitimate and determined Hindus or Buddhists and had no desire to be classified with "anonymous Christians." And to those who desired to be genuine professing and practicing Christians among the Buddhist or Hindu population, the idea of being anonymous proved to be equally offensive.[18] In other words, as open as the concept of anonymous Christianity hoped to be, it proved to be a judgment that suited neither Christians nor those outside the faith.

---

in Uppsala (1968): "Will Uppsala betray the two billion?" This concern served as one important reason for the founding of the Evangelical Movement in 1974. And when its manifesto, the *Lausanne Covenant*, was formulated at that time, it unequivocally affirmed the centrality and uniqueness of Christ in missionary proclamation and witness. See Stott, *Making Christ Known*, 16–19.

16 *Nostra Aetate* 2, in Abbott, *Documents of Vatican II*, 662.

17 *Lumen Gentium* 16, in Abbott, *Documents of Vatican II*, 35.

18 Yates, *Christian Mission in the Twentieth Century*, 175–77.

In recent years, the Vatican II statements have been qualified by the papal encyclical *Dominus Iesus* (2000), which takes recourse in pre-Vatican II claims.[19] *Dominus Iesus* argues for a Roman Catholic ecclesiology that determines not only relations to other religions but also relations to Protestant church bodies. It seems to return to pre-Vatican II statements, such as the one made in 1302 by Pope Boniface VIII, who had declared "it is absolutely necessary for the salvation of all men that they submit to the Roman Pontiff" and who passed the famous statement: "*Extra ecclesiam nulla salus est*" ("Outside the church there is no salvation").[20] It is debatable, however, whether *Dominus Iesus* actually may be seen as a truly fundamental change in Rome's theological position on religions. For in her anthropology and moral theology that affirms natural man's ability to contemplate the will of God in his conscience (*synteresis*), the back door in Roman Catholic theology remains open for religious pluralism.[21]

The preceding discussion offers a brief glimpse into current debate concerning Christianity's attitude to other religions. Lutherans should approach the issue from the perspective of the central doctrine of its theology—justification. It would be an incomplete discussion for Lutheran theology if one were to bypass this core doctrine of Christianity's attitude to other religions, belief systems, values, and practices.

A CAUTIOUS CONCESSION TO ALL RELIGIONS

The doctrine of justification provides us with a hermeneutic of mapping out Christianity's relationship to other religions. The doctrine of justification makes both certain concessions, albeit cautiously, and explicit dismissals of other religions. In terms of concessions, justification states the following position: First, all Christians share with every human being the fact that they are God's creation and that this is true as long as the world stands. Thus God has created both Christians and non-Christians alike, and He continues to hold His hand over all peoples of the world. Second, all humanity stems from the first parents; thus all share the fall into sin (Rom. 5:12; Heb. 7:9–10). Through the fall, all humanity suffers a loss of the perfect righteousness and image of God (Gen. 1:26–27; 5:1), which, if not repaired in Christ, will have eternal consequences. This loss of the image of God must be perceived to be a spiritual loss that can be restored

---

19 For example, McDonnell, "Unique Mediator in a Unique Church," 542–49; Solheim, "Vatican Statement Drawing Strong Reactions."

20 The bull states: "That there is only one, holy, catholic and apostolic Church we are compelled by faith to believe and hold, and we firmly believe in her and sincerely confess her, outside of whom there is neither salvation nor remission of sins" (Neuner and Dupuis, *Christian Faith in the Doctrinal Documents of the Catholic Church*, 210–11).

21 Schulz, "Lutheran Response," 5–8.

only though faith in Christ. Through the proclamation of the Gospel, the mission of the Church intends to restore that spiritual image in Christ, who clothes all believers in His own righteousness.

However, the loss of the perfect relationship with God in the fall does not imply that God has abandoned His creation.[22] This is evident in a broader use of the image of God. In other words, there is also the affirmation from Scripture that the image of God, though difficult to define after the fall, still applies to every human being in the sense that all are under God's continued providence and protection. This broader image of God, which remains, though marred (1 Cor. 11:7; James 3:9), serves as an important argument for the preservation of human life, including that of unborn children (Ps. 139:13–16).

The Lutheran Confessions also stipulate that all humans are potentially or theoretically able to acknowledge the existence of their Creator. In Rom. 1:19–20; 2:15, for example, Paul writes that God has revealed His existence through the outward visible creation and that He has inscribed His will as a form of natural law on the hearts of man. From this general revelation, it is assumed that the non-Christian has, to some extent, a knowledge of God's existence, though sin is said to have greatly inhibited such a natural knowledge. Potentially, reason could acknowledge what is prescribed in the Decalogue, especially what is demanded in the Second Table of the Law.[23] For it is true that prior to his conversion man is still a rational creature with both an intellect and will, and so to some extent reason and free will are able to lead to an outwardly virtuous life. This is a very positive affirmation that human beings, despite shameless abuses of their natural will, may together pursue a civil righteousness through outwardly good works.

Thus it should be possible for all humans to accept governments and rulers and be law-abiding citizens. Christians expect that those who are in power apply natural law for the good of all in such a way that it curbs chaotic and criminal behavior.[24] In outward or secular affairs, every human being can still discern good from evil or freely choose to act in such matters. Christians and non-Christians may thus join hands in pursuing specific ethical and social interests and so expect such temporal blessings as good government, peace, and security.[25] There is, however, a difference between Christians and non-Christians in that Christians see themselves as duty-

---

22 See the respective statements on this topic in the Lutheran Confessions: Ep I 2 (Kolb-Wengert, 488); SD I 10 (Kolb-Wengert, 533); LC II 57 (Kolb-Wengert, 438); and Wiebe, "Missionsgedanken in den lutherischen Bekenntnisschriften," 35.

23 For a few pertinent texts on general revelation and natural law in the Lutheran Confessions, see LC II 67 (Kolb-Wengert, 440); SD V 22 (Kolb-Wengert, 585).

24 SD VI 1 (Kolb-Wengert, 587).

25 LC II 15–16 (Kolb-Wengert, 432); SD IV 8 (Kolb-Wengert, 575).

bound to "serve and obey" God thankfully for all blessings received, an act that cannot be expected from non-Christians who Scripture claims fail to recognize and thank God.[26]

In view of what Christians and non-Christians have in common from creation, Christians need not promote a separate moral ethos—even if issues such as the blessing of gay couples and abortion have divided not only society but also Christians. The reality is that Christians do not withdraw themselves to create their own perfect Christian society.[27]

In a theological statement entitled "Guidelines for Evangelical-Lutheran Christians Living Together with Muslims in Germany," published by the consistory of the Independent Evangelical-Lutheran Church (SELK) in 2002, the following point is made concerning Christians and Muslims joining hands on certain issues:

> The Koran speaks frequently of Allah's love in connection with the moral life. We thus claim that Christian and Islamic values are often shared in common. Both see abortion, pornography, unrestrained sexuality, drugs, and alcohol abuse as harmful and sinful. This joint concern could provide points for discussion that could ease and promote the coexistence between Muslims and Christians, create trust and offer the opportunity to deepen theological discussions.[28]

AN EXPLICIT REJECTION OF ALL RELIGIOSITY

The Christian's positive estimation of other religions must change when considering the person and work of Christ. While writing about the doctrine of justification, Melanchthon pointed out that good works in Christless religions constitute a kind of idolatry. Luther proceeds from the First Commandment and uncovers the idolatry of non-Christians as a trust in a false god. Melanchthon and Luther's judgments that natural man either seeks merits through works or actually pursues idols are very dismissive toward Christ-less religions. The bottom line is that adherents of other religions do not give all honor and glory to God, who is revealed in Jesus Christ. The rejection of the atoning sacrifice in Jesus Christ constitutes the basic definition of false belief and worship.

Theologian Holsten Fagerberg interprets Luther's position in the explanation of the First Commandment not in view of "the problem of our natural knowledge of God." Rather, Luther was dealing with "the matter of true faith or false faith, whereby a man has either God or an idol as his

---

26 LC II 22 (Kolb-Wengert, 433).

27 Ap XXVII 27 (Tappert, 273–74); Ap IV 135 (Tappert, 125).

28 "Guidelines for Evangelical-Lutheran Christians Living Together with Muslims in Germany," 13, 31.

Lord."[29] As Luther speaks about true faith as the correct worship of God, he also rejects the general knowledge of God of the so-called monotheistic faith-systems of either Islam or Judaism. Both religions reject or obscure, and so are unable to provide a correct worship of, God.[30]

The SELK statement mentioned above conveys Luther's point in terms of worship with equal incisiveness:

> As much as we genuinely desire to approach Muslims by invitation and visitation and to improve human relations with them, we must make it equally clear that we can have no joint worship with them, nor engage in any joint prayer; because Allah in Islam is another god than the Father of Jesus Christ [*denn Allah im Islam ist ein anderer Gott als der Vater Jesu Christi*]. Muslims reject the Holy Trinity, and as a consequence also the Son of God, Jesus Christ. This is recorded 23 times in the Koran. This in turn questions the atoning sacrifice of Jesus on the cross because Allah does not need a mediator or a lamb (Sura 518, et al.). Crucifixion would be a disgraceful defeat for Allah and his ambassadors. Truthfulness in this matter requires that Christians, just as Muslims, do not conceal these fundamental differences; confessing Muslims also see them clearly.[31]

Non-Christians can only advance to a true understanding of God as Creator through faith in Jesus Christ. It therefore is not any easier to know God's creation than it is to know His redemption. Without Christ and the cross as the content of faith, all statements of God as Creator are incomplete and not praiseworthy.[32]

Paul Tillich's proposition on the religiosity of non-Christians (the latent church) is deficient. To be sure, such concerns as "death," "judgment," and "fear" seize natural man, on the basis of which God is brought into the equation.[33] We may concede some truth to Tillich's insights insofar as these show that God's revelation in Christ does not fall perpendicularly from heaven onto barren ground (*tabula rasa*).[34] However, in Tillich's case, we are dealing with a construct that attributes qualities to the realm of natural

29 Fagerberg, *New Look at the Lutheran Confessions*, 67.

30 This is evident in LC II 66 (Kolb-Wengert, 440), where Luther lists all religions together with those of a (monotheistic) faith such as the Turks or Jews. In fact, even those belonging nominally to the Church, namely, false Christians and hypocrites, are classified as heathen (LC I 35, Kolb-Wengert, 391). See also Ap XV 15 (Tappert, 217), Ap VII 15 (*Triglotta*, 233), Ap VII 9 (Tappert, 169), AC XX 24–26 (Kolb-Wengert, 56). See Nordling, "Large Catechism III, 66," 235–39.

31 "Guidelines for Evangelical-Lutheran Christians Living Together with Muslims in Germany," 15, 33.

32 Schlink, *Theology of the Lutheran Confessions*, 59.

33 Tillich, *Systematic Theology*, 1:211.

34 For Karl Barth's "christomonistic" approach, see *Church Dogmatics*, 1/2:302–3, 326–27. This Barthian approach was, it seems, also taken by Schlink, *Theology of the Lutheran Confessions*, 49, 57, and was debated by Fagerberg, *New Look at the Lutheran Confessions,* 64–67, and Brunstäd, *Theologie der lutherischen Bekenntnisschriften*, 32.

or general revelation that must be transformed and corrected through the special revelation of the Gospel. Moreover, it needs to be stated clearly that the Gospel does not affirm man in his worldly existence, but rather takes him out of it, confronts him with eschatology, and provides him with the certainty of salvation in view of Christ's return as Judge. The Gospel thus transforms man, and this is a much more radical concept than the sterile religiosity Tillich advocates. The Word of God addresses the conscience and corrects and rebukes all preexisting religious notions.[35]

Thus the ultimate purpose of sharing the Gospel with others is to bring the horizon of their reality to Christ as Judge and Redeemer. Christian witness brings others before the presence of the tribunal of God, who judges and accuses but who also resurrects through the Gospel to faith.[36]

ANTHROPOLOGICAL DEFINITION OF RELIGION

One important aspect of Luther's explanation of religion and the religiosity of natural man is that it is defined anthropocentrically. Every human being entertains some notion of "god"! This is evident in Luther's definition of religion in the broadest sense—namely, "anything on which your heart relies and depends, I say, that is really your God." The value of this definition is that it excuses no human being, even the most adamant atheist. According to Luther, every human being establishes and maintains some sort of worship, because "everyone has set up a god of his own, to which he looked for blessings, help, and comfort." As Luther says, "everyone made into a god that to which his heart was inclined."[37]

By correlating the heart to the First Commandment, Luther addresses contemporary religiosity, which in today's terms is argued not merely as the outward behavior but actually also the innermost core, what is called ultimate allegiance and worldview.[38] Although spoken more than four hundred years ago, Luther's words include also those who argue within the postmodern paradigm. For what is significant also of Luther's definition is that while traditional church bodies are experiencing losses, religiosity

---

35 For the discussion on the conscience as the point of contact in Gospel proclamation, see Leipold, "Anknüpfung I," 743–47, and Beyerhaus, "Walter Freytags Begriff des Gewissens," 147.

36 This fits the description of the Gospel as provided, for example, in the Confessions; see SD V 20–21 (Kolb-Wengert, 585); Brunner, "'Rechtfertigung' heute," 131. The danger of Tillich's thinking, particularly his method of correlation (see *Systematic Theology*, 1:59–65), is that it gives precisely the impression that the proclamation of justification is merely focused on meeting the existential needs of man. Joest, "Die Rechtfertigungslehre Luthers in ihrer Bedeutung," 41–55, and Martens, *Die Rechtfertigung des Sünders*, 141–44.

37 LC I 17–18 (Kolb-Wengert, 388).

38 LC I 18–21 (Kolb-Wengert, 388).

itself as a human phenomenon has not diminished; instead, it has taken alternative forms in place of traditional Christianity.

According to Luther, all religiosity is a fabrication of the heart, and as such it opposes the religion that truly and ultimately matters—namely, that which is revealed in Christ. Christ in turn is apprehended through faith as the Word is preached. All religions thus stand as one united front opposing Christianity. This may sound simplistic in view of the plurality of religions around the world. But that simplicity has been widely adopted by theologians after Luther, who stated that the false religions (*religiones falsae*) oppose the one true religion (*religio vera*), that is, Christianity.[39] The demarcation between truth and falseness represents an invisible line that only God can see, just as only God can see the true invisible Church. In fact, such idolatry transgresses all geographic boundaries; it runs through the world, through Christianity, and through the heart of every human being so that within even the circles of true Christians, heathenism still exists. This radical definition of heathenism draws attention to a missionary frontier in closest proximity to the Christian community; it exists within Christianity, and it lends a missionary dimension to all preaching. The only antidote to such an encroaching heathenism in the life of the Church is given through the preaching of the Gospel.[40]

It is particularly through the divisions of God's Word—namely, Law and Gospel—that the true demonic unbelief is detected and refuted. God fully reveals Himself through the preached Word—namely, through the proclaiming of the Law, which places the heathen before God as a sinner and exposes him to God's judgment.[41] The proclaimed Law thus has the function of exposing man as in need of the Gospel. Ultimately, therefore, the initially positive evaluation of heathenism is no longer viable.[42]

---

39 Pieper, *Christian Dogmatics*, 1:13. On Pieper's references to Max Mueller, the famous scholar of comparative religions in India, see Danker, "Non–Christian Religions and Franz Pieper's *Christian Dogmatics*," 215–21. The German mission theologian Walter Freytag finds a common characteristic in all religions, which he calls deceptive goodness ("Das Dämonische in den Religionen," 18).

40 LWF, *Together in God's Mission*, 27–28.

41 For the discussion of how this Law works, see, for example, SA III II 4 (Kolb-Wengert, 312).

42 Blauw, *Goden en Mensen*, 161. Conversion is therefore not merely "an ever [emotional] deeper experience of God's grace together with all God's people," namely, those of other religions (Saayman, "If You Were to Die Today," 171). The divine work of the Holy Spirit is thus essential (SD II 9, 24, Kolb-Wengert, 545, 548–49). Laiser, "Authority of Scripture," 64.

Christian Witness Affirms
the Visible Church

We should thus add some visibility and concreteness to this line of division. For it may be assumed that where the articles of the creeds are confessed and God's Word is being preached, such acts would bring true faith and worship of the triune God. Thus, for Luther, the "three articles of the Creed, separate and distinguish us Christians from all other people on earth." To Luther, all people—whether "heathen, Turks, Jews, or false Christians and hypocrites"—are those "outside the Christian church" who are not "illuminated and blessed by the gifts of the Holy Spirit."[43] We must agree with the classical statement that outside the Church (in the proper sense of the invisible, universal congregation of believers) there is no salvation (*extra ecclesiam nulla salus est*) by pointing out that salvation has everything to do with the Word being heard and proclaimed in the Christian Church. For with that very Word, the Lord Himself rules His Church and takes people into His midst. Outside of proclamation and apart from the Word, God's presence is absent, and there begins the demonic nature of heathenism.[44] Christians in their witness should point out this ecclesial reality to non-Christians and affirm that an allegiance to Christ cannot exist or be sustained without the Church, even if it may be claimed otherwise.[45]

---

43 See Luther's statements: LC II 66 (Kolb-Wengert, 440); Ap VII 14–16 (Tappert, 170); SA III VIII 10 (Kolb-Wengert, 323).

44 LC IV 69 (Kolb-Wengert, 465); LC III 62, 80, 104, 113 (Kolb-Wengert, 448, 451, 454–55); LC II 52 (Kolb-Wengert, 438); *Taufbüchlein* 2 (*BSLK*, 536); LC IV 83 (Kolb-Wengert, 466).

45 In a previous chapter, we discussed the debate surrounding the proposal of a churchless Christianity as proposed by Hoefer, *Churchless Christianity*, and LWF, *Mission in Context*, 28.

CHAPTER SEVENTEEN

CONCLUSION

God mediates His salvation to the world through His Word as the Church preaches, administers, and witnesses. And yet, as simple and as basic as this activity sounds, it is fraught with complexity. Discussions in literature and at meetings, conferences, and conventions demonstrate how mission can unite but can just as easily divide Christians over theology and practice. Thus the Church is always challenged to find a match between her theology and practice in order to reach a common consensus. It is good to see Christians respond to mission out of love and compassion for the neighbor, but it should not become blind activism. Christians should be informed about the Church's belief and confession as they assume a place in the Lord's mission.

This study seeks to contribute to the discussion. It has navigated and explored the theology, nature, context, and task of mission, and in the process I have regularly pointed to the connection between belief and practice. Not everything has been said, but I hope the argument for a stabilizing structure may be heard. True, mission is an open-ended endeavor: countries open and close their doors for the Gospel, time and context bring up new challenges, and the Church must constantly readjust. But the Church serves the world with the same Gospel that the Church has been entrusted to teach, and she will do so till Christ's return.

How should I end this study? Let us return to a reference to the four classical categories that define the Church's role in God's mission: the Church is missional, evangelical, confessional, and vocational.[1] These traits do indeed provide a good summary of how we as Christians present ourselves to the world and how our study has probed the nature of mission.

First, the Church is *missional.* As God's redeemed community, she continues to receive life from God but then also unselfishly passes on the gift of life in Christ to the world (John 3:16). The Church administers the precious lifelines of Word and Sacrament, not only in the context of worship but also in a kerygmatic-sacramental activity to the unbelieving world. In

---

1 Bliese, "Mission Matrix," 237–48.

a true missionary Spirit, Christians look upon non-Christians as people who can be freed by the Gospel from a "works-driven" attitude and a self-centered moralism that gives God little room.

Second, the Church is *evangelical* in that she possesses the salutary Gospel. This Gospel is the only remedy to sin, death, and the devil. Martin Luther taught and believed in the power of the Gospel five hundred years ago, and today the Church shares that conviction. The Gospel performs no other purpose today than it did during the days of Paul and during the time of Luther. Although the Church has many tasks, she may not forget that she exists for her evangelical role of sharing the Gospel with the world.

However, the evangelical character of the Church expresses the Gospel in a number of visible forms. The Church is evangelical through witnessing, preaching, and administering the Gospel. In this connection, we reiterate the brief yet powerful statement on the Gospel's nature and purpose made by the missiologist Walter Freytag: "In the biblical sense nothing can be called mission that is not geared towards conversion and baptism."[2] Moreover, proclamation and the visible act of Baptism lead to an existing, worshiping community. Being evangelical questions the kind of individualism that has reached an idolatrous level in our society. As the Gospel brings the gift of justification, it also creates the visible reality of church membership and worship. The importance that the Reformation sets on being evangelical would be misunderstood if it were isolated from the context of ecclesiology and the various visible forms of the Gospel: witness, preaching, teaching, Absolution, Sacraments, and worship.

Third, the Church is also *vocational* in her service to and in the world. In addition to the ordained ministry of the Church, mission includes the sanctified life of all Christians by structuring itself around the manifold vocations of Christians. Through their witness and conduct, all Christians serve the mission of the Church by extending the Word into all realms of society. Christians need not scout about for good works or purposes in their life; the call for specific kinds of good works comes along with each specific vocation.

Fourth, the Church's mission is *confessional* in that all proclamation and every Christian's vocational witness must be articulated clearly and with fidelity to Scripture. Jesus once asked His disciples the question, "Who do you say that I am?" Just as Peter confessed, "You are Christ, the Son of the living God" (Matt. 16:16), Christians give similar answers to people who still have need to hear of Christ. By being confessional, the Church reaffirms the teachings of Luther surrounding his discovery of the Gospel, and she professes the content of that discovery to a world that is still searching.

---

2   Freytag, *Reden und Aufsätze*, 2:85.

By being confessional, the Church shares a common message in a meaningful and coherent way.[3] Finally, by being confessional, the Church speaks the Gospel truth with confidence in a world that, as Lesslie Newbigin argues, rejects any assertions that the Gospel should be true for everyone.[4]

Many who serve as missionaries may despair over the Church's slowness or failure to respond to the urgency of bringing the Gospel to the world. The reality, however, is that the Church will never attain the level of perfection many desire or aspire for her; she cannot free herself from the battles against sin throughout her earthly existence. Although the Church must seek to overcome her own failures, those failures also make up part of the fabric of her life. Mission has many frontiers, and one of these runs right through her midst. True believers, hypocrites, and, yes, even unbelievers exist in the visible Church so that the message of the Gospel imparts its gifts to all who call themselves members of the Body of Christ.[5] The title *Mission from the Cross* was chosen for this study precisely to capture the thought that, as Christians engage in God's mission, they always remain simultaneously *passive* recipients of the gift of forgiveness that flows from the cross of Christ.

Finally, the Church recognizes the fact that her proclamation does not take place in a vacuum. Mission happens within a given context. In that context, mission engages in some form of dialogue, whatever the situation may be. The Church must learn to listen in order to respond to the cries and the crises in our time. That presents a daunting and challenging task indeed. And yet the Church is always assured of the Lord's presence, for He has promised: "And behold, I am with you always, to the end of the age" (Matt. 28:20).

---

3 Mattes, *Role of Justification in Contemporary Theology*, 184–85.

4 Newbigin, *Gospel in a Pluralist Society*, 242–44.

5 See, for example, LWF, *Together in God's Mission*, 27.

THE SPREAD OF LUTHERAN MISSION WORK

At the close of the Reformation, the famous Lutheran preacher and hymn writer Philip Nicolai wrote *A Commentary on the Reign of Christ* (1597). Nicolai's work provided a geographical survey of regions reached by the Gospel. He stirred Lutherans to increase foreign mission work.

Lutheran mission work spread in three basic ways: (1) publications of Gospel literature; (2) missionaries sent by Lutheran rulers, churches, and mission societies; and (3) Lutheran congregations established by immigrants. The map here highlights five centuries of work by Lutheran missionaries—only a sampling—which we hope will stir you to support further mission work.

1523—Luther writes *Jesus Christ Was a Jew by Birth* as a missionary tract; in 1529, he publishes the Small Catechism to support the instruction of converts to Christianity.

1557—Primus Truber translates and publishes the Gospels, the Catechism, and other resources for the Croats and the Wends.

1558—Estonian, Latvian, and Livonian Lutheran peasants are resettled in Russia.

1559—Swedish King Gustav Wasa begins and supports mission work among the Lapplanders.

1634—Peter Heyling begins mission work in Egypt and Ethiopia.

1648—John Campanius translates the Catechism for the Delaware Indians.

1706—Bartholomäus Ziegenbalg and Heinrich Plütschau begin mission work in Tranquebar (Tharangambadi), India.

1721—Hans Egede serves as missionary to the Eskimos in Greenland.

1742—Johann Philipp Fabricius begins mission work with the Tamil in Madras (Chennai), India.

1749—German Lutheran immigrants land at Halifax, Nova Scotia.

1762—Christian Frederick Schwartz conducts mission work at Trichinopoly (Tiruchirapalli) and, later, Tanjore (Thanjavur), India.

1839—August L. C. Kavel and congregation arrive in Adelaide, Australia.

1844—John Ludwig Krapf begins mission work in Zanzibar, Tanzania.

1845—August Crämer founds missionary colony in Frankenmuth, MI, to work with American Indians.

1851—Theodor Fliedner and four deaconesses begin relief work among Arab people in Jerusalem.

1854—The mission ship "Candace" (Hermannsberger Mission) reaches Port Natal (Durban), South Africa.

1861—St. Martin's Church organized in Cape Town, South Africa.

1864—Ludwig I. Nommensen begins mission work with the Bataks of Indonesia.

1866—John Engh and Nils Nilsen begin mission work in Madagascar.

1877—Synodical Conference begins mission work among African Americans.

1883—Daniel Landsmann begins mission work among the Jews in New York.

1886—Johan Flierl begins mission work in New Guinea. Missionary Union of Sweden begins work in Congo, Africa.

1887—Theodore Schmidt organizes congregation in Valdivia, Chile.

H. J. B. Gellmuyden serves a congregation in Buenos Aires, Argentina.

1892—James A. B. Sherer begins mission work in Japan.

1894—K. G. T. Naether begins mission work in Krishnagiri, India.

T. F. Mohn starts a mission station in Ambur, India.

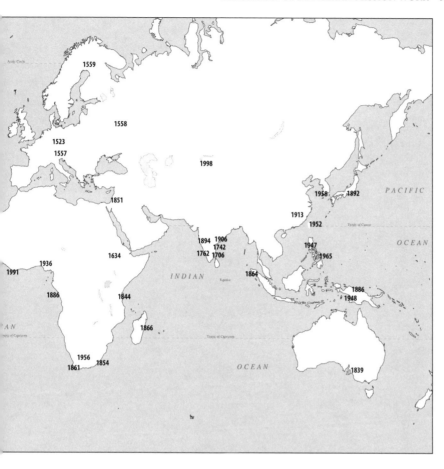

1901—Christian J. Broders and then William Mahler organize mission work in Brazil.

1913—Edward L. Arndt begins mission work in Hankow, China.

1936—Henry Nau and Jonathan Udo Ekong begin mission work in Calabar Province, Nigeria.

1947—Alvaro Carino and Herman Mayer begin mission work in Manila, Philippines. Lutheran World Federation (LWF) organized in Lund, Sweden.

1948—Willard Burce and Otto Hintze begin mission work in New Guinea.

1950—LCMS Texas District sends pastors to Mexico City.

1952—Taiwan Lutheran Mission organized.

1956—The Bleckmar Mission (Hannover) begins work among Indians living in South Africa. The Norwegian Lutheran Mission founds its radio mission, Norea Mediemisjion.

1958—Lutheran mission work organized in South Korea.

1965—Lutheran Bible Translators (originally, "Messengers of Christ") send Don and Mary Murray to the Philippines.

The Cold War (1948–91) interfered with the development of new mission work. Since the collapse of communism, Lutheran mission work has begun anew in parts of Eastern Europe and Asia (e.g., Kyrgyzstan, 1998), as well as in Côte d'Ivoire and Guinea in Africa. In 1993, the International Lutheran Council (ILC) was organized at Antigua, Guatemala, and is strengthening the bonds of confessional Lutheran Churches worldwide.

As Scripture and the Nicene Creed teach, Jesus Christ "will come again with glory . . . whose kingdom will have no end." Therefore, we boldly pray the words of Luther's mission hymn, "O let the people praise Thy worth, In all good works increasing; The land shall plenteous fruit bring forth, Thy Word is rich in blessing. May God the Father, God the Son, And God the Spirit bless us! Let all the world praise Him alone, Let solemn awe possess us. Now let our hearts say, 'Amen!'"(*LSB* 823:3).

PERSONS INDEX

Scripture Index

BIBLIOGRAPHY

Aagaard, Johannes. *Mission, Konfession, Kirche: Die Problematik ihrer Integration im 19 Jahrhundert in Deutschland.* 2 vols. Lund: Gleerup, 1967.

———. "Missionary Theology." Pages 206–27 in *The Lutheran Church, Past and Present.* Edited by Vilmos Vajta. Translated by Vanessa Dolbe. Minneapolis: Augsburg, 1977.

———. "Missionstheologie." Pages 250–74 in *Die Evangelisch-Lutherische Kirche: Vergangenheit und Gegenwart.* Edited by Vilmos Vajta. Frankfurt am Main: Evangelisches Verlagswerk, 1983.

Abbott, Walter M., gen. ed. *The Documents of Vatican II.* Translated by Joseph Callagher et al. Chicago: Follet, 1966.

Abraham, William J. *The Logic of Evangelism.* Grand Rapids: Eerdmans, 1989.

Afflerbach, Horst. *Handbuch Christliche Ethik.* Wuppertal: R. Brockhaus, 2002.

Allen, Roland. *Missionary Methods: St. Paul's or Ours?* Grand Rapids: Eerdmans, 1962.

———. *The Spontaneous Expansion of the Church and the Causes which Hinder It.* Grand Rapids: Eerdmans, 1962.

Althaus, Paul. *Fact and Faith in the Kerygma of Today.* Translated by David Cairns. Philadelphia: Muhlenberg, 1959.

———. "Um die Reinheit der Mission." Pages 48–60 in *Mission und Theologie.* Edited by Franz Wiebe. Göttingen: Heinz Reise, 1953.

Amstutz, Josef. *Kirche der Völker: Skizze einer Theorie der Mission.* Freiburg: Herder, 1972.

Anderson, Gerald H. "American Protestants in Pursuit of Mission: 1886–1986." *International Bulletin of Missionary Research* 12 (1980): 98–118.

———. *Biographical Dictionary of Christian Missions.* Grand Rapids: Eerdmans, 1998.

Andersen, Wilhelm. "Die kerygmatische Begründung der Religions- und Missionswissenschaft." *Evangelische Missionszeitschrift* 11 (March 1954): 29–37.

———. *Towards a Theology of Mission: A Study of the Encounter between the Missionary Enterprise and the Church and Its Theology.* London: SCM, 1955.

Aring, Paul Gerhard. *Kirche als Ereignis: Ein Beitrag zur Neuorientierung der Missionstheologie.* Neukirchen-Vluyn: Neukirchener, 1971.

Aulén, Gustaf. *Christus Victor: An Historical Study of the Three Main Types of the Idea of Atonement.* Translated by A. G. Hebert. New York: Macmillan, 1969.

Barna, George. *Growing True Disciples.* Grand Rapids: Zondervan, 1998.

Barrett, David, and Todd M. Johnson. *World Christian Trends AD 30–AD 2200: Interpreting the Annual Christian Megacensus.* Pasadena, CA: William Carey Library, 2001.

Barth, Karl. *Church Dogmatics.* Vol. 1/2. Translated by G. T. Thomson and Harold Knight. New York: Scribner's, 1956.

———. *Church Dogmatics.* Vol. 4, 3/1. Translated by G. W. Bromiley. Edinburgh: T&T Clark, 1961.

———. *Church Dogmatics.* Vol. 4, 3/2. Translated by G. W. Bromiley. Edinburgh: T&T Clark, 1962.

———. *Church Dogmatics.* Vol. 4/1. Translated by G. W. Bromiley. Edinburgh: T&T Clark, 1956.

———. "Theologie und Mission in der Gegenwart." Pages 100–126 in *Theologische Fragen und Antworten.* Vol. 3 of *Gesammelte Vorträge.* Zürich: Evangelischer Verlag, 1957.

Bayer, Oswald. *Living by Faith.* Translated by Geoffrey W. Bromiley. Grand Rapids: Eerdmans, 2003.

———. "Notae ecclesiae." Pages 75–90 in *Lutherische Beiträge zur Missio Dei.* Erlangen: Martin Luther Verlag, 1982.

Beck, William F. *The Holy Bible: An American Translation.* New Haven: Leader, 1976.

Beißer, Friedrich. *Hoffnung und Vollendung.* Gütersloh: Gütersloher Verlagshaus Gerd Mohn, 1993.

———. "Mission und Reich Gottes." Pages 43–56 in *Lutherische Beiträge zur Missio Dei.* Erlangen: Martin Luther Verlag, 1982.

Die Bekenntnisschriften der evangelisch-lutherischen Kirche. Herausgegeben im Gedenkjahr der Augsburgischen Konfession 1930. Göttingen: Vandenhoeck & Ruprecht, 1930.

Berger, Peter. *A Skeptical Affirmation of Christianity.* Oxford: Blackwell, 2004.

Berkhof, Hendrikus. *The Doctrine of the Holy Spirit.* Richmond, VA: John Knox, 1964.

Beyerhaus, Peter. *Aufbruch der Armen: Die neue Missionsbewegung nach Melbourne.* Bad Liebenzell: Verlag der Liebenzeller Mission, 1981.

———. "Christi Heilsangebot durch seine Gesandten." *Evangelisches Missionsmagazin* 116 (1972): 54–66.

———. *Die Grundlagenkrise der Mission.* Wuppertal: R. Brockhaus, 1970.

———. *Humanisierung: Einzige Hoffnung der Welt?* 2d ed. Bad Salzuflen: Verlag für Missions- und Bibel- kunde, 1970.

———. "Missionar I (Evangelisch)." In *Lexikon Missionstheologischer Grundbegriffe.* Edited by Karl Müller and Theo Sundermeier. Berlin: Dietrich Reimer, 1987.

———. *Missions—Which Way? Humanization or Redemption?* Translated by Margaret Clarkson. Grand Rapids: Zondervan, 1971.

———. "Die Predigt als Ruf zur Mission." Pages 16–38 in *Lutherisches Missionsjahrbuch für das Jahr 1968.* Edited by Walter Ruf. Nürnberg: Selbstverlag der Bayerischen Missionskonferenz, 1968.

———. *Die Selbständigkeit der jungen Kirchen als missionarisches Problem.* 2d ed. Wuppertal-Barmen: Verlag der Rheinischen Missions-Gesellschaft, 1956.

———. *Shaken Foundations: Theological Foundations for Mission.* Grand Rapids: Zondervan, 1972.

———. "Walter Freytags Begriff des Gewissens in der Sicht südafrikanischer Missionsarbeit." Pages 146–57 in *Basileia: Walter Freytag zum 60. Geburtstag.* Edited by Jan Hermelink and Hans Jochen Margull. Stuttgart: Evang. Missionsverlag, 1959.

Bieder, Werner. "Spiritus Sanctus Pro Mundi Vita." Pages 59–68 in *Fides pro mundi vita.* Edited by Theo Sundermeier. Gütersloh: Gütersloher Verlagshaus Gerd Mohn, 1980.

Bijlsma, Roelof. *Die Taufe in Familie und Gemeinde.* Munich: Chr. Kaiser, 1962.

Bingle, E. J. "The World Mission of the Church: A Survey." In *Missions under the Cross.* Edited by Norman Goddall. London: Edinburgh House Press, 1953.

Bizer, Ernst. *Luther und der Papst.* Munich: Christian Kaiser, 1958.

———. "Über die Rechtfertigung." Pages 11–30 in *Das Kreuz Jesu Christi als Grund des Heils.* Edited by Ernst Bizer, J. F. Gerhard Goeters, Wolfgang Schrage, Walter Kreck, and Walther Fürst. Gütersloh: Gütersloher Verlagshaus Gerd Mohn, 1967.

Blauw, Johannes. "The Biblical View of Man in His Religion." In *The Theology of the Christian Mission.* Edited by Gerald H. Anderson. New York: McGraw-Hill, 1961.

———. *Goden en Mensen: Plaats en Betekenis van de Heidenen in de Heilige Schrift.* Groningen: J. Niemeijer, 1950.

Bliese, Richard. "The Mission Matrix: Mapping Out the Complexities of a Missional Ecclesiology." *Word and World* 26.3 (Summer 2006): 237–48.

———, and Craig Van Gelder, eds. *The Evangelizing Church: A Lutheran Contribution.* Minneapolis: Augsburg Fortress, 2005.

Blocher, Henri A. "The Lutheran—Catholic Declaration on Justification." Pages 197–217 in *Justification in Perspective.* Edited by Bruce L. McCormack. Grand Rapids: Baker Academic, 2006.

Blöchle, Herbert. "Die missionarische Dimension in der Theologie Luthers." Pages 357–68 in *Die Einheit der Kirche: Dimensionen ihrer Heiligkeit, Katholizität und Apostolizität: Festgabe Peter Meinhold zum 70. Geburtstag.* Edited by Lorenz Hein. Wiesbaden: Franz Steiner, 1977.

Bohren, Rudolf. *Mission und Gemeinde.* Munich: Chr. Kaiser, 1962.

Bonhoeffer, Dietrich. *The Cost of Discipleship.* New York: Macmillan, 1959.

Bosch, David J. "Theological Education in Missionary Perspective." *Missiology* 10.1 (January 1982): 13–34.

———. *Transforming Mission: Paradigm Shifts in Theology of Mission.* Maryknoll, NY: Orbis, 1991.

———. *Witness to the World: The Christian Mission in Theological Perspective.* Atlanta: John Knox, 1980.

Boyd, Gregory A., and Paul R. Eddy. *Across the Spectrum: Understanding Issues in Evangelical Theology.* Grand Rapids: Baker Academic, 2002.

Braaten, Carl E. *The Apostolic Imperative.* Minneapolis: Augsburg Fortress, 1985.

———. *Justification: The Article by Which the Church Stands or Falls.* Minneapolis: Fortress, 1990.

————. "A Trinitarian Theology of the Cross." *Journal of Religion* 56 (January 1976): 113–21.

Brandt, Hermann. "Über den Beitrag lutherischer Mission zum Gemeindeaufbau: Mission als nota ecclesiae." In *Eschatologie und Gemeindeaufbau. Hermannsburger Missionsgeschichte im Umfeld lutherischer Erweckung.* Edited by Georg Gremels. Hermannsburg: Ludwig-Harms-Haus-Verlag— Missionshandlung, 2004.

Brecht, Martin. "Beobachtungen zum Gemeindeaufbau bei Luther." Pages 9–21 in *Reformation und Praktische Theologie: Festschrift für Werner Jetter zum siebzigsten Geburtstag.* Edited by Hans Martin Müller and Dietrich Rössler. Göttingen: Vandenhoeck & Ruprecht, 1983.

————. *Martin Luther.* Vol. 3: *Die Erhaltung der Kirche 1532–1546.* Stuttgart: Calwer, 1987.

Breytenbach, Cilliers. "Reconciliation Shifts in Christian Soteriology." Pages 1–25 in *Reconciliation and Construction: Creative Options for a Rapidly Changing South Africa.* Edited by W. S. Vorster. Pretoria: University of South Africa, 1986.

Brunner, Peter. "Die bleibende Bedeutung des lutherischen Bekenntnisses für die Mission." *Lutherische Blätter* 106 (1972): 8–22.

————. "Gott, das Nichts und die Kreatur. Eine dogmatische Erwägung zum christlichen Schöpfungsglauben." Pages 31–49 in vol. 2 of *Pro Ecclesia: Gesammelte Aufsätze zur dogmatischen Theologie.* Berlin: Lutherisches Verlagshaus, 1966.

————. "Das Heil und das Amt." Pages 293–309 in vol. 1 of *Pro Ecclesia: Gesammelte Aufsätze zur dogmatischen Theologie.* Berlin: Lutherisches Verlagshaus, 1966.

————. "Die Herrlichkeit des gekreuzigten Messias: Eine vordogmatische Erwägung zur dogmatischen Christologie." Pages 60–75 in vol. 2 of *Pro Ecclesia: Gesammelte Aufsätze zur dogmatischen Theologie.* Berlin: Lutherisches Verlagshaus, 1966.

————. "Ministerium Verbi, Ekklesia und Hirtenamt." Pages 17–46 in *Grundlinien für die Ordnung des Amtes in der Kirche: Arbeitsergebnisse des Theologischen Konvents Augsburgischen Bekenntnisses.* Fuldaer Hefte. Schriften des Theologischen Konvents Augsburgischen Bekenntnisses 11. Edited by Friedrich Hübner. Berlin: Lutherisches Verlagshaus, 1960.

————. "Die Notwendigkeit des neuen Gehorsams nach dem Augsburgischen Bekenntnis." *Kerygma und Dogma* 7 (1961): 272–83.

————. *Pro Ecclesia.* 2 vols. Berlin: Lutherisches Verlagshaus, 1962–.

————. "'Rechtfertigung' heute: Versuch einer dogmatischen Paraklese." Pages 122–40 in vol. 2 of *Pro Ecclesia: Gesammelte Aufsätze zur dogmatischen Theologie.* Berlin: Lutherisches Verlagshaus, 1966.

————. "Rechtfertigung, Wiedergeburt und neuer Gehorsam in Melanchton's Apologie." *Informationsblatt für die Gemeinden in den lutherischen Landeskirchen* 7 (1958): 302–3.

————. "Theologie des Gottesdienstes?" *Kerygma und Dogma* 22 (1976): 96–121.

————. "Vom Amt des Bischofs." Pages 5–77 in *Schriften des Theologischen Konvents Augsburgischen Bekenntnisses.* Edited by Friedrich Hübner. Berlin: Lutherisches Verlagshaus, 1955.

———. *Worship in the Name of Jesus.* Translated by Martin H. Bertram. St. Louis: Concordia, 1968.

Brunotte, Heinz. *Das Amt der Verkündigung und das Priestertum aller Gläubigen.* Berlin: Lutherisches Verlagshaus, 1962.

Brunstäd, Friedrich. *Theologie der lutherischen Bekenntnisschriften.* Gütersloh: C. Bertelsmann, 1951.

Bub, Wolfgang. *Evangelisationspredigt in der Volkskirche: Zu Predigtlehre und Praxis einer umstrittenen Verkündigungsgattung.* Stuttgart: Calwer, 1990.

Bürkle, Horst. *Missionstheologie.* Stuttgart: W. Kohlhammer, 1979.

Bultmann, Rudolf. "Ist voraussetzungslose Exegese möglich?" Pages 142–50 in vol. 3 of *Glauben und Verstehen: Gesammelte Aufsätze.* Tübingen: Mohr, 1947.

———. *Jesus Christ and Mythology.* Upper Saddle River, NJ: Prentice Hall, 1958.

———. "New Testament and Mythology: The Problem of Demythologizing the New Testament Proclamation." Pages 1–44 in *The New Testament and Mythology and Other Basic Writings.* Selected, edited, and translated by Schubert M. Ogden. Philadelphia: Fortress, 1984.

Bunkowske, Eugene W. "Luther, the Missionary." Pages 54–91 in *God's Mission in Action: A Booklet of Essays Delivered at the First Annual Missions Congress, Concordia Theological Seminary, Fort Wayne, Indiana, April 24–27, 1986.* Edited by Eugene W. Bunkowske and Michael A. Nichol. Fort Wayne, IN: Great Commission Resource Library, 1986.

Caemmerer, Richard R. "Kerygma and Didache in Christian Education." *Concordia Theological Monthly* 32.3 (March 1961): 197–208.

Callahan, Kennon L. *Effective Church Leadership: Building on the Twelve Keys.* San Francisco: Harper & Row, 1990.

———. *Twelve Keys to an Effective Church: Strategy for Planning Mission.* San Francisco: Harper & Row, 1983.

Calvin, John. *Institutio Christianae Religionis.* Vol. 2. Edited by A. Tholuck. Berlin: Gustav Eichler, 1834.

Carey, William. *An Enquiry into the Obligations of Christians to Use Means for the Conversion of the Heathens.* New facsimile ed. London: Carey Kingsgate Press, 1962.

Cheesman, Graham. *Mission Today: An Introduction to Mission Studies.* Belfast: Presbyterian & Reformed Publishing Co., 1989.

Cho, Paul Yonggi. *The Fourth Dimension.* Plainfield, NJ: Logos International, 1979.

Commission on Theology and Church Relations, Lutheran Church—Missouri Synod. *The Charismatic Movement and Lutheran Theology.* St. Louis: LCMS, 1972.

———. *The Joint Declaration on the Doctrine of Justification in Confessional Lutheran Perspective.* St. Louis: LCMS, 1999.

———. *The Lutheran Church and the Charismatic Movement: Guidelines for Congregation and Pastors.* St. Louis: LCMS, 1977.

———. *The Ministry: Offices, Procedures, and Nomenclature.* St. Louis: LCMS, 1981.

———. *The Ministry in Its Relation to the Christian Church as Seen on the Basis of the Holy Scripture and the Lutheran Confessions with Applications to Specific Problems of the Church in Our Time.* St. Louis: LCMS, 1993.

———. *A Statement of Scriptural and Confessional Principles.* St. Louis: LCMS, 1973.

———. *A Theological Statement of Mission.* St. Louis: LCMS, 1991.

Commission on Worship, Lutheran Church—Missouri Synod. *Lutheran Service Book.* St. Louis: Concordia, 2006.

Conn, Harvie M., ed. *Eternal Word and Changing Worlds: Theology, Anthropology, and Mission in Trialogue.* Grand Rapids: Zondervan, 1984.

———. *Theological Perspectives on Church Growth.* Nutley, NJ: Presbyterian & Reformed Publishing Co., 1976.

Copan, Paul, and Ronald K. Tacelli, eds. *Jesus' Resurrection: Fact or Figment?* Downers Grove, IL: InterVarsity, 2000.

Cullmann, Oscar. "Eschatology and Missions in the New Testament." Pages 42–54 in *The Theology of the Christian Mission.* Edited by Gerald H. Anderson. New York: McGraw-Hill, 1961.

———. *Salvation in History.* English translation drafted by Sidney G. Sowers and completed by the editorial staff of SCM Press. New York: Harper & Row, 1967.

Danker, William J. "Non-Christian Religions and Franz Pieper's *Christian Dogmatics.*" Pages 215–21 in *Fides pro mundi vita.* Edited by Theo Sundermeier. Gütersloh: Gütersloher Verlagshaus Gerd Mohn, 1980.

D'Costa, Gavin. *Theology and Religious Pluralism: The Challenge of Other Religions.* Oxford: Blackwell, 1986.

Deuser, Hermann. *Kleine Einfuehrung in die Systematische Theologie.* Stuttgart: Reclam, 1999.

Dörries, Hermann. "Luther und die Heidenpredigt." Pages 327–46 in vol. 3 of *Wort und Stunde: Beiträge zum Verständnis Luthers.* Göttingen: Vandenhoeck & Ruprecht 1970.

Drews, Paul. "Die Anschauungen reformatorischer Theologen über die Heidenmission." *Zeitschrift für praktische Theologie* 19 (1897): 1–26.

Dube, Dean Isashar. *Mit den bösen Geistern unter dem Himmel: Eine Kette unerklärlicher Ereignisse.* Gross-Oesingen: Lutherische Buchhandlung, 1992.

Eitel, Keith E. "The Way." *Criswell Theological Review* 4 (1989–90): 279–93.

Elert, Werner. "Augustin als Lehrer der Christenheit." Pages 174–83 in *Ein Lehrer der Kirche: Kirchlich-theologische Aufsätze und Vorträge.* Edited by Max Keller-Hüschemenger. Berlin: Lutherisches Verlagshaus, 1967.

———. *The Christian Faith: An Outline of Lutheran Dogmatics.* Translated by Martin H. Bertram and Walter R. Bouman. Columbus: Lutheran Theological Seminary, 1974.

———. "Gesetz und Evangelium." Pages 51–75 in *Zwischen Gnade und Ungnade: Abwandlungen des Themas Gesetz und Evangelium.* Munich: Evangelischer Presseverband für Bayern, 1948.

———. *The Lord's Supper Today.* Translated by Martin Bertram and Rudolph F. Norden. St. Louis: Concordia, 1973.

———. *The Structure of Lutheranism*. Vol. 1. Translated by Walter A. Hansen. St. Louis: Concordia, 1962.

Elfers, August. "Amt und Ämter in der Mission." Pages 35–40 in *Das Wort und die Völker der Erde: Beiträge zum lutherischen Verständnis der Mission*. Edited by Ernst Strasser. Uelzen: Niedersächsische Buchdruckerei, 1951.

Engel, James F., and H. Wilbert Norton. *What's Gone Wrong with the Harvest?* Grand Rapids: Zondervan, 1975.

Engle, Paul E., and Gary McIntosh, eds. *Evaluating the Church Growth Movement*. Grand Rapids: Zondervan, 2004.

Erickson, Millard J. *Making Sense of the Trinity*. Grand Rapids: Baker, 2000.

Etuk, Udo. "The Theology of Contextualization in Africa: A Cover for Traditional Cultural Revival." *Concordia Journal* 6 (November 1985): 214–22.

Das Evangelium und die Völker: Beiträge zur Geschichte und Theorie der Mission. Berlin-Friedenau: Verlag der Buchhandlung der Gosnerischen Mission, 1939.

Fagerberg, Holsten. *A New Look at the Lutheran Confessions (1529–1539)*. Translated by Gene J. Lund. St. Louis: Concordia, 1972.

———. *Die Theologie der lutherischen Bekenntnisschriften von 1529 bis 1537*. Göttingen: Vandenhoeck & Ruprecht, 1965.

Farley, Edward. "The Reform of Theological Education as a Theological Task." *Theological Education* 17 (Spring 1981): 93–117.

Feucht, Oscar. *Everyone a Minister*. St. Louis: Concordia, 1974.

Findeis, Hans Jürgen. "Missiology." Pages 299–301 in *Dictionary of Mission: Theology, History, Perspectives*. Maryknoll, NY: Orbis, 1997.

Flachsmeier, Horst. *Geschichte der Evangelischen Mission*. Giessen: Brunner, 1963.

Flogaus, Reinhard. *Theosis bei Palamas und Luther: Ein Beitrag zum ökumenischen Gespräch*. Göttingen: Vandenhoeck & Ruprecht, 1997.

Forde, Gerhard O. "Forensic Justification and the Law in Lutheran Theology." Pages 278–303 in *Justification by Faith: Lutherans and Catholics in Dialogue VII*. Edited by H. George Anderson, T. Austin Murphy, and Joseph A. Burgess. Minneapolis: Augsburg, 1985.

"A Formula of Agreement: A Theological Assessment." *Concordia Theological Quarterly* 62 (April 1998): 83–124.

Forsberg, Juhani. "Abraham als Paradigma der Mission in der Theologie Luthers." Pages 113–20 in *Lutherische Beiträge zur Missio Dei*. Erlangen: Martin Luther Verlag, 1982.

Foster, John. *After the Apostles: Missionary Preaching of the First Three Centuries*. London: SCM, 1951.

Franzmann, Martin. "Reconciliation and Justification." *Concordia Theological Monthly* 21 (February 1950): 81–93.

Freytag, Walter. "Das Dämonische in den Religionen." Pages 13–21 in vol. 2 of *Reden und Aufsätze*. Edited by Jan Hermelink and Hans Jochen Margull. Munich: Chr. Kaiser, 1961.

———. *The Gospel and the Religions*. Translated by B. S. Cozens. London: SCM, 1957.

———. "Mission im Blick aufs Ende." Pages 186–98 in vol. 2 of *Reden und Aufsätze*. Edited by Jan Hermelink and Hans Jochen Margull. Munich: Chr. Kaiser, 1961.

———. *Reden und Aufsätze*. Edited by Jan Hermelink and Hans Jochen Margull. Munich: Chr. Kaiser, 1961–.

———. "Sendung und Verheißung." Pages 217–23 in vol. 1 of *Reden und Aufsätze*. Edited by Jan Hermelink and Hans Jochen Margull. Munich: Chr. Kaiser, 1976.

———. *Spiritual Revolution in the East*. Translated by L. M. Stalker. London: Lutterworth, 1940.

———. "Das Ziel der Missionsarbeit." Pages 82–186 in vol. 2 of *Reden und Aufsätze*. Edited by Jan Hermelink and Hans Jochen Margull. Munich: Chr. Kaiser, 1961.

———. "Wie Heiden Christen werden." Pages 161–70 in vol. 1 of *Reden und Aufsätze*. Edited by Jan Hermelink and Hans Jochen Margull. Munich: Chr. Kaiser, 1961.

———. "Zur Psychologie der Bekehrung bei Primitiven." Pages 170–93 in vol. 1 of *Reden und Aufsätze*. Edited by Jan Hermelink and Hans Jochen Margull. Munich: Chr. Kaiser, 1961.

Fritz, John. *Pastoral Theology: A Handbook of Scriptural Principles*. St. Louis: Concordia, 1932.

Fung, Raymond, ed. *Evangelistically Yours: Ecumenical Letters on Contemporary Evangelism*. Geneva: WCC Publications, 1992.

Gäbler, Paul. "Der eschatologische Neuansatz in der Mission." Pages 41–47 in *Das Wort und die Völker der Erde: Beiträge zum lutherischen Verständnis der Mission*. Edited by Ernst Strasser. Uelzen: Niedersächsische Buchdruckerei, 1951.

García, Alberto L., and A. R. Victor Raj, eds. *The Theology of the Cross for the 21st Century*. St. Louis: Concordia, 2002.

Gensichen, Hans-Werner. "Ambassadors of Reconciliation." *Lutheran World* 20 (1973): 236–44.

———. *Glaube für die Welt: Theologische Aspekte der Mission*. Gütersloh: Gütersloher Verlagshaus Gerd Mohn, 1971.

———. *Living Mission: The Test of Faith*. Philadelphia: Fortress, 1966.

———. "Mission und Luthertum." Pages 546–48 in vol. 4 of *Die Religion in Geschichte und Gegenwart*. 3d ed. Edited by Kurt Galling. Tübingen: J. C. B. Mohr (Paul Siebeck), 1960.

———. "Die Taufe in der Mission." Pages 27–30 in *Das Wort und die Völker der Erde: Beiträge zum lutherischen Verständnis der Mission*. Edited by Ernst Strasser. Uelzen: Niedersächsische Buchdruckerei, 1951.

———. *Das Taufproblem in der Mission*. Gütersloh: C. Bertelsmann, 1951.

———. "Were the Reformers Indifferent to Missions?" Pages 119–27 in *History's Lessons for Tomorrow's Mission: Milestones in the History of Missionary Thinking*. Geneva: World's Student Christian Federation, 1960.

George, Carl F. *Prepare Your Church for the Future*. Grand Rapids: Fleming H. Revell, 1992.

Gerhard, Johann. *Loci Theologici*. Volume 2. Edited by Ed. Preuss. Berlin, 1864.

Gibbs, Eddie, and Ryan K. Bolger. *Emerging Churches*. Grand Rapids: Baker Academic, 2005.

Goppelt, Leonhard. "The Lordship of Christ and the World according to the New Testament." *Lutheran World* 14 (1967): 15–39.

Grane, Leif. *The Augsburg Confession: A Commentary.* Translated by John H. Rasmussen. Minneapolis: Augsburg, 1987.

Green, Lowell C. "Welchen Luther meinen wir?" *Lutherische Theologie und Kirche* 15 (1991): 2–19.

Greene, Colin J. D. *Christology in Cultural Perspective: Marking Out the Horizons.* Grand Rapids: Eerdmans, 2003.

Grenz, Stanley. *A Primer on Postmodernism.* Grand Rapids: Eerdmans, 1996.

Größel, Wolfgang. *Die Mission und die evangelische Kirche im 17. Jahrhundert.* Gotha: Friedrich Andreas Perthes, 1997.

Grotius, Hugo. *The Truth of the Christian Religion.* Translated by John Clarke. Kessinger, 2004.

Guder, Darell L. *The Incarnation and the Church's Witness.* Harrisburg, PA: Trinity Press, 1999.

————, ed. *Missional Church: A Vision for the Sending of the Church in North America.* Grand Rapids: Eerdmans, 1998.

Günther, Wolfgang. "Gott selbst treibt Mission: Das Modell der 'Missio Dei.'" Page 57 in *Plädoyer für Mission: Beiträge zum Verständnis von Mission heute.* Edited by Klaus Schäfer on behalf of the Theological Commission of the Evangelischen Missionswerkes in Deutschland (EMW). Hamburg: EMW, 1999.

————. *Von Edinburgh nach Mexico City: Die ekklesiologischen Bemühungen der Weltmissionskonferenzen (1910–1963).* Stuttgart: Evangelischer Missionsverlag, 1970.

"Guidelines for Evangelical-Lutheran Christians Living Together with Muslims in Germany." Independent Evangelical-Lutheran Church (SELK), 2002.

Hägglund, Bengt. *History of Theology.* Translated by Gene Lund. St. Louis: Concordia, 1968.

Hammann, Henry P. "The Translation of Ephesians 4:12—A Necessary Revision." *Concordia Journal* 14.1 (January 1988): 42–49.

Harrison, Milmon. *Righteous Riches: The Word of Faith Movement in Contemporary African American World.* Oxford: Oxford University Press, 2005.

Hartenstein, Karl. "Theologische Besinnung." Pages 51–72 in *Mission zwischen Gestern und Morgen: Vom Gestaltwandel der Weltmission der Christenheit im Licht der Konferenz des Internationalen Missionsrats in Willingen.* Edited by Walter Freytag. Stuttgart: Evang. Missionsverlag, 1952.

Hauerwas, Stanley, and William H. Willimon. *Resident Aliens: Life in the Christian Colony.* Nashville: Abingdon, 1989.

Heerboth, Paul. "Missouri Synod Approach to Mission in the Early Period." *Missio Apostolica* 1.1 (May 1993): 26.

Hendrix, Scott. *Luther and the Papacy: Stages in a Reformation Conflict.* Philadelphia: Fortress, 1981.

Heß, Willy. *Das Missionsdenken bei Philipp Nicolai.* Hamburg: Friedrich Wittig, 1962.

Hesselgrave, David J. *Communicating Christ Cross-Culturally*. Grand Rapids: Zondervan, 1978.

———. *Today's Choices for Tomorrow's Mission: An Evangelical Perspective on Trends and Issues*. Grand Rapids: Academie, 1988.

Heubach, Joachim. *Die Ordination zum Amt der Kirche*. Berlin: Lutherisches Verlagshaus, 1956.

Hick, John, and Paul F. Knitter, eds. *The Myth of Christian Uniqueness: Toward a Pluralistic Theology of Religions*. Maryknoll, NY: Orbis, 1987.

"Hilfe zur Unterscheidung von Geistesströmungen in Kirche und Welt: Das neue Fragen nach dem Heligen Geist. Biblische Orientierungshilfe." *Diakrisis* 1.14 (February 1993): 37–38.

Hoefer, Herbert. *Churchless Christianity*. Pasadena, CA: William Carey Library, 2001. Originally published 1991.

Hoekendijk, Johannes Christiaan. *The Church Inside Out*. Translated by Isaac C. Rottenberg. Edited by L. A. Hoedemaker and Pieter Tijmes. Philadelphia: Westminster Press, 1964.

———. *Die Zukunft der Kirche und die Kirche der Zukunft*. 2d ed. Stuttgart: Kreuz, 1965.

Hoffmann, Gerhard. "Gedanken zum Problem der Integration von Kirche und Mission in Deutschland." *Evangelische Missionszeitschrift* 25 (October 1968): 200–214.

Hogg, William Richey. "The Rise of Protestant Missionary Concern." Pages 95–111 in *The Theology of the Christian Mission*. Edited by Gerald Anderson. Nashville: Abingdon, 1961.

———. "The Teaching of Missiology: Some Reflections on the Historical and Current Scene." *Missiology: An International Review* 4 (October 1987): 487–506.

Holl, Karl. "Luther und die Mission." Pages 234–43 in vol. 3 of *Gesammelte Aufsätze zur Kirchengeschichte: Der Westen*. Tübingen: J. C. B. Mohr, 1928.

Holsten, Walter. "Die Bedeutung der altprotestantischen Dogmatik für die Mission." In *Das Evangelium und die Völker: Beiträge zur Geschichte und Theorie der Mission*. Berlin: Buchhandlung der Gosnerischen Mission, 1939.

———. *Das Kerygma und der Mensch: Einführung in die Religions- und Missionswissenschaft*. Munich: Christian Kaiser, 1953.

———. "Die lutherische Kirche als Träger der Sendung." Pages 12–17 in *Das Wort und die Völker der Erde. Beiträge zum lutherischen Verständnis der Mission*. Edited by Ernst Strasser. Uelzen: Niedersächsische Buchdruckerei, 1951.

———."Reformation und Mission." Pages 1–32 in *Archiv für Reformationsgeschichte* 44. Edited by Gerhard Ritter. Gütersloh: C. Bertelsmann, 1953.

Hopf, Friedrich Wilhelm. "Lutherische Kirche treibt Lutherische Mission." Pages 13–47 in *Lutherische Kirche treibt Lutherische Mission: Festschrift zum 75 jährigen Jubiläum der Bleckmarer Mission*. Edited by Friedrich Wilhelm Hopf. Bleckmar: Mission Evangelisch-Lutherischer Freikirchen, 1967.

———. "Zur Begründung unserer Hospitalarbeit." Pages 143–49 in *Lutherische Kirche treibt Lutherische Mission: Festschrift zum 75 jährigen Jubiläum der Bleckmarer Mission.* Edited by Friedrich Wilhelm Hopf. Bleckmar: Mission Evangelisch-Lutherischer Freikirchen, 1967.

Huff, Livingstone M. "The Crusades and Colonial Imperialism: Some Historical Considerations Concerning Christian-Muslim Interaction and Dialogue." *Missiology: An International Review* 22.2 (April 2004): 141–48.

Hunter, George III. *Radical Outreach: Recovering Apostolic Ministry and Evangelism.* Nashville: Abingdon, 2003.

Hunter, Kent R. *Foundations for Church Growth.* New Haven, MO: Leader Publishing Co., 1983.

Isichei, Elizabeth. *A History of Christianity in Africa.* Grand Rapids: Eerdmans, 1995.

Iwand, Hans Joachim. *The Righteousness of Faith According to Luther.* Translated by Randi H Lundell. Edited by Virgil F. Thompson. Eugene, OR: Wipf & Stock, 2008.

Jaeschke, Ernst. *Bruno Gutmann: His Life, His Thoughts and His Work.* Erlangen: Verlag der Ev.-Luth. Mission, 1985.

Jenkins, Philip. *The Next Christendom: The Coming of Global Christianity.* Oxford: Oxford University Press, 2002.

Ji, Won Jong. "Evangelization and Humanization." *Concordia Theological Monthly* 42 (March 1971): 163–72.

———. "To Be Lutheran: Lutheran Identity and Task in Light of the Doctrine of Justification and the Responsibility for the World." *Concordia Journal* 18 (October 1992): 315–38.

Joest, Wilfried. "Amt und Ordination—unüberholbare Strukturen?" *Kerygma und Dogma* 17 (1971): 75–85.

———. *Dogmatik.* Vol. 1: *Die Wirklichkeit Gottes.* 2d ed. Göttingen: Vandenhoeck & Ruprecht, 1987.

———. "Karl Barth und das lutherische Verständnis von Gesetz und Evanglium." *Kerygma und Dogma* 24 (1978): 86–103.

———. "Die Rechtfertigungslehre Luthers in ihrer Bedeutung für den modernen Menschen." Pages 41–55 in *Reformation heute: Bibelarbeit und Referate der internationalen Theologentagung des Lutherischen Weltbundes vom 29. 5. bis 2. 6. 1967 in Berlin.* Edited by Heinrich Foerster. Berlin: Lutherisches Verlagshaus, 1967.

Johnson, John F. "Justification according to the Apology of the Augsburg Confession and the Formula of Concord." Pages 185–99 in *Justification by Faith: Lutherans and Catholics in Dialogue VII.* Edited by H. George Anderson, T. Austin Murphy, and Joseph A. Burgess. Minneapolis: Augsburg, 1985.

"Joint Lutheran/Roman Catholic Declaration on Justification: A Response." *Concordia Theological Quarterly* 62 (April 1998): 83–124.

Jongeneel, Jan A. B. "The Missiology of Gisbertus Voetius: The First Comprehensive Protestant Theology of Missions." *Calvin Theological Journal* 26 (1991): 47–79.

———. *Philosophy, Science, and Theology of Mission in the 19th and 20th Centuries.* 2 vols. Frankfurt am Main: Peter Lang, 1995–2002.

Kähler, Martin. "Evangelisation der Welt—Gottes Wille." Page 101 in *Schriften zu Christologie und Mission*. Munich: Chr. Kaiser, 1971.

———. *Schriften zu Christologie und Mission: Gesamtausgabe der Schriften zur Mission*. Edited by Heinzgünter Frohnes. Munich: Chr. Kaiser, 1971.

Kandler, Karl-Hermann. "CA VII—Konzentration und Weite lutherischer Ekklesiologie." *Kerygma und Dogma* 35 (February 1989): 70–83.

———. "Kirche als Exodusgemeinde." *Kerygma und Dogma* 17 (1971): 244–57.

———. *Die missionarische Dimension der Gemeinde*. Berlin: Lutherisches Verlagshaus, 1963.

Kane, J. Herbert. *Christian Missions in Biblical Perspective*. Grand Rapids: Baker, 1976.

———. *A Concise History of the Christian World Mission: A Panoramic View of Missions from Pentecost to the Present*. Grand Rapids: Baker, 1978.

———. "The Work of Evangelism." Pages 564–68 in *Perspectives on the World Christian Movement: A Reader*. Edited by Ralph. D. Winter and Steven C. Hawthorne. Pasadena, CA: William Carey Library, 1981.

Keegan, Terence J. *Interpreting the Bible: A Popular Introduction to Biblical Hermeneutics*. New York: Paulist Press, 1985.

Keysser, Christian. *A People Reborn*. Translated by Alfred Allin and John Kuder. Pasadena, CA: William Carey Library, 1980.

Kimme, August. "Die Kirche und ihre Sendung." Pages 91–104 in *Lutherische Beiträge zur Missio Dei*. Erlangen: Martin Luther Verlag, 1982.

Kinder, Ernst. *Der evangelische Glaube und die Kirche: Grundzüge des evangelisch-lutherischen Kirchenverständnisses*. Berlin: Lutherisches Verlagshaus, 1960.

Kirk, J. Andrew. *What Is Mission? Theological Explorations*. Minneapolis: Fortress, 2000.

Kirsten, Hans, and Ida Näther. *Unsere lutherische Mission in Indien*. Gr. Oesingen: Verlag der Lutherischen Buchhandlung, 1984.

Klootwijk, Eeuwout. "Christian Approaches to Religious Pluralism: Diverging Models and Patterns." *Missiology: An International Review* 21 (October 1993): 455–68.

Knitter, Paul. *No Other Name? A Critical Survey of Christian Attitudes toward the World Religions*. Maryknoll, NY: Orbis, 1985.

———. *Towards a Protestant Theology of Religions*. Marburg: N. G. Elwert, 1974.

Köberle, Adolf. *Universalismus der Christlichen Botschaft: Gesammelte Aufsätze und Vorträge*. Darmstadt: Wissentschaftliche Buchgesellschaft, 1978.

Köstenberger, Andreas J., and Peter T. O'Brien. *Salvation to the Ends of the Earth: A Biblical Theology of Mission*. Downers Grove, IL: InterVarsity, 2001.

Koester, Robert John. *Law and Gospel: The Foundation of Lutheran Ministry with Reference to the Church Growth Movement*. Ann Arbor, MI: UMI Dissertation Services, 1989.

Kolb, Erwin J. "The Primary Mission of the Church and Its Detractors." *Concordia Theological Quarterly* 54.2–3 (April-July 1990): 117–29.

Kolb, Robert. "Contemporary Lutheran Understandings of the Doctrine of Justification: A Selective Glimpse." Pages 153–76 in *Justification: What's at Stake in the Current Debates*. Edited by Mark A. Husbands and Daniel J. Treier. Downers Grove, IL: InterVarsity, 2004.

———. "Luther's Smalcald Articles: Agenda for Testimony and Confession." *Concordia Journal* 14 (April 1988): 115–37.

———. *Speaking the Gospel Today*. Rev. ed. St. Louis: Concordia, 1995.

———, and Timothy J. Wengert, eds. *The Book of Concord: The Confessions of the Evangelical Lutheran Church*. Minneapolis: Fortress, 2000.

Koschade, Alfred. "Luther on Missionary Motivation." *Lutheran Quarterly* 17 (1965): 224–39.

Kraemer, Hendrik. *The Christian Message in a Non-Christian World*. London, 1938.

Kraft, Charles H. *Christianity in Culture: A Study in Dynamic Biblical Theologizing in Cross-Cultural Perspective*. Maryknoll, NY: Orbis, 1979.

———. *Communicating the Gospel God's Way*. Pasadena, CA: William Carey Library, 1979.

Kreider, Alan. "Beyond Bosch: The Early Church and the Christendom Shift." *International Bulletin of Missionary Research* 29.2 (April 2005): 59–68.

Kretzmann, Martin L. "Crosscurrents in Mission." *Lutheran World* 16 (1969): 354–57.

Krige, Eileen Jensen. *The Social System of the Zulus*. Pietermaritzburg: Shuter & Shooter, 1981.

Krispin, Gerald S. "Baptism and *Heilsgewißheit* in Luther's Theology." *Concordia Journal* 13 (April 1987): 106–18.

Krusche, Werner. "Die Kirche für andere: Der Ertrag der ökumenischen Diskussion über die Frage nach Strukturen missionarischer Gemeinden." Pages 133–75 in *Schritte und Markierungen: Aufsätze und Vorträge zum Weg der Kirche*. Göttingen: Vandenhoeck & Ruprecht, 1971.

———. "Das Missionarische als Strukturprinzip." Pages 109–24 in *Schritte und Markierungen: Aufsätze und Vorträge zum Weg der Kirche*. Göttingen: Vandenhoeck & Ruprecht, 1971.

Kuriakose, M. K. *History of Christianity in India: Source Materials*. Delhi: ISPCK, 1982. Reprinted in 1999.

Kurz, Alfred. *Die Heilsgewißheit bei Luther*. Gütersloh: C. Bertelsmann, 1933.

Kvist, Hans-Olaf. "Der Heilige Geist in den Bekenntnisschriften der evangelisch-lutherischen Kirche." *Kerygma und Dogma* 31 (1985): 201–11.

Laiser, Naaman. "The Authority of Scripture Provides the Basis for the Integrity of Justification." Pages 59–66 in *Rechtfertigung und Weltverantwortung*. Internationale Konsultation euendettelsau 1991. Edited by Wolfhart Schlichting. Neuendettelsau: Freimund, 1993.

Laman, Gordon D. "The Origin of Protestant Missions." *Reformed Review* 43 (Autumn 1989): 728–74.

Latourette, Kenneth Scott. *A History of the Expansion of Christianity*. Vol. 3. New York: Harper, 1939.

Lazareth, William H. *Two Forms of Ordained Ministry.* Minneapolis: Augsburg Fortress, 1991.

Leipold, Heinrich. "Anknüpfung I." Pages 743–47 in vol. 2 of *Theologische Realenzyklopädie.* Edited by Gerhard Krause and Gerhard Müller. Berlin: de Gruyter, 1978.

Lessing, R. Reed. *Jonah.* Concordia Commentary Series. St. Louis: Concordia, 2007.

Lieberg, Hellmut. *Amt und Ordination bei Luther und Melanchton.* Göttingen: Vandenhoeck & Ruprecht, 1962.

Lienemann-Perrin, Christine. "Theological Education." Pages 426–29 in *Dictionary of Mission: Theology, History, Perspectives.* Maryknoll, NY: Orbis, 1997.

Lindberg, Carter. *The Third Reformation: Charismatic Movements and the Lutheran Tradition.* Macon, GA: Mercer University Press, 1983.

Littell, Franklin. "Protestantism and the Great Commission." *Southwestern Journal of Theology* 2 (October 1959): 26–42.

Lochmann, Jan Milic. "The Lordship of Christ in a Secularized World." *Lutheran World* 14 (1967): 59–78.

Löhe, Wilhelm. "Drei Bücher von der Kirche (1845)." Pages 85–179 in vol. 5/1 of *Gesammelte Werke.* Edited by Klaus Ganzert. Neuendettelsau: Freimund, 1954.

———. *Gesammelte Werke.* Neuendettelsau: Freimund, 1954.

———. *Three Books about the Church.* Translated by James L. Schaaf. Philadelphia: Fortress, 1969.

Loewenich, Walther von. "Die Kirche in lutherischer Sicht." Pages 191–209 in *Von Augustin zu Luther: Beiträge zur Kirchengeschichte.* Witten: Luther Verlag, 1959.

———. "Zur Gnadenlehre bei Augustin und bei Luther." Pages 75–86 in *Von Augustin zu Luther: Beiträge zur Kirchengeschichte.* Witten: Luther Verlag, 1959.

Lose, David J. *Confessing Christ: Preaching in a Postmodern World.* Grand Rapids: Eerdmans, 2003.

Lüdemann, Gerd. *Jesus' Resurrection: Fact or Figment? A Debate between William Lane Craig and Gerd Lüdemann.* Edited by Paul Copan and Ronald K. Tacelli. Downers Grove, IL: Intervarsity, 2000.

Luther, Martin. *D. Martin Luthers Werke.* Kritische Gesamtausgabe. Vol. 6. Weimar: Hermann Böhlau, 1888.

———. *D. Martin Luthers Werke.* Kritische Gesamtausgabe. Vol. 10/3. Weimar: Hermann Böhlau, 1905.

———. *D. Martin Luthers Werke.* Kritische Gesamtausgabe. Vol. 43. Weimar: Hermann Böhlau, 1912.

———. *D. Martin Luthers Werke.* Kritische Gesamtausgabe. Briefwechsel. Vol. 6. Weimar: Hof-Buchdruckerei und Verlagsbuchhandlung, 1935.

———. *D. Martin Luthers Werke.* Kritische Gesamtausgabe. Briefwechsel. Vol. 7. Weimar: Hof-Buchdruckerei und Verlagsbuchhandlung, 1937.

———. *Luther's Works.* American Edition. Vol. 30. Edited by Jaroslav Pelikan. St. Louis: Concordia, 1967.

——. *Luther's Works.* American Edition. Vol. 31. Edited by J. J. Pelikan, H. C. Oswald, and H. T. Lehmann. Philadelphia: Fortress, 1957.

——. *Luther's Works.* American Edition. Vol. 36. Edited by J. J. Pelikan, H. C. Oswald, and H. T. Lehmann. Philadelphia: Muehlenberg, 1967.

Lutheran Church—Missouri Synod, The. *Convention Proceedings: 57th Regular Convention, The Lutheran Church—Missouri Synod.* St. Louis: Concordia, 1989.

——. *The Mission Task Force: A Mission Blueprint for the Nineties.* St. Louis: LCMS, 1991.

Lutheran World Federation. *Mission in Context: Transformation, Reconciliation, Empowerment: An LWF Contribution to the Understanding and Practice of Mission.* Geneva: Lutheran World Federation, Department for Mission and Development, 2004.

——. *Together in God's Mission: A LWF Contribution to the Understanding of Mission.* Hanover/Neuendettelsau, 1988.

——. "The 'Two Kingdoms' and the Lordship of Christ: A Working Paper of the Commission on Theology of the LWF." *Lutheran World* 14 (1967): 79–88.

Mahlmann, Theodor. "Zur Geschichte der Formel 'Articulus stantis et cadentis ecclesiae.'" *Lutherische Theologie und Kirche* 17 (November 1993): 187–99.

Manecke, Dieter. *Mission als Zeugendienst: Karl Barths theologische Begründung der Mission.* Wuppertal: Rolf Brockhaus, 1972.

Mannermaa, Tuomo. "In ipsa fide Christus adest: Der Schnittpunkt zwischen lutherischer und orthodoxer Theologie." Pages 11–93 in *Der in Glauben gegenwärtige Christus: Rechtfertigung und Vergottung, Zum ökumenischen Dialog.* Arbeiten zur Geschichte und Theologie des Luthertums, n.s. 8. Hanover: Lutherisches Verlagshaus, 1989.

——. "Why Is Luther So Fascinating? Modern Finnish Luther Research." Pages 1–20 in *Union with Christ: The New Finnish Interpretation of Luther.* Edited by Carl E. Braaten and Robert Jenson. Grand Rapids: Eerdmans, 1998.

Manns, Peter. "Amt und Eucharistie in der Theologie Martin Luthers." Page 68–173 in *Amt und Eucharistie.* Edited by Peter Bläser. Paderborn: Bonifacius-Druckerei, 1973.

Margull, Hans Jochen. "The Awakening of Protestant Missions." Pages 137–48 in *History's Lessons for Tomorrow's Mission: Milestones in the History of Missionary Thinking.* Geneva, Switzerland: World's Student Federation, 1964.

——. *Hope in Action: The Church's Task in the World.* Philadelphia: Muhlenburg, 1962.

Marquart, Kurt E. *The Church and Her Fellowship, Ministry, and Governance.* Confessional Lutheran Dogmatics 9. Edited by Robert Preus. Fort Wayne, IN: International Foundation for Lutheran Confessional Research, 1990.

——, trans. *Justification—Objective and Subjective: A Translation.* Fort Wayne, IN: Concordia Theological Seminary Press, 1982.

Martens, Gottfried. "Glaubensgewißheit oder Daseinsgewißheit?" Pages 171–79 in *Rechtfertigung und Weltverantwortung.* Internationale Konsultation Neuendettelsau 1991. Edited by Wolfhart Schlichting. Neuendettelsau: Freimund, 1993.

————. *Die Rechtfertigung des Sünders—Rettungshandeln Gottes oder historisches Interpretament?* Göttingen: Vandenhoeck & Ruprecht, 1992.

Mattes, Mark C. "A Future for Lutheran Theology?" *Lutheran Quarterly* 19.4 (Winter 2005): 439–57.

————. *The Role of Justification in Contemporary Theology.* Grand Rapids: Eerdmans, 2004.

Maurer, Wilhelm. *Historical Commentary on the Augsburg Confession.* Translated by H. George Anderson. Philadelphia: Fortress, 1986.

————. *Historischer Kommentar zur Confessio Augustana.* 2 vols. Gütersloh: G. Mohn, 1976–78.

————. "Der lutherische Beitrag zur Weltmission der Kirche Jesu Christi." *Evangelische Missionszeitschrift* (August 1969): 170–87.

————. "Die Lutherische Kirche und ihre Mission." Pages 183–205 in vol. 2 of *Kirche und Geschichte: Gesammelte Aufsätze.* Edited by Ernst-Wilhelm Kohls and Gerhard Müller. Göttingen: Vandenhoeck & Ruprecht, 1970.

————. "Reformation und Mission." Pages 20–41 in *Ihr werdet meine Zeugen sein: Festschrift Georg F. Vicedom zum 60. Geburtstag.* Edited by Walther Ruf. Nürnberg: Bayerischen Missionskonferenz, 1963.

Maurier, Henry. "The Christian Theology of the Non-Christian Religions." *Lumen Vitae* 31 (1976): 59–74.

McDonnell, Kilian. "The Unique Mediator in a Unique Church: A Return to Pre-Vatican II Theology?" *The Ecumenical Review* 52.4 (October 2000): 542–49.

McGavran, Donald A. "A Church in Every People: Plain Talk about a Difficult Subject." Pages 622-28 in *Perspectives on the World Christian Movement: A Reader.* Edited by Ralph. D. Winter and Steven C. Hawthorne. Pasadena, CA: William Carey Library, 1981.

————. *Understanding Church Growth.* Revised and edited by C. Peter Wagner. 3d ed. Grand Rapids, Eerdmans, 1990.

————, and Win Arn. *How to Grow a Church: Conversations about Church Growth.* Ventura, CA: Regal Books, 1973.

McGowan, A. T. B. "Justification and the *ordo salutis.*" Pages 147–63 in *Justification in Perspective.* Edited by Bruce L. McCormack. Grand Rapids: Baker Academic, 2006.

McGrath, Alister. *Iustitia Dei: A History of the Christian Doctrine of Justification.* 2 vols. Cambridge: Cambridge University Press, 1986.

————. *Justification by Faith: What It Means for Us Today.* Grand Rapids: Academie, 1988.

Medeiros, Elias Dos Santo. *Missiology as an Academic Discipline in Theological Education.* Ann Arbor, MI: UMI Dissertation Services, 1992.

Melanchthon, Philip. *Loci Communes 1543.* Translated by J. A. O. Preus. St. Louis: Concordia, 1992.

Meyer, Carl, ed. *Moving Frontiers.* St. Louis: Concordia, 1964.

Meyer, Heinrich. *Bekenntnisbindung und Bekenntnisbildung in jungen Kirchen.* Gütersloh: C. Bertelsmann, 1953.

Meyer, Johannes. *Historischer Kommentar zu Luthers Kleinem Katechismus.* Gütersloh: C. Bertelsmann, 1929.

Meyer-Roscher, Walter. "Die Bedeutung der lutherischen Bekenntnisschriften für die gegenwärtige ökumenische Diskussion." Pagse 19–34 in *Lutherisches Missionsjahrbuch für das Jahr 1966.* Edited by Walter Ruf. Nürnberg: Bayerischen Missionskonferenz, 1966.

Mildenberger, Friedrich. *Theologie der lutherischen Bekenntnisschriften.* Stuttgart: W. Kohlhammer, 1983.

Miller, Roland. *Muslims and the Gospel: Bridging the Gap.* Minneapolis: Lutheran University Press, 2005.

Mission Blueprint for the Nineties. Summary, Mission Task Force. St. Louis: The Lutheran Church—Missouri Synod, 1991.

"The Missionary Calling of the Church." A statement by the Willingen Conference of the International Missionary Council, held July 5–17, 1952, in Willingen, Germany. *International Review of Mission* 41 (1952): 562.

Molland, Einar. "Besaß die Alte Kirche ein Missionsprogramm und bewußte Missionsmethoden?" Pages 51–67 in *Die Alte Kirche*, vol. 1 of *Kirchengeschichte als Missionsgeschichte.* Munich: Chr. Kaiser, 1974.

Moltmann, Jürgen. *The Crucified God: The Cross of Christ as the Foundation and Criticism of Christian Theology.* Translated by R. A.Wilson and John Bowden. New York: Harper & Row, 1974.

Moorman, Donald. *Harvest Waiting.* St. Louis: Concordia, 1993.

Moreau, A. Scott, gen. ed. *Evangelical Dictionary of World Missions.* Grand Rapids: Baker, 2000.

Moritzen, Niels-Peter. "Der Missionar: Ein Berufsbild und seine Chancen." Pages 21–31 in *Jahrbuch Mission 1988.* Hamburg: Missionshilfe, 1988.

Mortensen, Viggo, ed. *The Role of Mission in the Future of Lutheran Theology.* Aarhus: Centre for Multireligious Studies, University of Aarhus, 2003.

Mostert, Walter. "Hinweise zu Luthers Lehre vom Heiligen Geist." Pages 15–45 in *Der Heilige Geist im Verständnis Luthers und der lutherischen Theologie.* Edited by Joachim Heubach. Erlangen: Martin Luther Verlag, 1990.

Muck, Terry C. "The Missiological Perspective: Is It Mission or Missions?" *Missiology: An International Review* 32.4 (October 2004): 419–20.

Müller, Gerhard. "Missionarischer Gemeindeaufbau bei Martin Luther." Pages 31–37 in vol. 2 of *Zwischen Reformation und Gegenwart II: Vorträge und Aufsätze.* Hannover: Lutherisches Verlagshaus, 1988.

Mueller, John Theodore. *Christian Dogmatics.* St. Louis: Concordia, 1955.

Müller, Karl. *Mission Theology.* Nettetal: Steyler, 1985.

———. *Mission Theology: An Introduction.* Nettetal: Steyler, 1987.

———, and Theo Sundermeier, et al., eds. *Dictionary of Mission: Theology, History, Perspectives.* Maryknoll, NY: Orbis, 1997.

———, and Theo Sundermeier, eds. *Lexikon Missionstheologischer Grundbegriffe.* Berlin: Dietrich Reimer, 1987.

Mundinger, Carl S. *Government in the Missouri Synod.* St. Louis: Concordia, 1947.

330 MISSION FROM THE CROSS

Myklebust, Olaf Guttorm. *The Study of Missions in Theological Education.* 2 vols. Oslo: Forlaget Land Og Kirke, 1955–57.

Nagel, Norman. "The Office of the Holy Ministry in the Confessions." *Concordia Journal* 14 (July 1988): 283–99.

Narum, William. "Preaching of Justification: A Self-Examination of the Church." *Lutheran World* 6 (1960): 369–87.

Needam, Nick. "Justification in the Early Church Fathers." Pages 25–53 in *Justification in Perspective.* Edited by Bruce L. McCormack. Grand Rapids: Baker Academic, 2006.

Neill, Stephen. *A History of Christian Missions.* London: Harmondsworth, 1986.

———. *The Unfinished Task.* 6th ed. London: Edinburgh House & Lutherworth, 1957.

Neitzel, Leonardo. *Mission Outreach and Households in the City of Fortaleza, Northeast Brazil.* Dissertation. Concordia Theological Seminary. May 2000.

Neuner, J., and J. Dupuis, eds. *The Christian Faith in the Doctrinal Documents of the Catholic Church.* Westminster: Christian Classics, 1975.

Newbigin, Lesslie. *Foolishness to the Greeks: The Gospel and Western Culture.* Grand Rapids: Eerdmans, 1986.

———. *The Gospel in a Pluralist Society.* Grand Rapids: Eerdmans, 1989.

———. "The Logic of Mission." In *New Directions in Mission and Evangelization II: Theological Foundations.* Edited by James Scherer and Stephen B. Bevans. Maryknoll, NY: Orbis, 1994.

———. *Trinitarian Faith and Today's Mission.* Richmond, VA: John Knox, 1963.

Nida, Eugene. *Message and Mission: The Communication of the Christian Faith.* New York: Harper, 1960.

Niebuhr, H. Richard. *Christ and Culture.* London: Harper & Row, 1952.

Nordling, John G. "Large Catechism III, 66, Latin Version." *Concordia Journal* 29.3 (2003): 235–39.

Nürnberger, Klaus. "Thesen zum Stellenwert der Rechtfertigungslehre im Kontext biblischer Soteriologien." Pages 67–86 in *Rechtfertigung und Weltverantwortung.* Internationale Konsultation Neuendettelsau 1991. Edited by Wolfhart Schlichting. Neuendettelsau: Freimund, 1993.

———. "Wider die Verengung der Rechtfertigungslehre." Pages 141–71 in *Jahrbuch Mission 1993.* Edited by Verband evangelischer Missionskonferenzen. Hamburg: Missionshilfe, 1993.

Núñez, Emilio A. *Liberation Theology.* Translated by Paul E. Sywulka. Chicago: Moody, 1985.

Oden, Thomas C. *The Justification Reader.* Grand Rapids: Eerdmans, 2002.

Öberg, Ingemar. *Luther and World Mission.* Translated by Dean Apel. St. Louis: Concordia, 2007.

———. "Mission und Heilsgeschichte bei Luther und in den Bekenntnisschriften." Pages 25–42 in *Lutherische Beiträge zur Missio Dei.* Erlangen: Martin Luther Verlag, 1982.

Oehler, Wilhelm. *Geschichte der Deutschen Evangelischen Mission*. Vol. 1. Baden-Baden: Wilhelm Fehrholz, 1949.

Ohm, Thomas. *Machet zu Jüngern alle Völker: Theorie der Mission*. Freiburg: Erich Wewel, 1962.

Olson, Jeannine E. *Deacons and Deaconesses Through the Centuries*. St. Louis: Concordia, 2005.

Pannenberg, Wolfhart. *Faith and Reality*. Translated by John Maxwell. London: Search Press; Philadelphia: Westminster Press, 1977.

———. *Jesus: God and Man*. Translated by Lewis L. Wilkins and Duane A. Priebe. Philadelphia: Westminster Press, 1968.

———. *Systematic Theology*. Translated by Geoffrey W. Bromiley. Grand Rapids: Eerdmans, 1994.

Pelikan, Jaroslav. *The Riddle of Roman Catholicism*. London: Hodder & Stoughton, 1960.

Peters, Albrecht. *Kommentar zu Luthers Katechismen*. Vols. 1–2. Göttingen: Vandenhoeck & Ruprecht, 1991.

———. "Die Vaterunser-Auslegung in Luthers Katechismen (III)." *Lutherische Theologie und Kirche* 3 (1980): 66–82.

Peters, Paul. "Luthers weltweiter Missionssinn." *Lutherischer Rundblick* 17 (1969): 162–75.

Pieper, Francis. *Christian Dogmatics*. Vol. 1. St. Louis: Concordia, 1950.

Plitt, Gustav Leopold. *Geschichte der lutherischen Mission nach den Vorträgen des Prof. D. Plitt*. Vol. 1. Edited by Otto Hardeland. 2d ed. Leipzig: A. Deichert'sche, 1894.

Pöhlmann, Horst Georg. *Abriß der Dogmatik: Ein Kompendium*. Gütersloh: Gütersloher Verlagshaus Gerd Mohn, 1975.

———. "Die Apologie als authentischer Kommentar der Confessio Augustana." *Kerygma und Dogma* 26 (July/September 1980): 164–73.

———. "Der Mensch und die Technik." Pages 81–93 in *Anthropologie und Christologie*. Veröffentlichungen der Luther-Akademie e.V. Ratzeburg 15. Edited by Joachim Heubach. Erlangen: Martin Luther Verlag, 1990.

———. "Das Problem der Ur-Offenbarung bei Paul Althaus." *Kerygma und Dogma* 16 (1970): 242–58.

Pragman, James H. *Traditions of Ministry*. St. Louis: Concordia, 1983.

Prenter, Regin. *Spiritus Creator*. Translated by John M. Jensen. Philadelphia: Muhlenberg, 1953.

Preus, Robert D. "Confessional Subscription." Pages 43–52 in *Evangelical Directions for the Lutheran Church*. Edited by Erich Kiehl and Waldo Werning. Chicago: Lutheran Congress, 1970.

———. "The Confessions and the Mission of the Church." *The Springfielder* 39 (June 1975): 20–39.

———. "The Doctrine of the Call in the Confessions and Lutheran Orthodoxy." *Luther Academy* 1 (April 1991).

———. *The Doctrine of the Call in the Confessions and Lutheran Orthodoxy.* Fort Wayne, IN: Luther Academy, 1991.

Priest, Robert, Terry Dischinger, Steve Rasmussen, and C. M. Brown."Researching the Short-Term Mission Movement." *Missiology* 34.4 (October 2006): 431–50.

Rad, Gerhard von. *Old Testament Theology.* Vol. 1. Translated by D. M. G. Stalker. New York: Harper & Row, 1962.

Rahner, Karl. "Grundprinzipien zur heutigen Mission der Kirche." Pages 46–80 in vol. 2/2 of *Handbuch der Pastoraltheologie: Praktische Theologie der Kirche in ihrer Gegenwart.* Edited by Franz Xaver Arnold. Freiburg: Herder, 1966.

———, and Herbert Vorgrimmler, eds. *Kleines Konzils-Kompendium.* Freiburg: Herder, 1966.

Rambach, Johann J. *Christliche Sitten-Lehre.* Leipzig: Schopp, 1738.

Ratke, David. *Confession and Mission, Word and Sacrament: The Ecclesial Theology of Wilhelm Loehe.* St. Louis: Concordia, 2001.

Raupp, Werner, ed. *Mission in Quellentexten.* Erlangen: Verlag der Evang. -Luther. Mission and Bad Liebenzell: Verlag der Liebenzeller Mission, 1990.

Recker, R. "The Concept of the Missio Dei." *Calvin Theological Journal* 11 (November 1976): 194.

Rengstorf, Karl Heinrich. *Apostleship.* Translated by J. R Coates. London: A&C Black, 1952.

Richardson, Don. *Eternity in Their Hearts.* Ventura, CA: Regal Books, 1984.

———. *Peace Child.* Glendale, CA: Regal Books, 1976.

Rittner, Reinhard, ed. *Was heißt hier lutherisch! Aktuelle Perspektiven aus Theologie und Kirche.* Hannover: Lutherisches Verlagshaus, 2004.

Roensch, Manfred, and Werner Klän. *Quellen zur Entstehung und Entwicklung selbständiger evangelisch-lutherischer Kirchen in Deutschland.* Frankfurt am Main: Peter Lang, 1987.

Rosenkranz, Gerhard. *Der christliche Glaube angesichts der Weltreligionen.* Munich: Francke, 1967.

———. *Die christliche Mission: Geschichte und Theologie.* Munich: Chr. Kaiser, 1977.

———. *Weltmission und Weltende.* Gütersloh: C. Bertelsmann, 1951.

Rosin, H. H. *Missio Dei: An Examination of the Origin, Contents and Function of the Term in Protestant Missiological Discussion.* Leiden: Inter-university Institute for Missiological and Ecumenical Research, 1972.

Roy, H. *Zinzendorfs Anweisungen für die Missionsarbeit.* Gütersloh: C. Bertelsmann, 1893.

Ruler, Arnold van. *Calvinist Trinitarianism and Theocentric Politics.* Translated by John bolt. Lewiston: Mellen, 1989.

Rzepkowski, Horst. "Creation Theology and Missiology." Page 90 in *Dictionary of Mission: Theology, History, Perspectives.* Maryknoll, NY: Orbis, 1997.

Saayman, Willem. "If You Were to Die Today, Do You Know for Certain That You Would Go to Heaven? Reflections on Conversion as Primary Aim of Mission." *Missionalia* 20.3 (November 1992): 159–73.

Samartha, Stanley J. *One Christ—Many Religions: Toward a Revised Christology.* Maryknoll, NY: Orbis, 1991.

Sanders, John. *No Other Name: An Investigation into the Destiny of the Unevangelized.* Grand Rapids: Eerdmans, 1992.

Sanders, Van. "The Mission of God and the Local Church." In *Pursuing the Mission of God in Church Planting.* Edited by John M. Bailey. Alpharetta, GA: North American Mission Board, 2006.

Sanneh, Lamin. *Translating the Message.* Maryknoll, NY: Orbis, 1989.

Sasse, Hermann. "Article VII of the Augsburg Confession in the Present Crisis of Lutheranism." Page 40–68 in *We Confess: The Church.* Translated by Norman Nagel. St. Louis: Concordia, 1986.

———. *"Ecclesia Orans."* Briefe an lutherische Pastoren n.5 (1949).

———. "Die Frage nach der Einheit der Kirche auf dem Missionsfeld." Pages 216–27 in vol. 2 of *In Statu Confessionis: Gesammelte Aufsätze und Kleine Schriften von Hermann Sasse.* Edited by Friedrich Wilhelm Hopf. Berlin: Die Spur GMBH & Co. Christliche Buchhandels KG, 1976.

———. "Heil außerhalb der Kirche?" Pages 315–27 in vol. 2 of *In Statu Confessionis: Gesammelte Aufsätze und Kleine Schriften von Hermann Sasse.* Edited by Friedrich Wilhelm Hopf. Berlin: Die Spur GMBH & Co. Christliche Buchhandels KG, 1976.

———. "Über die Einheit der Lutherischen Kirche." Pages 244–58 in vol. 1 of *In Statu Confessionis: Gesammelte Aufsätze und Kleine Schriften von Hermann Sasse.* Edited by Friedrich Wilhelm Hopf. Berlin: Die Spur GMBH & Co. Christliche Buchhandels KG, 1976.

Scaer, David P. "Augustana V and the Doctrine of the Ministry." *Lutheran Quarterly* 6 (1992): 403–23.

Schaibley, Robert W. "Lutheran Preaching: Proclamation, Not Communication." *Concordia Journal* 18 (January 1962): 6–27.

Schattauer, Thomas H., ed. *Inside Out: Worship in an Age of Mission.* Minneapolis: Fortress, 1999.

Scherer, James A. *Gospel, Church and Kingdom.* Minneapolis: Augsburg, 1987.

———. *Justinian Welz: Essays by an Early Prophet of Mission.* Grand Rapids: Eerdmans, 1969.

———. *Mission and Unity in Lutheranism: A Study in Confession and Ecumenicity.* Philadelphia: Fortress, 1969.

———. . . . *That the Gospel May Be Sincerely Preached throughout the World: A Lutheran Perspective on Mission and Evangelism in the 20th Century.* LWF Report 11/12. Stuttgart: Kreuz/Erich Breitsohl, 1982.

———. "The Triumph of Confessionalism in Nineteenth-Century German Lutheran Missions." *Mission Apostolica* I.2 (November 1993): 71–81.

———, and Stephen B. Bevans, eds. *New Directions in Mission and Evangelization.* Vol. 1: *Basic Statements 1974–1991.* Maryknoll, NY: Orbis, 1992.

Schlatter, Adolf. "Luther und die Mission." *Evangelisches Missionsmagazin* 61 (1917): 281–88.

Schleiermacher, Friedrich. *The Christian Faith*. Vol. 1. English translation of the 2d German ed. Edited by H. R. Mackintosch and J. S. Stewart. New York: Harper & Row, 1963.

Schlichting, Wolfhart, ed. *Rechtfertigung und Weltverantwortung: Internationale Konsultation Neuendettelsau 1991*. Neuendettelsau: Freimund, 1993.

Schlink, Edmund. *The Doctrine of Baptism*. Translated by Herbert J. A. Bouman. St. Louis: Concordia, 1972.

———. "Gesetz und Evangelium als kontroverstheologisches Problem." *Kerygma und Dogma* 7 (1961): 1–35.

———. *Theology of the Lutheran Confessions*. Translated by Paul F. Koehneke and Herbert J. A. Bouman. Philadelphia, Fortress, 1986.

Schmidt, Johann. "Die missionarische Dimension der Theologie." Pages 193–201 in *Das Wort und die Wörter: Festschrift Gerhard Friedrich zum 65. Geburtstag*. Edited by Horst Robert Balz und Siegfried Schulz. Stuttgart: W. Kohlhammer, 1973.

Schnackenburg, Rudolf. *Der Brief an die Epheser*. Evangelisch-Katholischer Kommentar zum Neuen Testament 10. Köln: Benziger, 1982.

Schöne, Jobst. *The Christological Character of the Office of the Ministry and the Royal Priesthood*. Plymouth, MN: Logia Books, 1996.

———. "Church and Ministry II: Systematic Formulation." *Logia* 2 (1993): 35–40.

Schreiner, Lothar. "The Legacy of Ingwer Ludwig Nommenson." *International Bulletin of Missionary Research* 24.2 (April 2000): 81–84.

Schulz, Georg. "Die Bedeutung des Bekenntnisses der lutherischen Kirche für die missionarische Verkündigung." 1980. A Presentation held at the International Convention at Heiligenstein, Elsaß, 4. September 1980. Unpublished article.

———. "Das geistliche Amt nach lutherischem Verständnis in der missionarischen Situation." Pages 162–74 in *Kirchenmission nach lutherischem Verständnis: Vorträge zum 100 jährigen Jubiläum der Lutherischen Kirchenmission (Bleckmarer Mission)*. Münster: LIT, 1993.

Schulz, Klaus Detlev. "Christ's Ambassadors." *Logia* VII.3 (1998): 13–18.

———. "In Search of the Proprium of Lutheran Mission: Eight Theses." *Logia* 15.1 (Epiphany 2006): 5–7.

———. "The Lutheran Debate over a Missionary Office." *Lutheran Quarterly* 19.3 (Autumn 2005): 276–301.

———. "Lutheran Missiology in the 16th and 17th Century." *Lutheran Synod Quarterly* 43.1 (March 2003): 4–53.

———. "A Lutheran Response to the Christology and Natural Theology of the Papal Encyclical Dominus Iesus." *Logia* 10.4 (Reformation 2001): 5–8.

———. *The Missiological Significance of the Doctrine of Justification in the Lutheran Confessions*. ThD dissertation. Concordia Seminary, 1994.

———. "Tensions in the Pneumatology of the Missio Dei." *Concordia Journal* 23.2 (April 1997): 99–121.

———. "Towards a Missionary Church for the City." *Missio Apostolica* 11.1 (May 2003): 4–13.

———. "Universalism: The Urgency of Christian Witness." *Missio Apostolica* 14.2 (November 2006): 86–96.

Schurb, Ken. *Does the Lutheran Confessions' Emphasis on Subjective Justification Mitigate Their Teaching of Objective Justification?* Fort Wayne, IN: Concordia Theological Seminary Press, 1983.

———. "The Resurrection in Gospel Proclamation." *Concordia Journal* 18 (January 1992): 28–39.

Schwarz, Hans. "Der missiologische Aspekt der Rechtfertigungslehre." Pages 209–17 in *Rechtfertigung und Weltverantwortung*. Internationale Konsultation Neuendettelsau 1991. Edited by Schlichting, Wolfhart. Neuendettelsau: Freimund, 1993.

Schwarzwäller, Klaus. "Rechtfertigung und Ekklesiologie in den Schmalkaldischen Artikeln." *Kerygma und Dogma* 35 (1989): 84–105.

Scott, Waldron. *Karl Barth's Theology of Mission*. Downers Grove, IL: InterVarsity, 1978.

Scudieri, Robert J. *The Apostolic Church: One, Holy, Catholic and Missionary*. Fort Wayne, IN: Lutheran Society for Missiology, 1995.

Seamands, John T. *Harvest of Humanity*. Wheaton, IL: Victor Books, 1988.

Seils, Martin. "Heil und Erlösung IV." Pages 622–37 in vol. 14 of *Theologische Realenzuklopädie*. Edited by Gerhard Müller. Berlin: de Gruyter, 1985.

Senior, Donald, and Carol Stuhlmueller. *The Biblical Foundations for Mission*. Maryknoll, NY: Orbis, 1994.

Siemon-Netto, Uwe. *The Fabricated Luther*. 2nd ed. St. Louis: Concordia, 2007.

Slenczka, Reinhard. "Die Erkenntnis des Geistes, die Lehre vom Geist und die Unterscheidung der Geister." Pages 75–104 in *Der Heilige Geist im Verständnis Luthers und der lutherischen Theologie*. Edited by Joachim Heubach. Erlangen: Martin Luther Verlag, 1990.

Smail, Thomas. "The Holy Spirit in the Holy Trinity." Pages 149–65 in *Nicene Christianity*. Edited by Christopher R. Seitz. Grand Rapids: Brazos Press, 2001.

Smalley, William A. "Cultural Implications of an Indigenous Church." Pages 494–502 in *Perspectives on the World Christian Movement: A Reader*. Edited by Ralph. D. Winter and Steven C. Hawthorne. Pasadena, CA: William Carey Library, 1981.

Smith, Gordon T. "Religions and the Bible: An Agenda for Evangelicals." Pages 9–29 in *Christianity and the Religions: A Biblical Theology of World Religions*. Edited by Edward Rommen and Harold Netland. Pasadena, CA: William Carey Library, 1995.

Smith, James K. A. *Who's Afraid of Postmodernism?* Grand Rapids: Baker Academic, 2006.

Smith, L. B. *The Contribution of Hadrian Saravia to the Doctrine of the Nature of the Church and Its Mission*. Dissertation. Edinburgh, 1966.

Solheim, James. "Vatican Statement Drawing Strong Reactions." *Episcopal News Service* (September 15, 2000).

Spitz, Lewis W. "The Universal Priesthood of Believers." Pages 321–42 in vol. 1 of *The Abiding Word*. Edited by Theodore Laetsch. St. Louis: Concordia, 1975.

Steffen, Tom A. *Passing the Baton: Church Planting That Empowers.* La Habra: Center for Organizational & Ministry Development, 1993.

Stephenson, John R. *Eschatology.* Confessional Lutheran Dogmatics 13. Edited by Robert D. Preus. Fort Wayne, IN: Luther Academy, 1993.

Stolle, Volker. *The Church Comes from All Nations.* Translated by Klaus Detlev Schulz and Daniel Thies. St. Louis: Concordia, 2003.

——. *Kirchenmission nach lutherischem Verständnis.* Münster: LIT, 1993.

——. "Über die Zielsetzung organisierter Missionsarbeit." *Lutherische Theologie und Kirche* 4 (December 1987): 132–36.

——. *Wer seine Hand an den Pflug legt: Die missionarische Wirksamkeit der selbständigen evangelisch-lutherischen Kirchen in Deutschland im 19. Jahrhundert.* Gross-Oesingen: Lutherische Buchhandlung, 1992.

——. "Zur missionarischen Perspektive der lutherischen Theologie im 17. Jahrhundert." *Lutherische Theologie und Kirche* 15 (1991): 21–35.

Stott, John. "Evangelism Plus." *Christianity Today* (October 2006): 94–99.

——, ed. *Making Christ Known: Historic Mission Documents from the Lausanne Movement 1974–1989.* Grand Rapids: Eerdmans, 1997.

Strasser, Ernst. "Das Hauptstück von der Mission." Pages 56–58 in *Das Wort und die Völker der Erde: Beiträge zum lutherischen Verständnis der Mission.* Edited by Ernst Strasser. Uelzen: Niedersächsische Buchdruckerei, 1951.

——. "Das Wesen der Mission nach lutherischem Verständnis." Pages 7–11 in *Das Wort und die Völker der Erde: Beiträge zum lutherischen Verständnis der Mission.* Edited by Ernst Strasser. Uelzen: Niedersächsische Buchdruckerei, 1951.

——. "Das Wesen des Heidentums." *Neue kirchliche Zeitschrift* 39 (1939): 77–105.

Sweeney, Douglas A. *The American Evangelical Story: A History of the Movement.* Grand Rapids: Baker Academic, 2005.

Take a Giant Step: Be a World Christian. What's New and What's What in World Missions Today. St. Louis: Lutheran Church—Missouri Synod, 1986.

Tappert, Theodore G., ed. and trans. *The Book of Concord: The Confessions of the Evangelical Lutheran Church.* Philadelphia: Muhlenberg, 1959.

Tennent, Timothy C. "The Challenge of Churchless Christianity: An Evangelical Assessment." *International Bulletin of Missionary Research* 29.4 (October 2005): 171–77.

Terray, Laszlo Geza. "Mission und Reich Gottes—Korreferat zu dem Referat von John Vikström." Pages 69–74 in *Lutherische Beiträge zur Missio Dei.* Erlangen: Martin Luther Verlag, 1982.

Thangaraj, M. Thomas. *The Common Task: A Theology of Christian Mission.* Nashville: Abingdon, 1999.

Thelle, Notto R. "The Legacy of Karl Ludwig Reichelt." *International Bulletin of Missionary Research* 5.2 (April 1981): 35–40.

Thesen für die Lehrverhandlungen der Missouri-Synode und der Synodalconferenz bis zum Jahre 1893. St. Louis: Concordia, 1894.

Thielicke, Helmut. *Theological Ethics.* Vol. 1: *Foundations.* Edited by William H. Lazareth. Grand Rapids: Eerdmans, 1966.

Thomas, Norman E., ed. *Classic Texts in Mission and World Christianity: A Reader's Companion to David Bosch's* Transforming Mission. Maryknoll, NY: Orbis, 1995.

Thomasius, Gottfried. *Das Bekenntnis der evangelisch-lutherischen Kirche in der Konsequenz seines Prinzips.* Nürnberg: August Recknagel, 1848.

Tillich, Paul. "Die Lehre von der Inkarnation in neuer Deutung." Pages 205–29 in *Offenbarung und Glaube.* Schriften zur Theologie II. Vol. 8 of *Gesammelte Werke.* Edited by Renate Albrecht. Stuttgart: Evangelisches Verlagswerk, 1970.

———. "Missions and World History." Pages 281–89 in *The Theology of the Christian Mission.* Edited by H. Gerald Anderson. New York: Abingdon, 1961.

———. *Systematic Theology.* Vol. 1. Chicago: University of Chicago Press, 1951.

———. "Wesen und Wandel des Glaubens." Pages 111–95 in *Offenbarung und Glaube.* Schriften zur Theologie II. Vol. 8 of Gesammelte Werke. Edited by Renate Albrecht. Stuttgart: Evangelisches Verlagswerk, 1970.

Tippet, Alan. *Introduction to Missiology.* Pasadena: William Carey Library, 1987.

Toward a Theological Basis, Understanding and Use of Church Growth Principles in The Lutheran Church—Missouri Synod. Prepared by the Church Growth Strategy Task Force, 1991.

Triebel, Johannes. *Bekehrung als Ziel der missionarischen Verkündigung.* Erlangen: Verlag der Ev.-Luth. Mission, 1976.

———. "Strukturen des Bekennens." *Kerygma und Dogma* 26 (1980): 317–26.

Triglot Concordia: The Symbolical Books of the Ev. Lutheran Church. St. Louis: Concordia, 1921.

Trillhaas, Wolfgang. "*Regnum Christi*: On the History of the Concept in Protestantism." *Lutheran World* 14 (1967): 40–58.

Tucker, Ruth. *From Jerusalem to Irian Jaya.* Grand Rapids: Zondervan, 1983.

Vajta, Vilmos. "The Confessions of the Church as an Ecumenical Concern." Pages 162–88 in *The Church and the Confessions: The Role of the Confessions in the Life and the Doctrine of Lutheran Churches.* Edited by Vilmos Vajta and Hans Weissgerber. Philadelphia: Fortress, 1963.

Valleskey, David J. *We Believe—Therefore We Speak.* Milwaukee: Northwestern, 2004.

Van Engen, Charles. *Mission on the Way: Issues in Mission Theology.* Grand Rapids: Baker, 1996.

Van Rheenen, Gailyn. *Missions: Biblical Foundations and Contemporary Strategies.* Grand Rapids: Zondervan, 1996.

Verkuyl, Johannes. *Contemporary Missiology: An Introduction.* Translated and edited by Dale Cooper. Grand Rapids: Eerdmans, 1978.

Vicedom, Georg F. *Actio Dei: Mission und Reich Gottes.* Munich: Chr. Kaiser, 1975.

———. *The Mission of God: An Introduction to a Theology of Mission.* Translated by Gilbert A. Thiele and Dennis Hilgendorf. St. Louis: Concordia, 1965.

———. *Die Missionarische Dimension der Gemeinde.* Berlin: Lutherisches Verlagshaus, 1963.

———. *Die Rechtfertigung als gestaltende Kraft der Mission.* Neuendettelsau: Freimund, 1952.

————. *Die Taufe unter den Heiden.* Munich: Chr. Kaiser, 1960.

Veith, Gene Edward, Jr. *The Spirituality of the Cross.* St. Louis: Concordia, 1999.

Vikstrom, John. "Mission und Reich Gottes—Erlösung und Reich des Friedens als Glaubensgegenstand und ethische Aufgabe: Ein Beitrag zum aktuellen zwischenkirchlichen Dialog." Pages 57–68 in *Lutherische Beiträge zur Missio Dei.* Erlangen: Martin Luther Verlag, 1982.

Voelz, Jim W. *What Does This Mean? Principles of Biblical Interpretation in the Post-Modern World.* St. Louis: Concordia, 1995.

Voigt, Gottfried. *Was die Kirche lehrt.* Erlangen: Martin-Luther-Verlag, 1991.

Waddell, James Alan. *The Struggle to Reclaim the Liturgy in the Lutheran Church: Adiaphora in Historical, Theological and Practical Perspective.* New York: Edwin Mellen Press, 2006.

Wagner, C. Peter. "Church Growth Movement." In *Evangelical Dictionary of World Mission.* Edited by Scott Moreau. Grand Rapids: Baker, 2000.

————, ed. *Church Growth: State of the Art.* Wheaton, IL: Tyndale, 1986.

————. *Spiritual Power and Church Growth.* Altamonte Springs, FL: Strang Communications, 1986.

Wagner, Herwig. "Die Kirche und ihre Sendung." Pagse 105–12 in *Lutherische Beiträge zur Missio Dei.* Erlangen: Martin Luther Verlag, 1982.

————. "Das lutherische Bekenntnis als Dimension des Missionspapiers des Lutherischen Weltbundes 'Gottes Mission als gemeinsame Aufgabe.'" Pages 149–61 in *Kirchenmission nach lutherischem Verständnis: Vorträge zum 100 jährigen Jubiläum der Lutherischen Kirchenmission (Bleckmarer Mission).* Münster: LIT, 1993.

Walther, Carl Ferdinand Wilhelm. *Americanisch-Lutherische Pastoraltheologie.* 5th ed. St. Louis: Concordia, 1906.

————. *Church and Ministry: Witnesses of the Evangelical Lutheran Church on the Question of the Church and Ministry.* Translated by J. T. Mueller. St. Louis: Concordia, 1987.

————. "Why Should Our Pastors, Teachers and Professors Subscribe Unconditionally to the Symbolical Writings of Our Church." *Concordia Theological Monthly* 18 (April 1947): 241–53.

Warneck, Gustav. *Evangelische Missionslehre.* Gotha: Friedrich Andreas Perthes, 1892.

————. "Mission unter den Heiden." Pages 125–71 in vol. 13 of *Realencyklopädie für protestantische Theologie und Kirche.* 4th ed. Leipzig: J. C. Hinrichs'sche, 1903.

————. *Outline of a History of Protestant Missions from the Reformation to the Present Time: A Contribution to Modern Church History.* Translated by George Robson. New York: Flemming H. Revell, 1901.

Warren, Rick. *The Purpose Driven Church.* Grand Rapids: Zondervan, 1995.

————. *Purpose Driven Life.* Grand Rapids: Zondervan, 2002.

WCC- CWME. *Statement on Urban Rural Mission,* 1986.

Weber, Christian. *Missionstheologie bei Wilhelm Löhe: Aufbruch zur Kirche der Zukunft.* Gütersloh: Gütersloher Verlagshaus, 1996.

Weber, H. E. "Mysterium Trinitatis." *Zeitschrift für systematische Theologie* 16, (1939): 355–63.

Weber, Wilhelm. "Die lutherische Tradition in Gottesdienst und Unterweisung als Faktor der missionarischen Entwicklung." Pages 175–96 in *Kirchenmission nach lutherischem Verständnis: Vorträge zum 100 jährigen Jubiläum der Lutherischen Kirchenmission (Bleckmarer Mission).* Edited by Volker Stolle. Münster: LIT, 1993.

Wenz, Gunther. *Theologie der Bekenntnisschriften der evangelisch-lutherischen Kirche.* Berlin: de Gruyter, 1998.

Werning, Waldo J. *Twelve Pillars of a Healthy Church.* Fort Wayne, IN: Fairway Press, 1999.

Wetter, Paul. *Der Missionsgedanke bei Martin Luther.* Bonn: Verlag für Kultur und Wissenschaft, 1999.

Wiebe, Franz. "Missionsgedanken in den lutherischen Bekenntnisschriften." Pages 15–71 in *Lutherisches Missionsjahrbuch für das Jahr 1955.* Edited by Walther Ruf. Neuendettelsau: Selbstverlag der Bayerischen Missionskonferenz, 1955.

Wilch, John R. *Ruth.* Concordia Commentary Series. St. Louis: Concordia, 2006.

Wingren, Gustaf. *Luther on Vocation.* Translated by Carl C. Rasmussen. Philadelphia: Muhlenberg, 1957.

Winter, Ralph D. "The Long Look: Eras of Mission History." Pages 168–69 in *Perspectives on the World Christian Movement: A Reader.* Edited by Ralph. D. Winter and Steven C. Hawthorne. Pasadena, CA: William Carey Library, 1981.

———, and Steven C. Hawthorne, eds. *Perspectives on the World Christian Movement: A Reader.* Pasadena, CA: William Carey Library, 1981.

Witte, Martin. "Kirche als Ziel der Sendung." Pages 18–26 in *Das Wort und die Völker der Erde: Beiträge zum lutherischen Verständnis der Mission.* Edited by Ernst Strasser. Uelzen: Niedersächsische Buchdruckerei, 1951.

Wittgenstein, Ludwig. *On Certainty.* Edited by G. E. M. Anscombe and G. H. von Wright. Translated by Denis Paul and G. E. M. Anscombe. Oxford: Blackwell, 1969.

Wyder, Heinrich. *Die Heidenpredigt.* Gütersloh: C. Bertelsmann, 1954.

Yates, Timothy. *Christian Mission in the Twentieth Century.* Cambridge: Cambridge University Press, 1994.

Your Kingdom Come: Mission Perspectives. Report on the World Conference on Mission and Evangelism. Melbourne, Australia 12–25 May 1980. Geneva: World Council of Churches, 1980.